SCHEMING
FOR THE POOR

SCHEMING FOR THE POOR

The Politics of Redistribution
in Latin America

William Ascher

HARVARD UNIVERSITY PRESS
Cambridge, Massachusetts, and London, England
1984

Library of Congress Cataloging in Publication Data

Ascher, William.
    Scheming for the poor.

    Includes bibliographical references and index.
    1. Income distribution—Government policy—Chile.
2. Income distribution—Government policy—Argentina.
3. Income distribution—Government policy—Peru.
I. Title.
HC195.I5A73   1984   339.5'2'0983   83-12866
    ISBN 0-674-79085-5 (alk. paper)

To the memory of my father,
Meyer S. Ascher

Acknowledgments

The funding of my travel to the countries covered in this study came from the Foreign Area Fellowship Program of the Social Science Research Council, the United States Information Agency, the Ford Foundation, and the Hudson Institute. A year at the World Bank on an International Affairs Fellowship of the Council on Foreign Relations increased my exposure to development thinking and the issue of income distribution. I am grateful to all these agencies for their support.

I have benefited from the research assistance of Laila Atallah, Charles Grice, and Flavia Sacchi. The coherence of my argument has been improved by critiques from Leonor Blum, Ronald Brunner, Matthew Crenson, John S. Fitch, Lars Schoultz, and Sidney Tarrow. Discussions with Latin American academics and policymakers, too numerous to list here, were invaluable. Michael Aronson of Harvard University Press deserves credit for editorial guidance. And my wife, Barbara, is responsible for making even the conception of this book possible.

Contents

I
INTRODUCTION

CHAPTER 1
Defining the Redistributive Issue

OF ALL THE REGIONS OF the world Latin America has the most unequal distribution of income and wealth.[1] Not surprisingly, the area has seen numerous redistributive efforts, several of which have resulted in dismal failure. Many redistribution-minded governments have been overturned; some have reversed their own progressive policies; and some have effected redistribution only by undermining the long-term prosperity of the country as a whole. Yet there have also been successful redistributions, a fact that is frequently overlooked in the justifiable lamentations over the socioeconomic disparities in Latin America.

Why do some redistributive efforts succeed better than others? There are a couple of obvious answers: the poor were or were not sufficiently strong; the government was or was not sufficiently strong; the government was or was not sufficiently committed to redistribution. But these answers are largely circular, and in any event they are inadequate for clarifying how to pursue equity without undermining long-range economic growth.

This book uses the cases of post–World War II Argentina, Chile, and Peru to explore some of the nonobvious causes. It focuses on the policymaking process involved in attempts to redistribute income and wealth, particularly the tightly interrelated tasks of policy formulation and coalition building. The policy process is, of course, far more complicated; the "prior" task of developing a macroapproach to economic growth, and the "subsequent" tasks of implementation and evaluation, are also important. The emphasis on formulation and coalition building in this study is motivated by their importance in triggering or averting the mobilization of opposition to redistribution—which proves to be an essential cause of redistributive failure in the cases under examination—and the very practical consideration that, to be feasible, a comparative study must restrict its focus.

Despite growing recognition of the need to overcome poverty in developing countries, there has been remarkably little study of the process of selecting and implementing redistributive policies. Although there are countless technical suggestions for achieving redistribution—and even for simultaneously achieving both redistribution and aggregate economic growth[2]—the understanding of political and institutional factors required for successful redistribution is quite underdeveloped.

This lack of attention to the policymaking process reflects the strong current of pessimism that runs through the prevailing literature. Most studies of redistribution over the past two decades have concentrated on dispelling the hope of the 1950s that both economic growth and equitable distribution could be easily achieved by developing countries. At a time when the optimism concerning *automatic* economic development and "takeoff" was high,[3] scholars like Gunnar Myrdal emphasized the chronic problems that lock sizable portions of Third World populations into poverty (Myrdal 1957, 1968; Elliot 1975). Such works established a paradigm for research on poverty by stressing the inadequacies of existing policy approaches, unmasking many of these policies as superficial, stressing the deep structural sources of inequality, and demonstrating how intractable the poverty problem is on both a world scale and within individual nations. This paradigm and the normative outlook of subsequent researchers have been wedded in a strange way; it is almost as if the commitment to be "against poverty" requires that the scholar portray poverty as virtually unyielding.

The ideological implication of this paradigm is clear: liberal democracy, once synonymous with reform in Latin America and in the developing world in general, has become the object of disdain and frustration for most advocates of redistribution. The flaw in liberal democratic practice is widely perceived as the power it accords upper-income and middle-income groups bent on blocking redistributive economic reforms. According to this view, although the rationale and rhetoric of liberal democracy are rooted in the strength of numbers, the power of the masses can be checked by the superior organization, finances, and access to policymakers enjoyed by the wealthy few. Well-organized and well-financed lobbying operations wield such power in the normal channels of liberal democratic legislatures and penetrable bureaucracies that advances in economic equality are easily vetoed. Short of revolution, the options for eliminating poverty are severely limited.

This pessimism is often accompanied by an equally strong current of fatalism. The distribution of wealth—and hence the continued existence of poverty—is seen as the deterministic result of either fundamental economic structures and long-term economic trends, or of basic political conditions and the corresponding balance of political power. Both the economic determinism and the political-power-balance determinism are discouraging to proredistribution activists. If, as the economic deterministic argument maintains, income distribution is locked into the enduring, slowly changing structure of the economy, one must be reconciled to the inequalities of underdevelopment. Many officials of developing nations, aid-granting nations, and international financial institutions have come to believe that the poor can be helped only through a general economic expansion, often mounted at the expense of the poor, that increases their incomes at a rate no greater than the increase in overall national income. If, as the political-power-balance determinism maintains, redistribution will occur if and only if those committed to it have sufficient political power, then success or failure of redistribution is a foregone conclusion, beyond the influence of strategy or effort.

In contrast to these deterministic outlooks, this book focuses on the policymaking process out of a conviction that it *does* make a difference. This is not simply a fond hope; both the questionable logic of the determinist arguments and a careful examination of the redistributive record reveal that pessimism and fatalism are unjustified. Although there is much more drama in exploring the clash of political forces than in investigating the complex and largely unexplored terrain of economic policymaking, the understandable reluctance to study the policymaking process in detail has serious costs. It ignores the necessarily prosaic aspects of promoting redistribution, thereby discouraging attempts to overcome the real obstacles. Because long-range economic changes do not predetermine income distribution, because the so-called balance of power does not really explain who gets what, at least some of the answers must lie in the process itself.

THE LIMITS OF ECONOMIC DETERMINISM

Beginning with Simon Kuznets in the 1950s, many economists have approached the problem of explaining distributive patterns by statistically exploring differences in income distribution either across nations or for the same nation over time. Given the usual weakness of time series information on income distribution trends,[4] most statistical analyses (including Kuznets' own Nobel Prize winning research) have relied on differences among nations. The presumption is that characteristics associated with countries having equitable distributions of

income will be the same as those linked to the dynamics of distributional change within each country. Thus, if more industrialized countries have more equal distributions of income, the implication is that
industrialization is causally related to progressive redistribution. Kuznets (1969) concluded that the level of equality diminishes as a country
moves from the least advanced economy to an intermediate stage of
development then improves again as the country becomes more fully
industrialized and modernized. Other studies, taking Kuznets' findings as a point of departure, have either supported or disputed this
conclusion—with considerable variation, presumably depending on
the particular cases, time periods, measures of inequality, and statistical methods employed.[5]

What is important for us at the moment is not the statistical pattern
(especially since there is no single pattern), but rather what is implied
by the general methodology. By its statistical search for the pattern that
best fits the "typical" distributive change, this approach conveys what is
usual but not what is unusual. It reveals that modernization, industrialization, and increasing aggregate wealth embody or create certain
changes in the structures of employment, productivity, compensation,
and the like that result in distributional changes. However, what the
approach does not logically imply is that all countries follow the same
pattern of distributional changes over the course of economic development, or experience the same structural changes. The very fact that
some cases do not fall on the curve representing the typical rise and fall
of income inequality as nations become wealthier means that development does not *determine* the level of income equality in any rigid way,
even if it is valid (and very useful to know) that development *affects*
income equality. These "outlying" cases are as interesting as the typical
cases, especially in understanding how to avoid the usual deterioration
of income equality.

LIMITS TO POWER-BALANCE DETERMINISM

It is indeed true that the poor face an uphill battle in molding economic
policy to improve their condition. When the wealthy control the
economic policy apparatus, policies tend to do little to ameliorate
uneven distributions of wealth and income. Even when government is
in the hands of genuinely committed redistributionists—a rare enough
circumstance—redistributive efforts are often thwarted by the economic and political reactions of the wealthy. There is, then, *generally* a
congruence between the power of an economic group and its ability to

secure policy outcomes favorable to its interests. It is also undeniable that there is *generally* a close connection between the wealth of a group and the power it can wield.

However, these observations do not warrant the strong determinist position that redistribution is guaranteed if the forces committed to it hold enough political power, and precluded if they do not. The factual basis for this proposition is questionable because of the circularity of attributing both commitment and power only after the fact. Certainly any particular instance of income redistribution effected through governmental policy demonstrates, by definition, the willingness of the government to pursue that policy and, again by definition, the power of the government to impose that policy in order to produce the redistributive effect. Yet this does not illustrate, or even address, what constitutes sufficient initial commitment or sufficient power. Post hoc attribution of commitment and power ignores the questions of whether other regimes with equal levels of commitment and power have failed in their redistributive efforts, or whether some regimes with far less power or commitment—judged by less circular standards—succeeded in redistributing income.

In terms of the logic of the argument, power-balance determinism is plagued by two problematic premises. First, the notion that the power of any group (or alliance of groups) is of fixed magnitude is an essential supposition of the argument, yet in fact that power is most often situational. Its capacity to achieve its objectives can vary greatly according to the forums, coalitions, and strategies it engages.

Second, the parallel supposition that commitment to redistribution is an intrinsic attribute of groups, governments, or individuals does not square with the reality of changing levels of commitment. As the political and economic reactions to redistributive efforts unfold, even genuine initial commitment of a regime can easily vanish. The fallbck argument that the regime was not sufficiently committed in the first place begs the question of whether commitment in any useful sense of the term encompasses all of the attitudes that must be taken into account to understand why some redistributive attempts succeed and others fail. It provides no insight into why conditions following redistributive efforts were threatening enough to chill the early enthusiasm.

There is a weaker form of the political determinist argument that avoids at least the logical flaws of the strong version. Given the array of power resources and strategies available to a government with a certain initial commitment to redistribution, it may be argued that the range of discretion among reasonable options is not great enough to make much difference in the distributional outcome.

In contrast, I hypothesize that the range of discretion is usually quite wide, because the characteristics of policymaking arenas which are manipulable have a significant impact on who has access to policymaking, on how much opposition is mobilized against redistributive efforts, and on whether redistributive instruments will be economically and politically feasible. Therefore, without denying the importance of the economic and political power structures as the *context* of the formulation and execution of economic policies, my focus is on the impact of various forms of policymaking and on strategies to mold these forms. There are at least three reasons why the politics and the decision-making procedures in effect in the course of policy formulation and implementation deserve much more attention:

1. In the course of policy formulation the power balance can change through the formation of new coalitions, which in turn are sensitive to how the process unfolds. Consequently the initial balance of power is not a fixed condition.

2. Particularly for developing countries, characterized by relatively poor economic information, the actual consequences of an economic policy are by no means always predictable or controllable. Policy objectives are thwarted by design flaws, by defensive reactions of economic actors threatened by the policy, and by uncontrollable external factors. The assumption that "where there's a will there's a way" does not necessarily hold for antiredistributionists or for proredistributionists. Hence initial commitment to redistribution neither guarantees nor precludes redistribution. The specifics of policymaking and the details of policy instruments are relevant.

3. To the extent that the policymaking process reveals the means by which the congruence between political power and policy benefits can be undermined or reinforced to the advantage of the poor, strategies for redistribution can be found. If certain policy instruments, forums, actors, or routines are discovered to facilitate redistribution when proredistributionists are in power, or to hinder regressive policy initiatives when others are in control, then guidelines for more effective redistributive efforts can be established.

Let us take a quick look ahead now at some of the possible ways in which the policymaking process can be structured to make a difference.

Policymaking personnel: The characteristics of governmental policymakers (their social background; the mix of partisans, bureaucrats, and *técnicos*; occupational training; and so on) influences access, economic ideology, and anticipation. To the extent that a policymaker carries with him (consciously or unconsciously) the orientation of his own social group, the interests of these groups have the advantage. Attempts by high-income groups to block redistribution can be short-circuited if policymaking positions are staffed by individuls who by background, training, or role conception afford greater accessibility to lower-income groups, reject antiredistributive economic orientations, and are unwilling to abandon or water down redistributive policies in the face of opposition.

Policy-making modes: Different routines and analytical approaches to economic policymaking have effects on the likelihood of redistributive outcomes that have barely been explored. The decision-making modes (comprehensive planning vs traditional budgeting, conciliatory bargaining vs combative confrontations, and so on) vary in terms of how much access is available to specific economic groups and which economic orientations are compatible with decision-making routines. Furthermore, the dominance of particular policymaking modes affects not only the mechanics of policy formulation, but also the mix of personnel involved. For example, comprehensive planning implies a relatively stronger role for technical experts, and hence greater prominence of their particular orientation toward redistribution.

Redistributive instruments: Even if two different policy instruments theoretically produce the same degree and type of redistribution, the nature of the instruments constrains the ways decisions are made and affects the capacity and willingness of the opponents of redistribution to react against it. Redistribution through government expenditures requires budgetary decisions, while redistribution through monetary policy may not. Confiscation of assets triggers reactions of a different magnitude than does manipulation of terms of trade, even though the latter may effect equally significant redistribution. The appropriate choice of policy instruments, made in policymaking arenas in which proredistributionists prevail and implemented without arousing catastrophic reactions, can dramatically facilitate effective redistribution.

Communication and symbol manipulation: Because perceptions depend on the flow of symbols more directly than on material outcomes per se, the latitude in symbol manipulation permits redistributive policy to be conveyed in very different ways—and hence to elicit very different reactions. Policies designed to secure the same degree of redistribution may arouse different levels of opposition, attract different levels of support, and engage or suppress various nonmaterial issues (such as the respect and prestige of affected groups) differently. When policymakers are viewed as "symbol specialists"—who shape material reality only indirectly, through the flow of communication—the mutability of the political impact and the success of policy can be better appreciated.

The ways policies are presented to the public constitute an aspect of policy design that has been largely neglected.

Fluidity of coalitions: "The rich vs the poor" is only one of a virtually infinite array of possible confrontations between coalitions. The balance of power depends, of course, on which groups come together to form coalitions on issues of both power sharing and policy outcome. The possibility of forming a proredistributive alliance that includes enough of the groups with wealth and power to win in policy battles contradicts the fatalistic assumption that the debility of the poor leaves them at the mercy of the united rich. Strategy based on selecting the policies and the rhetoric necessary to form and maintain a winning coalition thus becomes a key part of policy design. This, too, has an important symbolic or perceptual component: alliances are forged through common identifications as well as through common material interests; opposition coalitions form as much from feelings of threat as from actual deprivations.

Nonmaterial trade-offs: The fact that nonmaterial rewards are valued in addition to material ones provides the opening for progressive economic policies to be supported by relatively wealthy groups in exchange for nonmaterial benefits. Symbolic rewards that do not require major allocations of goods and services can cement coalitions or mitigate the dissatisfactions of groups undergoing economic deprivations.

In short, many facets of the policymaking process have potential importance for the progress of redistribution. My goals, then, are to demonstrate that the fatalistic argument can be rejected, and to develop a framework for strategic choice that will enable the policymaker to best serve the poor.

FOCUS ON ARGENTINA, CHILE, AND PERU

Two approaches can be employed to establish that policy choices do make a difference. The first is to examine concrete cases in detail to determine whether choices made by proredistributive regimes can be shown to lead to different outcomes than would other alternatives not selected. The second approach is to identify strategies that have led to success with enough consistency, under diverse enough conditions, to dispel the possibilities that the association is coincidental or simply reflective of a given level of power or commitment. In other words, the discovery of strategic choices that consistently produce greater redistributive success than other choices would confirm the importance of strategy itself and reject the fatalist position.

In this study I employ both of these approaches. By examining policymaking episodes in Argentina, Chile, and Peru, I assess the importance of specific historical choices. By finding strategies that hold in different countries, for different kinds of government, I affirm the second basis for rejecting the fatalist position.

Like many Latin American countries, Argentina, Chile, and Peru have undergone numerous attempts at redistribution, under both civilian and military regimes, and numerous reactions against redistribution, sometimes resulting in even more serious disparities of income. I shall look at some of these efforts only briefly and consider others in considerable detail (see Table 1). If the overall record of redistribution in the three countries I am examining seems unimpressive (particularly in recent years), this is typical of Latin America and of much of the developing world. The important point is that we can identify for each of these countries some instances of sincere attempts by regimes to effect redistribution, some successes, and some failures. A comparison of successes and failures resulting from roughly matching levels of regime commitment and strength provides the potential to discover inductively the nonobvious correlates of success (that is, factors other than the power of the redistributionists).

Why go beyond the careful analysis of redistribution in one country? The use of several core cases provides not only more explanatory power, but also a much greater capacity to frame important questions that might not arise when dealing with a single case, about which detailed historical knowledge conveys an obviousness to each event or outcome. For example, the massive disinvestments triggered by sharp redistributions under Juan Velasco Alvarado in Peru and Salvador Allende in Chile might seem too obvious a reaction to study in detail until it is noted that in other instances—Argentina under Juan Perón, for example—sharp redistribution did *not* induce massive disinvestment. It is possible that the difference lies in idiosyncracies of the counterexamples; yet it is also possible that the counterexamples are relevant for refining the "obvious" explanation, and even for formulating strategies to improve the chances of meaningful redistribution.

During the past few years there has been a remarkable improvement in the availability of published accounts of policymaking episodes for the three countries we shall examine.[6] Complementing the relatively strong literature and data on income distribution for Argentina and Chile has been an impressive growth of materials on income distribution in Peru.[7] It is now feasible, to a greater extent than before 1975, to

TABLE 1. REGIMES AND ORIENTATIONS EXAMINED IN THIS STUDY.

Country and years of regime	President	Basic initial orientation of regime	Qualification to basic orientation
ARGENTINA			
1945–1955	**Juan Perón**	Authoritarian populist	Retrenchment of workers' income during second term
1955	Eduardo Lonardi	Military caretaker	
1955–1958	Pedro Aramburu	Military caretaker	Expected economic "revenge" against workers did not materialize
1958–1962	**Arturo Frondizi**	Centrist reformist	Reversed progressive policy by the end of 1959
1963–1966	**Arturo Illia**	Centrist reformist	
1966–1970	Juan Carlos Onganía	Conservative military	Income-share freeze rather than regressive distribution
1970–1971	Roberto Levingston	Conservative military	Same
1971–1973	Alejandro Lanusse	Conservative military	Same
1973	Hector Campora	Radical	Forced resignation aborted program

CHILE			
1946–1952	Gabriel González Videla	Centrist reformist	Very modest redistributive emphasis
1952–1958	**Carlos Ibáñez**	Authoritarian populist	Reversed progressive policy by 1955
1958–1964	Jorge Alessandri	Conservative civilian	Some progressive policy elements
1964–1970	**Eduardo Frei**	Centrist reformist	Partial reversal of progressive policy by 1968
1970–1973	**Salvador Allende**	Radical	
PERU			
1945–1948	Jose Bustamente	Centrist reformist	Very modest redistributive emphasis
1948–1956	**Manuel Odría**	Authoritarian populist	Progressive policy effects overshadowed by effects by other policies
1956–1962	Manuel Prado	Centrist reformist	Very modest redistributive emphasis
1963–1968	**Fernando Belaúnde**	Centrist reformist	
1968–1975	**Juan Velasco Alvarado**	Radical (military)	Retrenchment in certain areas

NOTE: Administrations shown in bold face are those examined in greatest depth.

13

make contextually meaningful comparisons of the patterns of these three countries, relying on primary as well as secondary materials.

THE PATTERN OF REDISTRIBUTIVE EFFORTS

Considering the diversity of Latin American politics and the profusion of redistributive attempts in the region, it is striking that so many countries there went through a similar pattern during the post–World War II era. This pattern of redistributive efforts by, in turn, authoritarian populists, centrist reformers, and "radicals" is useful for comparative purposes, in that the political styles and the rules of the game vary in important ways across the three types.

The sequence is not rigid; in some countries, including Argentina, military interventions or other abrupt regime changes derailed governments that seemed to fulfill the sequence. Often the immediate successor to a redistribution-minded regime was a regressive one. In other cases, one or more phases never materialized (Venezuela and Colombia, for instance, have not experienced attempts at radical transformation). Furthermore, the distinctions among authoritarian populists, reformists, and radicals do not by any means constitute an analytical framework that explains the success of redistribution or accounts for the political dynamics of redistributive policymaking.

AUTHORITARIAN POPULISM

The first type, emerging right after the end of World War II, was the strongly personalist regime of a figure with populist but authoritarian leanings, usually (but not always) of military background, with at least some initial commitment to income redistribution. Brazil's Getulio Vargas, Venezuela's Marcos Pérez Jiménez, and Colombia's Gustavo Rojas Pinilla are a few examples. Because of the limited ability—or willingness—of these authoritarian populists to carry out their initial redistributive aims, this period in retrospect has become the "era of the dictators" rather than the "era of the populists." Many would-be populists found themselves repressing workers' movements and pursuing nonredistributive or even regressive economic policies. Nevertheless, the failure to achieve redistribution under many of the authoritarian populists does not negate the attempts, and in fact these failures illuminate the dynamics of redistributive attempts and the reactions they provoke.

Argentina, Chile, and Peru each had an authoritarian populist phase. Gen. Juan Domingo Perón was the champion of the Argentine *descamisados* ("shirtless ones"); Gen. Carlos Ibáñez was, until disillusionment set in, Chile's "General of Hope"; and Peru's Gen. Manuel Odría cast himself as the champion of peasants and workers both. Although these regimes differed in terms of the legal-political status (Odría came to power through a coup d'etat, Perón was elected after consolidating power in a military government, and Ibáñez was elected at the outset), there were striking similarities in political and policymaking styles: populist rhetoric, use of threats, attempts to take over the union movement, policy improvisation, and rejection of competitive pluralist politics. The initial policies also had much in common: reliance on massive public works (especially by Perón and Odría), tax reform, and expansion of social welfare, coupled with a willingness to resort to orthodox stabilization measures in the face of high inflation. These similarities were neither coincidental nor even independent, since both Ibáñez and Odría modeled themselves on Perón. Yet the success of these would-be populists differed markedly. Perón accomplished significant redistribution, whereas Ibáñez and Odría abandoned their populist aims in favor of regressive economic programs.

CENTRIST CIVILIAN REFORMISM

From the late 1950s to the mid-1960s another approach to redistribution emerged in much of Latin America, conditioned by the "twilight of the tyrants" and the advent of the Alliance for Progress. These redistributive efforts, promoted by the Alliance, were mounted by democratically elected civilian leaders trying to cultivate the support of the working class, employing a strategy of "industrialization with redistribution," along with moderate land reform. In quite similar contexts of open partisan political competition, their initial goals included administrative and tax reforms, progressive wage policies, stringent controls over foreign investment, and state-led (but not state-monopolized) growth. While these reformists permitted the state a major role in economic regulation and even allowed direct state economic activity (for example, autonomous state enterprises and governmental investment), they did not undertake fundamental or revolutionary transformations of the economic structure except insofar as land reform required changes in property rights.

This approach characterized the initial efforts of Juscelino Kubitschek in Brazil and Rómulo Betancourt in Venezuela. For the three countries covered in this study, the civilian reformists par excellence were Eduardo Frei in Chile and Fernando Belaúnde in Peru. The Argentine case is less straightforward, however, because Arturo Frondizi, the first civilian reformist to win election as a proredistributionist, reacted to an inherited economic crisis by adopting a sharply regressive economic program; his subsequent efforts to regain the support of the working class, cut short by the military coup of 1962, might or might not have resulted in an overall progressive redistribution. Another military intervention ended the civilian regime of Arturo Illia after only three years (1963–1966) and makes this era still less clear-cut as an illustration of civilian centrist reformism.

RADICALISM

Several reformist attempts perceived as failures gave way to periods of far more drastic efforts at economic revamping. This reaction occurred less frequently than the other two because some reformists were successful in preventing a subsequent victory by the Left (whether civilian or military), while others succumbed to antileftist military governments which prevented the radicals from assuming power. However, "radical" regimes have followed the overthrow of regimes other than civilian reformists. Fidel Castro in Cuba and the Sandinistas in Nicaragua fall into this category.

In Chile the radical regime was Allende's "experiment in Marxism"; in Peru it was the radical military government of General Velasco. The Argentine specimen of radical transformation, like the reformist attempts before it, was short-lived—the neo-Peronists began in 1973 with what appeared to be extreme redistributive policies under Hector Cámpora, but Perón himself intervened after a few weeks to change the direction of economic policy toward an "income share freeze."

The commonality of these efforts lay not in ideological uniformity, for neither Campora nor Velasco were Marxists, but rather in the provocativeness, abruptness, and lack of planning of each attempt. All intended, at least initially, to rely far more than previously on public ownership and state intervention in the economy, with the goal of substituting public investment for the private investment which the leadership knew would be withdrawn. All three relied heavily on leftist rhetoric and confrontations to mobilize workers beyond their electoral participation, in order to offset the adamant opposition of a private business sector that feared massive expropriation.

Although the distinctions among authoritarian populism, civilian reformism, and radicalism provide a convenient means for comparing redistributive attempts, we must remember that the framework of explanation need not change. The types are distinguishable in terms of strategies and political-climate factors that are relevant to the framework irrespective of the period or phase: the degree of provocativeness with which redistributive measures are introduced, the willingness of policymakers to improvise and calibrate their measures (that is, adjust their scope and strength) despite ideological qualms, the breadth of the groups targeted for redistributive victimization, the directness of redistributive policy, and so on. Redistributive success or failure reflects not the operation of different politicoeconomic dynamics for different regime types, but rather the consequences of strategic choices and situational differences as shaped by a common dynamic.

This dynamic is based on the interplay among (a) choices of policy instruments and tactics, (b) subjective trends, and (c) material changes. Success lies in the leader's capacity to shape the subjective climate, through selection of policy and tactics, in order to curb the motivation of groups facing deprivation to undermine or to retaliate against the government's efforts. Since each phase of redistributive effort creates a distinct subjective climate, and evolves in similar material contexts as well, each encounters broadly similar challenges for tactical and policy choices.

Thus, the provocative confrontationist style of the authoritarian populists permitted none of their redistributive efforts to escape the onset of the typical reaction sequence of inflation, balance-of-payments problems, and incipient disinvestment. The difference between the success of Perón and the failure of the others is that Perón did not permit these consequences to reverse the redistributive thrust of his policies, though his measures were recalibrated as economic conditions changed. The penchant for improvisation shared by all the populists saved most of Perón's redistributive thrust, but Ibáñez and Odría failed to maintain control over enough of the fundamental levers of economic policy. Moreover, by directing benefits and lucrative investment opportunities to a segment of the entrepreneurial class, only Perón countered the tendency of his populist rhetoric to provoke a coalition of the wealthy against redistributive policy (as it did in Peru and Chile).

The civilian reformists accomplished more redistribution than their declining popular support would indicate. Both their success, and their lack of credit for it, were due in part to the image of their redistributive policies as piecemeal and ineffectual. The legislative arena, where redistributive policy debate was centered, permitted antiredistributionists to penetrate the process of policy formulation itself in order to dilute the redistributive strength of any given piece of legislation. Nevertheless, significant redistribution was achieved through legislation linked to benefits for groups other than the poor, or through presentation of it as serving other objectives as well. Yet a good deal of significant redistribution was blocked by coalitions of the wealthy that formed, not because they were actually threatened by the specific redistribution objectives, but rather because they felt threatened by measures which implied a broad range of redistributive targets.

The radicals' efforts met with the expected reaction: massive capital flight and political and economic reprisals. Even so, the possibility of maintaining the support or at least acquiescence of certain segments of the nonpoor population was not cut off until appallingly poor planning ravaged the incomes of these groups and consolidated the coalition of middle class and wealthy in adamant opposition to the regimes in Peru and Chile. In neither country was state investment capable of making up the loss. The ideological rigidity of both governments, and their preoccupation with macropolitics rather than economic detail, inhibited the concrete planning and policy flexibility required to fend off the negative effects of the economic reaction sequence. Opposition to Allende, both domestic and external, quickly led to political and economic chaos, culminating in the 1973 military coup. In Peru, political retaliation against the government was initially limited by the military nature of the regime itself, but the unrelieved economic decline provoked Center and Right elements of the military to remove Velasco and reverse most of his redistributive policies.

The message of this historical survey, then, is disconcertingly unheroic. The virtues of forthrightness, openness, ideological consistency, and courage to face attack often turn out to be liabilities to successful redistribution. Progressive redistribution may be more readily effected when regime leaders indulge in improvisation, obfuscation, and even insincere threatening. Even strong commitment to redistribution, long considered the sine qua non of redistributive success, can be a liability if it is articulated forcefully. The regime's cry "To the barricades!" sends to their own barricades both those directly victimized by the redistribution and any others who feel even remotely threatened by it. In light of the capacity of the wealthy—when fully mobilized—to undermine the economy and topple a regime, and the disappointing levels of support forthcoming from the beneficiaries of redistribution, the first task of the successful redistributionist may be to avert opposition rather than to galvanize support.

In case after case the masters of redistribution prove to be the tacticians rather than the warriors. The best records of redistribution are held by the pragmatic politicians whose familiarity with the policy process enables them to manipulate the political atmosphere to lull, disarm, or intimidate the potential opposition, and to isolate the direct victims of specific redistributive measures from their potential allies among all other groups fearing drastic redistribution.

If it seems "undemocratic" to advise proredistributionists to manipulate policy levers far removed from the most open policymaking arenas, two other considerations should be noted. First, these undeniably important levers are inevitably set by someone. Someone must choose, or decide to let drift, the exchange-rate regime, pricing policy, bank discount rates, and so on. Traditionally they have been controlled, at least indirectly, by bankers, landowners, importers, exporters, investors, and other individuals of both wealth and economic expertise. I urge that their control of these levers not go unchallenged. Second, the "democratic nature" of a government and its operations exists on several levels. It need not be regarded as undemocratic for a democratically chosen government to pursue its mandate through all legal avenues, whether open or closed to interest groups and the public.

An equally important conclusion is more encouraging than disconcerting. The conventional wisdom holds that because of the failure of the most aggressive redistributive efforts, which presumably reflect the staunchest regime commitment, the outlook for redistribution is dim. Yet the postwar experiences of Argentina, Chile, and Peru suggest, to the contrary, that these efforts failed in part because they were conducted too openly. More subtle attempts meet the ironic fate of greater success but far less recognition; as a result, the true record of redistribution is considerably better than the apparent record based on the more prominent episodes.

INCOME REDISTRIBUTION IN PERSPECTIVE

What does a shift in the overall distribution of income signify? Does a temporary increase in the workers' share of national income for, say, one or two years, make a significant difference economically, socially, or politically? Some would argue that the changes required to overcome economic and political inequality in developing nations depend on long-term shifts in fundamental attitudes and political arrangements, which far outweigh the impact of temporary economic benefits. Policymakers who hold this belief may be tempted to trade off immediate benefits to the poor in exchange for greater resources and flexibility to pursue what seem to be longer-range changes in the structure of education and the economy. This compromise may have very unfortunate consequences by introducing the sort of complacency with the status quo that Myrdal (1968, pp. 765–766) noted among the Indian leaders who were willing to allow long-term educational plans to fulfill their commitment to resolving the awesome problems of poverty in India. But apart from the issue of whether preoccupation with long-term plans has negative effects, the question remains of whether attention to apparently short-term trends in income distribution is worthwhile for either the analyst or the policymaker. Our approach here must be to examine what income redistribution means, what it reflects (its causes and correlates), and what its impact is.

If income is viewed as the receipt of a broad range of goods and services as well as money, some of the apparent distinctions between changes in income distribution and changes in long-term trends of social development disappear. When the poor receive benefits such as expanded government-funded educational and health services, their incomes (broadly defined) increase just as their long-term prospects for social and economic improvement increase. Of equal importance, once additional economic benefits are conferred upon the poor, their moral and political claim to higher benefits is strengthened. Most ethical systems regard the withdrawal of rewards and rights from a still relatively deprived group as a greater injury than not having accorded these benefits in the first place. Politically, it tends to be far easier to mobilize a group in defense of existing benefits than to mobilize individuals who have not yet received such benefits, especially if their poverty is accompanied by political ignorance and apathy.

The considerable difficulty of finding monetary equivalents for the receipt of such benefits and opportunities should not obscure the fact that policies aimed at increasing the welfare of the poor through higher government expenditures in health, education, and the like— or through other means to promote the present and future flow of benefits to the underprivileged—are redistributive policies just as much as wage policies are. Consequently, if income measures could detect the impact of such benefits, "progressive" shifts in the overall distribution of income would signify improvements in both the immediate economic status of the poor and their long-term socioeconomic development. Unfortunately, the vast majority of the statistics available on income distribution in developing countries are based on money flows alone and disregard the income from governmental expenditures and even the impact of taxation. For example, an income redistribution effected by taxing the wealthy in order to finance an expansion of primary education is clearly redistributive, but may not show up at all in the statistics on "before-tax" income shares. My focus throughout this book is on policies that influence the flow of benefits rather than merely the flow of money earnings. When the statistics on changes in income distribution reflect even roughly the overall flow of benefits, I have used them; but I consider the specific nature of prevailing policies to be of greater importance, the more so when the aggregate trends in available data are misleading.

REDISTRIBUTION AND GROWTH

It is not my purpose in this book to contribute to the long-standing debate on the relationship between overall economic growth and the distribution of income. Nevertheless, it would be unconscionably shortsighted to focus exclusively on equitable distribution as a desired goal without taking into account the impact of redistribution on overall growth. If greater income equality were *consistently* contrary to overall economic growth, redistribution would be counterproductive in the long run, even for the poor. Fortunately this is not the case.

What is the relationship between equity and growth? Development economists have been engaged for decades in heated controversy over this question. There is no consensus even over what conditions are required for, or conducive to, growth. One body of literature asserts that long-term growth requires an income distribution equitable enough to provide a population with the physical capabilities and skills necessary for high worker productivity, as well as the capacity to both consume and save. Another body of literature emphasizes the higher investment potential of the wealthy, the greater profitability of industries paying low wages, the anti-inflationary effects of restraining popular demand, and a score of other rationales for unequal distribution.

The lesson emerging from the seemingly interminable debate among development economists and from the Third World's postwar economic record is that the controversy over "growth or equity" vs "growth with equity" seriously overestimates the connectedness of income distribution and aggregate growth. The stalemate results from three critical facts.

First, although many studies exploring the relationship between equity and growth imply (perhaps unwittingly) that income distribution per se is the crucial determinant of the pace of economic growth, in actuality authorities credit many other factors with greater impor-

comprehensive economic or political history, nor do I explain the ideological origins of the commitment to redistribution. I certainly do not
attempt to account for the motivations of political leaders, except to
emphasize that their commitment to redistribution can be quite
changeable. And I make no attempt to trace comprehensively how
other motivations impinge upon the pursuit of redistribution—except
to demonstrate that in the typical case the interactions among different
objectives are indeed important.

As I have said, this study is designed to illuminate the importance of
the policymaking process, not to specify precise tactics to achieve
redistribution in a particular case. Therefore, although I argue for the
policy-sciences approach in trying to understand a specific case, or in
attempting to formulate policies for that case, this book is not itself an
application of the policy sciences. It does not provide a comprehensive
policy analysis, even though its conclusions underline the need for such
comprehansive analysis in the actual formulation of redistributive
policy.

In pointing out the obvious considerations (such as the potency of a
unified coalition of the wealthy) and even the subtle ones (the lag
between the reality and the perception of economic deprivation) that
should enter into policy design and strategic calculations, it is important for a comparative and interpretive study to avoid giving the
impression that there is a single package of concrete redistributive
policy instruments and tactics applicable to any situation irrespective of
contextual differences. A useful framework, one that reflects the
importance of contextual variations, will point to the relevant considerations for policy design and analysis, not provide directions for
blind application.

CHAPTER 2
Matching Tactics, Context, and Theory

IN THE PRECEDING CHAPTER I stressed that the tactics of income distribution are important, a point that would seem obvious except that so many analyses and suggested approaches seem to disregard it. I also made a few general points concerning the often-neglected task of keeping the opposition from mobilizing, the utility of coalitions across income-class boundaries, and the importance of selecting instruments that take advantage of the peculiarities of the policymaking terrain.

To say that tactics count does not mean that tactics can be selected without regard to the context in which they are applied. On the contrary, my hesitancy in advocating the general application of one specific tactic over another stems from the importance of contextual variations, fully confirmed by the case studies. The framework developed in this chapter is designed to establish which contextual factors trigger which political or economic dynamics when redistribution is attempted. These dynamics account for the political and economic predicaments, the obstacles and opportunities, the possibilities for alliance and maneuver, that appropriate tactics must address. The "nature of the regime," in terms of the authoritarian-populist, reformist, or radical style of leadership, is only one aspect. In this chapter I explore the implications of several other contextual differences across countries and over time.

Such differences are inevitably fuzzy and, for purposes of attributing importance, inconveniently overlapping. For example, the maturation of the state's apparatus for making and enforcing economic policy is often a clear trend over time; but assessing its impact on the success of redistributive efforts is confounded by other changes such as shifts in leadership styles and international economic conditions. The matches we do find between tactics and contextual factors must therefore be regarded as tentative.

It is also necessary at this point to introduce a somewhat abstract and deductive theory of income redistribution. The examination of case studies requires theoretical guidance to separate the key factors from the infinity of detail and to identify fruitful comparisons for further exploration.

A FRAMEWORK FOR ANALYZING REDISTRIBUTIVE POLICY FORMULATION

Formally, the distribution of income is the outcome of the combined effects of (a) the prevailing structure of production, shaped to some degree by governmental economic policies (of which some are intended to be redistributive, others not); and (b) the extraction and reallocation of income received, effected through governmental policy and private charity.

All governmental policies and specific decisions impinging upon the distribution of income and wealth are formulated through the formal apparatus of government: executive, legislative, administrative—usually a combination of these entities. Different types of policy measures require different modes of information gathering, analysis, formal authorization, and implementation; hence different measures are formulated and implemented in somewhat different policymaking arenas.

In addition to its distributional objectives, the central economic policymaking team of every regime has a view of how the overall growth of the economy should be orchestrated. This growth model, or macrostrategy—either explicitly articulated or simply inferrable from the ad hoc economic measures adopted—includes views on the appropriate role of the state in the economy, on how to stimulate investment, and on how to regulate demand. These views are based on expectations of how responsive various economic actors will be to the overall package of economic policies and the political environment.

The proposal and subsequent enactment of economic policies elicit reactions, both direct and indirect. Economic interest groups and political entities attempt to influence the current formulation of policy. However, they also react to their perceptions of existing policies and the prospects of future events, by providing political support or opposition, or by complying to or ignoring the government's appeals for specific cooperation in economic behavior (for example, investing where the government calls for investment).

The fact that the reactions are to perceptions of policy effects is important, because several factors obscure who benefits and who loses from economic policy. Data on economic trends are often poor, the

operations and implications of arcane economic instruments are difficult to understand, and there is a chronic (and often justified) tendency
to assume that the government's "true" intentions work at variance
with its stated intentions. Equally important, there usually are competing efforts by the government and by those who feel threatened by
economic policy to influence public interpretation of the thrust of these
policies—the government, of course, emphasizing the common
benefits of its program, and the opposition trying to portray the
policies as victimizing a broad range of groups, who are called upon to
join the opposition. The government that neglects opportunities to
convey its interpretation is at a serious disadvantage, as the case of
Arturo Illia in Argentina demonstrates. Regardless of who is more
persuasive, there is often a substantial discrepancy between the reactions that might be expected in light of the actual impact of policy and
the reactions that do emerge. Not infrequently actors of a particular
economic sector will believe incorrectly that they have been targeted as
victims of redistribution, and their subsequent unwillingness to maintain the economic activity hoped for by the government will seriously
undermine the success of the redistributive policy.

Negative reactions are of three kinds: economic accommodation,
economic retaliation, and political retaliation. The choice of reaction
mode depends on how much is risked in escalating the reaction from
the "pure business" level of accommodating under prevailing policies
to the more openly political level of trying to undermine an economic
policy or provoke the replacement of the policymakers responsible for
its formulation. This risk, in turn, hinges on the government's willingness and ability to punish such defiance, politically or through further
economic deprivation.

To the degree that private-sector cooperation does not fulfill the
growth model's expectations, the government is likely to attempt to
expand the state's economic role. This expansion may come as increased
regulation over private-sector economic activity (wage-adjustment
decrees, for instance, rather than labor-management bargaining),
increased state investment effected by new governmental financial institutions or greater governmental control over existing financial institutions, or direct state involvement in production. Thus disinvestment,
price increases in defiance of governmental wishes, and other adverse
reactions to redistributive efforts tend to promote greater state intervention. However, the more stringent formal control over the economy
which a stronger state role implies does not necessarily translate into
more effective control. The state itself is an arena of economic actors
(such as public-sector employees and state-enterprise managers) whose

policy. Thus the types of instruments employed—and the tactical options for presenting, formulating, and implementing them—are important in determining who will be mobilized to support or oppose them.

Awareness and mastery of the implications of redistributive policy are enhanced by access to technical expertise in economics, which then becomes a resource in the politics of redistribution—a resource often dominated by the higher-income economic sectors. If, however, pro-redistributive groups can also enlist the help of such experts, the advantage of the wealthy can be neutralized.

The perception that only certain policies actually have distributional implications is an illusion of important political consequence. It allows the distributive impact of the ostensibly nonredistributive instruments to go largely unnoticed and unchallenged. Sometimes the decisive battle over income distribution is won by conservative forces who are able to formulate a "nondistributive" policy that has income concentration effects that swamp the effects of progressive measures.

THE PRINCIPLE OF DIFFERENTIAL ACCESS

The arenas in which redistributive policies are formulated and implemented offer differential access and influence to representatives of economic groups and interests. Different arenas are more or less conducive to the employment of different political resources (such as voting strength, personal connections, or technical expertise). As with awareness, access to the policy formulation process for specific economic instruments can be enhanced by enlisting technical expertise or deploying other resources. However, at any point in time the governmental policymakers face relatively stable differences in the access of proredistributive and antiredistributive groups with respect to different policymaking arenas, and therefore they can choose their arenas to increase the influence of whichever side they choose. Yet the selection of economic policy instruments to carry the brunt of the redistributive effort is more commonly guided by precedent and by what seem to be the more "obvious" vehicles of redistribution.

THE PRINCIPLE OF DIFFERENTIAL CAPACITY

Given that redistributive policies can be terminated because of declines in overall economic prosperity, economic sectors whose continued economic activity is vital for the success of the regime's growth strategy are less vulnerable to redistributive extraction than are other sectors. The determinants of such economic "cruciality" include not only the economic structure per se, but also the particular growth strategy undertaken by the regime, which relies more on the dynamism of certain economic sectors than others.

In addition, the spokesmen for some economic sectors, by virtue of their prestige or expertise, have a greater capacity to convince government leaders or other key actors that economic policy is misguided or that the economy is on the brink of collapse. Since the success or failure of current policy is never black and white, and the seriousness of a supposed crisis is often subject to interpretation, undermining policy through persuasion can be as potent as economic sabotage. The Peruvian example will illustrate this point forcefully.

THE PRINCIPLE OF MULTIPLE FUNCTIONS

The government does not advocate redistributive policies in isolation of its political objectives, nor is any government perceived as advocating redistributive measures strictly for economic or altruistic motives. The reactions to a redistributive measure are responses to its political implications as well. This is of particular importance when economic beneficiaries organized in political movements in competition with the regime refuse to support a redistributive policy because its successful enactment might strengthen the government's position.

Economic policy measures that entail significant changes in the distribution of income often serve other significant economic functions. For example, "tax reform" in addition to increasing the progressivity of taxes, can also increase the efficiency of the tax system. Land reform may be progressively redistributive, but it may also be intended to increase agricultural productivity. The fact of multiple objectives behind redistributive policies can be advantageous if used to cement coalitions between redistributionists and economic actors interested in furthering the other objectives. On the other hand, it can undermine the redistributive strength of such measures if they are tailored to achieve other objectives at the cost of redistributive impact.

CONTEXT

Six broad contextual elements are relevant to any instance of economic policymaking:

1. The productive and distributional structure of the economy;
2. The unity of the economic sectors and subsectors;

3. The scope and political status of organized labor vis-à-vis the regime;
4. The regime's political base, in terms of the economic sectors in support and in opposition;
5. The thrust of other economic policies in force at the time;
6. The strength and role of the state.

Each of these elements also has special significance for the conduct of redistributive policymaking. However, each needs to specified more narowly to identify its redistributive implications.

ECONOMIC STRUCTURE

Economic stratification. The connection between the economic act of redistributing income and the political act of eliciting support for such policies depends on the nature of "the poor" relative to their political resources. How poor are the poor? Do they occupy economic positions of enough importance to permit them to exact improvements in their situation? Does their geographic location permit political activism? Are they unified economically and politically? The economic stratification of any society is a complicated pecking order in which almost everyone is richer than some and poorer than others. Therefore the degree of poverty and the extent of inequality are complicated constructs, to say the least.

At the beginning of the postwar period income inequality was roughly the same in Argentina and Chile, then at comparable levels of industralization and urbanization. Manufacturing accounted for a quarter of Argentine production, and between a fifth and a quarter of Chilean production (Kaldor 1964, pp. 246–248; UN 1969, p. 126). Around 60 percent of the Argentine population and 55 percent of the Chilean population were urban dwellers (UN 1966, p. 13).[1] At these similar stages of import-substitution industrialization promoted by the lack of available manufactures from the industrial nations, workers' shares of national income were also similar. In 1948, 68 percent of Chilean families deriving income from wages and salaries received 42 percent of the national income, while the 70 percent of Argentine families earning wages and salaries received 45 percent of the national income in 1946 (UN 1949, p. 152; UN 1964, p. 76). In Peru, with less than 30 percent of the population living in urban settlements, manufacturing accounted for less than 15 percent of production at the end of the war (UN 1949, p. 152). Low income was more exclusively a characteristic of the small farmer in Peru than in Chile, and somewhat

more so in Chile than in Argentina.[2] The peasantry of Chile probably
lived as miserably as the peasantry of Peru (Loveman 1979, p. 262), but
the latter constituted a much larger proportion of the population:
almost 60 percent of the Peruvian work force was engaged in agriculture, compared to just over 30 percent in Chile (Kaldor 1964, p. 241;
Thorp and Bertram 1978, p. 258).

By 1950 the situation in Argentina was even more distinctive.
Manufacturing contributed 30 percent of production, and the 70
percent of the work force earning wages or salaries received more than
50 percent of the national income (UN 1968). Perón's second administration, and afterward his successors, faced a socioeconomic structure
of greater income equality, urbanization, and industrialization than
existed even much later in Chile and Peru. In those two countries the
peasantry still accounted for a large segment of the work force, of
nearly constant absolute size and only gradually declining proportions
(Kaldor 1964, p. 241; Webb 1977).

Although it would seem that the scope of poverty and the degree of
income inequality would be important contextual factors in determining the prominence of distributional issues, this is not the case in the
countries being analyzed here. Concern over income redistribution
and poverty alleviation has not been positively correlated with actual
levels of inequality and poverty. If concern is measured by the amount
of attention focused on distribution as a political issue, Argentina has
been no less concerned than Chile, nor Chile than Peru. If anything,
distributional issues could be considered less prominent in Peru than in
Argentina—labeled the zero-sum society (Silvert 1966)—or in Chile—
where the social question of the income distribution between labor and
capital has been named the dominant political problem since the turn
of the century (Loveman 1979, p. 218).

Political unity of forces favoring redistribution depends in part on
the socioeconomic similarities of groups that might stand to gain from
redistribution. Hence the "uniformity of poverty" is a resource for
proredistributionists. In Latin America uniformity signifies the absence of duality between the urban organized lower-income groups
and the rest of the poor, principally the peasantry, either because the
income differences between these two segments are minor or because
the latter segment is small in number.

In Peru and Chile the duality was and still is great. Guillermo
O'Donnell provides a rough indication of the size of the "peripheral"
or "primitive production" sector of South American nations by cal-
culating the proportions, as of 1965, of the agrarian population with:
less than U.S. $200 per capita income; per capita productivity under

power of the industrial elite, we can compare industrial employment in large industry. The data show rather high levels of concentration in Argentina and Chile, with much smaller-scale manufacturing in Peru. In 1946, 47.1 percent of all industrial workers in Argentina worked for firms of over a hundred employees; in 1954, the figure was 47.8 percent (Diaz Alejandro 1970, p. 504). The proportion of manufacturing employees in Chilean firms of over 100 employees was 57 percent in 1957 (UN 1966, p. 63). These figures are roughly comparable, since a greater number of the Chilean firms were of the state sector, and manufacturing generally entails larger-scale operations than the rest of "industry." In Peru, however, only 34.7 percent of manufacturing workers were in firms of even twenty or more employees (FitzGerald 1979, p. 274).

Dependence. The economic structure establishes the degree of dependence of the local economy on changes and decisions made abroad, specifically on the booms and depressions triggered by changes in the world economy. For Latin America the condition of the U.S. economy and decisions of U.S. economic actors (including the government) are particularly important.

The broad issue of whether a Latin American country is best served by exposing its economy to the opportunities and dangers of the world economy is not the focus of this study. Suffice it to say that the view that deviations from free trade are costly distortions interfering with comparative advantage is countered by the also arguable views that selective protectionism can nurture infant industries that will ultimately constitute comparative advantage, or that responses to immediate market signals can narrow a nation's economic diversity to the point of limiting its future adaptability. Whichever view is correct, redistributive efforts depend on a considerably narrower aspect of dependency: the degree to which foreign reactions to redistributive policies and their consequences affect the domestic economy. Note that this is very different from asking whether foreign decisions and conditions affect the domestic economy in general ways. Clearly, a recession in the industrialized world will color the domestic prosperity of any country with significant trade or investment ties to the developed nations. The issue, rather, is how much impact redistributive policies will have on the domestic economy via, first, the impact of these policies on foreign behavior (withholding or offering loans, aid, trade, or investment) and, second, the impact of foreign behavior on the domestic economy. Without such impact, even if foreign decision makers find a nation's redistributive policies abhorrent, they lack sufficient leverage or motivation to do anything about it.

The "foreigners" are diverse and act out of diverse motives. Foreign decision makers, whether they represent governments, international agencies, or private firms, may base their decisions on criteria ranging from the most stringently economic aspects of creditworthiness to the most political and ideological considerations of geopolitics. These decisions may be in response to specific redistributive measures (such as nationalization) or to the widespread economic conditions resulting from redistributive policies and other aspects of the economic policy regime. They may range from highly positive (such as the increased U.S. Alliance for Progress aid for governments viewed as more reform-minded) to highly negative (investors' reluctance and U.S. government boycotts during the early Perón administration and the Allende administration). Whatever the sources or nature of these reactions, the economy's openness to foreign decisions determines the breadth of analysis necessary for anticipating the consequences of redistributive efforts.

Argentina, Chile, and Peru, because of their dependence on exports and their shortage of domestic capital to maintain growth rates that are regarded as satisfactory, are all vulnerable to world economic fluctuations. Table 3 shows that Peru depended on exports for a fifth to a quarter of gross domestic product (GDP) from the beginning of the postwar period up to the beginning of the 1960s. Chile was somewhat less dependent on export in terms of the share of GDP, which was just under a fifth during the same period, although Chile's strong dependence on the single export of copper made the country more vulnerable to world price fluctuations. Argentina was both less dependent, with exports constituting less a tenth of GDP by 1950, and enjoyed a greater diversity of exports. Even so, it must be emphasized that exports have been pivotal for all three countries, since the import requirements to keep the process of industrialization going require good export performance if serious balance-of-payments problems are to be avoided. The UN Economic Commission for Latin America, though openly skeptical of the pitfalls of export dependence, declared

TABLE 3. EXPORT EARNINGS AS A PERCENTAGE OF GROSS DOMESTIC PRODUCT FOR ARGENTINA, CHILE, AND PERU.

Period	Argentina	Chile	Peru
1945–1949	14.5	18.8	18.5
1950–1954	9.6	14.2	19.3
1955–1961	9.8	14.2	25.0

SOURCE: United Nations 1964, pp. 86, 94.

in 1959 that for Argentina "the expansion of the export trade is just as vitally necessary as import substitution for the vigorous development of industry and, consequently, for the rapid growth of the per capita product" (UN 1959, p. 23).

Immediately after World War II export production and marketing was in private hands. Particularly in Chile, where the major copper mines were all foreign owned, multinational corporations also played an important role in export production and export trade. Argentine export production, basically in beef and grain, remained private and Argentine-owned, but during the Perón administration the marketing of agroexports was taken over by the government, only to be abandoned by Perón successors. After that, export was "regulated"—in general very badly—through export taxes and exchange-rate policy. In Peru the main exporting of sugar, cotton, and fish meal was by private, local groups, whereas the extractive industries, principally petroleum and copper, by 1950 were dominated by foreign firms (Thorp and Bertram 1978, chaps. 11 and 12).

The direct participation of foreign companies in the domestic economies was also substantial. If U.S. direct investment is used as a measure of the presence of multinational companies in Latin American countries, then the figures of Table 4 imply that Chile and Peru, with economies roughly one-fifth and one-eighth the size of the Argentine economy respectively, had greater proportional U.S. investment than did Argentina. However, the bulk of U.S. investment in Chile was in export-oriented mining, and over half of the U.S. investments in Peru were in mining and petroleum (U.S. Department of Commerce 1960, 1974). Thus in manufacturing the presence of foreign capital was proportionately greater in Argentina than in Chile throughout the period and started out greater than in Peru, although

TABLE 4. U.S. DIRECT INVESTMENTS IN ARGENTINA, CHILE, AND PERU (MILLIONS OF U.S. DOLLARS).

Year	Argentina All	Argentina Manufacturing only	Chile All	Chile Manufacturing only	Peru All	Peru Manufacturing only
1943	380	101	328	27.5	71	5.5
1950	356	—	540	—	145	—
1957	333	—	666	—	383	—
1959	361	158	729	21	427	31
1966	758	510	765	47	651	128

SOURCES: U.S. Treasury Department 1947; 1960, p. 92; 1974, p. 31.

the U.S. manufacturing investment in Peru grew rapidly in the 1950s and 1960s. In short, Argentina faced a greater penetration of foreign capital in domestically oriented industry, while Chile and Peru faced far greater penetration in export-oriented industry.

Any conclusions about the dependency of a nation must be tempered by recognizing that, to some degree, the importance of dependency varies according to the economic strategy adopted by its leaders. Some economic growth strategies are more heavily dependent on foreign inputs for their success; some tactics of redistribution are more likely to provoke withdrawal of pivotal foreign cooperation or retaliation from foreign actors. Even so, to understand the demise of regimes that for one reason or another became targets of U.S. retaliation (such as Velasco's regime in Peru or Allende's in Chile) the role of economic dependency cannot be ignored.

Unity of Economic Sectors

Unity has two dimensions: shared material interests, as when a given policy benefits or deprives two or more sectors; and perceived common interests. Both can be volatile. The composition of a sector can change over time (Argentina's industrial sector prior to Perón, for instance, was controlled by "old money," but was split thereafter by the emergence of "new-money" entrepreneurs operating on a smaller scale), and different policies can unify or separate economic sectors. A common threat can foster unity where it was absent before. Thus the unity of economic sectors changes as economic structures evolve, as new regimes rise, and as new policies are presented.

The unity of the high-income sectors at the beginning of the postwar period depended on the mingling of ownership of land and industry, and on the homogeneity of the efficiency and scale of operations within each of the sectors. In Argentina early industrialization was strongly connected to the agricultural export sector (Randall 1978, p. 120). By 1945 large-scale industry was well established in its own right, but the financial and emotional ties to agroexport persisted. Similarly, the financing of Peruvian industrialization, albeit limited, came primarily from the landed elite seeking diversification. Only in Chile was there a continuous separation of agricultural and industrial ownership.

As industrialization progressed, two factors decreased the unity of the industrial and agricultural elites. In Argentina and Peru new entrepreneurs with little connection to the old elites arose in nontraditional subsectors: small-scale and medium-scale import-substitution industries in Argentina, light consumer goods and fish-meal processing in Peru. The Argentine entrepreneurs depended on Perón's diversion of agroexport profits for their own subsidies, organizing themselves separately from the large-scale industrialists.[3] In the 1960s foreign investment in Peruvian industry added another division among the business-sector actors. Second, as the difficulties of going beyond the easy stages of import-substitution industrialization became evident in Chile and Peru, the inefficiency of the latifundia came to be regarded by other elite groups as the bottleneck holding back rapid economic progress. Thus by the 1960s the industrial sectors in both countries were favorably disposed to land reform designed along efficiency criteria, and in Peru even the coastal agricultural producers did not strongly oppose land reform in the Sierra region. In short, high-income sectors in all three countries had some fissures of potential advantage to the clever redistributionist. These were divisions across sectors, technological levels, and regions that hampered a grand coalition of the wealthy.

THE SCOPE AND STATUS OF ORGANIZED LABOR

Organized labor plays a special role in redistributive efforts because, first, it is organized—and therefore capable of articulating its demands and backing them with organized strength—and, second, the labor union is traditionally oriented to the "employer-vs-employee confrontation" mentality that takes for granted the progressive nature of increased real worker income. Three aspects of working-class organization are of critical importance in establishing the conduct of not only wage policy but redistributive policy in general. The *scope of organized labor,* reflected by the proportion of workers within the labor movement, is an important determinant of whether income increases to organized labor have progressive or regressive distributional effects. If large segments of the work force are not unionized, and because of their lack of bargaining power earn considerably lower incomes, then higher wages to unionized workers or other policy benefits (such as subsidized food prices imposed largely for the benefit of urban workers) may well reduce the purchasing power of poorer populations. Broader scope of organized labor thus fortifies its claim that prolabor policy and progressivism are synonymous. The size of the labor movement also tends to strengthen it politically.

Argentina, Chile, and Peru are clearly distinguishable in terms of the scope of organized labor. The organization of Peruvian labor—not surprisingly, given the country's lower level of economic development—is markedly less widespread. In the latter half of the 1960s roughly 9 percent of the entire work force (including white-collar workers) was unionized, and about 15 percent of the nonagricultural work force.[4] In Chile in the same period roughly 30 percent of the overall work force was organized, the proportions being 40 percent in industry, 60 percent in mining, and 14 percent in agriculture (Angell 1972, p. 45). In Argentina, the half-million organized workers of the pre-Perón era increased fivefold under Perón, so that by the 1960s Argentina had fully one-third of its total work force (45 percent of total employees) organized in the umbrella Confederación General de Trabajadores, or CGT (General Labor Confederation), with a substantial number of workers organized in competing unions.[5]

The *strength of organized labor* is the second important characteristic. While the proscription or the support of organized labor by particular regimes has some effect, the overall power of organized labor is stabilized over time by other durable characteristics such as labor scarcity, industrial modernity, class awareness, and the historical development of the labor movement.

Judging the strength of organized labor obviously is more difficult, and more situation specific, than assessing its scope. Chilean labor long was tightly organized, legally recognized, legally recognized, militant, and well represented in partisan politics by the Communist and Socialist parties that vied for dominance within the Central Federation of Chilean Workers. Its bargaining power was somewhat limited, however, by the surplus of labor. Argentine labor, since its elevation in political and economic status by Perón, has been very strong by general Latin American standards; some would label it "the best organized and most militant in Latin America" (Reed 1972, p. 2). The scarcity of labor has strengthened its bargaining position; and politically labor has maintained its unity through Peronist dominance, though rivalries within Peronism have occasionally reduced that unity. However, Peronist dominance has motivated government intervention and interference in the labor movement by anti-Peronist regimes. It would be difficult to make a blanket statement that either Chilean or Argentine labor is stronger than the other in any overall sense. Peruvian labor, because of its smaller scope and greater labor surplus, is considerably weaker in economic terms. In general it has also been weaker in organizational and legal standing, depending on the fortunes of the Alianza Popular Revolucionaria Americana, or APRA movement. Yet APRA, which represents a large portion of organized labor, has never been out of contention in the struggles for governmental control.

The third aspect of organized labor is the *competitiveness of its current leadership* with the leadership of the government, an ongoing struggle that provides labor leaders with an additional political motive to reject the government's redistributive measures. In contrast, when the executive already controls large segments of organized labor, he can use their loyalty to gain compliance with his own guidelines. Obviously this competitiveness is a changeable characteristic, depending on who holds the reins of government and whether the regime's leadership aspires to gain control of organized labor as well. Three situations have existed in the countries under examination: (a) the executive, or his political party or movement, already has established control over much of organized labor (the cases of Allende and Perón); (b) the executive attempts to increase his control over organized labor through efforts seen by established labor leaders as major challenges (Frondizi in Argentina; Ibáñez and Frei in Chile; Odría, Belaúnde, and Velasco in Peru); (c) the executive does not control the bulk of organized labor and makes no major effort to gain such control (Illia in Argentina; the Radical party presidents in Chile; José Luis Bustamante and Manuel Prado in Peru). It must be emphasized that almost all regimes attempt to increase their influence over the labor movement to some degree; the question is whether the efforts are perceived as a major political issue.

The Regime's Political Base

Although most regimes seek and claim broad-gauged support, typically an administration comes to be identified as representing certain socioeconomic groups. The support afforded the regime is a complex outcome of its concrete policies and this identification. However, the image is often self-fulfilling, as governments attempt to preserve their support by the policies they formulate.

The regime that develops a working-class base faces different dilemmas and opportunities than one dependent primarily on the middle sectors. The implications of the base of support, only partially captured by the adoption of populist, centrist, or radical approaches by each regime, are best elaborated on a case-by-case basis. Broadly speaking, though, the dependence on middle-sector support obligates government leaders to preoccupy themselves with balancing redistribution with growth. The working-class-based regime is less likely to reverse its own redistributive measures out of concern for the decline in overall economic growth, but it is more susceptible to attempts to topple the regime by higher-income groups who fear the collapse of their economic positions. The working-class-based regime is also less likely to be able to convince the business sector that it has a credible growth strategy. By the same token, the middle-class-based regime is less capable of convincing labor that its redistributive intentions are sincere.

THE CONTEXT OF OTHER POLICIES

The redistribution-minded optimist might hope for a complete separation of production and distribution, anticipating that the state's actions to channel income and wealth could be conducted without interfering with the impact of policies designed to stimulate production, or with production itself. If this were the case, the government could select the growth-stimulating strategy conducive to the highest rate of overall growth, then redistribute the after-production incomes in accordance with its equity objectives.

In practice, however, the separation cannot be sustained. It has long been recognized that the distribution of income and wealth affects the volume and structure of production via effects on income disposable for investment and consumption;[6] furthermore, production policies affect the capacity of the opponents of redistribution to undermine the redistributive effort. This can come about dramatically, when the economy declines (as under the Peruvian military radicals), or simply when the leaders come to believe that their redistributive efforts are inconsistent with growth objectives.

Moreover, redistributive policies themselves influence decisions to produce and invest. The profit-maximizing investor looks at the net incentives for investment in various areas. Policies motivated by redistributive goals influence his production decisions as well. And, of course, the economic actor who tries to change policy is even more likely to base his investment and production decisions on his reactions to redistribution-oriented policies.

Just as different economic structures afford different economic sectors the opportunity to undermine redistributive policy, different economic growth strategies are vulnerable to undermining by different economic sectors. For example, inward-looking industrialization requires the cooperation of local investors. If, by contrast, the impetus for economic exansion is expected to come from exportation controlled by the private sector, the actions of the export sector and its foreign counterparts will have a disproportionately important role in determining the overall prosperity of the economy and the perceived soundness of economic policy. If foreign investment is given a central role in the government's development strategy, then the pivotal actors are the multinational corporations, foreign bankers, the U.S. government, multilateral development agencies, and the domestic actors from whom these external actors get their cues regarding the viability and political ramifications of investment in that country. It is worth noting, however, that external decisions on foreign loans and aid can foster redistribution as well as block it. In Chile alone, U.S. support through official aid and the facilitation of private foreign investment was a significant factor in Frei's successes, whereas U.S. opposition, entailing the suspension of most aid and the discouragement of private investment, was even more significant in Allende's failure.

The macrostrategy of a government's economic policy is part of the context to the extent that only certain strategic options will be perceived as viable for a given country in a given era. However, the strategy chosen from within this range will generally have some congruence with the regime's ideological position, and government leaders must also consider whether a specific macrostrategy (a) benefits the economic sectors from which the regime expects support; (b) places greater disruptive power in the hands of antagonistic sectors; and (c) benefits the beneficiaries of redistribution by directly increasing their productivity. Like so many elements that condition the success of redistributive policy, the configuration of economic policies is partially constrained but by no means entirely so.

The range of macrostrategies perceived as viable in Argentina and Chile has been very broad. Regime changes and economic downturns have brought many sharp reversals from previous policies. Inward-looking approaches have alternated with internationalism, modest reversions to laissez-faire with increased statism, expansionism with tight-credit austerity. Despite these changes, a basic pattern of protected industrialization financed through the export earnings of other sectors (Argentine agroexport and Chilean copper) can be discerned. Light and medium industry grew basically in private hands, and heavy industry through the state; but in Chile the state moved steadily into the former subsectors as well. To augment the financing channeled away from the export sectors, agricultural wealth was also diverted into industry.

This process of industrialization established some of the basic vulnerabilities of each regime's growth strategy. In Argentina the extraction from agroexport to finance industrialization was more ticklish than extracting copper-export earnings in Chile because the Argentine agroexporters were politically powerful; their profits and hence their willingness to export were precarious, and they could turn to the domestic market to dump some of their production in order to avoid high export taxes. The large Chilean copper mines, in contrast, were steadily profitable, making it easier for the state to tax copper exports without killing the incentive to keep up production, which moreover could not be significantly diverted to domestic markets. Naturally the fluctuations in world copper prices made huge differences in the Chilean government's revenues, but the government was not dependent on the cooperation of the copper companies to the degree that Argentine prosperity depended on the willingness of the agroexporters to maintain cereal and beef production.

Although industry obtained financing from other sectors, largely through government policy, the typical government could ill afford to antagonize the industrialists. The importance of industrial growth as a mark of economic success obliged many governments to encourage industrial investment from all quarters, not the least of which was the industrial sector itself. The importance of industrial production also made the compliance of industrial labor a critical factor for smooth economic growth. The labor strike and the "investment strike" in industry became potent weapons, even though industry was by and large a favored sector.

In Peru the range of macrostrategies undertaken by the various regimes was narrower, with consistent emphasis on export promotion and on privately controlled industrialization encouraged by industrial promotion laws designed to offset the liabilities of the limited internal market. Even though several Peruvian administrations attempted to expand the role of the state, Peru remained markedly more laissez-faire—and private-ownership-oriented—than either Chile or Argentina. Although the extraction of resources from export sectors into industry was minimal in comparison to Argentina and Chile, the Peruvian exporters themselves often placed profits earned through export into industrial ventures. They were thus more pivotal to the success of government policy than their counterparts in Argentina or Chile.

THE ROLE OF THE STATE

Finally, we must establish the links among production, redistributive policy, and the role of the state. The government's functions with respect to redistribution have four components:

1. Regulation of remuneration and pricing;
2. Extraction and reallocation of income derived from existing productive arrangements (fiscal policy, for example);
3. Regulation of production to reorient it into activities providing greater income for designated beneficiaries;

4. Direct state production or involvement in finance, marketing, and so
on.

Earlier in this chapter I proposed that the government's intervention
and the state's direct economic participation grow not only out of an
ideological preference for socialism, but also from the government's
desire to gain greater control, to rely on economic instruments of
presumably surer effect, and to reduce the private sector's capacity to
undermine redistributive efforts. Any such theory of the state's role
must take into account, for each of the above-mentioned components,
both the extent of the state's presence and its effectiveness. These are
sometimes regarded together under the rubric "the strength of the
state." However, if we wish to distinguish between governmental
effectiveness and the strength of the state, the latter is most usefully
defined in a way parallel to the definition of the strength of foreign
actors: that is, the capacity of the state sector to shape the structure of
the economy in terms of its sectoral allocations, investment levels and
allocations, technological directions, emphasis on domestic or foreign
market production, and so on.

In theory, one could contrast the actual pattern of the economy's
evolution with the hypothetical course it would have taken in completely private hands. Still, we cannot presume that the changes in the
economy produced by state-sector actions will be faithful to the objectives of the central government's leadership. Certainly the scope of the
state sector can be a major determinant of the government's effectiveness in achieving its objectives, but only if the central government is
willing and able to wield the economic power of the state sector
effectively.

With respect to government effectiveness per se, a general pattern
of learning to manage economic problems can be detected, countered
only partially by occasional declines in governmental control as anti-
statist regimes tried to dismantle existing interventionist mechanisms.
It is important to note that a government's effectiveness is not a single
characteristic; a government is effective or ineffective with respect to
each particular task. For example, the Allende government was able to
enforce price controls more effectively than any preceding Chilean
administration, yet it could not contain wage demands of state employees or prevent decapitalization in the state sector. The evaluation of
governmental effectiveness is useful principally in assessing the prospects for achieving particular objectives.[7]

The overall strength of the state is an important contextual factor in
that the dilemma facing the strong state controlled by a redistribution-
minded regime is the danger of redistributing income to a greater

degree than intended, with the consequent problem of deteriorating production. The dilemma facing the weaker state is that its redistributive attempts tend to evaporate in the fact of accommodative reactions on the part of the targeted victims; its redistributive promises often cannot be kept. Whereas the strong state faces the danger of a rightist reaction if its efforts go too far, the weak state risks alienating the left when its claimed commitment to redistribution appears false.

In one respect, the strength of the state in the economy is simply the obverse of the strength of the private sector. If we recall Table 2, it is clear that the Chilean state had a far greater share of investment and thus had a greater capacity to channel investment into activities according to the visions of the governmental and state leaders rather than in accordance with private-sector priorities. Moreover, this was done basically through one huge agency, the state development corporation CORFO. Markos Mamalakis argues: "The basic agent in the government's development effort, CORFO has acted as a financier, entrepreneur, investor, innovator and researcher, and frontierman. As such, it has dominated economic life since 1939" (1965, p. 18).

Table 2 also indicates that until the late 1960s the scope of the Argentine state was greater than the Peruvian. However, the Argentine state sector never had the coordination that CORFO provided in Chile, nor did it gain legitimacy as an appropriate source of economic dynamism. Despite Perón's development of state enterprises in production and a large state apparatus in marketing and finance, governmental economic management was still largely a matter of regulating the private sector. The same was true in Peru until the 1968 military government expanded the state sector as part of its attempt to restructure the economy.

CONCLUSIONS

Although it is easy to see why many leaders might have felt trapped by the contextual limitations they had to face, the factors enumerated above are notable for the predominance of aspects which are neither unalterable nor completely manipulable. Redistributive policy obviously cannot be formulated in an ivory tower—country-specific limitations cannot be ignored. But it is equally true that the redistribution-minded leader can to some degree mold his context—through the selection of macrostrategy in addition to specifically redistributive measures, through coalition overtures to particular economic sectors, and through changes in the role of the state sector.

II
THE
AUTHORITARIAN
POPULISTS

THE LIBERAL DEMOCRACIES and conservative oligarchies of Latin America in the 1930s and 1940s, because of rising urbanization and literacy, were vulnerable to "men on horseback" who could appeal to the masses. The liberal democracy of the era was dominated by struggles within and between the upper and middle classes; the poor had little involvement and little to gain. Although in theory the numerically strong masses should have been favored in electoral politics, even where suffrage was broad, working-class groups were rarely well enough organized to compete effectively. In addition, the frequent legislative-executive stalemates increased the yearning for strong leadership to replace weak democratic regimes.

The conservative oligarchies, largely military-dominated governments supported by the landed elite, offered even less hope for the poor. Instead, their use of dictatorial power in defense of the economic status quo fueled the commitment of their opponents to employ authoritarian means of their own to redress the imbalance of wealth. And in their preoccupation with fending off the political claims of the middle-sector parties, the oligarchical regimes were often caught off guard by the emergence of populism.

Juan Perón in Argentina led the way, not only in preceding most other populists but also in the strength of his grip on the workers' movement and in the prominence of his efforts as a paradigm of populism. In Peru the economic and political collapse of a civilian regime in 1948 brought in Gen. Manuel Odría, while Chile's former dictator, Gen. Carlos Ibáñez, rode into office on a wave of opposition to the established parties in 1952. Thus, in the space of six years these three countries all acquired strong presidents of military background, with Odría and Ibáñez more or less consciously emulating Perón's style and policies. Let us begin, then, with the master.

CHAPTER 3
Argentina's Machiavellian Master

I N MANY RESPECTS significant income redistribution in Argentina began and ended with the regime of Juan Perón, from 1946 to 1955.[1] Perón carried out the most sweeping redistribution of any initiated in the three countries covered by this study, but still encountered a number of difficulties. On the one hand, the magnitude and durability of redistribution effected under Perón, the duration of Perón's own rule, and his ability to reverse the economic decline encountered in the middle period of his administration would certainly qualify the Peronist period as an impressive *relative* success. The workers' share of national income increased dramatically, from less than 40 percent during World War II to a high of over 50 percent reached in 1950–52; it remained fairly high through the Perón years and during the first three years after Perón was deposed.[2] By 1947 average real wage rates for urban workers—the low-income group in Argentina because of its predominantly urban population and capital-intensive agriculture—had risen 40 percent over the previous period, and they have never slipped back below this level (Diaz Alejandro 1970, p. 538). Workers rose from virtual powerlessness before the Perón era to a position of bargaining strength that to this day has not been completely eroded, despite the strong antiunion actions of later military governments.

Yet this decade had its share of economic difficulties and political turmoil. Perón's economic management was widely attacked as incompetent, especially by critics more concerned with the economy's aggregate growth than with its income distribution.[3] Perón also polarized Argentine politics in such a way that after 1955 representation of working-class interests was severely hampered by the prohibitions on the political activities of the Peronist movement. In assessing the redistributive gains made under Perón, we need to bear in mind that his political and economic record was by no means an unqualified success.

Nevertheless, it is worth noting that criticisms of Perón's economic measures have themselves been severely challenged. The economic

historian Laura Randall (1978, p. 158) points out: "To a great extent,
Perón achieved the economic results he desired." On the basis of new
studies, revised data, and a perhaps more sensitive appreciation for the
international context in which Perón had to operate, there has been a
remarkable reappraisal of Perón's economic performance. Robert
Alexander, often critical of Perón, recently expressed his revised
assessment: "The economic policies of the Perón government have
been severely criticized by its opponents and by foreign economists.
However, there is little doubt that in general terms they were justified
by the state of Argentine economic development and the world situation at that period"(Alexander 1979, pp. 63–64). Moreover, the economic growth statistics calculated just after Perón's ouster, which
showed economic stagnation for the period, have been called into
question; subsequent calculations of economic growth rates for the
same period show considerable progress (Randall 1976).

More to the point, many of the events and policies widely acknowledged as responsible for the economic problems of the era (for
example, nationalization of British-owned railways, wasteful public-
works projects, severe droughts, and falling export prices) had very
little to do with the objective and means of redistributing income. The
economic weaknesses of Peronist policies, however great they may
have been, do not demonstrate that income distribution could only
have been effected at the cost of severely damaging the economy. That
the Argentine economy has declined relative to its promise is undeniable; but the idea that Perón's redistribution destroyed the Argentine
economy for future generations disregards both the malaise of the
economic structure prior to Perón's administration and the fact that
succeeding regimes attempted a wholesale dismantling of the Peronist
economic structure, expunging its strengths as much as its weaknesses.[4]

It is also important to challenge a widespread impression that the
second half of the Perón era was marked by a regression in income
distribution, a myth that arose from the fact that when the economy
was beset with difficulties from 1949 to 1952, Perón pressed the labor
unions to accept lower real wages and to desist from strikes. It was
widely perceived (though of course never expressed publicly by the
government in these terms) that the rise in real wages had overshot the
level at which both high production and low inflation could be
achieved. The labor movement complied enough to reduce the strike
level dramatically for the 1951–1953 period (Wynia 1978, p. 72), and
real wages went down by more than 20 percent of their 1950 level and
by nearly 30 percent of their highest level in 1948 (Silverman 1969, p.

245). Yet the crucial point is that these declines in real wages occurred in a period of general economic decline, in which *total* income decreased even more. In terms of income shares, even conservative estimates show the 1952–1954 workers' share at or near the 1950 high, with only 1951 showing a modest decline. According to less conservative estimates, even the 1951 workers' share was higher than in prior years, and the 1952 level was still greater (Silverman 1969, p. 243). Thus, the reduction in real wages did not drop the wage level back to what it had been prior to Perón, and, as the statistics reveal, wage earners did not suffer more than other sectors from the economic decline of the early 1950s.

THE PERONIST INITIATIVES

When Perón emerged in 1945 as the dominant figure of the military government that had seized power in 1943, the Argentine economy still revolved around beef and grain exports. This was reflected in an income distribution favoring large-scale agricultural producers, and a political structure that protected their control over economic policy since 1930, when a succession of autocratic conservative governments replaced the middle-class-based, urban-oriented Radical party.

In recognition of the agroexport producers' claim that the vitality of the export trade was critical to Argentina, several vital levers of economic policy had been placed in their hands. The grain and meat marketing boards established through the efforts of large-scale producers in the 1930s remained under their control until 1946. Via price floors established by these boards the government paid grain producers more than world market prices during the bleak trading years of the 1930s (Randall 1978, p. 101). The Central Bank, too, was directed by private bankers concerned primarily with facilitating international trade through monetary policies that kept the Argentine currency stable (Randall 1978, pp. 64–66).

Through these mechanisms the agroexport producers had managed to guarantee their own requirements for credit, not infrequently at the expense of credit availability for small-scale agriculture and for manufacturing. The manufacturing sector, which had emerged during the First World War and again during the Great Depression when importation of foreign manufactures was limited, grew up largely without government support. Beef and grain exporters had used these same mechanisms to ensure that the profits from export sales in good years would go directly to the agroexport producers and export middlemen with little government interference, and that in years of low world market prices their losses would be cushioned.

Because of the economic and policy dominance of land-intensive beef and grain production, the income distribution problem facing Perón was quite different from the problems of Chile and Peru. Since European immigration to the cities, reinforced by internal urbanization during the export-market collapse during the depression, had provided the bulk of Argentina's lower-income families, the primary welfare problem in Argentina was urban poverty. The solution apparent to Perón, to encourage urban-centered economic growth, would not have addressed the welfare problem of rural impoverishment that was predominant in Peru and relatively important in Chile as well.[5]

In short, for Perón to redistribute wealth to his low-income followers, he had to divert the profits flowing to agroexport producers into industry, at the same time ensuring that industrial workers shared in the resulting wealth. A policy of wage increases alone would have had two serious liabilities: it would have driven many marginal manufacturing firms into bankruptcy, and it would have left untouched the large number of urban unemployed and the remaining rural landless ready to migrate to the cities (Merkx 1968, chap. 8).

Perón's grand scheme, then, was to shift wealth away from the cattle and grain producers and into subsidized, largely private-sector industrialization. Along with public works for infrastructure, this industrialization would raise workers' incomes through the enforcement of high government-controlled wage and benefit levels. Five mechanisms were central to this scheme:

1. An institution for capturing the agricultural export profits;
2. A system of industrial subsidies;
3. A massive public works program;
4. A wage-setting and enforcement apparatus;
5. A social security tax system.

To accomplish the first objective of transferring income from agricultural producers to urban wage earners, Perón, in characteristically ad hoc fashion, used the grain and meat export marketing mechanism to siphon off agroexport profits. In March 1946—after his presidential election victory, but before his inauguration—Perón had outgoing president Edelmiro Farrell decree the establishment of the Institute for Trade Promotion (IAPI) to replace the existing marketing boards, for the ostensible purpose of providing Argentina with more unified bargaining power in setting export prices. IAPI did succeed in selling

Argentine agricultural exports at fairly high prices through most of the Perón era, but the prices it paid to the agroexport producers were far below the prices it received on the world market, resulting in huge IAPI gains which were then applied as governmental subsidies to new industrial enterprises. These industries, in turn, provided employment openings for both the existing urban unemployed and the poor pouring into Buenos Aires and other cities from the countryside.

The bulk of the redistributed income thus came from the agricultural sector:

> The shift was not . . . a straightforward one from profits to wages . . . it rather involved a substantial income shift from rural to urban families, with most, but not all, of the gain going to wage-earning families within the latter group. While agricultural families received 22.3 per cent of all personal income in 1946, their share was only 14.2 per cent in 1949; by contrast, the share of non-agricultural families (not including *rentiers* or the retired) rose from 69.9 to 79.6 per cent. (UN 1969, p. 130)

What made this shift a truly progressive redistribution was the fact that such a large proportion of the Argentine rural population consisted of well-to-do independent farmers, who were victims of the redistribution. Farm workers also lost income through declining agricultural prices, but unlike almost all other Latin American countries, Argentina had a small enough proportion of farm workers and owners of small plots known as *minifundia* to ensure that income shifts from agriculture would benefit the urban poor more than they would deprive the remaining rural poor.[6]

There is some controversy about whether the export producers realized from the outset that IAPI would be used to extract wealth from the agricultural sector. Whether or not they did, the incongruity of using this institution as a redistributive device certainly caught rural interests off guard.

The employment of IAPI to redistribute income was disarming to its opposition for two reasons. First, marketing boards were not new to Argentina, and in fact the boards, previously dominated by the export commodity producers, had served this segment well. It would have been difficult and embarrassing for the producers to attack the *principle* of such boards; their complaint was simply on the pragmatic ground that the institution was being misused. Second, since Perón's policies were perceived by the producers as abuse of an otherwise useful institution, the creation of IAPI provoked efforts by the producers to educate the government to the error of its economic ways, rather than leading to an out-and-out producers' boycott against a relatively blatant attempt to wrest away their power and wealth. The pages of the

Review of the River Plate (a conservative journal) and the pronouncements of the Sociedad Rural (the leading rural elite society) were
marked by almost plaintive calls for reevaluation of IAPI policy, as if it
were merely technically misguided. These attacks on IAPI have been
interpreted as an indication of the rural elite's adamant opposition to
the Peronist policies. While this is undoubtedly true, it is of equal
importance that the opposition was channeled into defensive com-
plaining in the public media rather than into economic boycott and
sabotage or open political revolt.

Once IAPI was established, Perón turned to his industrial promotion program. Partially outlined in the two Five-Year Plans, in fact the
program lay more in the profusion of regulations, concessions, and
exceptions on tariffs, taxes, permits, and the like, than in any coherent
plan. The majority of large, well-established industrial enterprises
received little because their owners opposed the Peronist unionization
movement and, besides, they had been operating rather profitably
without subsidies prior to Perón's rule. The major interest-group
organization of the large businesses, the *Unión Industrial Argentina,* or
UIA (Argentine Industrial Union), complained continually about the
lack of coherence and efficiency of the new industrial development, the
growing "anarchy" of the labor-management arena, and the favoritism
the government showed to union demands vis-à-vis those of employers.

This opposition by UIA left small and medium-sized industries to
gain under Perón's industrial protectionism. Organized at Perón's
instigation into the *Confederación General Económica,* or CGE (General
Economic Confederation), to rival UIA, undercapitalized small-scale
entrepreneurs relied heavily on the government for cheap credit—
usually at negative interest rates—and particular advantages to ensure
survival in an otherwise too-competitive environment (Freels 1968,
chap. 2; Mallon and Sourrouille 1975, p. 144). New industrial jobs
initially grew out of the rapid, helter-skelter expansion of these modestly scaled enterprises, though the general expansion of the economy
from 1946 to 1950 stimulated greater employment in established
industries as well.

To meet the infrastructural needs of this burgeoning industry and
to absorb more labor, Perón launched a massive public works program
that was widely criticized for its extravagance. Critics saw the frenetic
building of roads, ports, monumental buildings, and the like as a
wasteful expression of Perón's egotism, but there were also important
macroeconomic effects, principally an increased demand for construction materials and a tightening of the labor supply. Argentine employ-

ers could not count on a virtually unlimited labor pool, but instead had to compete for relatively scarce labor.

This was possible because during the 1943–1945 period Perón had revamped the wage-setting system that had previously afforded tremendous advantage to employers. Before Perón became the first secretary of labor in November 1943, unionization had been hampered by the refusal of employers to recognize or bargain with unions, dismissals of union activists, and other acts of harrassment usually abetted by the government. Perón changed the mechanism of wage setting by involving the Secretariat of Labor in collective bargaining conferences. Ostensibly the conferences were to permit management and labor to negotiate freely. Yet the secretariat not only ensured that unionists could bargain without risking reprisals, it also had the power to arbitrate if there was a deadlock. The secretariat's known prolabor leanings frequently induced the unions to adopt recalcitrant positions so that the government would intervene in their favor (Alexander 1962, p. 193). Until the government decided that real wages had risen beyond their optimal level, the secretariat consistently imposed higher real wages. Beginning in 1952 the government imposed greater control by setting wage levels directly, without much pretense of labor-management negotiations, but by this time higher real wages were regarded as inflationary; thus the imposition of direct control was as much to rein in the unions as to reduce the bargaining power of the enterprises.

Several qualities of the Peronist approach to wage policy help to clarify how it was received politically. By manipulating wage levels through many separate, governmentally influenced collective bargaining agreements, rather than by legislating broad, industry-wide wage adjustments, Perón's wage policy was *differentiated.* That is, different rules applied to different conditions—and therefore to different cases. Instead of having the same wage adjustment for all workers, imposed directly by the government, each bargaining outcome was unique. Therefore the full weight of the industrial owners could not be mobilized for or against a sweeping package; nor was the government held responsible for a blanket wage increase disappointing to the workers. Equally important, industrialists in one subsector, or workers in another, could be favored or deprived without the necessity of treating all industrialists or all workers in like fashion.

The wage-setting structure was also *indirect,* in that the bargaining outcome, though manipulated by the government, nevertheless was colored by the struggle between workers and owners. The government was involved, to be sure, and was undoubtedly held responsible for some of the outcomes, but it was not the sole accountable decision maker.

Finally, the outcome at any point in time was *segmental*, in that each decision affected only a small portion of the total population—the relevant group of workers and their employers.

These qualities reinforced the ambiguity of the apparent net results of wage and price changes. The welter of bargaining agreements (*convenios*) defies straightforward translation into overall wage increases, even to economists with the benefit of data and hindsight. To the contemporaneous observer, even the direction of favoritism or bias of governmental intervention can be unclear. As Richard Webb points out, with reference to wage policy in general:

> Wage policy is particularly subject to ambiguity. It is difficult to pin down the (net) direction of policy bias, and more so, its intensity. The intensity of policy effort is as important to establish as its bias, particularly in a situation of mixed inputs where the net output is a resultant determined by both the direction and strength of different inputs. The ambiguity of labor policy results first from the variety of instruments that are relevant to wage levels and that may easily operate in conflicting directions. Ambiguity also results from the *continuous* nature of labor policy-making, especially when price levels are not stable. Even in non-inflationary environments, wage levels are being decided continuously by the market and by a succession of collective bargaining agreements so that governments can easily modify, and even reverse over short periods, the intensity and direction of their intervention. (Webb 1974, p. 8)

It should be noted, however, that the ambiguity of the government's impact on real wages can be sharply reduced if the government decrees blanket wage adjustments. Perón avoided doing this and thereby preserved his capacity to "divide and control" both the industrial sector and the labor movement.

It may seem strange that the Peronist regime, which was quite open in its suppression of political opposition—strangling the opposition press, intervening in the universities, and undermining the political freedoms of the opposition parties—resorted to such indirection in economic strategy.

The first reason is that Perón, who had no use for political cooperation beyond the army, church, and labor movement he dominated, could not dispense with the economic cooperation of groups that were outside this alliance. Agricultural producers, industrialists, and private investors were necessary to keep the economy functioning because the state, though its economic role was increasing, could not have provided adequate capital by itself. The private sector was too important to be destroyed and too powerful to be dominated; a massive flight of capital or economic sabotage would have been disastrous for Perón's economic plans. Perón had to reserve the participation of these sectors in the Argentine economy through either incentives or threats, while at the same time transferring vast amounts of resources. This task was eased considerably by effecting such transfers through what seemed to be slapdash arrangements. As such, they could not be interpreted as signs that the new regime was irrevocably committed to stripping all capital from the wealthy. Through the machinations of IAPI, Perón was able to provide incentives for certain industrialists who demonstrated that cooperation could yield huge benefits, to paralyze some landowners who feared a fate far worse than reduced profits, and indeed to reverse the direction of subsidy when it was necessary to encourage greater agricultural investment. The convoluted, improvised nature of his other income transfer institutions and arrangements gave Perón the flexibility to threaten, woo, or co-opt—without, however, dooming any economic group to crushing defeat.

REACTIONS TO PERÓN

Since the groundwork for Perón's economic changes was laid before his inauguration as president in early 1946, the first crucial period for the anti-Peronist opposition was this prepresidential period of 1943–1945, during which Perón rose from unknown to hero. Yet the opposition was conspicuously disorganized and ineffective. Certainly the rule of an interim military government that had suspended constitutional rights and kept Congress closed was somewhat intimidating to potential leaders of the opposition. Equally important was the climate of uncertainty that prevailed throughout this period. Although many subsequent accounts have erroneously assumed that the intentions of Perón and his fellow officers were obvious from the beginning, presumably because Perón's impact turned out to be so pronounced, contemporaneous accounts reveal quite a different climate. For example, the Argentine economist Felix Weil, in the preface to his aptly named 1944 book, *Argentine Riddle,* implied that the ranchers (*estancieros*) triggered the 1943 military coup in order to derail the growing political power of the industrial sector, and that Perón's presidential predecessors, Gen. Pedro Ramírez and Gen. Edelmiro Farrell, as well as Perón himself, continued to serve the interests of the rural elite (Weil 1944). As late as 1953 the American observer George Blanksten (1953,

p. 249) reported that "some analysts have even come to regard Perón as a champion of the country's *estancieros* or major landowners, although conclusive evidence of this remains to be established."

Even as Perón's transformation of labor relations was well under way, his rivals in the armed forces were trying to check his rise; if his imprisonment in October 1945 by army officers who briefly seized power had not provoked the massive worker demonstrations that swept him back to power, Perón's changes might have been reversed. The landowners and large-scale industrialists, though never confident that Perón and the other young ascendant officers would faithfully represent their interests, were hopeful that the intramilitary struggle would ultimately lead to a government that favored their interests. In light of the probable affront to these presumably idealistic military leaders that blatant pressures from the wealthy elites would engender, an all-out confrontation must have seemed very risky for the wealthy.

In this atmosphere of uncertainty, in which the rhetoric of Perón and his associates seemed almost equally likely to be bluff as serious threat, in which both the objectives and the prospects for survival of the governing clique were murky, and in which three different generals briefly held the highest governmental position before Perón emerged on top, it is understandable that the ultimately victimized groups did little to stop these economic initiatives. They concentrated, instead, on winning the 1946 general election, trying to capture the presidency or at least to mount significant legislative opposition. The anti-Peronist groups united in a Democratic Front that gave them hopes of victory right up to the election—which Perón won handily.

By 1946, then, the anti-Peronists had to give up on legislative obstruction as a strategy of opposition, since the Peronists had captured over 60 percent of the seats of the Chamber of Deputies and all but two of the Senate seats. The opposition did attempt a sort of social intimidation in the legislature, with Conservative and Radical legislators mocking the awkward speeches and clumsy maneuvers of neophyte Peronist lawmakers. Though the Peronists' insecurities came through clearly in their rather poignant appeals for respect, they were not intimidated; these attempts only infuriated them and prodded the Peronist majority into impeaching several opposition legislators.

Despite Perón's overwhelming legislative majority, very few of the Peronist reforms were carried out through new legislation. Even after his overwhelming majorities in both houses had been assured by the February 1946 general election, Perón had Farrell establish IAPI before the legislature convened. By 1946, then, Perón could maintain that adequate legislation for the protection and benefit of workers was already on the books and required only implementation. Indeed, during the uncertain, confusing years of 1943–1945 Perón had secured the passage of all the legislation he needed.

Perón's opponents turned also to the international arena. Argentina, despite Perón's nationalism, was still dependent on the willingness of other nations to accept Argentine exports of beef and grain, and increasingly on the willingness of foreign investors to fill the gap left by the tapering off of private domestic investment. The United States, a major potential source of investment, had been antagonistic to the pro-Axis government since its inception in 1943. Therefore the opposition thought it had an effective ally in U.S. Ambassador Spruille Braden, scion of a wealthy American family (which owned copper mines in Chile, among other holdings), who was on good terms with the Argentine economic elite and an ardent opponent of Perón's authoritarianism. Through Braden both the economic elite and the critics of Perón's political repression attempted to turn U.S. policy even more strongly against Perón.

As it happened, Braden's intervention reinforced Perón's appeal by heightening nationalist sentiment. Economic opposition, in the form of a U.S. investment boycott, would have been far more effective, particularly in the early 1950s when Argentina's foreign reserves and local capitalization were rapidly declining. Yet when Perón decided to reverse his policy and woo foreign investment (despite maintaining rhetorical attacks on economic imperialism), the U.S. government's Export-Import Bank came through with a large loan for an ambitious military-run steel complex after presidential envoy Milton Eisenhower visited Argentina in 1953 (Randall 1978, p. 140). Apparently, as memories of Argentina's pro-Axis stance during the war faded, and the need to cultivate cold war allies grew, the U.S. position was to overlook Perón's verbal bellicosity. Perón also succeeded in getting a huge automobile complex financed by Henry Kaiser, and a few other major investments by U.S. firms were attracted by Argentina's largely untapped consumer-durables market.

The opposition to Perón was economic as well as political. The stock exchange, the UIA, the Sociedad Rural Argentina, and conservative journals such as the *Review of the River Plate* published gloomy reports on the Argentine economy which, if they had been persuasive, would have discouraged investment by both local and foreign sources. Actually, they were successful, in conjunction with Perón's rhetoric, in scaring off most foreign investment. These efforts fell short of concerted attempts to mount a boycott, which would have risked reprisals. Rather, they represented a combination of genuine perceptions of

calamity (the economy *was* turning sour—for certain groups) and a
strategy of manipulating perceptions so as to convince investors that
their economic interests, as well as the campaign against Peronist
policy, would be best served by withdrawing from the economy.

It is not surprising, then, that their analyses of the economy were
incomplete and misleading without being strictly false. When the
amount of land cultivated for the traditional export crops of wheat and
corn declined, this was trumpeted as proof of agricultural stagnation.
Because agricultural disinvestment was a plausible result of the sort of
policy Perón had adopted, this negative appraisal of the effects of
Perón's agricultural policy went practically unchallenged for decades
after Perón was ousted.

In fact, the statistics carried in the press disregarded the shift to
newer crops (such as rye, sunflower, and peanuts) and to increased
grazing acreage for greater beef production. Contrasting the reductions in acreage devoted to traditional export grains with the increases
devoted to other agricultural pursuits, Jorge Fodor concludes:

> It was not true that land was being abandoned. What had happened was
> simply that beef production had increased ... The total decline in
> cultivated area in Buenos Aires, Cordoba, Santa Fe, La Pampa and Entre
> Rios between 1936–7 and 1956–7 had been 7.2 milion hectares. Between
> 1937 and 1947 cattle had increased in these same provinces by 7.4
> million heads, an addition in land terms of slightly over 8 million
> additional hectares. (Fodor 1975, pp. 153–155)

The agricultural shifts documented by Fodor, to new export crops,
industrial-related crops, and meat production, reflect income-
maximizing adaptations of the agricultural sector to market incentives
created by the Peronist economic program. The expansion of industrial demand for agricultural inputs was growing, as was the domestic
demand for meat by a working population increasingly able to afford
better food.

A comparison of investment rates just prior to and after the takeover
by Perón reveals that total investment increased substantially. Recall
that the biggest jump in industrial workers' income in relation to total
national income took place in 1948 and 1949. Yet the investment rate
(the proportion of new investment to gross domestic product) was
higher in 1948 (27.3 percent of GDP) than in any other year from 1935
to the present. It went down somewhat in 1949, but was still considerably higher than it had been prior to Perón's regime. The additions
to domestic fixed capital in 1949 were 30 percent higher than in 1945
(in real terms) and 15 percent higher still by 1955—even though the

flow of foreign fixed capital, presumably responding to the negative image of Argentine investment opportunities conveyed by both Perón's opposition and Perón's own rhetoric, dropped dramatically from over U.S. $4 billion (in 1950 dollars) in 1945 to less than U.S. $2 billion by 1955. By 1955, *accumulated* fixed capital exceeded U.S. $230 billion (in 1950 dollars) compared to U.S. $173 billion for the 1940–1944 period (Ferrer 1967, pp. 229–230).

This can be explained by three factors. First, the coalition of support for Perón included not only urban (and some rural) workers, but also the emerging industrial sector that regarded Perón's policies as opening up industrial opportunities and thus improving the investment climate. In fact, the rapid expansion of industry in a relatively labor-scarce country meant that government-backed wage increases, rather than being "needless" costs from a strictly economic point of view, helped industry compete for labor. Perón's subsidies for industrial operations eased the transition from low-paid to moderately-paid labor for many entrepreneurs.

Second, state investment, complemented by subsidized state credit for the industrial sector, made up for the investment decline on the part of large-scale industry. This was quite different from the pattern seen in other cases (for instance, Allende in Chile, or even Brazil in the 1970s) of state enterprise squeezing out—either in reality or in perception—private domestic enterprise. Again, the CGE-affiliated businesses were encouraged, so that the state did not have to take on the herculean task of being the sole investor in an otherwise disinvesting economy. As Richard Mallon and Juan Sourrouille (1975, p. 144) point out: "In the early part of the Perón administration the expansion of bank credit to the private sector, usually at interest rates that were negative in real terms, was probably sufficient to offset the drying up of other sources of external enterprise financing."

The third factor explaining the absence of net disinvestment in Argentina under Perón was simply the lack of concerted economic retaliation or sabotage. Judged retrospectively, the changes in class relations wrought by Perón were so great that one might expect that his initiatives would have aroused an equivalent reaction. Yet the groups victimized by Perón's economic changes faced a less desperate situation in tolerating Perón than they would have in rebelling against him.

Consider, for example, the fact that Perón, despite much bombast about the necessity for land reform, did not actually enact a sweeping land reform program. This unrealized threat became a key instrument in gaining compliance for other measures. Throughout the Peronist period the regime gained—perhaps cultivated—an image of being vindictive, capricious, and inconsistent. It was plausible for landowners to hope that quiescence would enable them to escape retaliation, and to fear that high-profile opposition would bring down the wrath of the government in the form of land reform, expropriation, or other crushing punishments. As it turned out, Perón never pushed any economic group to the point where it had no hope of recovering within the existing economic regime. In his prepresidential period the prospects of reversing the Peronist measures through internal military shakeups or an anti-Peronist election victory inhibited desperate action by the opposition; after Perón was elected, the omission of both serious land reform and industrial expropriation left the wealthy quite aware that their sufferings could have been even greater. Perón has been criticized for mounting a half-hearted revolution that raised expectations without adequately shifting the control of the economy to satisfy those expectations. Yet in fact, whether out of design or aimlessness, Perón found a politically viable economic approach that forced significant redistribution without driving the victims to political rebellion or economic sabotage.

Thus, the economic opposition to Perón failed, as the expectation of disinvestment and economic ruin was not self-fulfilling after all. The economy staggered in the early 1950s, more from drought and inefficiency than from disinvestment, and recovered by 1954–1955. Perón was ousted for antagonizing the military and the church, rather than for essentially economic reasons. The overall level of investment was maintained by the increase in state economic activity, the dynamism of the smaller and medium-sized industrial firms that could afford to disregard dour diagnoses of the economy's prospects because they enjoyed direct governmental support, and those sources of foreign investment that responded more to their own perceptions of opportunity than to the intelligence offered by Perón's economic opposition. As more recent and balanced statistical studies have pointed out, the agricultural sector reacted neither with economic retaliation nor with withdrawal, but rather by shifting investments within the agricultural sector according to income-maximizing profit incentives.

AFTERMATH

Before we turn to Perón's emulators in Chile and Peru, it will be useful to examine the aftermath of the Peronist regime, both to assess Perón's success and to understand *post*redistributive dynamics. The image and the reality of the three-year period of military rule following Perón's downfall diverge sharply: it is remembered as an era of stern revenge (*La Revancha*) against the working class for its support of Perón (Rock 1975), while in fact the economic position of the workers improved in absolute terms and their relative position declined only slightly if at all. A reevaluation of this period from a distributive perspective paints a very different picture than do the standard histories.

The major political events of the period were the replacement of the first provisional president, the conciliatory Gen. Eduardo Lonardi, and the ultimately unsuccessful efforts by his successor, Gen. Pedro Aramburu, to dismantle the Peronist political and economic structures. These political events explain the image of the era and even help to explain, though indirectly, why the "revenge" in fact did *not* extend to economics.

A fascinating historical riddle now arises. In 1955 the Peronist regime and its urban working-class allies were thoroughly defeated; the former was discredited as incompetent and corrupt, while the latter was exposed to a strong desire for retribution on the part of the middle and oligarchic groups treated harshly by the Peronists in the name of the workers. Yet manufacturing workers' real wages during the 1956–1958 period—from the ouster of Perón to the restoration of elected government, under Arturo Frondizi—were *higher* than during any previous three-year period with the sole exception of 1948–1950. Moreover, relative to overall per capita income, favoritism to labor in 1956 was higher than in any year since 1950, and in both 1957 and 1958 the favoritism ratio (that is, the ratio of average wage to per capita income) was still higher than what it had been prior to 1948. Remarkably, workers' real wages increased 17 percent in 1956 despite a slight decline in per capita gross national product (GNP). Although workers' real wages dropped back to the 1955 level in 1957 (while per capita GNP remained roughly the same), they increased 10 percent in 1958, while GNP per capita rose only 6 percent. In short, organized labor did slightly better after Perón's ouster than it did under Perón's "austerity" measures of 1951–1955, and suffered—at the most—only a very modest decline in real income after the extremely high 1956 increase in workers' wages (Merkx 1968).

There are two qualifying considerations. First, even in 1956 workers' incomes were lower than they had been in the heyday of huge wage increases in the first few years of Perón's rule. Workers still looked back at this earlier period as the *really* good old days, and the post-Perón period was not perceived as a high point for workers' benefits. Second, the bans on trade union activities imposed both the immediate deprivation of political restriction and the possibility of future economic deprivation for a labor movement less capable than before of defending its interests.

It is also worth noting that memories of this era cover the late 1950s, or even the whole period from the fall of Perón through the early 1960s. The drastic decline of workers' income resulting from the Frondizi devaluation of 1959 is often folded into the appraisal of the reaction of the immediate post-Perón era. In actuality this consequence was not due to the military government or any supposed "revenge," but rather to the later action of a civilian president elected on a populist platform. The 1955–1958 post-Perón military government, in contrast, left wageearners in roughly the same position as in the previous three-year period, in terms of both real wages and share of national income.

There are, then, two puzzles: how was labor able to save itself from a severe decline in earnings, and why did the impression develop that indeed a revenge against the workers was being sought? These enigmas have a shared explanation, which begins with the imperfection of information concerning the economic situation, and the ways people try to make sense of an economic situation under a condition of partial ignorance. Economic statistics for Argentina, as for almost all developing countries, have been incomplete, often inaccurate, and highly suspect when they are compiled and analyzed during or shortly after the period to which they refer. In the case of post-Perón Argentina, the fact that the earlier Central Bank figures for national income and its distribution issued contemporaneously differ from later figures calculated by the planning agency (CONADE), as well as from those of the United Nations Economic Commission for Latin America, is more than just a headache for economic historians; it was also an important source of uncertainty for all who participated in the public controversies and political struggles over economic policy.

The effect of political events, in contrast, is often much clearer and more pronounced. When the government "intervenes" in a labor union, or a political party is banned, or the president makes a provocative speech, the "facts"—though not necessarily their interpretation or implications—are more certain than are the economic trends of the moment. Consequently it is quite natural to impute economic trends from apparently related political occurrences, using plausible but not necessarily valid rules of thumb to connect politics to economics.

Undoubtedly it would have come as a surprise to industrial workers of this supposedly antilabor period that the percentage of manufacturing income going for the payment of wages and salaries *increased* slightly during 1956–1958 as compared to 1953–1955. The conciliatory stance toward labor of the first interim president, Gen. Eduardo Lonardi ("Neither victors nor victims"), led to his ouster by hard-line military leaders after less than two months as president. His successor, Gen. Pedro Aramburu, reinforced his hard-line reputation by rejecting a policymaking role for the labor movement negotiated under Lonardi, banning union activity on the part of Peronist union leaders and imposing a provocative but largely ineffective eighteen-month wage freeze. The General Confederation of Labor, the umbrella union organization, was also banned. Finally, a currency devaluation, always a conspicuous act, penalized urban consumers by making imported goods and domestic products depending on imported inputs more expensive.

As an example of an attempted redistribution—though in this case regressive—Aramburu's ineffective effort, particularly the wage freeze and the devaluation, may be characterized as direct, ostensibly general rather than differentiated, and highly provocative. As a consequence, the intended victims (namely the urban workers) were inadvertently mobilized to oppose government policy.

The very fact that the new generation of union leaders (who took over the positions vacated by the Peronist leaders banned by Aramburu) regarded the government as antagonistic led to an even greater resolve to fight for wage increases, as the extraordinarily high level of strikes in the period indicates. The irony was that the same unions which had loyally acquiesced to Perón's occasional wage restraint measures were provoked to strong and ultimately effective stridency by the new government's presumed antagonism to labor. Perhaps the most important redistributive legacy of Perón was the inextinguishable power of the labor movement.

The increase in real wage rates for industrial workers was thus accomplished through the myriad collective bargaining agreements hammered out between organized labor and employers, despite the formal wage freeze, often through quite militant and combative union actions. Once again, the ambiguity of the net effects of wage settlements was heightened by the absence of a centrally imposed wage adjustment.

The preoccupation with politics rather than economics also prevented the Aramburu regime from lifting all price controls, as the famous Prebisch report commissioned by Aramburu had recommended. Price ceilings on key consumer goods kept the cost of living from rising precipitously to wipe out the "illegal" wage gains. Despite Raúl Prebisch's warnings that these price controls created untenable

distortions in the economy, Aramburu may have been loath to remove
them because he feared that economic dissatisfaction would lead to a
Peronist resurgence in the scheduled 1958 election. As it happened, by
the time of the election the anti-labor *reputation* of the Aramburu
regime, even without actual economic deprivations imposed upon
organized labor, rescued Peronism from its discredited state of only a
few years before. The elected candidate, Arturo Frondizi, won only by
promising to restore Peronists' political rights in subsequent elections.

CHAPTER 4
The Debacle of Chile's General of Hope

W HEN THE AGING GEN. CARLOS IBÁÑEZ was reelected president of Chile in 1952 as the populist, "antiparty" candidate, he carried a legacy of populist economic reforms from his first administration.

Though Ibáñez was by no means a political reformer or advocate of democratic rule, as dictator from 1927 to 1931 he had reformed the public administration, increased public works and state economic intervention, expanded the educational system, and undertaken modest measures of land reform (Gil 1965, pp. 60–61; Kinsbruner 1973, p. 131). Until the Great Depression devastated the Chilean economy in 1930, Ibáñez had succeeded in wresting a large degree of economic control from the wealthy landowning, mining, and commercial interests—at the same time maintaining prosperity. As industrialization had gained pace, foreign investment had flowed into a Chilean economy under firmer state direction than had been feasible before. During his first administration Ibáñez had drawn support from the emerging urban working class and the other relatively low-income economic sectors benefiting from his economic changes. The end of this reformist experiment had come when the depression struck Chile as hard as any country in the world. Considering the widespread conventional view that it was necessary to cut back on wages and government spending to combat the depression, the deterioration of workers' benefits in 1930–1931 did not indicate insincerity in Ibáñez' redistributive stance.

In 1952, then, Ibáñez already had bona fide credentials as a populist, redistributionist reformer. His political backing reflected this stance: he received his principal support from the politically and economically excluded: "non-unionized workers, the peasants, the women and the young" (Gil 1965, p. 69). As the antiparty candidate, the General of Hope, as he was known, attracted the support of voters disaffected by the major parties, in large part because the parties were seen as instruments of the politically established groups—landowners, businessmen, foreign interests, bureaucrats, and organized labor. Even the leftist parties, with power bases in the industrial and mining unions, were seen as excluding unorganized workers in both the cities and the countryside. Industrial workers rejected the ideological parties of the Left to embrace Ibáñez' improvised populism, while the peasantry rebelled for the first time against the political control of rightist landowners (Gil 1965, pp. 74–77). Ibáñez gained the support of these groups by attacking the competence, the position, and even the morality of the "establishment," thus earning him the unqualified animosity of this powerful element.

It is important to underscore the strength of Ibáñez' commitment to economic reform and his political need to carry out redistribution, because subsequent events led many to discredit him as a hypocrite whose promises to the poor were no more than campaign rhetoric.[1] By 1958 any temporary economic gains of the poor under the Ibáñez administration had been completely eroded by inflation and by the conservative economic policy measures adopted to combat it. Even though during the Ibáñez years many more workers were incorporated into organized labor and thus into a much stronger political position, his initial efforts to direct economic gains to the poor failed so utterly that his initial commitment has been cast in doubt. There is little question that as Ibáñez' support faded away, he was willing to sacrifice the interests of the poor to maintain himself in office. But because his populist impulse was strongly manifested earlier, and because the political rationale for satisfying at least some of the aspirations of his lower-income supporters was obvious, it is unfair to label Ibáñez' populism as a pose. It is far more useful to explore why this initial impetus was blunted and to determine whether subsequent events were inevitable or avoidable.

THE BACKGROUND OF IBÁÑISMO

Carlos Ibáñez was not the first president of Chile to attempt redistribution, nor the first to fail. The frustration of redistribution plans has been a principal motif of the Chilean postwar period. Of the three Radical party administrations receding Ibáñez' 1952–1958 term, the experience of the last one, Gabriel González Videla, was not only the most immediate background of Ibañismo but also the most poignant of the failures.

Chile emerged from World War II with a high level of industrial expansion fed by wartime shortages and strong demand for Chilean exports of copper and nitrates. With financing from the state-owned development corporation known as CORFO, private-sector industrialists continued to expand light industry to replace imported manufactured goods, in keeping with the pattern of "easy" import substitution industrialization occurring throughout postwar Latin America.

Chile also emerged without a resolution to its "social question": the disparities in wealth and power among the social classes, and the attendant conflicts that had dominated Chilean politics for decades. Unlike Argentina and Peru, the politics of class had been in the forefront of Chilean politics throughout the interwar period. Major leftist parties (the Communist and the Socialist parties specifically) played prominent roles, making it clear that the challenge to existing economic relations could neither be ignored nor easily repressed, though attempts at suppression had been common ever since the nitrate workers had banded together in the northern mines during the nineteenth century. The postwar period was marked by both the continued prominence of the so-called social question and the promise of prosperity through industrial expansion.

The Radical leaders who occupied the presidency from 1938 to 1946, Pedro Aguirre Cerda and Juan Antonio Rios, tried to accommodate both the problem and the promise. They were publicly committed to improving income distribution via an economic expansion that would permit wage and salary increases without destroying the dynamism of industrialization. This qualified assurance of redistribution resulted in a very mixed record, since the two administrations were at least as sensitive to industrialists' claims that high labor costs and union activity impeded industrialization as they were to workers' demands for higher wages. By 1946 white-collar workers (*empleados*), both in industry and in government, had improved their real salaries, but the real wages of blue-collar workers (*obreros*) remained constant despite the overall industrial expansion.[2] Industrialization thus was not translated into concrete benefits for the industrial worker, as it was to be in Argentina under Perón. Despite their proworker rhetoric, Chilean Radicals failed to capture the labor movement from the leftist parties; the party's strength remained with the white-collar sector.

Moreover, the industrial expansion came at the expense of workers in the rural sector, where the real incomes of peasants declined significantly after 1940. To appease industrial workers, as well as to keep down the pressures for higher industrial wages, the Radical administrations and the regimes before them had stringently controlled the price of food, while at the same time a system of subsidies and tax exemptions had been erected to promote agricultural production. The large landowners were the principal beneficiaries of these concessions, as well as of the stricter restrictions on rural unionization than on urban unionization. Clearly the redistribution effected by Aguirre Cerda and Rios was so-called easy redistribution, and hardly progressive, in that the government extracted wealth principally from the politically weak peasantry.

Gabriel González Videla, a Radical who won the 1946 presidential election with the backing of the Communist party, promised—tentatively—to be different. Three Communist leaders held important cabinet positions, and the Radical ministers were chosen from that party's more progressive wing. In particular, the minister of economy, Luis Bossay, set the tone by identifying "the unequal distribution of wealth as the main cause of the country's economic troubles ... the capitalist class accumulates an excessive amount of resources."[3] However, the cabinet also included representation of the rightist Liberal party, which had supported González Videla's bizarre electoral coalition. Given his centrist Radical and rightist Liberal backing, González Videla's need to satisfy the Left through progressive redistributive economic policy was less essential for maintaining his organized political support and was perhaps a potential liability.

Like so many Chilean economic policies, González Videla's initial plan was defined in terms of the battle against inflation, which reached 30 percent in 1946 in contrast to the previous year's rate of less than 8 percent. The preceding Radical administrations had provided huge amounts of investment capital to industrial entrepreneurs at low interest rates; but because of delays, inefficiency, and profit taking, productive capacity did not increase as much or as fast as was expected. The expansion of money and demand (previously pent up by wartime shortages, now reinforced by higher middle-income salaries), without a corresponding increase in actual production, launched Chile into a new and more serious inflationary phase that was exacerbated by low world copper prices.

Thus the initial policy package introduced by the González Videla regime was a stabilization program emphasizing tighter credit for private entrepreneurs and stricter controls on price increases (as opposed to wage increases). Both measures could be enacted through the apparatus of the executive branch rather than the legislature, since the price-control agency (the Commissariat of Staples and Price Control) was already in existence, and the control of credit was an executive function overseen by the Central Bank. While this meant that legislative interference was precluded (the Radicals lacked even a plurality in

Congress), it did not follow that the president had complete control over policy implementation; for any agency has at least some degree of autonomy and capacity to defy the wishes of a chief executive and his cabinet.

The González Videla program was soon in ruins. The program's credibility, crucial to its success, was undermined at the outset by criticisms from the Central Bank. Its leaders took advantage of their virtually autonomous position to argue that credit restrictions and price controls would not work, but wage restrictions could. The Central Bank's board of directors, by law dominated by representatives of private banks and producers' associations, had no tolerance for policies restricting bank credit to private entrepreneurs. Beyond their own self-interest, the powers behind the Central Bank adhered to orthodox economic principles that construed the problem of inflation as a problem of excessive demand.

Through a combination of defiance by producers and retailers, and the utter incapacity of the public administration to enforce the regulations, price controls were simply ineffective. The Commissariat of Staples and Price Control, founded in 1932 but permitted an active role in penalizing price violations only in 1939, was quickly swamped with cases. Without a dedicated, efficient, and powerful price-control bureaucracy, the enforcement of rigid price controls, especially when applied in the midst of ongoing wage and salary adjustments, is extremely difficult—and the cost of compliance together with the ease of getting away with violations make voluntary compliance highly unlikely. The bureaucracy under the González Videla regime, bloated with Radical party loyalists, was neither efficient nor particularly enthusiastic about enforcing controls on producers and merchants. In 1947, after intense opposition by the manufacturers' associations, the commissariat was rendered practically powerless (Cavarozzi 1975, p. 169).

What made compliance by producers and merchants so costly was the enormous increase of strike actions in the pursuit of higher wages. Union leaders interpreted the assumption of power by a Communist-backed president as an affirmation of their right to press for a bigger share of a supposedly expanding industrial economy, when in fact the slow maturation of large-scale industrial projects had not yet yielded greatly increased production.

The political rationale for heightened strike activity was the reluctance of Communist party leaders to allow González Videla to take full credit for whatever improvements in workers' incomes were to emerge from his program. The harder the unions pressed for wage hikes in excess of levels in line with the administration's hopes for dampening the wage-price spiral, the more the victory for the workers would be attributable to the Communist party and the union organizations rather than to the Radical regime.[4] The Communists saw the opening as a chance to press for higher wages, and also to consolidate their control over the labor movement. Their strong showing in the 1947 municipal elections indicated that they were succeeding politically— for the moment. Their success, however, heightened the threat to both the Right and to González Videla's Radicals.

Confronted with this onslaught of wage demands and strikes backed by political might, most firms granted large wage increases. These increases, along with the production losses stemming from the strikes, heightened the inflationary pressures. Real GNP in 1947 plummeted by 14 percent and the 33 percent inflation rate was over twice that of the previous year. In reaction to the eroding economic and political situation, González Videla had the Communist cabinet ministers resign in mid-1947, and signaled that real wage increases were at an end by canceling an announced salary raise for public employees. With even more labor unrest resulting, and a continuing high inflation rate, González Videla called in Jorge Alessandri, the industrialists' foremost spokesman, to become minister of finance and head a new cabinet. The traditional policies of wage restraint and industrial promotion were immediately applied, leading to a quick but temporary economic recovery in 1948.

For the next four years, despite the general sluggishness of the economy, the Radical government clung to orthodox measures without attempting progressive redistribution to stimulate growth. The combination of González Videla's brief flirtation with redistribution, followed by the frustration of anti-inflationary austerity that neither controlled inflation nor brought prosperity, left the Radicals without a credible economic approach to attract their traditional supporters. This crisis of confidence led to the reemergence of Ibáñez as an alternative to the tired party politicians.

THE ECONOMIC CONTEXT

Although it was almost universally accepted that Chile's major economic problem of the era was inflation (Kaldor 1964, p. 267), the diagnosis was misleading inasmuch as the inflation was itself the manifestation of a deeper problem: the difficulty of adjusting to the decline in Chile's trade position following the end of the Korean War and the subsequent decrease in world demand for copper. The year 1953 saw a decline of nearly 30 percent in Chile's export capacity (Instituto de Economía 1963, vol. 2, p. 27). During the first half of 1954 the problem was so serious that Chilean copper could not be sold (*Hispanic American Report* 7 [1954], p. 35). This was a major blow, since taxes on copper exports constituted nearly 20 percent of central government revenues, while taxes on the external sector in general (that is, import and export taxes) constituted just over half of government revenues (Instituto de Economía 1956, pp. 176–180). Since the beginning of World War II, the Chilean economy had been fueled by copper export earnings, which were largely plowed back into import-substitution industrialization rather than expansion of the export base. This pattern resulted in extremely high industrial growth rates (Kaldor 1964, p. 264), but at the same time it increased Chile's dependence on export earnings because the capital machinery and intermediate inputs for Chilean industry still had to be acquired from abroad. The cutback in export earnings following the Korean War created serious balance-of-payments problems. In short, the export-earned wealth on which Chile had depended during the previous period for its relative prosperity and high consumption levels was no longer available. Someone had to cut back. As shown in Table 5, the lack of success in

TABLE 5. INFLATION AND DISTRIBUTION IN CHILE
UNDER CARLOS IBAÑEZ.

Year	Monthly sueldo vital in Santiago (1950 pesos)	Increase in sueldo vital over previous year (percent)	Increase in cost-of-living over previous year (percent)
1950	3,800	25.0	20.6
1951	3,818	22.9	16.7
1952	4,082	30.0	23.3
1953	4,025	24.4	12.1
1954	3,958	53.6	56.1
1955	3,561	58.6	71.1
1956	3,146	46.5	83.8
1957	3,181	30.2	37.7
1958	3,031	20.0	17.3
1959	2,990	36.7	32.5
1960	3,080	15.0	33.3

SOURCE: Instituto de Economía 1963, vol. 2, p. 46.

combating inflation changed the initial redistributive gains of low-income groups into serious losses by 1955, with another very steep decline in 1956.

One of Ibáñez' first victories was to secure extraordinary powers from Congress to enact new economic legislation for a six-month period. The willingness of Congress to grant such powers certainly reflected the fears of legislators (particularly the Radicals whom Ibáñez had accused of being the root of Chile's corruption) that Ibáñez would seize on their opposition as a justification for dissolving Congress and establishing a dictatorship. It is also likely that many legislators were happy to leave Ibáñez with the burden of responsibility for economic policymaking in extraordinarily difficult economic times.

IBÁÑEZ' INITIATIVES

The economic strategies of the Ibáñez administration prior to 1956 are difficult to summarize succinctly, because of the multiplicity of plans and measures applied (or in some cases only proposed) before they incurred so much opposition or failure that they were dropped.[5] Nevertheless, it was clear that wage, credit, and exchange policy and tax reform were the primary preoccupations of the Ibáñez administrators, even though the various teams of policymakers attempted quite different strategies for each. On the other hand, some of the traditional progressive instruments were not considered. Social spending was limited by the consensus on bringing it in line with the government's reduced revenues. There was no serious effort to address urban-rural disparities, which could have been attacked by a growth model other than import-substitution industrialization, or by reducing the urban drain on rural resources represented by the price control and import of foodstuffs. And, generalized price controls, ineffective under previous administrations, were given little emphasis.

WAGE POLICY

After an initial flurry of rural wage improvements enacted through the establishment of a rural minimum wage, successive cabinets vascillated between trying to improve real incomes of wage earners and trying to limit, in the name of the fight against inflation, the increases that workers were able to bargain for themselves. One nearly constant element of policy was the commitment to keeping food prices low—largely through subsidized imports—in order to preserve the purchasing power of wages.

As far as the institutional structure of wage negotiation was concerned, the early Ibañista efforts closely resembled Perón's, in that wage disputes were channeled to the bargaining boards under the Ministry of Labor, which had been purged of its most obvious proemployer functionaries, and which, for the first year of Ibáñez' administration, consistently favored workers' demands. This approach was altered, however, whenever the economic team in office was sympathetic to the diagnosis of inflation offered by the business community, namely that in addition to labor-cost pressures on prices, inflation was basically due to excess demand by wage earners.

Finally, Ibáñez' wage policy cannot be separated from his labor policy, which began promisingly like Perón's but ended up in confrontation. When Ibáñez took office in late 1952, the apparent disarray of the labor movement made the opportunity for unification under Ibáñez' own leadership look attractive. He was to learn, however, that the major difference between Chilean and Argentine labor was that the Chilean work force, even though divided, was highly organized and militant. The Communist party and its labor confederation were operating openly (despite the fact that the anti-Communist "Law for the Defense of Democracy" was still formally in effect), and the Socialists and Radicals could rely on their own loyal unions.

Thus, when Ibáñez called union leaders together in November 1952 to form two labor organizations, one for white-collar and the other for blue-collar workers, the effort was boycotted by the major labor leaders of all existing movements. They countered Ibáñez' initiative by calling for a united Central Unica de Trabajadores de Chile (CUTCh).

The Ibáñista labor leaders were invited to participate in CUTCh, but when the Communists proved powerful enough to secure the election of a sympathetic independent, Clotario Blest, as CUTCh president, Ibáñez called back his representatives and announced that he was withdrawing his pledge to repeal the Law for the Defense of Democracy, on the grounds that the Communists were engaging in "social agitation." Although Ibáñez maintained the skeleton of his own confederations throughout his term, it was CUTCh that captured the vast majority of union support. It later confronted the administration not only with numerous industry-wide strikes, but ultimately with several successful general strikes. Opposition to Ibáñez' attempt to take over the union movement unified the competing factions of labor more solidly than had ever been possible prior to this threat.

CREDIT POLICY

The Ibáñez administration went further than previous Chilean governments in gaining control over the levers of credit policy. Ibáñez used his extraordinary powers to consolidate the state's credit institutions into the State Bank, and he expanded the Central Bank's power to include the imposition of credit limits on private banks. This last power was used only sporadically; over the 1952–1955 period, the supply of money increased 261 percent, partly to validate price increases and cover the fiscal deficit, but also to meet the requirements of banks sometimes allowed to lend money at interest rates far below the rate of inflation. Whereas the previous problem of controlling credit in Chile was the lack of coordination and centralized control, the problem now became that of deciding how to balance the objectives of controlling inflation—which obviously called for more stringent limits on credit—and maintaining economic activity through more lenient credit policy.

EXCHANGE AND TRADE POLICY

The emergency powers were also used to create the National Institute of Trade to regulate foreign trade and to consolidate the public sector's purchases abroad. The Foreign Trade Council, entrusted with the responsibility for deciding which of the multiple exchange rates would apply to individual import-export transactions, was used in the same fashion as Perón's foreign trade entities such as IAPI, to subsidize certain kinds of imports at the expense of export profits. Rather than supporting productive activities in any coherent way, the Foreign Trade Council primarily subsidized food imports, although it also granted favorable exchange rates to raw material imports.

A major technical flaw in import management, besides the multiple-exchange-rate system that was often applied arbitrarily to favor particular importers, was the use of import quotas rather than duties to accomplish the basic objective of reducing imports. The quota system was inefficient, inasmuch as it created shortages when import needs were underestimated and allowed domestic producers to operate with little or no competitive pressure from the outside. It was also highly susceptible to corruption; quotas frequently were increased on particular items as special favors, defeating the stated purpose of holding down imports.

Overall, trade policy clashed with the anti-inflationary efforts. While the balance-of-payments problem could not be ignored, it ended up being interpreted and approached in its narrowest form. Instead of trying to reduce the fundamental sources of import dependence, the Ibáñez government struck at only modest components of import demand. Thus in April 1954 the government restricted credit available for finished-goods imports, but not for the import of industrial inputs and food; banned automobile imports and foreign travel of government officials; and created more red tape for private citizens seeking to obtain passports for foreign travel (*Hispanic American Report* 7 [1954], p. 33).

TAX REFORM

The emphasis on tax reform was certainly not surprising, and in fact it had every advantage a progressive reform could have—except that it was not politically feasible. Outside observers of the Chilean economy agreed that the tax system was woefully inadequate in stemming the consumption of the well-to-do. The counterargument that money in the hands of the wealthy was more productive because it induced a higher level of savings and investment was simply negated by the data on Chilean consumption. Nicholas Kaldor (1964, p. 266) points out:

> Despite the growth of profits (by 56 per cent. in real terms excluding stock appreciation), there has been no increase in the proportion of savings and gross investment in the national income; and the volume of investment in fixed capital by the private sector has actually declined after 1946–48. Net investment in fixed capital has remained extremely low and . . . could not have amounted to more than 3 to 4 per cent. of the net national income; it has tended to decline moreover after 1946–8, and the decline in private net investment in fixed capital has been considerably greater than the decline in total net investment . . . The reason for this is to be found in the high propensity to consume of the capitalist class who appear to have spent on personal consumption more than two-thirds of their gross income, or three-quarters of their net income after taxes. In comparison with other countries, the luxury consumption of the property-owning classes appears to take up an altogether disproportionate share of the national resources, part of which would be automatically released for investment purposes if a more efficient system of progressive taxation were introduced.

Every economic policy recommendation for Chile, from the most conservative sources to the most progressive, highlighted the importance of tax reform. Moreover, a tax increase would have had the political advantage of leaving Congress in the position of having imposed the sacrifice, since only Congress could legislate tax changes. The major criticism that can be leveled against Ibáñez' economic teams is not that they focused their efforts on a theoretically minor or even counterproductive vehicle for redistributing income and improving Chile's aggregate growth prospects at the same time, but rather that they put so much emphasis on this vehicle without adequately employing other instruments of greater practicality though less theoretical importance.

Ibáñez policymakers in every major policy package featured a tax reform designed to increase the rates and efficiency of tax collection. From a political perspective, the emphasis on tax reform in an anti-inflation package was well advised in that it represented the contribution of the wealthy to the shared sacrifices necessary to stop the inflationary struggle over income shares (Hirschman 1963, p. 199). However, each time a package was presented for congressional approval, the tax increase aroused adamant opposition. The extraordinary powers of the first six months were not used to change the tax laws, because these months did not span the period for considering the next budget, which was the time most tax changes had traditionally been formulated. Ibáñez could have pressed for broader extraordinary powers, but he chose not to do so. With some of his support coming from business elements of the Agrarian Labor party and other politically independent businessmen, it appears that Ibáñez did not want to bear the full responsibility of raising taxes.

STYLE

It was particularly difficult for a government like that of Ibáñez' to deliver the message that cutbacks were essential. The Ibáñez appeal was the mystique of will, and of broad heroic visions that transcended the morass of day-to-day detail that apparently had dispirited the Radical presidents preceding him. Consequently, when a brief effort at restricting credit or demand proved to be politically unrewarding, the thrust of Ibáñez' economic orientation turned to stimulating activity instead of adjusting for the decline that began in late 1953. He alternated between proposing stringent plans that would have enforced some economic sacrifice by various income groups, and reacting passively to expansionary and inflationary demands to allow unionized labor to press wage demands and the business sector to secure easy credit and pass cost increases on to consumers.

It is not clear that Ibáñez planners were aware of the discrepancy between the scope of the problems they faced and the superficiality of the instruments they employed. In fairness to these individuals, it must be noted that they rarely had the time or the backing from Ibáñez to undertake thorough consideration or prolonged action on the problems they confronted. Donald Bray (1961, p. 5) points out that 135 cabinet ministers were appointed during Ibáñez' six-year term.

The extremely rapid turnover of cabinets is illuminating in two respects. First, the resignations, which on the whole were undoubtedly demanded rather than voluntary, reflected a certain conception of economic management. Negative economic performance was presumed to indicate either incompetence—although it should have been obvious to everyone aware of Chile's deteriorating export situation that the basic problems were not the fault of that month's policymaker—or an intolerable political embarrassment requiring a change in personnel. Yet the fact that the cabinets were shuffled so frequently brought political embarrassment to Ibáñez in quite the opposite way. The instability of the government, the implication that the economic situation was bad enough to necessitate cabinet changes, the further suggestion that the situation was due to mismanagement by the outgoing ministers, and Ibáñez' evident inability to select competent ministers, all conveyed the image of desperate thrashing about.

Second, the cabinet changes also resulted from battles within the Ibáñez inner circle. Marcelo Cavarozzi's interviews with Ibañistas reveal a bitter struggle among the various factions, including the two major parties initially supporting Ibáñez (Agrarian Labor and Popular Socialist), the entrepreneurial faction, right-wing authoritarian populists, and the young "technocrats" (Cavarozzi 1975, pp. 223–241). This factionalism was one of the prime weaknesses of the Ibáñez coalition strategy of eschewing the major political parties in favor of alliance with the more numerous smaller factions.[6]

REPEATED EFFORTS

In the euphoria of his election victory Ibáñez began with populist measures that completely disregarded the fiscal and macroeconomic constraints necessary to prevent a resurgence of inflation. Legislation created a social security service that extended its coverage to workers receiving one-sixth the income level previously needed to qualify. Increased benefits and a family allowance were added, with the bulk of the contributions to be made by the employer. By 1954 employer contributions to social security had risen from the 1952 level of 7.7 percent of basic remuneration to 24.2 percent. Most important from the perspective of poverty alleviation, a minimum agricultural wage was established in 1953, applicable to more than a quarter of a million agricultural laborers. Neither these measures nor the newly legislated automatic wage adjustment formulas for public employees were enacted with secure revenue sources, and the liquidity of the social security service was also precarious (Ffrench-Davis 1973, pp. 192–199).

These measures assuredly helped the lower-income sectors, but with the encouragement of high-wage labor settlements and loose credit and exchange restrictions, they also triggered higher inflation. The redistributive question became the issue of how the burden of sacrifice for controlling inflation would be shared. At the risk of imparting an impression of greater coherence than actually prevailed, let me point to five initiatives during the 1953–1955 period.

The first initiative, known as the Herrera plan after finance minister Felipe Herrera, was a package of budgetary restraint and tax reform (Herrera argued that the tax system in effect was highly regressive); monetary and credit restriction; and a decrease in imports (many of which were considered luxury items). Herrera argued that if monetary expansion and easy credit enabled the wealthy to borrow at cheap interest rates, thereby debasing the currency earned by the working-man, monetary restraint would signify the end of this special privilege (Bray 1961, p. 55).

The Herrera plan was submitted to Congress in mid-1953, where it encountered stiff opposition. Herrera, though noted as a brilliant economist, showed little political acumen in presenting his program. As Albert Hirschman (1963, p. 195) points out: "While an increase in taxes was orthodox anti-inflationary policy, the proposal never got any-where in Congress, especially since the Finance Minister advocated it with the slogan 'Let the powerful also pay.'" Radical party senators and deputies, politically threatened by the implication that previous Radical governments had used inflation to erode the income share of the working class, attacked the Herrera plan as based on faulty premises (arguing that the workers' share had not declined under their adminis-trations). Liberal and Conservative legislators, who along with the Radicals constituted the bulk of the majority opposition, opposed the plan's goals as well as its logic. The Liberals openly acknowledged that the plan would indeed redistribute income—and opposed it because, they argued, income redistribution would reduce private investment. The Conservatives, who labeled the plan Marxist, argued that the austerity program should focus on reducing government employment rather than distort the economy through manipulations of credit and taxation (Bray 1961, p. 56).

When it became clear that the Herrera plan would not pass, Ibáñez replaced Herrera with Guillermo del Pedregal, who under Radical administrations was a founder of Chile's development corporation (CORFO) and a leading advocate of monetary expansion. Del Pedregal had held a variety of key posts, including that of interior minister, in which capacity he was entrusted with the early union-forming initiatives. As economics and finance minister he reflected the *inflacionista* position within the cabinet. The Popular Socialists, taking this shift as an indication that Ibáñez had abandoned the struggle to save the wage earner from the ravages of inflation, left the government coalition. Del Pedregal proceeded to allow a massive increase in credit.

It is not implausible that Ibáñez and del Pedregal expected that this expansionary policy would lead to the same (initially) happy results as in Perón's Argentina, where pro-Peronist small-scale and medium-scale entrepreneurs responded to the availability of credit to take advantage of the expansion of mass consumer demand (Cavarozzi 1975, p. 232). This position was supported by financiers, many of whom were reaping huge profits, and also by certain businessmen who, without easy credit, feared that they could not sustain their operations. The unions were strong enough to press for higher wages, leaving employers in a squeeze unless currency expansion and price increases were also permitted.

Another reading of the shift to del Pedregal's inflationist policy is that Ibáñez may have decided that the union demands, now representing (in his eyes, at least) the efforts of the Communist-dominated CUTCh to undermine the economy's stability, the government, and the capitalist system, could not be allowed to succeed. Monetary expansion meant that whatever wage gains were won through labor's militancy would be eroded through inflation, thus denying the CUTCh any lasting victory. Labor leaders naturally reacted bitterly to the mounting inflation that seemed to erode their gains while enriching the *especuladores*.

However, del Pedregal's efforts at economic expansion were limited by the lack of responsiveness of the mainline business owners. Because he did not call for any sacrifice on their part, del Pedregal gained a more favorable reaction from businessmen than had any other pre-1955 Ibáñez minister (Cavarozzi 1975, p. 255). Still, they feared, apparently with justification, that the availability of credit would be steered predominantly to Ibáñez' supporters.

Because the Herrera plan had been defined by the Right as a leftist initiative, the del Pedrgal policy was seen by some observers as an effort to appease the entrepreneurs (Cavarozzi 1975, p. 255). Whether or not this was accurate, it had the peculiar effect of setting up the expectation that the success of the new effort ought to be judged in terms of whether entrepreneurs reacted favorably by holding back on price increases or increasing investment. This gave the business sector the tactical advantage of controlling the evaluation of the government's policy.

The hoped-for recovery did not materialize and, not unexpectedly, inflation gained momentum. The most obvious reason for the lack of recovery is that basic economic conditions, aside from the credit policy, were simply not ripe; higher inflation was expected, strikes and demands for higher wages were on the rise, the "easy" phase of import-substitution industrialization was over, and the trade outlook was gloomy. Furthermore, available credit was never properly matched to investment conditions. There were, indeed, Ibañista business elements clamoring for the opportunities to expand. But Ibáñez did not resort to a major siphoning mechanism like Perón's IAPI to finance a new industrial sector from the potential profits of another sector. Subsidized credit was available. For this policy to succeed without provoking even worse disequilibrium, it would have had to be delicately balanced so that interest rates were slightly above or below the inflation rate. Instead, the interest rates were kept so low in comparison to inflation that resources which otherwise could have gone into productive investment were funneled into speculation by those who had the connections to secure bank loans (Ffrench-Davis, 1973, p. 25). Since credit was limited and yet not enough seemed to be directed toward productive activities, most industrialists considered all of the Ibáñez policies of 1953–1955 as antientrepreneurial (Cavarozzi 1975, p. 300). Their "preference" for the del Pedregal approach was a preference only in the negative sense that it was for a lesser evil than the other initiatives taken during the period.

From Ibáñez' perspective, of course, del Pedregal's inability to reactivate the economy, even with higher inflation, was the worst outcome. Ibáñez then turned to Senator Eduardo Frei, later Chile's Christian Democratic president, to head a new cabinet. Frei did not belong to the Ibañista coalition (his party had not supported Ibáñez in the 1952 election), but Ibáñez presumably believed that it was time to go beyond the narrow partisan base that had limited cooperation with his programs thus far. Frei formulated a plan of striking comprehensiveness: under a new grant of extraordinary powers, the executive would impose stringent restrictions on government spending and credit, stricter controls on banking and exchange dealings, and basic reforms in the tax system and administration of government.

However, Frei insisted on the prerogative of choosing the other key cabinet ministers, claiming that his choices would be made on the basis of technical expertise, not political connections. The fact that Frei and his own party were rivals to the Popular Socialists and Agrarian Laborites in the Ibáñez coalition meant, of course, that a Frei cabinet, even if manned strictly by tecnicos, would have been a political defeat for Ibáñez' coalition partners. Hirschman (1963, p. 197) notes that Frei's program would have given him power rivaling that of Ibáñez himself.

Ibáñez rejected Frei's cabinet demands and the deal fell through. The explanations for the failure make this otherwise inconsequential episode quite illuminating. Obviously, Frei's rising power and the opposition from progovernment parties provided motives for refusing to accede to Frei's conditions. Bray (1961, p. 57) reports that the strongest opposition to the Frei plan came from "members of the PAL [Agrarian Labor Party] who feared the loss of some of the personal emoluments of power."Aside from these "personal" considerations, it is likely that the comprehensiveness of the program itself was recognized as politically implausible. Hirschman (1963, pp. 197–199) notes that congressional approval was doubtful; the Frei program was certainly more threatening to established interests than the Herrera plan, which had already been rejected by the legislature. The comprehensive approach to a problem that nearly everyone would agree deserved comprehensive treatment was simply infeasible politically. Much of the time wasted in formulating plans for treating the problem of inflation in Chile can be attributed to the unwillingness to face up to this unpalatable reality.

Nevertheless, in 1954 the administration proposed yet another package that entailed both credit restrictions and wage restrictions in order to allocate the burden more evenly. The new finance minister, Jorge Prat, reimposed the credit restrictions that del Pedregal had lifted, maintaining that they were not standing in the way of recovery; recovery simply was not to be expected in such inflationary and highly uncertain times. More controversially, Prat proposed the establishment of a Council of Economic Stabilization to supervise a limit on 1955 wage and salary adjustments that would keep the increases at no more than 60 percent of the cost-of-living increase of 1954. In addition, all strikes were made illegal, but unions could submit claims for higher wages to binding arbitration. To balance these worker sacrifices, Prat proposed higher taxes and lower dividends. Finally, the package would include the establishment of a minimum wage along the lines of—though at a lower level than—the minimum salary already in effect (Hirschman 1963, p. 197; Cavarozzi 1975, p. 257).

In mid-1954 Prat applied the measures which could be undertaken by the executive alone, particularly the ceiling on expansion of bank loans. The level of public confidence seemed to rise, and by September

the inflation appeared to be moderating slightly (Instituto de Economía 1956, p. 215; Hirschman 1963, p. 197). But when the whole
program was submitted to Congress in November 1954 for the 1955
budget and wage-adjustment deliberations, at a time when a state of
siege was in effect because of strikes in key industries, congressional
reaction was negative. In fact, Congress had countered Ibáñez' request
for extraordinary powers by voting to lift the state of siege, despite
Ibáñez' claims that the situation was explosive.

Ibáñez railed against legislative obstructionism, contemplated an
"auto-coup d'etat," but discovered the lack of enthusiasm among his
own factions and the readiness of the opposition to resist him with
paralyzing strikes. In early 1955 he replaced Prat with an Agrarian
Labor cabinet; the new advisers further antagonized labor by enacting
a wage adjustment of "only" 60 percent, which was lower than the rate
of inflation. However, the Central Bank decided to ignore finance
minister Sergio Recabarren's request for lower credit ceilings
(Cavarozzi 1975, pp. 260–261). Since the request was widely attacked
by the banks and by production groups, the Central Bank had enough
backing to defy the minister. The Ibáñez government had become so
weak with the withdrawal of Popular Socialist support, widespread
strikes, and unabated inflation that Ibáñez recognized the necessity for
an altogether new coalition.

The Radicals were still to be left out of the new alliance, but Ibáñez
could align himself with the antiredistributive Liberal and Conservative legislators. This he did in late 1955, signaling the end of any
semblance of populist effort. Ibáñez suddenly had the legislative
majority necessary to pursue the attack on inflation, but it had to be a
rightist attack. In January 1956 Congress approved credit restrictions,
a price freeze at levels of two months before, and limited the cost-of-
living wage increase to only half of the previous year's inflation rate. To
bolster the authoritativeness of these programs, the administration
brought in U.S. consultants, the famous Klein-Saks mission. This
group endorsed the strategy of austerity through wage restraint, which
was immediately labeled as reactionary by the labor unions and all the
political groupings of the Left.

REACTIONS AND OPPOSITION TACTICS

Prior to the Klein-Saks mission, the most vocal opposition to Ibáñez'
economic policies came from the industrial sector, particularly from
SOFOFA. This organization of the major producing firms, like the

UIA under Perón, saw only threat in the president's alliance with up-and-coming entrepreneurs who were dependent on government subsidies. Established businesses already had their inside connections. The head of the Central Bank, Arturo Maschke, agreed with the mainstream businessman's interpretation of inflation as primarily due to wage and salary increases (Cavarozzi 1975, p. 241). The Central Bank was traditionally dominated by private business and finance representatives, who held six of the thirteen positions on the board (six others were for the government and only one for labor).

Prior to Ibáñez' election, the real income of wage earners had been seriously eroded by his predecessor's shift to wage restraint. The economic growth of previous years had gone largely to profits and, in lesser proportions, to white-collar employees (Caldor 1964, pp. 242–250). Once Ibáñez was installed, organized labor was powerfully disposed to strike for higher wages and was probably encouraged by Ibáñez' populist rhetoric. In mid-1954 the volume of strikes was high enough to provoke the government to declare a state of siege. Once Ibáñez had labeled CUTCh as the enemy, strikes in defiance of the government were politically as well as economically motivated. The strikes in major industries and the two general strikes were indirectly responsible for the final abandonment of the Prat plan, since the militancy of the unions convinced Ibáñez that the state of siege was essential.

There were several ways in which Ibáñez' initiatives were undermined. The business sector unremittingly promoted its own standards of appraisal of government performance. When by 1954 it was widely accepted that an inflation policy had to have the acquiescence of the business sector, the Herrera and Prat plans became vulnerable to easy undermining by this sector, which had merely to express its opposition in order to severely reduce the credibility of the plans.

Another tactic was to play upon the divisions within the Ibáñez coalition. One of SOFOFA's early antagonists, labor minister Clodomiro Almeyda, withstood the direct attacks by SOFOFA, but was forced out by the intercession of Nicolas Yarur, head of the Yarur textile empire, who had close personal ties with Ibáñez (Cavarozzi 1975, p. 235). In several instances the initiatives undertaken by one faction of the Ibáñez coalition were vetoed by the threat of others that their faction would pull out, as indeed the Popular Socialists did in 1953 (Drake 1978, p. 305). This group had at first threatened to withdraw unless the original finance minister, Juan Rosetti, resigned, which he was forced to do in April 1953 (Bray 1961, p. 41).

Finally, and perhaps most obviously, there was the legislative opposition. It was clear from the start that the Radicals, who were not in principle opposed to progressive redistribution (as indicated by their own aspirations of the previous decade), were very much opposed in principle to cooperating with their political rival Ibáñez in any way. Thus those who opposed progressive policies could count on the Radicals to obstruct Ibáñez' initiatives in this direction; and they could of course depend on the Conservatives and Liberals to oppose any such initiatives for their thrust, if not their authorship.

We come back, then, to Ibáñez' puzzling reluctance to conduct economic policy in arenas outside of Congress. Although he certainly entertained the possibility of dissolving Congress, Ibáñez' never tried to circumvent it to pursue his economic goals. Both the Ibañistas and the opposition saw his problems as essentially political; as so often happens, economic tactics were relegated to secondary status.

AFTERMATH

Ibáñez may have felt exhilarated in being able, finally, to take decisive action through both executive and legislative channels. That the actions were not addressed to the original ends—lower inflation and improved income distribution—is a commentary on the mutability of objectives, an object lesson on the folly of regarding commitment to redistribution as a fixed entity. The battle against inflation and the recovery of effective power became the objectives which, in the new political calculations of the Ibáñez administration, warranted the sacrifice of distributional equity.

At last Ibáñez could act decisively. A state of siege was again declared throughout most of the country. Several hundred people were arrested in January 1956, emasculating a general strike threatened by CUTCh. As a result of wage restrictions and implementation of other elements of the Klein-Saks recommendations, the wage earners' share of national income declined still more than before Ibáñez had taken office. Even when the cabinet was reshuffled in mid-1956, there were no objections from the Liberals and Conservatives "so long as the anti-inflation program was continued and was not altered so as to include tax reform or other measures which would redistribute national income (Bray 1961, p. 121).

By 1958 antiparty populism, and in particular Ibañismo, were as discredited as the parties had been in 1952. After riots in Santiago in 1957, severe recession, and continued bitterness between Ibáñez and the labor movement, the Right was victorious in the 1958 presidential election. Under Arturo Alessandri, the most straightforwardly pro-business president since the depression, progressive redistribution was neither expected nor undertaken.

CHAPTER 5
The Faltering Redistributionist Impulse in Peru

THE REDISTRIBUTIVE record of Gen. Manuel Odría's eight-year rule in Peru from 1948 to 1956 was a disappointment without being a disaster. Unlike the typical abortive redistribution effort, which crashes down upon the regime, Odría's populist impulse simply sputtered; the policies had little ultimate effect. With strong world demand for Peruvian exports and a doubling of foreign investment propelling the economy at an annual growth rate of 6 percent (a per capita rate of nearly 4 percent), the opportunities for a significant increase in the working-class share of national income existed but were not realized. Although real wages rose modestly, they probably did not keep pace with the overall expansion of the economy (UN 1959, p. 11). In addition, the impoverished agricultural sector fell even further behind the expanding modern sectors of mining, commerce, and banking.

Odría's administration has gone down in Peruvian economic history as a "business-oriented conservative government" (Kuczynski 1977, p. 117). This would come as less of a surprise if Odría had not cast himself as a champion of the workers and peasants. His political strategy was to capture the loyalty of low-income groups through highly visible, direct largesse from the president to the people—to establish a rapport between the general and the masses that was based on paternalism rather than power sharing.

THE BACKGROUND

At the very outset of the post–World War II period the populist and "progressive" elements in Peruvian politics, for once united, succeeded in electing José Luis Bustamante y Rivero, a professor of law serving as ambassador to Bolivia. Following the wartime period of high inflation, foreign exchange crisis, food shortages, and declining real wages that had discredited the economic approach of conservative president Manuel Prado, Bustamante had the advantages of popular support and control of both houses of the legislature as long as the APRA party remained within his National Democratic Front. Moreover, during the first year of Bustamante's administration the markets for Peruvian exports were quite favorable, leading to a 20 percent increase in export earnings and thus a windfall improvement in the foreign exchange situation (Dragisic 1971, p. 53).

The first major economic policy change by the APRA-dominated Congress was an abrupt tax reform, entailing immediate increases in profit taxes (a 33 percent increase for the highest bracket, to 20 percent of profits) and in income taxes (a 20 percent increase for the highest bracket, to 30 percent of income). There were also increases in the tax rates on stock dividends and on sugar exports (Dragisic 1971, p. 54). The sugar export tax was new; it claimed between 20 percent and 50 percent of export sales above the level calculated from a base price. This tax consequently had the potential to draw off a large part of the export profits earned when the world market price of sugar—Peru's second most important export—was at a high level.

The second step was to change the institutional structure of economic policymaking. By shifting the regulation of credit from the Central Bank to the Bank Superintendency, formal control over credit regulation was taken out of the hands of the export-commodity producers (who had dominated the Central Bank) and put under the head of the superintendency, who was appointed by the president. This constituted a significant threat to the wealthy. The freewheeling lending practices of the half-dozen private banks controlling the bulk of deposits were strongly based on favoritism; insiders could readily finance their own operations, whereas it was very difficult for outsiders to gain access to credit. François Bourricaud (1969, p. 33) has even labeled control of credit as *the* major source of power of the oligarchy.

Yet strangely this institutional change attracted far less attention than the proposal of the APRA members (Apristas) to form a "Socioeconomic Council" to provide for broad participation in economic policymaking. APRA claimed that the intent of the Socioeconomic Council was simply to supply advice and consultation to the policymakers, yet Bustamante himself denounced the proposal as an attempt to negate the constitutionally established rights of the executive and his subordinates to make economic policy. The Apristas also initiated discussions of changes in the conduct of business, promoting government control of corporation statutes and abolition of bearer stocks (Dragisic 1971, p. 55). Even though the Aprista-dominated legislature ultimately made little change in the structure of the economy, it developed an unambiguous image of pursuing the course of fundamental change.

While these proposed institutional reforms were attracting attention and criticism, the price controls and other interventionist regulations that had proliferated as emergency measures during the war years were left intact. This absence of action was as important in its concrete economic effects as the Aprista reforms. Both domestic industrialists and exporters complained bitterly that the controls, out of place in a period of international peace, were strangling the local economy. The Apristas, countering that these measures were essential to keep inflationary pressures in check, even increased the controls. Full exchange control was adopted in 1946. The government refused to devalue the Peruvian *sol* because higher-priced imports (and import-competitive goods) would increase the cost of living for the lower-income groups, even though serious shortages of foreign currency began to block importation and the higher cost of Peruvian exports (along with a poor sugar crop) depressed export revenues (Dragisic 1971, p. 58).

The economic reaction of both the export-oriented economic elite and the smaller domestic producers was to cut their losses in the increasingly chaotic environment. As inflation and balance-of-payments problems increased, private investment in Peru decreased; real investment in 1947 was only three-fourths that of the previous year (Dragisic 1971, p. 58). Peruvian capital went abroad and foreign capital stayed away.

Furthermore, the reaction of the private business sectors to Bustamante's policies had a strong element of economic boycott. Leading private-sector institutions were quite blatant in advocating that the entire business community abstain from economic activity. In early 1948 the private Banco Internacional stated: "The difficulties with which capitalists, agriculturalists, merchants and industrialists have to contend in the development of their activities are so numerous that the times are unfavorable for undertaking any work of importance."[1] Sugar planters, incensed by tax reforms that seemed to single them out, played a particularly active role in mobilizing the opposition, going so far as to discourage foreign investment from coming into Peru (Thorp and Bertram 1978, pp. 173, 201, 394–395).

The attack on the government was not limited to economic action.[2] In mid-1947 the opposition members of Congress refused to attend congressional sessions, thus precluding a quorum (at that time 55 percent of the members). The immediate cause for such extreme action was justifiable outrage over the assassination of a prominent right-wing, anti-Aprista editor, and the government's failure to discover the killers. Yet a more basic rationale was the conviction of the Right that they had everything to lose and nothing to gain from minority participation in the legislature. There was less to fear from the president acting alone than from the Aprista legislative program. At the same time, their refusal even to go through the formalities of the legislative function was a dramatic symbol of censure, stating that normal politics were at an end.

The immediate political effect of this legislative boycott, in addition to tarnishing the legitimacy of the regime, was to drive a wedge between Bustamante and the Apristas. Since the latter could no longer determine the governmental program through legislation, Bustamante's rule by decree antagonized the APRA leadership. They retaliated against what they saw as Bustamante's abandonment of their legislative program by calling a general strike in August 1947, which for a week severely hampered manufacturing and commerce. The president countered by having labor leaders arrested and constitutional rights suspended.

By the beginning of 1948 Bustamante's progressive economic position was untenable. Inflation rose to nearly 30 percent in 1947; investment and production declined. The president imposed a conservative stabilization program by decree, appointed a military cabinet to counter the violent opposition his program was bound to arouse among the Apristas, and tried to conciliate the business community. The exporters were not satisfied with the severity of the stabilization program, and the anti-Aprista military was not satisfied with Bustamante's refusal to abolish the APRA organization. In September of 1948 he imposed a harsher stabilization package, and after two abortive military revolts Bustamante was forced to outlaw the APRA. In October the military, under the direction of Gen. Manuel Odría, ousted Bustamante, who by then had no support from any quarter.

Inasmuch as Bustamante was widely perceived as a very proper man with "no stomach for the political infighting" (Pike 1967, p. 280), his failure to control or sidestep either APRA or the conservative opposition was taken by many as a sign that Peru's old style of conspiratorial politics was still more viable than the new democracy that Bustamante was supposed to represent. And indeed Bustamante's unwillingness to engage in political machinations must be ranked an important factor in his demise. Although Bustamante's own writings are rather convincing about his commitment to economic reform (Bustamante y Rivero 1949, chap. 5), his major challenge, at which he ultimately failed, was to keep the radical economic demands of the Apristas from polarizing the political system. Despite the fact that the Apristas may have been considered the natural constituency of a progressive reformer, their refusal to accept Bustamante's moderate program was at least as important to its failure as was the opposition from the potential victims of redistribution.

ODRÍA'S PROGRAM

Confronted with the economic chaos inherited from Bustamante, Odría chose what he hoped was a balanced economic strategy to resolve the financial crisis without precluding the possibility of a populist program that could draw off Aprista support. The technical, abstruse task of effecting monetary stabilization was given over to Pedro Beltrán, the most prominent proponent of the laissez-faire export-led growth strategy favored by the cosmopolitan economic elite. Odría himself attempted to mold the distribution of income, allocating government benefits and establishing wage levels directly. The business sector (dominated by the producers of sugar, cotton, copper, and other export commodities) therefore was left to establish the macroeconomic structure, in the hope that a positive business climate would bring general prosperity, which in turn could be channeled through narrower specific measures to benefit the poor. The interventionist and nationalist stance of the Peruvian governments since the 1920s was to be reversed, and the flow of foreign capital and repatriated funds to be freed; credit restrictions and regulations were to be lifted along with the price controls that had stultified production during the Bustamante period. Workers were to be protected from this economic restructuring not by the government's interference with the market mechanism itself, but rather by offsetting measures of government expenditures and wage policy that were designed to impinge as little as possible upon the natural dynamic of production and trade.

The net result was hardly what Odría had promised. The wealthy export sector reaped enormous benefits; domestic industry, suffering from the export elites's near monopoly on access to credit and from the onslaught of imported manufactures, eked out some gains from the general economic expansion (Thorp and Bertram 1978, p. 261). White-collar workers benefited from government expansion and the availability of consumer goods. Organized blue-collar workers were aided by the offsetting measures, but these barely kept up with the cost of living and could not match the increases in profits enjoyed by the export sector. Unorganized and traditional-sector workers and peasants were virtually untouched by the boom, which left them in the same impoverished state as the marginals in other Latin American countries like Bolivia where the opportunities for rapid expansion had not materialized. Nonetheless, it was possible for Odría to legalize land takeovers of the urban squatters in Lima without affecting the macroeconomic balance. Although his administration was the first to be serious about the government's obligation to provide social welfare, the benefits were limited to urban areas and particularly to Lima. The eventual consequence was mass migration, which by the 1970s turned Lima into a city of sprawling slums.

The cynical interpretation of these events is that Odría deliberately limited the benefits for lower-income groups to the superficial, while catering to the interests of the wealthy on the more important matters of economic policy. Yet it is entirely possible that Odría sincerely saw himself as a champion of the people. After all, he was doing what Perón seemed to be doing so successfully in Argentina. In fact, both Odría in Peru and Ibáñez in Chile patterned themselves more or less consciously after Perón. Like Perón, each sought to create a controllable labor union structure through wage increases negotiated by hand-picked labor leaders loyal to the president. Each relied on massive public works projects to provide employment for the workers and prestige for the regime. General Odría, like General Perón, legislated improvements in workers' benefits and conditions: profit sharing, Sunday pay, mine safety, and employee placement (Hilliker 1971, p. 119). Odría's administration was the first in Peru to establish a full-fledged ministry of labor. Odría also instituted *blanket* wage increases designed to protect all workers from the ravages of inflation, and resorted to such increases seven times during his term of office despite the absence of the hyperinflation that elsewhere made such adjustments essential rather than optional.

CONTROLLING ODRÍA

There is a far more compelling explanation for the disparity between Odría's verbal populism and the actual bias of his economic policy in favor of the wealthy. The wealthy were very successful at controlling the economic levers fundamental to their interests, at the same time

acceding gracefully to Odría's populist impulses on what were in the
final analysis superficial matters. The levers entrusted to the economic
elite were simply more potent than the levers manipulated on behalf of
the poor. This implies that the economic elite enjoyed a superior
understanding of the dynamics of the economy—and employed a
superior mastery of persuasion. As Rosemary Thorp and Geoffrey
Bertram (1978, p. 201) point out:

> Having supported, if not contrived, the right wing military coup in 1948,
> the elite from then on left nothing to chance. A careful watch was kept
> over policy, and with skillful use of their foreign friends and manipula-
> tion of external pressures, the Government of General Odría was gently
> prodded in the desired direction. Step by step the exchange rate was
> totally freed in response to pressure, import restrictions were lifted the
> moment appreciation of the *sol* appeared likely, and contact maintained
> with the U.S. advisory mission called in to make recommendations on
> stabilization, so as to make sure that the proposed policies tallied with
> elite interests. Major laws were encouraged guaranteeing and facilitating
> investment in mining and oil ... By the early 1950s all signs of the 1940s
> experiment had disappeared, and Peru's system of trade and exchange
> was the freest in Latin America.

This gentle prodding of the government was accomplished by three
means. First, the economic philosophy of the elite was presented with
coherence and flair; it came to be regarded as equivalent to economic
rationality. Their arguments of laissez-faire and international division
of labor were, of course, reinforced by the export boom and the
foreign investment forthcoming during the Odría period. For those
who saw laissez-faire vs interventionism as a simple dichotomy, the
interventionist debacle of the Bustamante era implied that laissez-faire
was the only viable alternative. While liberalization can take many
forms, not all benefiting the economic elite, the version of export-
promoting free-trade liberalization propounded by the Peruvian wealthy was promoted as *the* orthodox version of laissez-faire.

Second, the key policymaking positions in establishing the exchange-rate regime and trade regulation were controlled by representatives of or sympathizers with the economic elite. Not only the Central
Bank, but also the treasury and economic policymaking institutions not
normally associated with conservative economic philosophies were
"captured" by the ideology of *beltranismo*. As late as the 1960s Jane
Jacquette (1971, p. 76) found that "the basic tenets of *criollo* liberalism,
the reliance on foreign investment and the congruence between private sector dominance and natural economic laws, are accepted at the
highest levels of the Central Bank, the Banco de la Nación and even the
National Planning Institute."

Finally, the elite's concrete reactions to economic policy were of such crucial importance to Peru's prosperity, given the existing economic structure, that governmental policymakers had to compensate for any damage done to the export producers even if the latter did not resort to economic boycott or political retaliation. The sequence of policies applied during this period is a fascinating example of the quandary of a regime whose leaders believe they cannot afford to antagonize or dislocate the wealthy through populist policies. Deficit budgets to support social welfare programs were followed by restrictive monetary policies to counter the potential inflationary pressure of deficits financed by the printing press, in turn leading to liberalization of the export-import regime to placate exporters' complaints about credit restrictions. Wage adjustments leading to higher demand for imports prompted further export-promotion liberalization in order to alleviate balance-of-payment deficits. Through five separate stabilization programs the effects of social spending and price controls for the middle class and the organized working class were countered by still further liberalization to ward off inflation, foreign reserve deficits, and production inefficiencies (Dragisic 1971, pp. 66–118). Through this sequence of countermeasures Peru ended up with not only the purest free-market-oriented regime in Latin America, but with the greatest vulnerability to the fortunes and temperament of the export interests and their foreign contacts.

AFTERMATH

The period following Odría's eight years of ultimately conservative policy is noteworthy for three reasons. First, an utterly different sort of regime—a civilian centrist government under Manuel Prado— encountered the same problems and responded in much the same way that Odría had. This suggests that whether regimes are dictatorial or democratic in nature is less important than is generally thought in accounting for the reactions to redistributive attempts and the success of these attempts.

Second, the striking similarities between the specific measures employed by Odría and by his successor illustrate an important characteristic of the economic policymaking process in Peru and in Latin America in general: the very limited degree of learning. While it is conceivable that these measures were no more futile than any others at that particular stage of Peruvian economic and political development, the lack of experimentation with other approaches reveals a certain historical blindness to past failures.

Finally, the completion of the APRA party's swing to the right following Odría's departure is a sobering example of the deterioration of redistributive support by groups that have already been elevated economically. While the alignment of proredistributive and antiredistributive forces at any given moment is usually perceived as fixed, it is in fact quite fluid.

When Odría reluctantly acceded to holding the presidential election of 1956, another unlikely coalition emerged victorious. With the support of APRA, whose leaders recognized that the military still would not permit an Aprista candidate, past president Manuel Prado defeated a conservative candidate and the rapidly growing reformist party of Fernando Belaúnde, the Acción Popular. Prado, a member of one of Peru's most patrician families, had overseen a bland and conservative administration from 1939 to 1945. By the time he was deposed by the military (a few days before the normal end of his second term) to annul the 1962 APRA victory, Prado's record on economic policy had been conservative enough for historians to regard his second term as "a business-oriented conservative regime" like that of Odría (Kuczynski 1977, p. 217). Looking back over the second Prado administration, most historians have focused on the conservative policies applied by Pedro Beltrán, once again permitted a nearly free hand in economic policymaking. Yet the first three years of the administration had a very different policy complexion; economic reform was promised and policies were designed to be at least modestly redistributive (Thorp and Bertram 1978, p. 260). It was only after these policies failed that Prado installed Beltrán, in mid-1959, to oversee a major shift in economic policy.

To be sure, Prado's commitment to redistribution for its own sake was mild at best, if the record of his previous administration is any indication. But there were significant political considerations that led Prado to begin his second administration with somewhat populist policies. For one thing, he had been elected with the support of APRA, whose leadership was pleased with the opportunity to make inroads against the Communist unions, but whose trade union membership could be kept satisfied only by concrete economic measures of wage bonuses and profit sharing, which Prado did implement in the early days of his administration. In return, APRA agreed to cooperate in the legislature (though in the beginning there were few APRA legislators) and to desist from politically embarrassing strike activity while still pursuing wage demands in a less politicized fashion. Through this accord—*La Convivencia*—the Prado administration was able to steer clear of much of the political unrest that could have been anticipated in such a setting, since (as was later shown) the military and APRA were still bitterly at odds, the pressure for meaningful land reform was mounting, and the range of groups capable of disrupting the political or economic systems had grown. In essence, Prado's commitment to economic reform was more politically compelling than Odría's; the general had relied on repression, whereas Prado had to face APRA and the rest of the Left in a fairly open liberal democratic framework.

Prado's initial economic program was dictated in part by policies he inherited. Many large public works projects had been initiated by Odría as a parting shot; they continued to drain the treasury, but for Prado to abandon them would have meant a very visible reduction in employment. The expansion of the bureaucracy under Odría saddled Prado with extensive budget obligations to pay for public-sector employees. Prado also implemented the modest profit-sharing plan that Odría had formulated but not put into effect; this, too, was a policy of vital concern to APRA, with its large following in the factories. Finally, Prado continued to observe the practice of blanket wage increases despite relatively low inflation rates and the widespread elite opinion that these increases were inflationary.

Prado attempted to meet these commitments through budget deficits—by 1957 in excess of revenues by 5 percent.[3] One result was that the inflation rate of roughly 7½ percent for 1957 and 1958, though modest by international standards, was still higher than the 5 percent average for the three years prior to Prado's administration and created a serious financial and production problem because of Prado's unwillingness to permit devaluation of the sol. While the Apristas opposed devaluation on the grounds that cheaper soles would make consumer imports more expensive, the export sector favored devaluation to make Peruvian exports more attractively priced on world markets, particularly because of the decline in demand occasioned by the recession in the United States. But instead of devaluing, the regime sought to bolster the value of the sol by restricting the money supply and the availability of credit.

The business sector responded to these policies with a combination of heated criticism—especially from Beltrán's newspaper, *La Prensa*, and its competitor, *El Comercio*—and concrete economic adjustments to minimize the damage. There was considerable flight of local capital in 1957 and 1958; an increasing volume of funds was devoted to currency speculation, and there was a rush by producers (as well as consumers) to purchase cheaper imported goods, creating a serious balance-of-payments deficit. The economic adjustments were not confined to "making do" within the ground rules established by the government, however. After the government had raised the marginal reserve requirements for commercial banks (that is, increased the amount of money the banks had to withhold from lending), the banks simply defied the administration by running up deficits with the Central Bank in order to grant more credit than the restriction allowed.

The government's measures and the ensuing reactions led to a sharp economic contraction by the second half of 1957, worsened by small harvests and poor export prices. Production dropped, and the Central Bank's reserves of foreign exchange were almost completely depleted. The likelihood of a devaluation became so clear that the unions began to demand higher wages to compensate, even before the devaluation was announced. A partial devaluation at the very end of 1957 did not free the sol but did reduce its value.

Parallel measures to increase government revenues through more efficient taxation procedures, higher tax rates, and new taxes on luxuries were submitted to Congress, but not much more than the procedural changes were passed despite Prado's presumed control over the legislature. The International Monetary Fund urged wage restraint, but in the face of strikes and strike threats Prado granted another blanket wage increase in May 1958, including raises to public employees that exacerbated the budgetary problem. The government had to rely on the limited devaluation, on a twelve-month wage freeze after the adjustment, and on reducing the budget for 1958—but even so, the budget deficit was a huge 15 percent. The hope for raising government revenues to match expenditures was frustrated yet again in early 1959 by the refusal of the legislature to increase taxes sufficiently. The administration's tax package was diluted to the point where the projected revenue increase was only a sixth of what was implied by the original proposal. Under other circumstances legislative obstruction might not have been surprising, but considering the crisis atmosphere and the supposed allegiance to Prado of most legislators, the administration's failure is noteworthy.

At this point—mid-1959—Prado found that the limited prospects for wage restraint, export growth, and increased revenues under the existing economic regimen would result in large budget deficits for 1959 and 1960. Inflation was running at over 12 percent, resulting from shortages rather than increased demand. The economic elite had withdrawn all of its support and willingness to cooperate, with the consequent problems of disinvestment and sluggish production looming for the foreseeable future.

There was an "easy" solution to these problems: in mid-1959 Prado called in Pedro Beltrán, his chief critic, to again take over the direction of economic policymaking. As premier and finance minister, Beltrán proceeded to restore the economic liberalism that had prevailed during the Odría period, this time without the grandiose public works projects and blanket wage increases that had partially balanced the regressive effects of Odría's macroeconomic policies. Under Beltrán the budget deficits were eliminated by cutting back on construction projects, food-price subsidies, and public-employee wage increases. To raise revenues and to avert the International Petroleum Corporation's threatened production halt, Beltrán increased domestic oil prices—an action that affected rich and poor alike. Congress finally passed a major industrial promotion law, which granted tax exemptions and other subsidies to industry. With the resumption of private investment, increased export earnings (partly due to the coincidental expansion of copper and fish-meal production), and reduced currency speculation, the economy recovered dramatically. From 1960 to the end of Prado's administration the balance of payments turned positive, the inflation rate remained below 6 percent annually, real growth averaged more than 8 percent, and all the budgets yielded surpluses.

This sort of economic miracle following the abandonment of a redistributive program (or even a program designed to protect the income share of the lower-income groups) is not uncommon. In Chile, for instance, economic recoveries followed the abandonment of redistributive policies under González Videla and Ibáñez. This tendency has several causes unrelated to the long-term merits of income-progressive and income-regressive policies. Redistributive policies are often abandoned during cyclic downturns (frequently caused by external factors such as low world-market prices), which reverse themselves shortly after the regressive policies have been applied. Less coincidentally, higher-income groups that have been holding back investment and political support from the government are far more likely to reinvigorate the economy and strengthen the government's capacity to restore an attractive climate for foreign investment as well. This does not necessarily mean that a regressive policy in place for a protracted period would do better than a progressive policy over the same period. Nevertheless, progressive policies have suffered in comparisons with the economic performance following their suspension. In the Peruvian case Beltrán's success confirmed for many Peruvians that there was a clear trade-off between growth and equity. This presumption was to have unfortunate consequences, not only in the willingness of the Right to sacrifice equity for growth, but in the willingness of the 1968 military government to sacrifice growth for equity.

Beltrán's policies, in spite of their negative impact on the wage share of income, were accepted by the Apristas. APRA's political foundation over the years had come to be concentrated in the blue-collar and white-collar unions (Hilliker 1971, pp. 88–94). Satisfying the highly organized, politically powerful unions through *selective* wage increases and other benefits was enough to keep APRA's support intact. Above all, APRA was concerned with seeing the Prado administration through to its completion, so that APRA's cooperation with the government could gain it enough respectability to permit it to assume power in 1962 (Werlich 1978, pp. 266–267). Current economic objectives were traded—it turned out futilely—for future political advantage.

As Peter Klaren (1973, p. 154) puts it, "By the 1960s the Aprista working-class clientele, not only on the plantations but also in the mining and manufacturing sectors, had clearly become a select elite within the broad spectrum of the nation's laboring population." This is, in fact, a not uncommon phenomenon that contributes to the self-liquidation of redistributive commitment and efforts. As initially low-income groups win the benefits of redistribution, their own commitment to further redistribution wanes, or is even replaced by opposition to redistribution, for they come to see their own gains as jeopardized by additional changes. By the 1960s, just as the first sincere attempts at fundamental tax reform were getting under way, the APRA slogan became "No more taxes!"

CHAPTER 6

Interpreting the Authoritarian Populists

THE FATE OF THE authoritarian populists hinged on their ability to prevent or surmount the reactions of opposition. Their choice of a populist style of governance virtually ensured their popular appeal and made it easy to mobilize mass support—but at the cost of provoking those who feared populist goals. In contrast to the centrist's dilemma of trying to arouse support from working-class groups that have little enthusiasm for the watered-down policies of compromise offered them, the authoritarian populist's predicament is that a mobilization of support touches off a mobilization of opposition.

The opposition's reactions can be political, economic, or both; they can be accommodative or punitive. The political dynamics are clear enough, illustrated in concrete cases and by comparisons among episodes. The dynamics of economic reaction, though, are better expressed in more abstract terms. Before examining the tactical differences among Perón, Ibáñez, and Odría, we shall find it useful to survey the economic reaction sequence in broad outline.

THE ECONOMIC REACTION SEQUENCE

Our few examples are sufficient to outline the most common economic dynamic that threatens redistributive efforts. Even in the absence of political or economic retaliation, economic *accommodations* by both the victims and the beneficiaries of redistribution can steer initially well-intentioned leaders like Ibáñez, Odría, and Prado into adopting regressive policies. Accommodations, defined as income-maximizing or profit-maximizing behaviors that take existing policy as given, can cause the abandonment of redistributive policy without any deliberate attempt by economic actors to undermine the economy or the existing regime—though that may be the ultimate outcome. The results of accommodations include:

1. Inflation—price increases, induced by higher demand and often
   provoked by wage increases.
2. Disinvestment—shifting capital out of domestic investment, either
   deliberately by the wealthy whose investment incentives have declined, or through a shift of income to the less-investment-prone
   poor.
3. Balance-of-payments deficits—caused by greater purchases of imports combined with investment shifts away from export
   production.

Ironically, none of these potentially devastating economic consequences entail direct conflict between the redistribution-minded regime and its potential victims, nor any deliberate damage to the
economy on the part of these potential victims. Inflation may emerge
from accommodative price increases intended merely to cover increased wage costs and to benefit from the greater demand that
progressive redistribution generally brings. Disinvestment can likewise
be a purely defensive rather than punitive reaction if investors simply
divert their capital from threatened enterprises whose expected profits
are no longer high. Similarly, incentives to import and disincentives to
export hold, even without any motivation to discomfit the government
by engineering a balance-of-payments crisis.

Consequently, although political, retaliatory intentions *may* reinforce and exacerbate these problems, their emergence and the reactions to them require only accommodative economic self-interest. The
results are disconcertingly "natural" if interpreted as drawbacks of
redistributive policy by those involved in policy appraisal. Without
confrontation, the emergence of economic problems following redistributive measures can less easily be attributed to "political struggle";
antiredistributionists have a promotional advantage in labeling redistribution "bad economics" if these consequences materialize. If inflation, disinvestment, and balance-of-payments deficits become acute
when redistributive policies are in effect, the common reaction of even
an initially redistribution-minded government is to impose a stabilization program consisting of sharp devaluation and austerity measures
with regressive effects.

INFLATION

Progressive redistribution tends to increase the overall demand for
goods and services. Schemes to encourage or force higher savings by

low-income groups do little to offset the propensity of the poor to devote more of their incomes proportionately to consumption than the wealthy do. The poor can less afford to save and invest. The increased demand due to redistribution brings different economic effects, depending on how much unused capacity exists and how much new capacity can be created. Commonly, considerable excess (unused) capacity exists at the time of redistribution and is capable of meeting some increased demand. If total capacity does not decline in the aftermath of redistributive measures, a certain degree of higher demand can therefore stimulate the economy without overly straining its ability to meet the new level of demand at prevailing prices. Increased demand may even induce further investment to boost productive capacity, as long as private investors respond to the market-expansion opportunities or the state enlarges its own production role.

When, however, redistribution creates more consumption demand at prevailing prices than productive capacity can meet, and investment incentives do not yield expansions of capacity, then inflationary pressures mount. Unless effective price controls can be imposed, which is rarely the case, inflation occurs.

The likelihood of capacity expansion, which could turn excess demand into a virtue rather than an inflationary force, is often limited by the fact that redistributive programs tend to discourage private investors confronted with higher wage costs, the expectation of inflation, and perhaps the fear of more extreme redistribution leading to expropriation. State expansions of productive capacity frequently are also limited during periods of redistribution because increased wages and other benefits for state workers, and higher social service and transfer payments to the poor, leave many state enterprises short of investment capital.

The task of carrying out redistribution without triggering inflation becomes a matter of *timing, calibration,* and *presentation.* Timing is of obvious importance because demand-increasing redistribution will be less inflationary if implemented when excess capacity exists. Calibration, or the fine-tuning of the magnitude of policy effects, is critical because the extent and rapidity of increases in demand will determine whether existing capacity will be strained, and whether expansions in capacity will come soon enough to prevent or at least diminish the inflationary effects of demand that exceeds existing capacity.

The presentation, or symbolic context, of redistributive measures is important to their inflationary prospects for very similar reasons. Inflation can be fueled by a wide variety of perceptions often associated with redistribution, yet the ways redistributive measures are presented

can modify these perceptions. First, the expectations that often provoke inflation through the dynamic of the self-fulfilling prophecy can
be expected to rise in proportion to expectations of how extreme the
redistribution will be. Second, the perception of threat on the part of
potential investors, as much as the actual existence of threat, influences
how much capacity-expanding investment will be forthcoming if demand increases. Third, if redistribution is presented in such a way as to
kindle stronger immediate demands for even more redistribution,
rather than to satisfy the aspirations of low-income groups at least
partially, then the redistributive measures already enacted can trigger
additional inflationary pressures, such as still higher wage demands.

As even the Peronist experience indicates, the balance of timing,
calibration, and presentation is rarely successful enough to eliminate
all inflationary pressures. The round of policymaking following the
initial imposition of redistributive measures tends to be characterized
by a preoccupation with the issue of inflation and a presumption, often
cultivated by antiredistributionist forces, that the redistribution per se
is responsible for the inflation. Whether this is true in any particular
case is an open question, but it is important to note that redistribution is
neither a necessary nor a sufficient condition for inflation. It has
already been noted that redistribution that does not boost demand
beyond existing and forthcoming capacity is not necessarily inflationary; and it is equally true that inflation can result from causes other
than redistribution (for example, from higher import prices, or from
offsetting wage and price increases). Therefore, an important component of the promotional side of the *appraisal* of redistributive policy is
the effort of antiredistributionists to lay the blame for inflation onto
redistributive instruments, and for the proponents of redistribution to
argue against this diagnosis.

The stakes of this debate are very high, because if the stabilization
measures adopted to combat inflation are predicated on a diagnosis of
the inflation as due to "excess demand" on the part of the poor, then
the stabilization package is likely to contain austerity measures that
attempt to reduce inflation by lowering the wages and other income of
the poor.

DISINVESTMENT

The "supply side" of the impact of redistribution hinges on changes
in investment devoted to maintaining and augmenting productive
capacity. Increased demand left unsatisfied by the activation of unused
capacity must be taken up by capacity expansions, we have seen, if
inflationary pressures are to be avoided. Even if demand remains

constant, a drop in investment can lower production and trigger inflation, thereby stigmatizing the government with the double failure of maintaining neither growth nor monetary stability.

The first question is whether redistribution per se creates economic disincentives to investment. Disinvestment can, of course, be punitive, if the wealthy or their allies are willing to withdraw their capital irrespective of the profitability of its current uses *in order* to bring on an economic crisis. In Peru particularly, there are graphic, well-documented instances of punitive disinvestment. Still to be resolved is the question of whether, political effect aside, redistribution deters domestic or foreign investors out of economic rationality.

The answer is complicated by the fact that the general propensity to invest and the propensity to invest in one's own economy can be quite different. We know that the wealthy save and invest more of their income than the poor do. The starting point of many theoretical considerations of the impact of redistribution on economic growth, accordingly, is to assume that investment declines, at least in the short run. Yet the relevant question is not whether various economic actors have more or less savings which could be used for investment, but whether they are encouraged to or deterred from directing it to productive investments in their own country. If redistribution can be structured so as to enhance investment opportunities within a country and minimize the flight of capital out of the country, the reduction in disposable capital due to the redistributive income shift can be offset.

What accounts for investment and disinvestment on the part of the private sector? E. V. K. FitzGerald's comment on Peru holds generally as well:

> It would appear that the rate of private capital formation in Peru is determined by the perceived investment opportunities rather than by the availability of finance, while these "oportunities" will clearly depend upon both the real state of the economy (particularly export growth and domestic demand) and the expectations of the investors themselves, particularly in reference to future political conditions and profit rates. (FitzGerald 1976, p. 21)

Disinvestment, then, has three possible sources or motivations:

1. Conscious design to induce changes in government or in governmental policy;
2. Reaction to reduced expected returns in activities or sectors adversely affected by implemented governmental policy;
3. Reaction to perceived threats to the return or ownership of investments not adversely affected by governmental policy up to that point in time.

These sources are often difficult to attribute to particular instances of disinvestment. Investors obviously may act out of a blend of motives, and furthermore that which constitutes a real drop in profitability is hard to distinguish from that which is perceived as a drop in profitability. Yet the distinctions are important in considering policy design and presentational strategy. An administration with particular redistributive objectives must expect that its measures will make some areas of investment or economic activity less remunerative and attractive than before, if only because certain practices of favorable governmental treatment for businesses or financiers are eliminated in the wake of redistribution. Consequently the second source of disinvestment, response to "the real state of the economy," is practically inevitable, though it can sometimes be mitigated through the government's capacity to mold perceptions of what reality is. Government statistics are highly suspect for this very reason. The government has more leverage in trying to avoid the other two sources of disinvestment, because it can control (often to a large degree) how much it will provoke retaliation and how widespread are the fears of even greater deterioration of investors' prospects.

To minimize capital flight from areas for which the government has no intention of reducing profitability, the choice of instruments and the presentation of policy must clarify what is definitely beyond the target of redistribution. But to avert politically motivated disinvestment, policy design and presentation may be directed toward linking such disinvestment to future retaliatory measures on the part of the government.

The flight of capital, in the concrete sense of actual transfer of assets from within a country to outside, in most cases is simply not preventable if capital owners are determined to remove their liquid assets. As Arnold Harberger notes:

> There can be little doubt that most wealthy people, in any less-developed country in the world, can and do find ways of having bank accounts and securities portfolios abroad. In many cases, the capital-market movements involved are perfectly legal; in others, the black market is used as a vehicle for transferring funds. But in any event the funds do get abroad ... If the economic return to capital becomes more unfavorable for home-country investment, this will carry as a consequence a greater flow of funds overseas. (Harberger 1977, p. 260)

This is not to say that investors who otherwise would remove their assets cannot be pressured into maintaining their investment levels, keeping their businesses open, or cultivating their farms. The fate of their *fixed* assets can be pivotal—they need to be convinced that their ownership of immovable assets such as land, buildings, or machinery can be safeguarded only by "cooperating patriotically" with the government's program by keeping these operations well financed. For example, agricultural taxes that penalize undercultivation, land reform measures that permit the expropriation of uncultivated land, or regulations that permit government intervention in factories operating below previous production levels can deter disinvestment, but only if the government's threat is not perceived as so excessive that investors come to regard their fixed assets as irretrievably lost anyway.

In addition to these possibilities for adopting disinvestment-minimizing strategies, the prospects for maintaining an adequate level of investment are improved by the fact that the increased demand that usually accompanies redistribution can itself provide stronger incentives for investment. Again, *if* demand is boosted by redistributive policies that are not seen as threatening to investment in general, then a positive investment climate can emerge. Of course, redistribution's victims can also play the promotional game to try to alter this climate. In short, there is no fixed macroeconomic rule that inextricably links redistribution with either increased investment or disinvestment on the part of the private sector. The investment level will vary according to at least partially controllable elements of the climate such as confidence, risk, and perceived opportunities.

The state's own investment of capital could, under some circumstances, fill the gap left by private-sector disinvestment. Increased state investment has often been posed as the simple way to escape the problem of having to attract continuing cooperation from a private sector that is likely to be both resentful and frightened. Yet the overconfidence of leaders who presume that the state's investment level is highly responsive to their own wishes is frequently unjustified, because governmental and autonomous state-enterprise resources are subject to several other claims as well. Public-sector wage demands impinge upon both the central government and state enterprises. Social service agencies draw off funds from the central budget that otherwise might go into investment. These competing resource needs are always present and may be exaggerated in periods of redistributive policy. Moreover, the expedient of resorting to government budget deficits in order to finance investment has its own inflationary consequences. The potential for increased state investment, though obviously important, is not necessarily reliable.

BALANCE-OF-PAYMENTS DEFICITS

The increase in the disposable income of lower-income groups effected through redistribution leads to higher demand for imports, as

well as for goods and services in general. If, as is usually the case, a fixed
currency exchange rate prevails, then the domestic inflation and
heightened import demand lead to overvaluation, as the local currency
loses its real (free-market) value vis-à-vis international currencies such
as the dollar.

The negative effects of an overvalued currency—the bias against
exports and favoring of imports, with the resulting deterioration of the
balance of payments; "indiscriminate import-substituting incentives"
(Bhagwati 1978, p. 209); and bottlenecks to overall growth due to
foreign exchange scarcity—call for devaluation before the degree of
overvaluation becomes extreme. Yet devaluation is generally resisted
by proredistributionists and not a few conservatives who fear its
political consequences, until extreme overvaluation compels a sharp
devaluation that often obliterates redistributive gains.

Devaluation in most instances is anathema to proredistributionists
because of its presumed regressive distributional effects. Devaluation
raises price levels—first of imports that must be purchased with less
valuable local currency, then of locally produced goods that depend on
imported materials and machinery or compete with imported goods.
The burden of these higher prices falls more on the poor than on the
wealthy for several reasons. The wealthy producers for the domestic
market can recoup their higher costs through higher prices, and they
profit through higher sales because competing imports are more
expensive. Wealthy producers for export, and export middlemen,
profit handsomely when their foreign currency earnings are converted
into local currency.

The distributional effects of mild devaluation can be compensated
by other measures. Moreover, a balanced exchange rate does not
condemn overall economic policy to regressivity, since it does not
preclude other measures from imparting a progresive effect. Serious
distributional damage, on the other hand, does occur when severe
overvaluation triggers a devaluation too extreme for politically feasible
compensatory measures to counter. This is most likely to happen when
policymakers come to believe, because of the "artificially" low prices
workers enjoy under the predevaluation condition of cheap imports,
that they must bear the burden of sacrifice entailed by the devaluation.
This is the rationale for stabilization policies that combine devaluation
with wage restraint: the inflationary effects of the devaluation are
contained by supressing the wage component of the price-wage spiral.
The balance-of-payments crisis that accompanies overvaluation, as
both cause and effect, gives further impetus to austerity measures that
penalize workers while providing incentives for export investment.

The stabilization sequence that has been so damaging to redistribu-

tion in Latin America can be understood only by accounting first for
the prevalence of severe overvaluation despite its well-known economic liabilities (which are summarized in Krueger 1978). As the
official exchange rate diverges from the falling free-market rate,
policymakers are understandably reluctant to unleash the inflation and
(at least temporarily) lowered purchasing power that devaluation
would bring on. Nonetheless, the drawbacks of serious overvaluation
are so obvious to economic policymakers that factors other than
straightforward economic considerations must play a major role.

The first of these factors is the symbolism that devaluation conveys.
It is widely regarded as an admission of failure—that the government
has not been able to pursue its economic policies effectively or even to
maintain the integrity of the national currency. Viewed as a sign of
economic malaise, it poses a threat to investors' confidence (Krueger
1978, p. 50).

Second, devaluation per se is generally *perceived* as more inherently
damaging and more regressive than its reality, taking into account the
overall effects. With respect to the perceived economic deprivations
due to devaluation, the most obvious is the almost immediate decline in
purchasing power, not its subsequent expansionary consequences.
Politicians therefore fear that inflation resulting from devaluation will
be viewed as an otherwise avoidable mistake, rather than as "corrective
inflation" necessary for reducing economic distortions. The inflation
may be attributed to the devaluation rather than to prior conditions
whose inflationary effects were temporarily restrained by
overevaluation.

With respect to regressivity, the benefits of devaluation that do
emerge for some relatively low-income groups—probably outweighed
considerably by the sacrifices of other low-income groups—register
hardly at all in softening the regressive image of devaluation. Although
workers involved in export production may benefit from the export-
promotion effects of devaluation, and some of the formerly unemployed may gain jobs in local industries that increase their production
to supply no-longer-importable goods, public attention tends to focus
predominantly on the windfall profits of the wealthy export producers.

This combination of short-sighted reluctance to reduce redistributive gains, heightened symbolism of failure, and fear of adverse
political reaction to devaluation has made extreme overvaluation a
common precursor to the crash of a redistributive effort. Once a
government has made an adamant, symbolic public commitment to
resist devaluation, redistribution-created increases in demand often
force overvaluation to a point where it is no longer economically
tenable. The government then faces the inescapable need to devalue

(in many instances forced by the International Monetary Fund) and stuns its trusting supporters with a crushing devaluation. What makes the "betrayal" all the more bitter is that the government usually denies to the last minute that it intends to devalue, in order to forestall currency speculation. To make matters worse, people with liquid assets who understand the game often play and win through speculation despite the government's coyness. On occasion, it has been argued that leaders deliberately encouraged pressures for extreme overvaluation in order to be "forced" into a devaluation that otherwise would have been politically too costly. When rigid refusal to undertake even partial devaluation, or devaluation before the currency is highly overvalued, is a sincere redistributive strategy, it is at best a poorly calibrated one.

HOW PERÓN WAS DIFFERENT

The economic reaction sequence was every bit as much a danger for Perón as it was for Ibàñez and Odría. Perón had to confront the possibility of massive disinvestment by both the large-scale agricultural producers and the established industrialists. Beef and grain producers had cause to undermine Perón's economic program as soon as it became apparent that the government was going to retain a large part of the profits of agricultural exports; the industrialists opposed Perón's support for upstart entrepreneurs and his expansion of state intervention and state enterprises. Perón also had to face balance-of-payments deficits during the years of drought that destroyed the export harvests. The expansion of working-class consumption demand meant that Argentina could have experienced explosive inflation as well. And even Perón tolerated an overvalued currency in order to avoid the humiliation of a major devaluation.

Therefore the demise of redistribution in the wake of economic and political reaction under Ibáñez and Odría, and the escape of Perón's policy from the same fate, permit a comparative examination of the concrete conditions and strategies that impel or fend off disinvestment, intolerable inflation, political retaliation, and all the other components of the redistributionist's nightmare. The same factors—political tactics, policymaking style, and ideological character—that account for Perón's relative economic success also account for his political success, a fact that should not be surprising in view of the intertwining of political and economic expectations and realities.

Perón's greater success in avoiding the trade-off between disinvestment and inflation resulted, first, from his unapologetic alliance with one segment of the well-to-do, the emerging industrial entrepreneurs.

Industrial firms, earning bigger profits during the Perón era than ever before, expanded vastly in terms of total assets (Silverman 1968, p. 244). While providing these attractive investment opportunities with unmistakable partiality, Perón also made sure that he had a mechanism for adding state-directed investment through a fairly noninflationary means: the extraction of wealth from rural producers. If direct state investment and credit subsidies had been financed without extracting capital or forcing savings, the resulting inflation would have eroded the industrialists' gains along with those of the urban workers. Apparently Perón was not at all discomfited by the lack of "evenhanded" sacrifice on the part of the wealthy, let alone the absence of balanced burdens for the wealthy and the poor.

Perón reduced politically motivated disinvestment and direct political opposition not only by aligning himself with the increasingly powerful nouveau riche, but also by refraining from destroying or ostracizing the victims of his redistribution *to the point of incurring their unrestrained retaliation*. This may seem strange to those familiar with Perón's burning of the prestigious Jockey Club and his speeches denouncing the landowners, but Perón's own ideology of *Justicialismo* and his concrete economic measures never signaled the economic doom of any group. In fact, to some Perón was an ideological nonentity: certainly not a democrat; hardly a Marxist or coherent socialist; not even a fascist. Irrespective of ideological aesthetics, Perón was politically effective with an ideology of such eclecticism and outright vagueness that it constrained him not at all.

This is of particular importance in light of the fact that Perón seemed to be a corporatist, and his emulators patterned themselves after this image. Yet Perón, in both thought and action, departed sharply from the corporatist paradigm of integrating all economic groups into an "organic" structure of economic cooperation and joint policymaking direction (Kenworthy 1973, pp. 17–46; Wynia 1978, pp. 55–60). Instead, Perón knew from the start that governing was struggle; that there would be winners and there would be losers. The Peronists' commitment to particular economic groups, despite the rhetoric of common benefit and common sacrifice, ensured that compensatory measures for the rural producers would not be allowed to erase completely the redistributive gains of the Peronist unions.

Another factor was the improvisational nature of Perón's approach to economic matters. No economic ideologue, Perón was willing to adapt an economic institution or policy designed for one purpose to serve utterly different functions. What in retrospect may seem to have been shrewdly deceptive may well have been merely expedient. The effect was to keep the threatened economic groups continually off

guard, never quite sure whether the worst had already occurred or
whether the government might be provoked by challenges into even
harsher attacks on those already somewhat victimized by Perón's
redistribution.

The importance of improvisation should not be dismissed simply
because it may have been second nature to Perón. Whether the result
of strategy or unselfconscious style, improvisation creates a quite
different climate for the reception of policy than does a widely publicized, ideologically based blueprint that clearly labels who is to lose
utterly. For all of Juan and Evita Perón's verbal attacks on the "oligarchy," no domestic economic group was entirely stripped of its income
or assets. Perón did *not* galvanize the opposition into desperate action,
as the blatantly ideological thrusts of Chile's Allende did in later times.
Even Ibáñez, with his relatively (compared, that is, to Allende) mild
redistributive program, lacked the improvisational impulse to circumvent legislative opposition.

When economic difficulties did set in for Perón, he adapted his
policies; adjusted the rates of taxes, subsidies, and interest; and even
temporarily reversed the rural-to-urban flow of resources—all without
flipflopping from a rigidly progressive structure to an irredeemably
regressive one. In contrast, Ibáñez' so-called fall into the hands of
conservative economic forces can be explained as much by his prior
refusal to compromise as by his subsequent cave-in to the rightist
position. Odría, too, brought in a Klein-Saks mission to counsel worker
austerity, rather than adjust his own redistributive mechanism.

Furthermore, Perón's chosen instruments of economic policy were
much more differentiated and segmented than those of Ibáñez and
Odría, with the result that Perón had more maneuverability in pin-
pointing benefits and deprivations in order to keep the well-to-do from
uniting against him. Under Ibáñez and Odría *general* wage adjustments
were among the most prominent and publicly debated instruments of
economic policy, exposing both governments to plain view as to the
direction of their wage policies, and thus to criticism by employers or
workers en masse when the wage adjustment exceeded or lagged
behind the rate of inflation. Similarly, the *general* tax increases that
Ibáñez and Odría hoped would place roughly equal sacrifice upon all
wealthy sectors provoked, expectably, united opposition from these
sectors. Perón's tax "reform," on the other hand, was a jumble of social
security tax increases, byzantine variations of corporate taxes, and
sundry other forms that infuriated the advocates of streamlined taxation. The result was, as usual, exasperation by Perón's critics, but
hardly united opposition.

If indeed Ibáñez and Odría were also operating initially within a political style (namely, populism) that permitted improvisation, why did they not avail themselves of the opportunities to modify instead of dump their redistributive programs? Their latitude in shifting to programs of totally different distributional implications turned out to be the downfall of redistribution rather than an aid for preserving it. Aside from unsubstantiable speculation on whether Ibáñez and Odría were sufficiently committed and clever, two broad considerations may be offered as explanations: inflexibility and incomplete control.

The same reluctance to impose uneven sacrifices was responsible for the lack of flexibility shown by Ibáñez and Odría. Perhaps because they were modeling themselves after an illusory image of Juan Perón as the ideologically committed corporatist, Ibáñez and Odría maintained their positions unyieldingly, until they were so untenable that the underlying principles had to be jettisoned.

To the extent that the behavior of Odría and Ibáñez illustrates the nature of corporatism and corporatist-grounded populism, corporatism reveals two serious liabilities for redistribution: first, the weakness of the corporatist-populist connection; second, the rigidity of any ideological position on the flexibility of policy choice. A corporatist may begin with the premise that the workers' contribution to society justifies their receipt of greater rewards. But when the corporatist faces the political and economic liabilities of progressive economic policy, especially if he cannot minimize these liabilities with flexible adjustments, he is easily tempted into abandoning the populist version of corporatism for the reactionary version that decries the struggle of the workers as dissonance in the otherwise harmonious workings of society. Since neither Odría nor Ibáñez came to power owing any particular debt to the trade unions or other working-class organizations, neither felt enough obligation to or dependence on the working class to forgo a complete reversal of progressive policy.

Although corporatism can accommodate *either* progressive *or* regressive policy direction at any one point in time, and swing abruptly at moments of economic or political crisis, this ambivalence is not translated moment by moment into pragmatic adjustment. In contrast, Perón had a clear clientele—organized labor—and never made any pretense of pleasing everyone.

CALIBRATION

Why is ideology so often antithetical to flexible adjustment of economic measures? The logic required to calibrate policy instruments properly in order to achieve a desired magnitude of redistributive effect calls for intricate compromises that few ideologies can rationalize.

While each policy instrument carries with it an a priori image of moderation or drastic change, nonetheless policymakers must decide how extreme each measure ought to be in order to *approach* the ideal accomplishment of objectives without bringing on an economic or political backlash. A government has to decide how much to devalue and how much to increase wages; tax changes must specify precisely what the new rates shall be, and so on. If the coverage of such governmentally regulated benefits as pensions and minimum wages is to be extended, the government must choose the scope of coverage as well as the particular magnitudes of the benefits.

Straightforward as this may seem, calibration involves much more than simply deciding what result is desirable. The magnitudes and parameters embodied in the design of policy initiatives change in the further stages of formulating and implementing policy; hence the initial design often reflects attempts to calibrate these magnitudes to offset further changes. Government agencies almost universally pad their budget requests; tax proposals are submitted to the legislature with higher tax rates than the administration actually prefers to see enacted; and so on. Similarly, policy design may reflect considerations of discrepancy between what is eventually formulated as policy and what the net impact will be. Wage increases are set with an eye to erosion due to inflation, just as tax rates are formulated in light of the potential for evasion.

Therefore the question of calibration has two components: calibration to achieve the "ideal" magnitude and rate of change, and the issue of what magnitude and rate are politically and economically optimal. These considerations often clash, and the image of ideological commitment in general is better served by attending to the former than to the latter.

It is clear that overshooting the redistributive goal through instruments that prove (with hindsight) to have been excessive can be as much of a problem as unanticipated dilution of redistributive effect. Perón's overestimation of the sustainable level of labor's share of national income by 1950 necessitated a politically costly retrenchment thereafter. Ibáñez did much the same thing by boosting government spending far more than state revenues would have justified. The crucial difference is that Perón recalibrated; Ibáñez did not.

The logic of calibration, then, requires the committed redistributionist to pursue his goals obliquely, without the all-out, go-for-broke measures that would clearly demonstrate ideological commitment.

However, to cast the scope and magnitude of initial policy objectives deliberately at variance with what ideology would dictate leaves the policymaker vulnerable to two charges: first, that he is deceptive rather than forthright about his goals; second, that he is too weak or too cowardly to brush aside the obstacles blocking a straightforward pursuit of goals through measures that impose by fiat precisely the called-for effects.

SCOPE OF CONTROL

Perón was able to manipulate himself out of political and economic difficulties more successfully than Ibáñez and Odría because he secured much more complete control over the economy. Perón, unlike Odría, never fell prey to the convenient rationalization that control of only a partial set of policy instruments would be sufficient to direct more resources to the poor. He had the audacity to believe that he and his close associates could reign over the entire Argentine economy without regarding any level of policymaking as too arcane—or too petty—to leave to others. The Peronists did not leave gaping loopholes by which the redistribution-targeted rich could escape or recoup their losses. And Perón, for a host of reasons including his personal outlook and his economic allies among the industrialists, never felt compelled to return control of economic policymaking to the wealthy economic groups.

The inability of Ibáñez and Odría to maintain overall control of the economic policy levers had two consequences. First, they both lacked an effective means to finance income transfer without an offsetting inflationary adjustment. Odría left the formulation of investment incentives (read loopholes) to the economic elite, while Ibáñez simply could not control taxation. Second, they had insufficient means to threaten or carry out economic deprivations upon those who defied their policies. Legislative defiance in Chile, and simple disinvestment in Peru, were not very costly reactions for the potential victims of redistribution, since the governments had few punishments at their disposal.

III
THE DEMOCRATIC
REFORMISTS

I N 1958 THE ARGENTINE electorate chose Arturo Frondizi. In 1963, the same year that Arturo Illia was elected president of Argentina after the military removed Frondizi, Fernando Belaúnde was elected president of Peru. The next year Eduardo Frei won a lopsided electoral majority to become Chile's president. Despite important differences in their approaches, all four of these men can be considered democratic centrists: willing to play (more or less) by the liberal-democratic rules of the game and, at least initially, committed to progressive economic reform.

The emergence of such regimes in all three countries during the 1960s was no coincidence. The United States, through the Alliance for Progress, was both rhetorically and financially supporting democratic reformists. In the context of the "revolution of rising expectations," the unimpressive performances of the conservative regimes that had followed the authoritarian populists guaranteed strong electoral backing for anyone who could take on the mantle of economic progressivism. The Argentine and Peruvian militaries, not yet ready to attempt to rule indefinitely themselves, proscribed the "dangerous" populist movements of Peronismo and Aprismo but did not prevent centrist figures like Frondizi and Belaúnde from seeking mass electoral support. In Chile the business-oriented Alessandri government (1958–1964) gave way to the broadly supported Christian Democratic regime of Eduardo Frei, who also promised both economic growth and greater equity.

Whereas the authoritarian populists depended almost entirely on mobilization of the urban masses, the democratic reformists conceived their base as also encompassing the rural poor and the middle class. The breadth of the economic objectives implied by this breadth of support was a sure indication that any explicitly articulated program of the reformists would quickly be revealed as overly ambitious. For, in addition to improving the economic status of organized labor and the urban marginals, the reformists were committed to land reform and higher incomes for the rural poor. Unlike both the authoritarian

populists and the later radicals, the reformists were also deeply concerned with improving economic efficiency and the business climate
for attracting domestic and foreign investment. In three cases confrontation with foreign capital was avoided through compromise solutions
on the ownership of natural resources: Frondizi extended exploration
contracts to the multinational oil companies; Belaúnde reached agreement with the International Petroleum Corporation (an agreement
that the military subsequently overturned); and Frei "Chileanized" the
major copper mines through generous compensation to the U.S.
owners. Only Illia was unenthusiastic about cultivating foreign investors and canceled the oil-exploration contracts upon reaching office.

In striving for such a wide appeal, all but Illia tried to incorporate
organized labor within their own movements. Consequently, government-labor relations took on an element of competition beyond the
strictly economic issues. The democratic reformist typically had to
balance the objectives of growth and equity in an atmosphere of rivalry
with established labor leaders of the Left, legislative opposition from
powerful populist or leftist parties, and skepticism on the part of the
private business sector.

On the positive side, however, was the widespread sentiment in all
three countries in favor of economic reform. The experiences of the
reformists can be viewed as lessons in the formulation and political
management of such reform. With little concern for political accommodation or for economic counsel outside a small circle of advisors,
each reformist launched his own model of economic reform and
managed, with greater or lesser success, to neutralize the reaction that
such an imperious aproach was bound to trigger.

CHAPTER 7

Gradualism in Chile

PRIOR TO 1970 THE ONLY successful redistribution in Chile was launched by President Eduardo Frei, author of the progressive anti-inflation Frei plan during the Ibáñez government. Jerome Levinson and Juan de Onis (1970, p. 8) point out that during the 1960s Chile was the only major South American country which seemed "to have accomplished a significant redistribution of income in favor of the poor." The bulk of this progress was accomplished by the 1964–1970 administration of Eduardo Frei, given that Frei's fairly conservative predecessor, Jorge Alessandri, reigned over the early 1960s. However, the Frei regime's success was tempered by both the erosion of its redistributive gains in the second half of his six-year term and the decline of political support for Frei's Christian Democratic party.

The redistributive record under Frei certainly cannot be regarded as a failure. Yet in terms of the distributive aspirations of Frei and his closest collaborators, and certainly in terms of the electoral fortunes of the Christian Democrats, his regime did not meet initial expectations. Frei managed to increase wage levels impressively during his first three years, but from 1968 to 1970 the pretax and pretransfer *relative* position of wage earners disintegrated to the point where their income share was no better than when Frei first came to power. Politically this was devastating. The inability of the administration to protect wage gains of unorganized or poorly organized workers from inflationary erosion, and the unwillingness of the government to back wage demands that it regarded as contrary to its anti-inflationary stabilization program, ruptured the link between Frei and organized labor.

All the same, Frei's record of income transfers through the budget was impressive, even though the budget deficits were somewhat inflationary. Berating, cajoling, and manipulating Congress, Frei more than doubled the effective tax rates, whereby the Chilean state could assume a far greater role in both industrial promotion and the provision of social services. The tax rate increases—much more important than shifts in the forms of taxes, or any movement from indirect to direct taxes—had the backing not only of the target groups of social service programs for which the rate changes were earmarked, but also of the adherents of budget balancing.

Frei had considerable success in land reform, even though his well-publicized targets were not met. He resettled some 28,000 peasant families on land encompassing 10 percent of all agricultural property and 16 percent of all irrigated property (Edwards 1972, p. 25). This was certainly impressive compared to the nearly negligible expropriation under Alessandri, but paled before Frei's *target* of 100,000 resettled families. His failure to reach this target is partly explicable by the enormous costs involved in resettling such a huge number of families.[1] If our assessment of agrarian reform is based solely on the extent to which the *economically feasible* volume of expropriable land was in fact expropriated, Frei's record is quite impressive.

However, the agrarian reform effort detracted from other aspects of Frei's redistributive program. The manner in which land reform was pursued diminished the effectiveness of the anti-inflation campaign, designed to protect wage gains for both industrial and agricultural workers. Businessmen in the industrial and commercial sectors, whose cooperation in holding down price increases was essential for the anti-inflation program, were antagonized by the threat to private property they saw in the constitutional amendment that was introduced for the land reform act. Instead of taking advantage of the isolation of the landed elite from the industrial and commercial sectors, Frei inadvertently triggered a coalition of the wealthy that doomed his cherished wage policy.

THE BACKGROUND

Eduardo Frei came to office with what was, for Chile, a strong electoral mandate. He was the first Chilean president in twenty years to receive a majority of the popular vote, having won 56 percent in a three-way contest. The Radical party candidate, Julio Durán, initially backed by the rightist parties, was abandoned by the rightist Democratic Front coalition so that its support could be thrown to Frei, whom they saw as the surest hope of checking the rise of the Marxist Left (led by Salvador Allende). These preelection maneuvers were triggered most immediately by a by-election victory of Allende's Frente de Acción Popular (FRAP) coalition, but more fundamentally by the growing realization that the balance of political power was moving to the left, and that some "preemptive" support for reform was a concession necessary to stave off more radical changes represented by the Marxist Left.

Consequently, Frei's majority was an exaggeration of the support for Center-Left reformism, but it did represent a widespread consensus that the prime political question was not whether there would be change, but rather how much. This shift began under Alessandri, whose striking ideological contrasts with Frei and Allende obscure the fact that his *relative* conservatism was in several respects reformist. As Jay Kinsbruner (1973, p. 153) points out, "The Alessandri administration served as a transition period in which serious reforms were undertaken and formerly radical positions were sponsored in the most respectable circles."

For example, Alessandri's tax reform proposals reflected not only the typical conservative concern for efficiency and for mobilizing capital, but also considerable concern for equity. Tax reform was viewed as a way of stimulating development capital that otherwise would have gone into "frivolous" consumption by the wealthy, who had previously avoided or evaded their fair share of taxes. Since the payment lag between income earning and tax payment had permitted individuals subject to high direct taxes to pay with far cheaper currency (because of inflation), Alessandri pushed through legislation to reduce the payment lag and to index tax liabilities to the rate of inflation (Sommerfeld 1966, p. 183).

Thus Frei inherited an atmosphere in which even the Right had embraced mild reform. Moreover, several of the most obvious potential victims of redistribution had become politically isolated. Unlike Peru, where the landed, industrial, and mining elites were thoroughly intermixed, in Chile there was enough distance between elite groups to permit alliances of redistributionists and certain wealthy sectors against other upper-class sectors. The large mines were owned by U.S. corporations that were not looked on with much favor by the local elites. Large landowners were also isolated. Virtually all other groups agreed that land reform was essential—whether for economic growth (because lagging production of the latifundia had become a serious bottleneck), economic justice, social peace, or as a precondition for American aid (McCoy 1969, pp. 16–19; Loveman 1976, p. 223).

FREI'S INITIATIVES

Frei's impressive electoral victory in 1964 hastened his initiatives in four major areas of domestic economic reform: social services targeted to the economically marginal population, tax reform, land reform, and wage policy designed to raise real wages without triggering an inflationary spiral.[2] These were all interrelated in that they required, or were part of, a much more dominant role of the Chilean state. Expanded social services and land reform with compensation to former landowners required the state to channel greater resources through its administration than ever before. Tax reform was designed to provide these resources. Wage policy, to improve real wages without triggering an inflationary spiral, required the state to control the rate of wage increases and somehow to forestall price increases.

Let us start by analyzing the macroeconomic model on which this enlargement of state activity depended. The Frei administration expected, correctly, that foreign investment and foreign aid would be available, for Frei was a favorite of U.S. policymakers interested in the reformist option in Latin America. He also expected the Chilean government, through the state industrial development agency CORFO, to contribute to the capitalization of the country, rather than becoming a drain on the central treasury. However, the magnitude of the resources to be channeled into areas without short-term payoffs was so great that the government had to count on the private domestic sector to maintain high levels of economic expansion. Consequently the overall economic initiative of the Frei administration, in addition to its redistributive aims, was to foster private as well as state economic expansion. This ultimately made the regime vulnerable to private-sector disinvestment when a large part of the business community was antagonized by some of the administration's policies (and its anticipated policies).

ACTIONS AND REACTIONS

The "mandate" of an election majority prompted Frei to submit a combined reform package to Congress in 1964, even before his Christian Democratic party gained control of the legislature. This haste left the definition of communal property vague and the source of resettlement financing unspecified. Wage policy, a combination of real-wage targets and anti-inflation measures, was similarly formulated with inadequate forethought, as reflected by the lack of consideration of the impacts of labor-management wage negotiations, stagnant savings rates, and price increases (Ffrench-Davis 1973, p. 59).

This combination was so ambitious that it has been interpreted as a deliberate attempt to provoke legislative rejection in order to highlight the need for a Christian Democratic victory in the 1965 congressional elections (Sigmund 1977, p. 36). The program was beaten down, but the Christian Democrats were indeed able to use legislative obstructionism as a cause célèbre to win the congressional elections. Frei ended up with a Christian Democratic majority in the Chamber of Deputies, though not in the Senate.

Frei's package of reformist initiatives had another notable characteristic. Although it was much farther to the left than any postwar economic program in Chile, workers' representatives and leftist political groups (besides elements within the Christian Democratic party) had little to do with its formulation. The technocrats of the party and the administration, themselves satisfied with the progressive merits of the program, attempted to impose it without permitting input from— or political credit to—others. The program, particularly in its wage policies and land reform, aroused the suspicion and competitiveness of the leftist parties, the non-Christian Democratic unions, and often the proposed beneficiaries themselves. Ricardo Ffrench-Davis (1973, p. 60), not unsympathetic to the Christian Democrats, notes with regard to the wage policy:

> In the technical sense, the program was clearly redistributive. But this did not constitute a sufficient condition for its success. The workers did not participate in the elaboration or the application of the program. Moreover, during the campaign certain "populist" images were created . . . As a consequence of these factors, the government suffered intense opposition on both flanks; the leftist opposition centered its action against the wage policy. The result was that, in contrast with the theoretically redistributive content of the program, the government policy appeared in practice as identified with the employers' side.

SOCIAL EXPENDITURE

Frei took full advantage of Chile's peculiar budget system to increase social spending, through both the central budget and the decentralized agencies. Spending in education increased by more than 15 percent, health by 80 percent, and housing by 75 percent. Considering that overall economic expansion for the 1964–1970 period was around 30 percent (Mamalakis 1976, p. 92), these expenditure increases far exceeded the pace of economic growth.

The structure of the budget system made social service expenditure a path of least resistance for redistributing income. However, spending increasingly slipped out of central control through the same dynamic, contributing to the precariousness of economic management that eventually plagued both Frei and his successor Allende.

The "details" of the budget law determined to a large extent who would get the political credit for extending social services to the poor. The breakdowns of the draft budget were not fine enough to enable congressmen to know precisely how each budget line would be spent. Decentralized agencies and state enterprises, even though they received massive central budget transfers, were beyond congressional budget review. Congress could not add programs without providing new taxes, nor without the president's assent. And the president always used the item veto to eliminate projects "suggested" by congressmen (Cleaves 1974, p. 326).

Congress from the very start had no discretion over the half of national government expenditures controlled by decentralized agencies and state enterprises. Yet, ironically, Congress could only gain political credit for social services by furnishing decentralized programs with their own earmarked funds. This dynamic shifted increasing proportions of public expenditure out of central budgetary control (usually with the hearty approval of the agencies involved, since they gained protected sources of revenue), and thus outside the control of both the executive and the legislature.

With respect to social expenditures within the central budget, congressmen could not claim that their initiatives were decisive, because of the greater initiative accorded the executive. Legislators got some short-term political mileage out of sponsoring public works measures, but these were almost always vetoed by the president, and (at least during the Frei era) the legislators who proposed such measures rarely tried to override the veto (Cleaves 1974, p. 80).

Without enjoying the credit for increased social service legislation, opposition congressmen still risked losing support if they opposed such legislation. To criticize central budget spending programs was thankless—it simply antagonized program recipients—and to block them was nearly impossible. Cleaves has demonstrated that during the Frei and Allende administrations the executive's polished budget proposal (*oficio final*) differed very little from the budget law adopted by Congress, both in terms of its overall level and its sectoral distribution—despite Frei's lack of majority in the Senate and Allende's lack of control in either chamber (Cleaves 1974, p. 54).

The ease with which Frei dominated the policymaking process in establishing central budget levels illuminates the importance of the "process" (as distinct from the leader's political power conceived as an overall attribute) in accounting for policy outcomes. As Frei's struggles over wage policy and land reform abundantly indicate, his political power per se, even with an electoral majority, could not account for such dominance. It was, rather, a result of the structure of the budgetary process—which Frei and later Allende inherited quite apart from any exercise of political power. There was a strong incentive for congressmen to adopt the role of defender of the taxpayer, even when increased taxes were clearly necessitated by the same expenditures these legislators had accepted. It was politically safe to oppose taxes without opposing any particular spending program. Consequently, legislative opposition was not a significant factor in restraining the expansion of spending, although legislative opposition to tax increases (eventually surmounted) caused the government to lose some of its control over the directions and scope of spending.

The executive's budgetary dominance did not mean that its objectives were easily achieved. Most important, spending in housing was considerably less than had originally been planned, a reflection of the interconnectedness of the different policymaking arenas. By 1967 the overall economic situation, because of the weakness of the wage and investment-promotion policies, forced Frei to forgo further major increases in social service spending. With an inflationary spiral threatening, and little prospect for expansion of the construction materials industry, the housing program seemed too "costly," even if the government could get the funds to finance it. Altogether, the housing program yielded just over 70 percnt of the 360,000 units planned, but the drop-off in housing starts in the last two years of Frei's administration was a major disappointment to housing planners and a serious political liability for the Christian Democrats. Lack of control over setting real wage levels, the weakness of the executive's control over the money supply because of the autonomy of the Central Bank, and the inability of the government to encourage more private investment all blunted the housing program despite the fact that the Frei administration controlled the "social" budget.

Another problem detracted from the progressive impact of the housing program. The state housing corporation CORVI had an initial objective not only of increasing the total volume of state-constructed housing units,[3] but of assigning a larger proportion of state-built housing to the poor. In 1965, 46 percent of the dwellings built by CORVI were "minimum" rather than "medium" or "superior," as opposed to a percentage of only 27 percent during 1962–1964 (Merrill 1968, p. 13). Yet as the pressures from relatively higher-income groups mounted, the caliber and real costs of CORVI-built houses rose too, as indicated by both their size and their cost (Merrill 1968, pp. 14–15; ODEPLAN 1971, pp. 325–326). "Low-income" as opposed to medium and superior housing constituted a consistently smaller proportion of CORVI's efforts, and even the low-income housing was more expensive and larger than had been planned. The consequence was to disqualify the lowest income groups.

These pressures were reinforced by the attitudes of professionals within CORVI (principally architects) who were accustomed to designing and overseeing more sophisticated housing.[4] Because of CORVI's status as a semiautonomous agency, its internal decisions on such matters were largely beyond the influence of the Congress and even the executive.

TAX REFORM

One could search the legislative record of the Frei years in vain for a clear-cut victory of "tax reform." Yet to judge by the outcries against overtaxation heard by 1967, and the increased support for the right-wing National party on the part of "middle-class voters who were disillusioned with reform programs that increased their taxes and gave them no direct benefits" (Sigmund 1977, p. 59), Frei had indeed penetrated the defenses of obstruction, avoidance, and evasion.

In an atmosphere of high concern over government social spending unquestionably requiring major tax changes, several attempts at tax reform were made, beginning with an ambitious package of measures submitted (and rejected) in 1964, and piecemeal changes introduced each year after that. What makes Frei's record of tax reform so difficult to assess—and yet so interesting—is that so little change in the *form* of taxes resulted in a much greater burden on the upper-income and middle-income groups to finance programs directed in good part to the poor. Frei basically increased the *rates* of existing taxes. The sales tax remained the most significant source of tax revenue, and in fact increased in importance (ODEPLAN 1971, pp. 386–390). And while some assessments of the Frei years point to a relative increase in direct over indirect taxes as a sign of increased progressivity,[5] a closer look indicates that the domestic incidence of direct taxes (that is, direct taxes excluding the revenues from the largely foreign-owned mining companies) increased only slightly more than domestic indirect taxes (indirect taxes excluding customs duties). Direct taxes excluding mining revenues increased from 23.5 percent of total revenue in the Alessandri period to 26.5 percent in the Frei years, while indirect taxes less customs duties rose from 45.0 percent to 47.3 percent. It is obvious from these figures that indirect taxes remained the major source of tax revenue under Frei (Stallings 1975, pp. 521–522).

Regardless of the source of taxes, the enormously increased level of tax-funded programs in health, housing, and basic education directly benefited the poor. Frei was able to claim in his message opening the

1966 congressional session that he had increased the taxes collected from the "upper classes" by 40 percent (Sigmund 1977, p. 50). By 1967 tax revenues reached 18 percent of the gross national product, and exceeded 21 percent by 1970, from a base of less than 13 percent in 1964 (Ffrench-Davis 1973, pp. 252, 329). Together, tax-rate increases, new taxes, and stricter enforcement of previously legislated tax-evasion penalties (for example, the first prosecutions for tax fraud in Chilean history!) more than doubled tax revenues under Frei's administration.

In each legislative confrontation, some pieces of Frei's tax programs won and other pieces lost.[6] In some instances (such as the property tax), the rates were decreased while the tax base was expanded, or the rates increased but the deductions expanded. Thus the overall "progress" in tax reform was hardly impressive, which is probably one of the reasons why whatever progress did occur was permitted to proceed without stiffer resistance. In short, Frei's tax initiatives achieved the sort of clouded, indirect results that are typical of many relatively effective redistributive attempts.

Frei's first foray into tax reform came in his initial legislative program of 1964, presented to a Congress still dominated by the opposition of Alessandristas and the Left. The program included across-the-board increases in tax rates. Using the anti-inflationary program as the vehicle and justification for raising taxes, Frei emphasized reducing the fiscal deficit by ensuring that new programs were introduced with adequate provisions for funding (Arbildua and Lüders 1968, pp. 37, 98). In some instances this meant including the legislation for new taxes within the legislation for new programs; in other words, "earmarking" the taxes.

Frei could present the need for higher taxes either in terms of the general need to meet the government's total fiscal obligations, or in terms of the opportunities to launch specific programs. Earmarking taxes to specific funding obligations affects the policymaking structure in two ways. First, the tax changes become more segmented, in that the identifiable groups which stand to benefit from the passage of each tax are narrower than the beneficiaries of government spending in general. Therefore the intensity of support for such measures, on the part of the benefiting interests, is likely to be high. At the same time, the interests supporting a segmented piece of legislation will be restricted. Second, earmarking is but one way of linking different components of economic policy. Making these linkages explicit engages economic actors in debate over the whole linked package, rather than isolating the participation of each to ostensibly separate issues. This seemingly paradoxical combination of segmenting taxes by earmarking each for a different purpose, and thereby combining revenue concerns with spending concerns, tends to increase the obviousness and directness of redistribution. To the extent that the connections between specific taxes and specific expenditures are made explicit, those who pay the tax become more aware that their contributions are going to the beneficiaries of that spending program. Thus the political trade-off in earmarking taxes to specific programs is the same as the trade-off of mobilizing intense though narrow support at the cost of provoking intense though narrow opposition.

Since the poor are often politically weak, particularly when confronted with the ability of the rich to obstruct legislation, earmarking taxes to specific social service expenditure programs would seem a risky approach. Yet for Frei (unlike Belaúnde in Peru), two factors tipped the equation in favor of seeking separate financing for programs in education, health, and housing. First, Chilean budgetary arrangements afforded political credit to Congress as well as to the president only when new funds were established. Second, middle-class groups standing to benefit from administering or supplying these services to the poor could be expected to support not only the social service expenditures, but also the tax increases linked to them.

Thus it was not simply a case of the supplicating poor vs the tax-shy rich. It was, instead, a confrontation between the *combination* of social service recipients and middle-class service suppliers, against the particular interests threatened by the specific tax obligations involved in greater expenditures. In short, it was an excellent opportunity for an interclass alliance in support of individual pieces of social service legislation *and* of the taxes to finance such legislation, as well as for logrolling agreements between different groups of service providers (teachers, health professionals, construction contractors) to support one another's funding requests. Frei's strategy increased the obviousness of the connection between extraction and allocation, but the political costs of making this clear were offset by the breadth of the coalition Frei was able to form in support of his measures.

More controversial than the earmarked indirect taxes was a new "wealth tax" (*impuesto patrimonial*), to be levied on the presumed income of capital assets including real estate, vehicles, and company shares. The wealth tax revenues were earmarked for a broad "program of transformation" to finance improvements in health, education, housing, and agrarian reform. The tax was to apply only to individuals with incomes at least nine times greater than the minimum wage, at rates ranging from 1.5 to 3.0 percent of the assets.

The Right objected vehemently to the entire tax reform package, but focused its attack on the wealth tax through a public campaign which implied that the tax would apply to the wealth of peasants and all small proprietors, when in fact it would have applied only to roughly 3 percent of the population. The opposition portrayed the tax package as a threat to anyone with land or other property. This hyperbole paid off in producing a certain degree of furor, yet the defeat of the tax legislation in 1964 contributed to the strength of the Christian Democratic plea for a majority in 1965.

When Frei resubmitted his tax plan in 1965, he still could not gain passage of the package intact, despite his majority in the Chamber of Deputies. Since Frei desperately needed support for his land-reform and copper-nationalization programs, he chose to avoid bitter confrontation over taxes. As Frei's finance minister, Sergio Molina (1972, p. 127), later recounted, "The governmental measures were consciously designed *not* to open many simultaneous fronts in the struggle [for income redistribution], because it was known that the affected sectors would become tenacious enemies out to frustrate them." Frei therefore accepted three dilutions of the wealth tax: first, the tax was to apply only in 1965; second, the rates were cut back to 1.2 to 2.1 percent; and, third, other tax liabilities were to be deducted from the base upon which the wealth tax was calculated. All in all, these dilutions reduced the yield of the wealth tax in 1965 to half of what it had been designed to yield.

Was this defeat? Later in the same year an earthquake and flooding provided the pretext for an additional program of reconstruction that secured funding through an extension of the wealth tax for two more years, at rates ranging from 1.6 to 2.8 percent. Then, in 1968, when the initial wealth tax expired, new legislation reimposed it at a lower rate (1.0 percent).

It would be difficult to find a more graphic example of a successful "foot in the door" strategy. Not coincidentally, amid the furor over the wealth tax, the changes of greatest significance in terms of the volume of revenues were taking place in the *rates* of the income and sales taxes. The controversy over the wealth tax made the more mundane increases in the rates of other taxes less noteworthy, and hence less subject to debate and prolonged resistance.

LAND REFORM

A nearly opposite pattern prevailed with respect to Frei's land reform initiative.[7] Whereas tax reform seemed to stagger from one setback to another even though the objective of revenue expansion was in fact accomplished, the land reform legislation seemed to be an instance of overkill (inasmuch as it entailed a constitutional amendment that strengthened the state's power to expropriate *any* property), which nonetheless resulted in far less than the targeted volume of land transfers.

Frei had promised to resettle 100,000 landless families—roughly half of the total—on their own private or communal farms. It was evident that new legislation would be required, since Alessandri's 1962 law required such prompt cash compensation for expropriated land that the government could not hope to pay quickly enough for the extensive expropriation contemplated. Moreover, under the existing legislation landowners could easily tie up their cases in the courts for years, if not indefinitely. Frei submitted land reform legislation in 1964 and included a proposal to amend the constitution's definition of property rights, despite objections within the Christian Democratic party to submitting the controversial amendment.

It is by no means obvious that a constitutional amendment was necessary for an agrarian reform law with the magnitude of effect that the Christian Democrats had in mind. It may be argued (though there was dissent on this question as well) that the particular land reform act that passed in 1967 did require a constitutional amendment to guarantee its constitutionality, but that is not to say that other formulas of expropriation and compensation having equivalent results could not have been accommodated under the existing constitutional arrangement.

It is even less clear that constitutional changes to legitimize the expropriation of farm property had to change the status of property rights as a whole. The generality of the constitutional amendment, which applied to all forms of property, could easily be construed as the first step in a broad attack on private property beyond land reform, despite assurances of the government to the contrary. This threat eroded Frei's support from the industrial and commercial sectors and weakened his ability to contain inflation.

What can account for the government's approach? There was a precedent in that Alessandri had amended the constitution to accommodate his land reform act (Loveman 1976, p. 229). However, Alessandri's political problem was different from Frei's; Alessandri had only to worry about appearing too conservative, whereas Frei ran the risk of seeming too conservative for the peasants and workers *and* too radical for the industrial and commercial interests. Nonetheless, it may have seemed "natural" to follow Alessandri in amending the constitution as a preliminary to land reform legislation.

Another consideration was that Chilean constitutional theorists preferred general provisions to particular detail. If, for political or legal reasons, the rights to certain types of property had to be redefined in the constitution, then rights to property in general should be redefined.

Finally, looking to his left flank, Frei may have believed that he too needed the appearance of radicalism. Changing the general definition of property rights and altering the constitution to promote the welfare of the peasant would appear far more forceful than subtle maneuvering to circumvent existing constitutional obstacles. In other words, Frei's strategists may very well have seen the "requirement" to amend the constitution more as a political asset than as a political liability. If so, they were reflecting the common bias of greater preoccupation with cultivating support than with avoiding the mobilization of opposition.

During the first half of Frei's term, then, the land reform agency (Corporación de Reforma Agraria, or CORA) in effect paralleled Perón's approach to extracting agricultural profits, in that the terms of the actual deprivation of the victims of redistribution were not as harsh as other viable options could have been. Perón's victims faced the choice of putting up with low profits or, perhaps, triggering land reform. Frei's victims faced the choice of yielding some land under the relatively generous compensation terms outlined in the existing agrarian reform law (which had been promulgated by Alessandri) or, perhaps, provoking a harsher land reform act. Until 1967 this combination of moderately strong action and even harsher threat was successful in keeping resistance to land reform at a minimum (Loveman 1976, p. 240).

After 1967 the government, armed with the new agrarian reform legislation, picked up the pace of expropriations, resettling 20,000 more families. There were three sour notes, though. First, the pace of resettlement was obviously much slower than what had originally been projected. Although it is doubtful that the targeted rate could have been achieved, if only because of the government's limitations in financing resettlement, another factor was the three-year delay in getting the legislation through Congress. While Christian Democratic officials such as Sergio Molina (1972, p. 89) have rather querulously placed the blame on the legislative opposition, "which held back the whole process," it is hard to imagine that the consideration of such a fundamental issue as property rights, in open legislative forum, could have proceeded much more rapidly.

Second, illegal land takeovers (*tomas*) were also on the increase, at once pointing up the government's inadequacy and defying its authority. This, of course, contributed to the polarization of the classes and detracted from the Christian Democratic party's credibility as a vehicle for bridging class differences.

Third, the legislative victory on agrarian reform, instead of pleasing the industrial and commercial interests that had supported land reform, in fact antagonized these groups. This turnabout can be explained in large part by the breadth of the constitutional amendment.

WAGE POLICY

For the Frei policymakers, wage policy constituted their major frustration and disappointment. Molina (1972, p. 127), minister of finance from 1965 through 1967 and probably the most influential government official in setting macroeconomic policy during this period, expressed the policymakers' bitterness in the following terms:

> It would not seem too optimstic a hypothesis to expect to gain the solidarity of the majority, as much by the content of the policy undertaken, clearly differentiated from that traditional in the past, as by the support shown by the people first in the presidential election of September 1964 and then in the parliamentary election of March 1965 ... The events demonstrated that the electoral support of the people does not necessarily signify support for the concrete measures of the elected government, especially when it attempts to set labor remunerations. This is one of the most difficult aspects to control in the application of an economic policy in Chile.

This was, however, an ironic disappointment. The target of a 20 percent increase in real wages had in fact been accomplished and even exceeded, despite the higher inflation and lower growth rates of the late 1960s. The overall index of real remunerations went up 38 percent from 1965 to 1969, with additional increases in 1970 (Stallings 1978, p. 250). The minimum wages in industry and agriculture, which reflect the wage levels for lower-income workers, did not fare as well; nonetheless both *increased*—the industrial minimum by 2.5 percent, the agricultural minimum (starting from a much lower level) by 33 percent, again not counting the substantial increases in the transition year of 1970.

The disappointment, then, was not in failing to raise wages. Rather, it was that the wage increases were secured at the cost of inflation and reduced overall economic expansion. Growth was inhibited first through tight credit policies for business, designed to restrain the inflationary impact of high wage increases, and later through the reluctance of investors to respond to improved investment opportunities when looser credit was instituted. Another disappointment was that the wage gains, though intended by the government, did not redound to the government's credit. As we shall see, the government was cast in the role of opposing wage advances. Finally, the real wage increases came in the first half of the Frei administration, leaving only negligible or even negative growth of remunerations in the second half, when the Christian Democrats needed support for the all-important 1970 presidential election. By then the Frei record was being criticized by major factions of his own party as insufficiently revolutionary. Instead of satisfying wage earners' aspirations, the administration encouraged demands for greater change than it could deliver and thereby discredited Frei's reformist approach.

The constraints on producers notwithstanding, the cornerstone of the strategy was, quite clearly, to control the workers (rather than the producers) in order to preserve what would have to be a rather delicately calibrated movement of wages just beyond the existing rate of inflation. If, instead, the unions took the general wage adjustment as the starting point for even higher wage demands, the inflationary pressures would be irrepressible. This was a possibility, because the president's general wage adjustment was not binding. As Barbara Stallings (1978, p. 169) points out:

> The President had the power to set the minimum wage and salary; in addition, he determined the level of the general cost-of-living increase, which was legally mandatory for the public sector and a recommendation for private firms. *In practice, however, this recommendation served only as a starting point for both public and private sector bargaining.* [emphasis added]

Thus, even though Frei's wage policy promised to be progressive, workers had the legal and political wherewithal to reject the restraint that Frei called upon them to show. The "agreement" (*compromiso*) mentioned by Molina was an electoral understanding rather than a formally negotiated agreement with legal standing. Once Frei had unveiled his gradual redistributive wage policy, he could only hope that union leaders and their members would see the dangers of squeezing employers too hard on the issue of wages.

As early as 1965, actual wage increases exceeded the guidelines set for that year. Organized workers, in particular, secured wage increases far above the cost-of-living increase of 1964: their average adjustment was 47 percent instead of the 38.4 percent calculated as the appropriate cost-of-living adjustment. In 1966, remunerations which were to be adjusted according to the previous year's official 25.9 percent rate of inflation far exceeded the guidelines, averaging approximately 40 percent overall. Thus, in the first two years, real wages of both the private and public sectors increased by about 10 percent *each year,* accomplishing the 20 percent real wage increase planned for the entire six-year period of Frei's administration (Ffrench-Davis 1973, pp. 210–213).

This was, of course, no cause for real joy within the government, although Frei's speeches naturally took credit for improving the welfare of the working man so quickly and so dramatically. It was recognized that the budget deficits created by higher public-sector wages, combined with higher private-sector labor costs and the unplanned leap in consumer demand, were so inflationary that declining inflation rates could not be sustained.

Moreover, the wage increases won by labor unions did not benefit the poorer segments of the working class, even leaving aside the peasantry. According to Chilean labor law, only workers in firms employing twenty-five or more persons could form full-fledged unions; only workers in firms of ten or more could form "union committees" of limited function. Consequently, even by 1970 only about 30 percent of Chilean employees (white collar and blue collar) were unionized, using the most liberal definitions and estimates of union membership (Angell 1972, pp. 45–47). The workers who were organized into labor unions by and large constituted the best-paid segment of the working class, because they were employed in the "modern sector" of relatively efficient and productive firms that could afford to pay more than the small-scale operator, and of course because the unionized workers could strike for higher pay. According to the 1967 industrial census, average incomes of workers in factories employing twenty or more workers were more than twice as great as those in factories employing between five and nineteen workers (Stallings 1978, p. 169). Negotiated wage increases hammered out between unions and employers meant higher incomes for only the wealthier segments of the work force.

The situation for nonunionized workers was indirectly affected by union wage gains, but not always positively. Nonunionized workers had to rely on the minimum wage (*salario minimo*) set by the government, which served as the wage floor for 40 percent of blue-collar workers around the middle of Frei's term (Stallings 1978, p. 250). The impact of negotiated wage increases on the real value of the minimum wage was manifested in three effects: (1) inflation, due to increased labor costs passed along as price increases, diminished the real purchasing power of any given level of minimum wage; (2) the combination of inflation and the higher wages of organized workers created some pressure on the president to raise the minimum wage for considerations of politics and equity; (3) the fact that the minimum wage was more controllable by the president than was the level of union-workers' wages made limitation of the rate of increase in the minimum wage one of the few dependable levers to restrain inflation. On balance, then, as inflation—caused in part by negotiated wage increases—eroded the value of the minimum wage, the president adjusted the minimum wage upward in nominal terms, but at a lower rate of increase than that of negotiated wages or the ensuing rise in the cost of living.

At first glance the behavior of the organized workers in both public and private sectors would seem shortsighted and even perhaps unpatriotic. However, there was a fascinating "extenuating" circumstance that illuminates the complexities of the triple stream of real, perceived, and official events. The official statistics for the cost-of-living increases were based on the controlled prices, ignoring the black market and differences in product quality. Price controls were used to engineer official statistics to serve the government's political and policy purposes. Not only did lower "official" inflation rates make the government appear more successful than it really was, they also limited the wage increases tied to the official cost-of-living increase (Edwards 1972, p. 31).

A careful independent study of pricing changes conducted by Jorge García and Hugo Freyhoffer calculated an actual cost-of-living increase of 44 percent as opposed to the official 29 percent for 1965, and 37 percent as opposed to the official 23 percent for 1966.[8] This discrepancy, too large to go unnoticed, was used as a justification for the unions' wage demands when the government criticized these demands as excessive (Angell 1972, p. 202).

Whether the unions would have been content to settle for adjustments equaling the actual rates of cost-of-living increases is a moot question. Certainly as the earning power of wages visibly eroded, union members wanted to at least keep up with the climbing prices. There was also a political consideration. Communist and Socialist unions, as in the days of González Videla, feared that an entente between Frei and the labor movement would threaten the position of the Left. The artificiality of the official statistics gave the Left a means to rally the labor movement against the Frei government.

RECESSION AND RETRENCHMENT

Domestic private investment plummeted in 1967. Fixed domestic capital investment in manufacturing fell from 294 millions of 1965 escudos in 1966 to only 92 millions in 1967. While this decline was

Democrats and because the proposals threatened the white-collar public employees who constituted a large segment of Radical party support (Angell 1972, p. 168).

The impossibility of securing passage of this package marked the turning point of the Frei administration's commitment to gradual real wage increases. Molina, considerably more progressive on the wage issue than succeeding ministers of finance, resigned in January 1968 after Frei withdrew the capitalization fund package from Senate consideration. His successor, Raúl Sáez, resigned a few months later when all vestiges of the bond program were deleted from the further-watered-down proposal he had introduced.[10] At that point Frei agreed to a wage adjustment package that conceded the full cost-of-living wage adjustment for public employees, expunged the prohibition on strikes, and lacked any provision for capitalization bonds. This was hardly a victory for the lower-income segments of wage earners, because it left the government to balance the problems of inflation and lack of investment with little help from, or sympathy for, the wage-earning sectors.

Therefore, after the failure of the forced-savings plan, the Frei administration pulled a policy lever far removed from public awareness and widespread understanding. The strict limitations on credit for private industry were removed in mid-1965. Henceforth businesses had access to abundant and relatively cheap credit, justified on the grounds of the need to stimulate production and investment (Edwards 1972, p. 34). It was certainly easier to apply this new policy than to restrain the wage demands of the unions. Yet the government's near monopoly on authority and understanding of credit policy, shared only by the banking and business sectors, had as much impact on *real* wages as any increase or restriction in nominal wage rates.

Unlike Ibáñez, Frei's change of orientation was to yield to inflationary pressures rather than to stifle them through regressive austerity measures. Although Frei's shift was not blatantly regressive, since attempts to restrict nominal wage gains were lessened rather than strengthened, the rise in prices touched off by looser monetary policy was hardly compensated by subsequent wage increases. Ironically, in giving up on efforts to constrain wage increases, the Frei administration gave up on protecting real wage gains. Because of increasing inflation, wage increases negotiated for 1968 actually lost ground in real terms for most of the wage-erning sectors, though negotiated wage increases gained in real value for the remainder of the Frei administration. The levels set for the minimum salary, minimum agricultural wage, and minimum industrial wage all lost real value during 1968 and 1969 (Stallings 1978, p. 250).

All in all, however, the policy reversal was not extreme. Price controls were maintained, but with substantial flexibility in permitting selective price increases to anticipate and preempt black-market operations or suply bottlenecks. Instead of triggering runaway inflation, the Frei administration was able to maintain what Ffrench-Davis (1973, p. 62) has termed "regulated inflation"—an inflation that cannot be extinguished but is held within bounds.

It is important to point out that the government's change of heart was the result also of two broader political factors. First, the polarization within Frei's own Christian Democratic party had intensified by early 1968 to the point of open confrontation (Sigmund 1977, p. 66). The radical faction, which along with a more moderate "third position" faction took over the party leadership in mid-1967, openly criticized the government's inability to achieve its progressive objectives and was especially critical of what they saw as Frei's move to the right. At the same time, the business sector's not inconsiderable support for the Christian Democratic party gave it a strong voice within the party's conservative wing—which, as the attacks on Frei mounted, came to be the *oficialista* (progovernment) faction. Although Frei's program to that point was far more menacing to private business than that of any previous government, including the threat to private property and the tax reform, open attacks by the Christian Democratic party's Left fostered, incredibly, an identification between Frei and the party's Right.

Stallings (1978, pp. 185–188) points out that there were three major tools for regulating demand: government spending, wage policy, and credit policy. Government spending increases were curtailed by 1967. Further reductions were difficult because of state-enterprise autonomy, and because of the large wage component of central government expenditure. State enterprises were proving disappointing as investors, because so much of their capital was "escaping" in the form of wages to public employees. Moreover, limited government spending would not fill the investment gap and, if the complaints of the industrialists' group SOFOFA were to be believed, more spending would antagonize private investors fearful of state encroachment. Wage policy was ineffective; as long as wages could not be held down drastically to provide a cheap-labor incentive, wage policy could do little to attract investment.

This left credit policy, which had been used until 1968 as the only major effective check on inflation. Disenchanted with wage policy, and disillusioned about the prospects of controlling inflation without killing off the economy's vigor, the Frei policymakers decided that controlling inflation was too costly. If real wages then suffered erosion through inflation triggered by expanded credit to the business sector, it could be argued that the unions had brought the problem upon themselves. Like Ibáñez before him, Frei had shifted from a populist to a probusiness strategy, though with far more subtlety than Ibáñez had shown when he invited in the Klein-Saks mission to advise drastic austerity. The new policy of ample credit for the business sector upset the balance of purchasing power among wage earners, private producers, and the state—a balance that had kept inflation at realtively low levels prior to 1968. Producers could now gain more, at the expense of the erosion of real wages through increased inflation.

INVESTMENT

The policy shift of 1968 conceivably could have set investment back on track, allowing the government to resume expansion of domestic fixed investment. Table 6 shows that this did not occur. To isolate the pattern of private-sector reaction to economic and political conditions, I have excluded foreign investment (which during the Frei period flowed mainly into the mining sector) from these statistics. The gnawing fears of inflation, inadequate credit, and expropriation outside the rural sector undermined the confidence of individual investors; the decline in private fixed investment was unrelenting.

The question, then, was whether this investment gap could be filled by a combination of foreign funds and state resources. The private sector's steady decline of investment was barely compensated by the

TABLE 6. DOMESTIC INVESTMENT IN CHILE, 1961–1969 (GROSS FIXED CAPITAL IN MILLIONS OF 1965 ESCUDOS).

Year	Direct public investment	Indirect public investment	Private investment	Total investment
1961	993	194	1,358	2,545
1962	1,332	259	1,035	2,626
1963	1,245	203	1,386	2,834
1964	1,296	178	1,260	2,735
1965	1,441	301	1,117	2,859
1966	1,594	289	1,017	2,900
1967	1,492	543	906	2,941
1968	1,589	710	867	3,166
1969	1,619	839	808	3,286

SOURCE: Calculated from ODEPLAN 1971, table 279.

public-sector increase, which came both directly and indirectly (that is, through loans and stock acquisitions). The fact that the state sector could increase savings and investment despite tremendous pressures to raise public-sector wages is impressive. Yet the growth in investment was a far cry from the 70 percent target that Frei's planners believed necessary for the growth and redistribution targets they had projected. Foreign investment could not fill the gap, and "forced savings" of workers (channeled into investment via the state) was simply not politically feasible after the heavy-handed attempts of 1967.

The critical point is that in 1968 Frei presented attractive investment opportunities and credit sources to domestic entrepreneurs, and they refused the call. When the hoped-for expansion of production did not materialize, credit was retightened in an effort to reduce the damage of inflation triggered by the jump in the money supply. But by then it was clear that the industrialists' unwillingness to respond to the incentives had foreclosed Frei's chances to regain the economic momentum of his first three years. It is useful to explore the reasons behind this unwillingness.

THE ESTRANGEMENT OF THE INDUSTRIAL SECTOR

The support and trust that Frei could command from the industrial sector was a key element of initial appeal and success. As one who promised to modernize Chile, Frei received the backing of those industrial leaders who viewed structural reform as essential, even if that required challenging the powerful landed elite. While Frei was never able to count on the full support of the industrial sector, the pro-Frei elements within the business community kept the industrial and commercial business organizations at least neutral in the first years of the Frei administration, despite the increases in real wages, taxes, and government spending. The estrangement came later, in 1967–1968. One apparent explanation must be dismissed at the start: the rejection of Frei by the industrial producers did *not* stem from a deterioration of their incomes. After a slight drop in profits for 1965, following the extraordinarily high profits of the previous year, industrial profits rose steadily in 1966 and 1967, increased dramatically in 1968, and then, after a minor decline in 1969, boomed again in 1970. The income *share* of industrial producers remained almost constant throughout the Frei era, while the gains of the workers came at the expense of the self-employed (Stallings 1975, p. 486, 498). The simple explanation that the industrialists were reacting in the inevitable manner of any victimized group is not sustainable.

It seems that the fear of future deprivations, rather than the imposition of sacrifice, must be invoked. Expectations of the producers were influenced by four very badly staged incidents and circumstances.

First, the temporary capture of the Christian Democratic party's formal leadership by factions of the party's Left in 1967 weakened the business sector's support for the party and the regime, a loss that was not fully recovered even after Frei reasserted his control over the party.

Second, the battle over the constitutional status of "property" left many industrialists and investors concerned that the breadth of the amendment passed in 1967, which did not focus exclusively on agricultural property, could be used to expropriate nonagricultural property as well. After several years of accepting the necessity for agrarian reform, the manufacturers' Society for Industrial Promotion (SOFOFA) began to meet jointly with the landowners' National Agrarian Society (SNA). The head of SOFOFA argued: "For three years of Christian Democratic government, each sector looked with indifference on the others' problems. Now we realize the interdependency of the private economy."[11]

Third, Frei's claims of revolution, and his tendency to exaggerate the unspectacular strides actually made in the area of income redistribution, antagonized the business community even as they disappointed the Left. For example, in his May 1967 state of the nation address, Frei boasted of the increase in workers' share of national income from 43 to 50 percent (Sigmund 1977, p. 60). Although the president was of course entitled to seek all the political credit he could get, this assertion at a time when inflation was again mounting and production faltering must have confirmed many fears that Frei was the problem rather than the solution.

A final explanation for the estrangement of the business sector concerned the more concrete matter of maintaining investment levels. Although Frei's policymakers believed that Chile needed increased investment from all sources (Molina 1972, pp. 81–82), whenever the private sector showed reluctance to invest, the government was quick to fill the gap with state investment, channeled primarily through semiautonomous enterprises overseen by the industrial development agency CORFO. Increased state investment then fueled private-sector fears that the state would encroach on future investment opportunities or jeopardize the future profitability of private investments in general. The 1967 anti-inflation budget cutbacks in housing and public works were pivotal in convincing the private sector that state investment was competitive rather than complementary to private investment.

Whereas no significant cutbacks occurred in the financing of state enterprises in industry itself (since the central government had already lost control over those policies), the reductions in *infrastructure* investment eroded the private sector's tolerance for state intervention (Stallings 1978, p. 111). By the time the government reduced the importance of the anti-inflation drive in order to free up credit for private investment, the private sector was unenthusiastic about further commitments to what they saw as an increasingly socialist economy.

CONCLUSIONS

The Frei experience is a rather clear example of the operation of economic constraints on the progress of redistribution. Compared to other redistribution-minded leaders, Frei enjoyed enormous (but obviously not absolute) political power, because of both the magnitude of his electoral victory and the Chilean institutional structure (for instance, the president's dominance over the budget process). Although conflicts within the Christian Democratic party had some bearing on economic policy choices, by and large the weakening of the redistributive momentum can be traced to problems in dealing with economic sectors rather than with political groups. Frei could not force the business community to maintain its level of investment, and failed to persuade them to do so. Nor could he convince organized labor to forgo strikes (which, to be sure, also had political motives) for what Frei argued was the long-term good of workers themselves.

These economic reactions were sufficient to erode redistribution, by forcing trade-offs between strengthening the gains of lower-income sectors and pursuing other important objectives—most notably continued economic expansion. As regards the issue of whether growth and equity are necessarily antithetical in the short run, the first half of the Frei period saw both redistribution and aggregate expansion, while the second half saw stagnation of both. Of course, the economic reactions triggered during the first three years affected the course of growth for the next three, making the relationship between growth and equity highly complex.

Frei's efforts to redistribute through wages ended when he stopped trying to prevent inflationary erosion of wages, in part because the restrictions constraining inflation were also limiting overall economic expansion, and in part because wage earners were hardly reciprocating Frei's efforts by giving him their support.

While the reactions to redistributive policy were basically economic, the immdediate triggers for these reactions were expectations and images as much as concrete actions of the administration. Frei squandered political capital in his handling of the constitutional amendment for land reform, antagonizing industrialists who were not ready to be subjected to redistributive attempts. The coalition of the wealthy that formed in about 1968 was a far more formidable opponent to redistribution than was the isolated landowning sector prior to the land reform effort.

In striving to attain his self-imposed targets, Frei achieved a great deal in comparison with other redistributive attempts. Yet his ambitious goals, so prominently displayed both during and after the presidential campaign, imposed political and economic costs. Those among the wealthy who took him seriously became reluctant to expose themselves to economic risk, and many of the expectant poor were disappointed in the gains actually made. The fear of the wealthy and the disappointment of the poor interacted. Low investment rates (the increase in gross investment up to 1969 was only 22 percent instead of the targeted 70 percent, despite large infusions of capital from foreign investors and the Alliance for Progress—see Edwards 1972, p. 50) made rapid, sustained expansion of productive capacity impossible and thereby dashed hopes for increased benefits without inflation. The government's inability to meet its targets provided an opening for the political opposition to attack the government for incompetence, bombast, and insincerity.

The government's flaunting of ambitious targets would have been more plausible if, say, the targets had been feasible but were simply undershot because of unforeseeable circumstances. Economic conditions were, on balance, favorable; yet the targets, apparently not screened for plausibility, were unobtainable. Brian Loveman (1979, p. 316) points out that effective implementation of the entire Frei program through legal means was a "practical impossibility." The targets probably were regarded by Frei and the Christian Democrats more as harmless campaign hyperbole than as sources of future embarrassment.

Moreover, the pursuit of redistributive targets over a six-year period was bound to run into the problem of administrative rigidity. The inability to target state housing more directly to the poor, the delays in carrying out land reform, and all the rest, constituted expectable reasons to fall short of the targets enunciated at the beginning of the Frei era.

The final lesson here is that trying to mobilize the support of workers is more thankless than one might expect. As was the case with Arturo Illia in Argentina, organized labor was not satisfied with what Frei considered to be more than ample rewards, given the economic situation of the country. The beneficiaries of redistribution ultimately added to the political problems of the redistributive regime. This lack of support detracts considerably from the logic of risking the mobilization of opposition to redistribution through attempts to rally the support of its beneficiaries.

CHAPTER 8

Reform in Peru

FERNANDO BELAÚNDE, LIKE his Chilean contemporary Eduardo Frei, seemed to be the quintessential progressive reformist. Yet although Belaúnde's specifically distributive policies were progressive, overall income distribution in Peru continued to deteriorate, and the gap between the rich and the very poor continued to grow. The first riddle of the Belaúnde experience is why the clearly redistributive efforts of this administration are not reflected in the income distribution trends, which show a steady concentration of income with the wealthier, modern, urban segment of the Peruvian population.

The second riddle is why the extremely promising and largely successful administration of the first few years changed so abruptly into the apparently ineffectual regime of the last few years. Belaúnde began with one of the highest rates of aggregate economic growth in the world, a vigorous poverty-alleviation program that seemed capable of satisfying the populism of military radicals, and immense popularity. The guerrilla threat was extinguished, Belaúnde's most visible development projects progressed impressively, and the country maintained a modest but positive rate of growth. Nevertheless, by 1967 the regime encountered a paralyzing fiscal crisis and took on the appearance of ineffectiveness, without any major external economic shocks to account for the change. Although world market prices fluctuated as usual, no drastic decline in export earnings can be found to account for the economic problems (Thorp and Bertram 1978, chap. 12); the United States did not sabotage the Belaúnde administration in any major way; there were no disastrous harvests. One must look to the internal dynamics to understand the reversal of Belaúnde's fortunes.

BELAÚNDE'S RECORD

Belaúnde's accomplishments in the spheres he emphasized seemed quite impressive. David Werlich (1978, p. 282) provides the following summary:

> During the Belaúnde years, enrollment in the primary grades grew by 41 percent, attendance at the high-school level jumped by 127 percent, and

the number of students receiving vocational training doubled. Between 1961 and 1972 illiteracy was reduced from 40 to 33 percent nationally. In the five predominantly Indian departments of the Sierra the rate of illiteracy fell from 71 to 57 percent ... Belaúnde took greatest personal interest in his Jungle-Margin Highway ... When completed in 1979, about five million acres of land would be available to 500,000 Peruvian colonists ... The government undertook several public housing programs and opened a network of small clinics in provincial towns. An increase of 400 percent in expenditures for irrigation between 1962 and 1965 supported projects designed to water 1,575,000 arid acres and improve existing systems serving 675,000 acres.

This constitutes impressive evidence of "physical progress" toward alleviating poverty. And calculations of the net impact of governmental instruments traditionally considered as distributive (pricing, fiscal, wage, and asset-reallocation policies) reveal that these instruments did actually improve the distribution of income. Richard Webb, who has done the most exhaustive study of income distribution and transfers during the Belaúnde era, developed the balance sheet shown in Table 7. Since in Peru the "modern" sector is far richer on a per capita basis than the "traditional" sector, the increase in transfers out of the modern sector constitutes a significant strengthening of net redistributive policy.

In Table 7 positive entries indicate the dollar values of transfers to the average worker in each sector; negative entries are the flows out of each sector. Thus in both 1961 and 1970 the average modern-sector worker

TABLE 7. INCOME TRANSFERS PER WORKER IN PERU, 1961–1970 (U.S. $ PER WORKER).

| | 1961 | | | 1970 | | |
| | | Traditional | | | Traditional | |
Type of Transfer	Modern	Urban	Rural	Modern	Urban	Rural
Net budget transfers	−300	60	20	−540	10	30
Taxes	−530	−70	−30	−800	−160	−50
Education	60	50	20	100	100	50
Health	100	50	10	100	50	10
Public investment	70	30	20	60	20	20
Price effect	40	10	−30	80	30	−70
Property transfers	—	—	—	20	0	0
Wages	—	—	—	140	0	15
Profits	—	—	—	−120	0	−15

SOURCE: Webb 1977, p. 78.

lost income through government spending ("budget transfer") inasmuch as his taxes ($530 and $800 for 1961 and 1970, respectively) exceeded his benefits from education, health, and public-investment expenditures. Traditional-sector workers, both urban and rural, were net beneficiaries of government spending, since their tax burdens were lower than their benefits from government spending. However, government price policies (such as food price controls) added to modern-sector incomes at the expense of rural-traditional incomes. Finally, property transfers (such as profit sharing and land reform) effected by 1970 had benefited modern-sector wage earners at the expense of modern-sector profits, and traditional-rural workers gained, though more modestly, from rural profits.

Webb concludes that distributive measures under both Belaúnde and his successor Velasco were "mildly progressive," primarily because of redistribution downward *within* sectors. Modern-sector workers gained from higher wages and profit sharing; urban traditional workers gained from government spending and food subsidies. Subsistence farmers gained from government spending and were not sufficiently involved in the market to suffer from depressed food prices. Commercial agricultural workers under Belaúnde broke even and gained considerably from Velasco's land reform (Webb 1977, p. 87).

In referring to specific instruments of obvious distributive import, the record therefore seems positive. The land reform (albeit very modest), the social service budget shifts, and the belated tax reform definitely were progressively redistributive. If one focuses on their long-term impacts on literacy and on rural productivity, they are more than superficial compensatory gestures designed to disguise regressive macroeconomic policies.

Nonetheless, the same government oversaw aggregate economic changes, originating in the early years of the post–World War II period if not sooner, that entailed a worsening of income distribution. Belaúnde's own economic theorists acknowledge that the Belaúnde era did not reverse the overall trend of income concentration resulting from the continued expansion of the modern industrial sector and the stagnation of the traditional sector. The significant aggregate distributional changes strengthened the city (industry, construction, and services) against the countryside; the urban working class and middle class gained relative to both rentiers and the rural population. Pedro-Pablo Kuczynski (1977, p. 72) concludes that "paradoxically, for a President, one of whose major interests was developing the interior, economic growth during 1963–1968 was largely an urban phenomenon."

Can one say, then, that the entire set of economic policies, of which the progressive measures were only a part, was regressive, inasmuch as income distribution did worsen? At one level, the answer depends on whether we distinguish the effects of policy from the effects of long-term change in economic structure. Kuczynski asserts that the income distribution trends in Peru were "as much the result of the trend of economic modernization as of deliberate government policy"; and, speaking of the urban orientation of growth during this period, that "this pattern of development is not surprising and is similar to that of most developing countries in the post-war period" (Kuczynski 1977, pp. 23, 72).

Kuczynski's argument can be countered by the consideration that this particular form of modernization can proceed only if government continues the "metapolicy" of encouraging or at least acquiescing to it. Obviously, Belaúnde did not overturn the entire economic system; and it was that system, in combination with the existing differences between the modern and traditional sectors of the Peruvian economy, which exhibited the common pattern of a growing gap between the dynamic modern sector and the relatively stagnant traditional sectors. Concentrating investment in the dynamic urban sector could be justified by arguing that given the low potential growth rate of the Peruvian Sierra, expansion of the modern sector was beneficial to the long-term prosperity of the country as a whole.

The Belaúnde administration passed up several important opportunities to redress the economic imbalance. One was in the area of pricing policy, which according to Webb (1977, p. 73), was one of the two chief *potential* instruments of horizontal income transfer (that is, from the modern, industrial sector to the traditional, agricultural sector). Instead of stimulating domestic food production and strengthening farm income by keeping food prices higher and applying existing tariff provisions against food imports, Belaúnde followed the standard policy of keeping food prices low by permitting cheap food imports (Kuczynski 1977, p. 11). This policy was not only traditional, it was politically expedient in light of the power of urban food consumers. Because Peru was predominantly agricultural, low food prices and heavy imports denied the poorest segments of the population (who lived in the rural areas) the opportunity to increase their incomes by selling their agricultural surplus at a profit. Low food prices kept many farmers at the mere subsistence level.

Another lost opportunity of Belaúnde's program was a balanced development of social service expansion. We shall see how overspending in education precluded spending in other areas.

Finally, the Belaúnde administration neglected to steer investment to the hinterland. This was not for lack of investment incentives, which were indeed provided, but rather because of equal or greater incentives in the intrinsically more attractive urban centers.

Adding to the complexity of assessing Belaúnde's measures is the fact that they laid the groundwork for the succeeding military regime to carry out further redistributive reform. It may be argued that the radical military faction that took over from Belaúnde in 1968 did not need the Belaúnde precedent to initiate its own redistribution, and therefore Belaúnde deserves little credit for initiatives that did not bear fruit during his own term of office. Could not the military simply impose, by executive decree, what Belaúnde had to eke out laboriously (and only partially successfully) through legislative clashes?

For this to be valid, one would have to make three highly questionable assumptions: (1) that radicalism within the military would have developed equally strongly if reform had not been in the air throughout the 1963–1968 period; (2) that the radical faction of the army would have prevailed against more conservative factions if Belaúnde had reversed the "inexorable" march toward equality; and (3) that the military's fervor for redistribution would have remained high if, instead of having Belaúnde's ready-made redistributive measures at hand (the tax reform and land reform legislation, for instance), it had been required to formulate the technical details of these policies itself.

In fact, Belaúnde's rhetoric, actions, and programs constantly focused the attention of the military on the problems of socioeconomic inequality—particularly in the College of Higher Military Studies, where the ideas of the 1968 revolution were developed. Both the progress made under Belaúnde, and the frustration of not accomplishing more, molded the military's role conceptions, virtually creating the redistributive commitment that was taken for granted once the military began to implement redistributive programs. For it was Belaúnde's land reform formula that the military applied, Belaúnde's tax structure that it enforced, and Belaúnde's program of Acción Popular that the military's own mobilization efforts sought to outdo.

THE BACKGROUND

The most immediate political circumstance conditioning Belaúnde's five years of confrontation with an intransigent opposition was the fact that Belaúnde and his Acción Popular party, in formal coalition with the small Christian Democratic party, won the presidency only after the military annulled APRA's victory the previous year. Even though APRA leader Victor Raúl Haya de la Torre had been denied the presidency in 1962, the military's action did not necessarily preclude the possibility of future APRA victories that might be allowed to stand, and the party's political position remained strong. The legislative seats won by APRA in the 1963 election—roughly 40 percent in each chamber[1]—were allowed to stand by the military. In coalition with the conservative Unión Nacional Odriista (UNO) party of Gen. Manuel Odría, APRA legislators could have a majority in both houses of Congress, whereas in coalition with Acción Popular, APRA would guarantee the legislative success of the administration's program. Moreover, the Peruvian constitution established the same six-year terms for legislators as for the president, thereby precluding the possibility that the president could engineer an electoral test of strength (as Frei did in Chile in 1965) in which congressional obstruction could result in the defeat of opposition legislators. Consequently, for many APRA members there was not only resentment against Belaúnde for having in effect usurped the rightful power of APRA, but strong motivation for continued competition. On the other hand, the rightward movement of APRA from its early radical positions meant that it was no longer bound to reject reformism as inadequate. The Belaúnde program, in broad outline, was not repugnant to the Apristas.

The question was whether Belaúnde himself necessarily had to be repugnant to the Apristas. As a progressive reformist, he naturally hoped for the support of populist-oriented political groups, of which APRA was by far the largest and best organized. Historians almost universally take for granted that the competitiveness between Acción Popular and APRA poisoned any hopes for cooperation. Yet APRA had become accustomed to cooperating with its political rivals as long as the party could claim some credit for the program. The experience of the Prado administration was a clear indication that APRA could be enlisted to support a non-APRA administration. However, Acción Popular was intended to be a mass populist movement and therefore was a greater organizational threat to APRA than Prado ever was. Even so, APRA's cooperation was so obviously necessary for the success of the administration's legislative program that APRA would have received much of the credit for successful reforms, at a time when there was a broad societal consensus that reforms were essential.

This near-consensus was the second important feature of the political climate. In the midst of economic expansion, Peruvians were

becoming more aware not only that the country was relatively backward in terms of economic equity and the well-being of the poor, but
also that the nation's wealth could be used to redress the problems of
the poor. The view that Peru was not a declining country for which
redistribution was an unaffordable luxury was becoming more prevalent. This can be seen from the fact that the two populist parties, Acción
Popular and APRA, received the overwhelming majority of support in
the elections of 1962 and 1963. François Bourricaud (1970, p. 254)
points out also that the church and major segments of the oligarchy
itself were attracted to Belaúnde's reforms.

The relatively high cohesiveness of the economic elite was another
important background factor. The prior lack of government support
for local industrial entrepreneurs left industrialization to the wealthy
export-producing sectors in agriculture (sugar and cotton) and in
mining, who had enough access to credit to finance large industrial un-
dertakings when the opportunities finally arose (Bourricaud 1970, p.
45). Thus the owners of the coastal plantations and the mines—or their
relatives and friends—became the industrial elite to a much greater
extent than in Argentina or Chile, where industrial entrepreneurs did
not share the same social circles and objectives as the agricultural and
mining elites. However, as the land reform struggle revealed, this
agricultural-industrial nexus did not extend to the major landowners
of the Sierra. They had been unable or unwilling to extract investment
capital from their agricultural operations; hence they were isolated
from the industrialists, who (as in Chile) looked upon hacienda agriculture as a serious stumbling block to the nation's economic progress.
Although the unity of the economic elite extended across sectors, it
broke down regionally, with the coastal elite having little in common
with the land-based elite of the Sierra.

The final major background factor was the economic expansion just
prior to the unsettled political conditions of 1962–1963. The export
boom, marked by both expanded volume and favorable world market
prices, filled the Central Bank's coffers, bolstered Peru's credit standing, and increased the tax base. However, it also set a baseline of high
aggregate growth (8.8 percent annual real GNP growth for the years
1960–1962) that would make reasonable future growth rates pale in
the comparison. It created a strong temptation to take advantage of
Peru's credit rating to borrow extensively from abroad, and it made the
export sectors seem the indisputable source of Peru's future growth,
even though the peculiar combination of export expansions (especially
in fish meal) during this period was unique and highly unlikely to
continue (Thorp and Bertram 1978, p. 206–207).

BELAÚNDE'S INITIATIVES

The redistributive initiatives of the Belaúnde government concentrated on the pursuit of concrete objectives: more roads, more teachers, more land for peasants. The previously neglected hinterland was to be opened up—partly through anticipated private investment, but principally through government spending.

Belaúnde immediately proposed legislation to increase government expenditures in almost all areas and sectors. The initial budget surplus (a result of the recent export boom and Prado's fiscal conservatism) encouraged the administration to boost spending immediately, without much concern for expanding revenues. For the long run, though, it was apparent that revenues had to increase. Given the two options for increasing revenues, expanding the tax base through aggregate growth or increasing the tax rates on the existing base, Belaúnde's initial policies strongly favored the former and the industrial promotion policies of previous governments were expanded.

How does this emphasis on industrial promotion conform to Belaúnde's commitment to, and image of, progressive redistribution? After all, the industrial sector had always been the advantaged one; promoting industry certainly had no prima facie progressive implications in a country where the vast majority of the very poor lived an agricultural life. Yet Belaúnde was publicly committed to treating the interests of the Sierra as primary (Bourricaud 1970, p. 244).

The administration's answer was that industrial promotion was to bring the benefits of modern-sector growth to the hinterland through *decentralized* industrialization. Without adequate means for channeling investment away from the Lima-Callao area, the industrialization program could not be progressively redistributive. The first, and by far the most publicized, facet of the decentralization program was the construction of the Marginal Highway (*Carretera Marginal*), a massive road project for the penetration of the Amazon, to facilitate migration from the resource-poor, overpopulated mountain region (the Sierra) to the potentially rich jungle region (the Selva). However, the productivity increases to accrue from the Marginal Highway were still far in the future, if they were to emerge at all, and depended on follow-up investments.

The second aspect of the decentralization policy was to modify the long line of industrial promotion laws generated by Belaúnde's predecessors to include incentives for investment outside the greater Lima area. Investment in both the Amazon and the Sierra was to be promoted by granting virtually complete tax exemption on profits from operations in these areas (Kuczynski 1977, p. 22).

THE INVESTMENT MODEL

The economic model underlying these policies seems to have come more from the heart than from methodical calculation of the financial requirements for the program. The state was prepared to fill the private investment gap that emerged as a result of the political uncertainties of 1962–1963 and the fears of redistribution. This made political sense for Acción Popular, since the state's deficit spending kept up demand and urban prosperity, even while contributing to higher inflation. The Belaúnde administration acknowledged the fact of sluggish private investment, and so other policies (such as tax exemptions) were designed to stimulate private investment.

The massive increases in government spending required revenues, yet the revenue-generating capacity of the government was limited from the very beginning by the conflicting need to change tax policy in the direction of promoting greater investment. Under other circumstances this combination might not have been problematic, but with Acción Popular's patent lack of control in Congress, the government risked running short of funds because of revenue slippages due to legislative obstruction or its own tax exemptions.

In an effort to marshal more extensive resources, in 1963 the Belaúnde administration, lacking a public bank, nationalized the Caja de Depósitos y Consignaciones, the social security treasury formerly administered by the commercial banks. As the new Banco de la Nación, this institution's funds came under direct central administration control and were thus available to cover part of the deficit, irrespective of whether it made fiscal sense to use them in this way (Kuczynski 1977, pp. 98–99). As the administration's capacity to control the levers of the economy grew, the temptation to manipulate them for short-term purposes grew correspondingly.

Clearly, the major preoccupation of economic policy was the budget and the tax changes required to pay for it. But there were other instruments with major impacts on income distribution: exchange policy, pricing policy, and credit policies.

Exchange policy was intended to cement Belaúnde's support from the urban working and middle classes, which otherwise might have been wary of his rhetorical emphasis on the development of the hinterland. The key to the exchange policy was overvaluation of the sol, kept at a constant conversion rate with the U.S. dollar until its devaluation was unavoidable in 1967. Overvaluation kept imports inexpensive despite inflation. Because of the favorable balance of trade, the government was able to maintain the exchange rate without elaborate controls.

As for the redistributive effects of the overvaluation itself, the exporters (most of whom were "old money," except for some entrepreneurs of the fish meal industry) undeniably suffered, while the urban consumer benefited. The direct economic effects on the rural poor are difficult to gauge, particularly for those in the Sierra outside of the market economy. It is important to note that overvaluation served the political purpose of gaining urban consumer acquiescence to Belaúnde's spending programs for the poor. The maintenance of the urban consumer's purchasing power, and the low food prices resulting from relatively cheap imports, made the rest of Belaúnde's policies far more palatable. This redistribution from the top (exporters) to the middle (the urban consumers) facilitated the acceptance of redistributive policies for the poor.

A complementary aspect of exchange policy was fairly easy credit (which kept up overall economic activity). Although on several occasions the government was moved to apply "stabilization" programs to control credit (Dragisic 1971), it never did so with much stringency; and in fact it was convenient politically for the austerity measures not to work, at least until the acute crisis of 1967.

A significant element was left out of the design of redistributive policy: There was no pricing policy that benefited the rural poor. Food pricing actually aided the urban consumer; however, the damage to the subsistence farmer was limited by virtue of his minimal integration into the market economy (Webb 1977, p. 87). There was no wage policy designed for redistributive purposes, which was just as well, considering that the bulk of the Peruvian population (and virtually all of the very poor) did not fall under wage-setting legislation. More important, the basic development strategy followed by previous administrations continued with little alteration. As Rosemary Thorp and Geoffrey Bertram (1978, p. 205) point out:

> The economy from 1948 until the end of the 1960s was the example *par excellence* in Latin America of that dream of orthodox development economists: an export-led system in which cyclical balance-of-payments difficulties were handled by domestic demand restraint and exchange devaluation, in which the entry of foreign capital and the repatriation of profits were virtually unrestricted and in which government intervention and particiation were kept to a minimum.

This characterization is somewhat exaggerated, since overvaluation prevailed until 1967 and export taxes were increased—hardly the ideal model of orthodox development! Even so, Belaúnde's economic policy was far closer to the orthodox approach than that of the reformists of any other major Latin American country.

Why? One possibility is that the administration consciously sought to balance its progressively redistributive policies with "orthodox" macroeconomic policies designed to maximize aggregate growth. There is evidence, however, that the established pattern of promoting export-led industrialization was taken for granted and not explored rigorously to assess its distributive implications. For example, even members of the economic team acknowledge that the national plan for 1966–1970 was little more than a listing of public investment plans, without coordinating economic measures (Kuczynski 1977, p. 105). It was, in fact, a Peruvian tradition to ignore the distributive aspects of macroeconomic parameters in framing explicitly redistributive (or poverty-alleviating) policies.

THE ECONOMIC STYLE

Although Belaúnde's macroeconomic approach was more in keeping with orthodox economic thinking than that of other populists, his economic approach ironically came to be regarded as a dangerous departure from orthodoxy.

Belaúnde seemed to regard the stuffy field of finance as somehow intrinsically conservative, as if consideration of financial constraints was tantamount to abandoning progressive objectives. The administration's "romanticism" allowed the conservative, export-oriented orthodox approach of Pedro Beltrán to continue to monopolize the status of "the sensible alternative." The Belaúnde approach was often called "heroic," in contrast with the "sound" approach of the orthodox economics still represented by the indestructible Beltrán and his newspaper, La Prensa. Belaundismo was depicted as unconcerned about overspending; Beltrán's La Prensa was concerned. The government was cast as ingenious in coming up with funds, whereas the opposition urged "sound public finance." The Marginal Highway was derided as an extravagant waste of resources (despite partial financing through low-interest loans from the U.S. Agency for International Development, or USAID) (Kuczynski 1977, p. 55), and Belaúnde's flamboyant presentation of the highway scheme contributed to this portrayal. The net effect of this juxtaposition of images was to make the orthodox model seem "correct"; the government's policies, by implication, were daring, humanitarian, but ultimately irresponsible. This depiction encouraged the idea that eventually, perhaps when the international environment (that is, world prices for Peruvian exports) changed, it would be necessary to revert to sounder economic policies. This concept hurt the administration in several ways. When economic problems emerged in 1966, the government's own solutions lacked credibility and its image of ineptness was reinforced. All of this is especialy ironic inasmuch as the Beltrán approach subsequently has come under attack. Thorp and Bertram (1978, pp. 206–207) assert that "export growth for the first time began to encounter serious physical or structural bottlenecks." Whether this interpretation is correct is subject to heated debate. What was notable about the orthodox approach was the extent to which it was accepted as the sane alternative to Belaúnde's romanticism.

THE POLITICAL STYLE

Belaúnde's cavalier attitude toward economic details was matched by his reluctance to become embroiled in the complexities of coalition politics and intricate bargaining. Shortly before his inauguration, Belaúnde's offer to APRA of a few cabinet positions was promptly rejected. Haya de la Torre announced an opposition coalition with the UNO which lasted into 1968 and attained dominance over both houses of Congress. There are indications that Belaúnde's overture to the APRA leadership was not very meaningful. The few cabinet posts offered to Haya de la Torre hardly constituted a partnership commensurate with Belaúnde's potential gain from a cooperative Congress. Furthermore, Belaúnde offered the same deal to Manuel Odría, implying that the offer to join the government as a minor coalition member was a courtesy offered to the losers, not an acknowledgment of the importance of the partner's role.

Throughout his campaign and presidency, Belaúnde sent out ample signals that he regarded his presidency as Acción Popular's day in the sun, and that he had no need of inhibiting political compromises. The formal alliance with the Christian Democratic party was a different matter, since the Christian Democrats had joined formally with Acción Popular in endorsing Belaúnde. But the idea of catering to his defeated opponents struck Belaúnde as unnecessary and incompatible with the role of president.[2]

This was very much the mentality of Bustamante, and of Illia in Argentina, who refused to recognize that his 26 percent plurality and lack of legislative majority would block his effectiveness unless he compromised with other political forces (Chapter 9). In Belaúnde's case, this exclusivity undermined his economic strategy. His most

serious economic problem, the budget deficit, grew out of the competition with APRA, as each side tried to outdo the other in providing social
benefits. Yet APRA had additional motives: embarrassing Acción
Popular in the legislative arena, and protecting the interests of APRA's
increasingly important middle-income white-collar and skilled blue-
collar supporters. This competitiveness led APRA to an almost instinc-
tive attempt to outbid Belaúnde's social service programs in the legislature; the other motives resulted in APRA's opposition to Bealúnde's
attempts to finance the escalating expenditures.

THE UNFOLDING OF BELAÚNDE'S MAJOR
PROGRAMS

SOCIAL SERVICE SPENDING

Spending for social services increased markedly under the Belaúnde government, because Belaúnde, like Frei, was able to capitalize
on the support of middle-class service providers. Whereas in 1963
social service spending of the public sector constituted 32 percent of
total spending, it increased to 35 percent in 1964, to nearly 40 percent
in 1965, and finally to its highest level of over 41 percent in 1966
(República Peruana 1966, p. 87). But it was a Pyrrhic victory politically,
because the fiscal crisis brought on by deficit spending contributed in
large measure to Belaúnde's overthrow by the army in 1968. Moreover, the uncontrolled increase in educational expenditures precluded
a more balanced approach to improving social services.

Belaúnde's proposals to increase government spending in health,
education, and rural development were the only progressive initiatives
that appealed to a politically relevant constituency other than the direct
beneficiaries. Social services required teachers, physicians, nurses,
builders, and bureaucrats—a large part of the politically aware middle
sector. These segments could be expected to applaud large increases in
social services, which implied greater demand and compensation for
their services. But APRA had the same political motive for cultivating
the support of these crucial voters. Belaúnde's ultimate problem
turned out not to be securing higher levels of spending, but controlling
the APRA–Acción Popular competition, as each tried to outdo the
other as populists who could also aid important middle-sector groups.
An unmanageable budget burden resulted. The administration made
little effort to earmark expenditures to new tax sources, or to insist

(using the threat of presidential veto) that only expenditure proposals backed by tax sources would be enacted—which would have obligated the legislature to accept higher taxes if it was to gain political credit for greater outlays.

With respect to public works for "development" projects, the administration was encouraged by the apparent ease of obtaining foreign loans and aid, based on the credit rating Peru had earned through the export boom. Coupled with Belaúnde's "physical" conception of development, this presumed opportunity led the administration to propose major public works projects with the expectation that long-term loans and aid would be forthcoming. There was little legislative opposition to these projects, but neither was there the expected long-term foreign funding. Peru was unable to come up with sufficiently well-planned projects to qualify for much multilateral aid, and the United States, at odds with the government over the expropriation of the International Petroleum Corporation, did not produce the expected amount of USAID financing (Kuczynski 1977, p. 95). Peru did qualify for much shorter-term (three years or less) lending from foreign commercial banks, which naturally limited the government's capacity to put off the financial burden as longer-term loans would have permitted. With its image of developmental activism on the line, the administration dramatically increased its short-term indebtedness through this less-than-ideal source of funding.

Another blow to Belaúnde's progressive objectives came in the failure of his decentralization program. Kuczynski (1977, p. 22), a central figure on the Belaúnde economic team, reports that despite the planning office's push for investment in the Sierra and the Amazon, and the virtually complete profits-tax exemption for new industries there, private investment still went to Lima. Not only was Lima more attractive because of its proximity to suppliers and markets, there were generous tax exemptions as well for industries being established in the capital area. The key point is that although investments outside Lima were encouraged through incentives, even more attractive incentives for Lima-centered development were allowed to persist (Frankman 1974). The soundness of the industrial promotion laws of previous regimes was taken for granted, with no evidence of recognition that metropolitan incentives would drive out the riskier investment opportunities in the interior. Analyzed in isolation, the decentralization incentives may have been evaluated as promising; but in the broader context that included more attractive incentives for other pursuits, they were obviously inadequate.

In public health, the health ministry's budget was a priority in 1964.

The Ministry of Health, and Social Assistance, as distinct from other channels of health-care services such as clinics for state employees, at least in theory offered its services to the very poor (although the scarcity of ministry hospitals in the countryside was a severe problem). Central government expenditures in public health rose more than 20 percent in 1964. However, public health still represented a rather small proportion of the national budget (roughly 8 percent), and government spending in health still favored the relatively well-off urban white-collar and skilled blue-collar workers covered by social security or public-employee health plans. By 1965 the budget of the health ministry had to be cut in real terms, because of the burgeoning expenditures in education. Despite an increase in 1967, it declined over the course of Belaúnde's term, with the share of the national budget devoted to health dropping below the levels of the 1950s (República Peruana 1966, p. 89; 1971, p. 389).

In housing, the administration had little enthusiasm for slum up-grading. It has been suggested that Belaúnde believed urban improvements would only exacerbate the problem of migration to the cities, and that resources for the poor should be directed to the rural areas where poverty was greatest. The state's modest efforts consisted in channeling private bank loans to slum dwellers and building some public housing which (as was increasingly the case for Frei's far more ambitious program in Chile) was ultimately too costly for the urban poor (Collier 1975, pp. 140–141).

The expansion in education expenditures, which forced the administration to limit spending in the other social service areas, was the most perverse outcome of the competition between Acción Popular and APRA. The government's educational proposal of 1964, developed by education minister Francisco Miró Quesada, called for moderate salary increases for public school teachers. APRA countered that if Miró Quesada was serious about his commitment to "giving the teachers dignity" (la dignificación del magisterio), the low pay of teachers had to be rectified dramatically. It so happened that the 60,000 public-school teachers and their families constituted roughly 6 to 8 percent of the voting electorate (Kuczynski 1977, p. 89). The legislature decided upon 25 percent pay increases for each of the next four years, in addition to improved fringe benefits and the guarantee of employment for all graduates of teachers' colleges. The administration, naturally wishing to avoid attack by so influential a group, endorsed the measure. After only two years the budgetary drain was so great that the administration was forced to cancel the remaining two increases; even so, the boost in educational spending, which reached nearly 30 percent of government expenditure by 1965 as compared to 20 percent in

1960, was a major cause of the fiscal crisis that plagued Belaúnde from that time on (Hunt 1971, p. 398).

The teachers' salary increase was a classic case of poor calibration—a failure to achieve an appropriate *magnitude* of policy impact. Certainly, upgrading teachers' pay and status was a commendable objective that served the interests of the poor, who stood to gain from an expansion of the eductional infrastructure. Yet the legislated increase so obviously overshot any reasonable level that the budgetary damage was far in excess of the benefits to the poor. A more balanced approach to the service needs of the Peruvian people would not have stressed education to the detriment of the other social services, since even by 1963 the GNP share devoted to education was the third highest in Latin America, exceeded only by Puerto Rico and Cuba (Hunt 1971, p. 394). It is reasonable to interpret the education expenditure as poor calibration rather than as simple political opportunism, because there is evidence of a glaring lack of insight into the effects of the measures. Kuczynski (1977, pp. 89–92) points out:

> Few politicians realized at the time what its costs would be, although it should have been obvious that the four annual across-the-board raises of 25 percent provided in the bill for 1965 to 1968 would by themselves lead to a mushrooming appropriation for education ... The Executive had not thought through the financial consequences of the measure.

The fact that the educational expenditures were indeed miscalculated is strikingly indicated by the degree to which budgeted expenditures for education were far exceeded by actual outlays, as indicated in Table 8. The excess amounts actually spent indicate that the administration

TABLE 8. BUDGETED AND ACTUAL EXPENDITURES OF THE MINISTRY OF EDUCATION OF PERU, 1960–1969 (BILLIONS OF SOLES).

Year	Budgeted	Actual	"Excess" (percent)
1960	1.31	1.43	9.2
1961	1.70	1.86	9.4
1962	2.14	2.22	3.7
1963	2.68	2.90	8.2
1964	3.56	3.60	1.1
1965	4.28	5.73	33.9
1966	5.56	7.15	28.6
1967	8.05	9.84	22.2
1968	6.69	7.11	6.3
1969	6.31	6.27	−0.1

SOURCE: Calculated from República Peruana 1971, p. 389.

badly underestimated the budget requirements generated by the new law. It was not until 1968, when the pay increases had been canceled, the employment guarantee annulled, and the regime ousted by the military, that actual and budgeted spending in education really coincided.

LAND REFORM

The agrarian situation facing Belaúnde in 1963 bore some similarity to the one facing Frei in 1964. In Peru, as in Chile, there seemed to be consensus support on the part of political groups for significant land reform, going far beyond the token colonization plans implemented earlier. Even Beltrán's newspaper, *La Prensa*, advocated land reform (Bourricaud 1970, pp. 325–327). Thorp and Bertram (1978, pp. 282–283) note the "abandonment of opposition to agrarian reform in principle by the ruling group in national politics." As in Chile, the inefficiency of hacienda agriculture was seen as a major bottleneck to economic expansion, and there was little disagreement about which types of landholdings were inefficient (namely the large, nonplantation holdings), whereas the plantations of the Peruvian coast were considered relatively efficient. Thus, the coastal sugar and cotton plantations were placed in a different category than the typical hacienda, just as the Chilean vineyards were considered different from the typical hacienda there.

One crucial difference in the positions on land reform was whether the efficient holdings should be included in land redistribution. This was not a simple trade-off between efficiency and equity, for the plantations could have been transformed into cooperatives without necessarily dismantling their efficient modes of production. Another facet, as in Chile, was how much compensation the landowners were to receive, which encompassed questions of the form and speed of compensation. It was evident in both cases that the equivalence of landholding dimensions could be established, in order to compensate for differences in land quality and access to irrigation, by using a measure of "basic irrigated hectares," but this was a cumbersome and time-consuming technical task. Finally, in order to compensate landowners through deferred payments, as in Chile a necessity for the fiscal viability of a major land redistribution, the Belaúnde administration had to change a constitutional provision requiring immediate compensation (Kuczynski 1977, p. 67).

It would thus seem that land reform in Peru was just as feasible, technically, as in Chile. Still, there were several political differences.

Although the Sierra landowners were politically isolated, the coastal plantation owners were an integral part of the economic elite that spanned the industrial, financial, and commercial-agricultural sectors. Second, although Belaúnde had campaigned on the importance of land reform, he had not specified precise targets for redistribution, whereas Frei had promised to give land to 100,000 families. Finally, Belaúnde had less leverage over the legislature than Frei, in terms of achieving his land reform measures.

The land reform bill introduced into Congress in 1963 was the culmination of years of campaigning, by Belaúnde and the APRA candidates, for extensive land redistribution *including* the coastal estates.[3] The vehemence of the demands for land reform since the late 1950s, and the rising strength of the groups behind these initiatives (APRA and Acción Popular), convinced many landowners that expropriation was inevitable. Massive agricultural disinvestment resulted.[4]

Most congressmen were at least rhetorically committed to agrarian reform, not only because of their campaign positions but also because significant land invasions in the mountains and on the coast were regarded as potential sparks of all-out revolution. But very few legislators, other than the Acción Popular and a few Christian Democratic allies, were disposed to accept the Acción Popular version. Some observers (Bourricaud 1970; Jacquette 1971, p. 150) have argued that the opponents of radical land redistribution had won even before Belaúnde took office, because the Acción Popular—Christian Democrat platform had committed Belaúnde to an agrarian reform devoted to efficiency and increased agricultural production, precluding transfers to effectively exploited properties. Certainly Belaúnde's vice-president, Edgardo Seoane, the advocate of more radical land reform, took the efficiency emphasis literally. Yet the transformation of the coastal estates into collectives or state-run enterprises was not necessarily obviated by a rhetorical or even a real commitment to efficiency and increased agricultural production, unless one accepted Beltrán's premise that unencumbered operation of the export-oriented plantations was essential for maintaining agricultural production. Alternatively, the platform's reference to efficiency could have reflected a desire to invoke a positively connoted principle (who could object to efficiency?), or to offset rhetorically what was really intended to be a strong reform effort. Whatever the private view of the Belaúnde administration, acceptance of Beltrán's premise was not evident in the legislative proposal itself, which did include the coastal estates as targets of expropriation.

The fears of the large landowners turned out to be unjustified. Because the administration bill was introduced hastily, presumably to take advantage of Belaúnde's initial popularity and the sense of urgency created by the disruption of illegal land seizures, it was awkwardly formulated, with cumbersome implementation machinery and an unwieldy set of 240 articles. The technical deficiencies of the land reform bill provided an opening for conservative forces. The bill was criticized by UNO, which had its own agrarian reform proposals emphasizing colonization of virgin territories and immediate cash payment for expropriated properties, and by APRA, which to its embarrassment had no well-thought-out, comprehensive counterproposal of its own. The technical deficiencies of the administration proposal saved APRA from having to reject the bill simply because it was not APRA's—which would have been politically costly because of APRA's past commitment to land reform and the growing perception that it had abandoned its former principles. In actuality, APRA opposed sugar plantation expropriation because APRA's support from plantation workers would have been jeopardized if the viability of the plantations was threatened by legislation for which APRA was held responsible. This was an ironic, yet not uncommon predicament for APRA (recall its opposition to redistributive efforts by Prado): its worker constituency, having achieved some economic gains already, stood in the way of efforts to aid still poorer segments, even though the APRA constituency was not the primary victim of the prospective redistribution (in this case the plantation onwers were). The technical weakness of the government's bill allowed APRA to call for "more time to reformulate," rather than opposing it for obviously political reasons.

The legislative majority of UNO and APRA held up the administration's land reform bill until December 1963, when Belaúnde called a special legislative session to resolve the issue. Peasant activists strengthened the administration's bargaining position by seizing more land illegally, increasing fears of a peasant revolution. In some cases the administration expropriated and redistributed this land, using its decree powers permitted in emergency circumstances (*Hispanic American Report*, August 1963, p. 798); this pressured conservative elements to opt for a legal land reform process whereby the landowners would at least be assured of compensation. Probably the special session would not have produced any legislation without the looming threat of more land seizures and massive rural disruption.

In preparation for the special session the Chamber of Deputies formed a committee, composed of six proadministration deputies, six opposition deputies, and one deputy of the radical Frente de Liberación Nacional, to formulate a compromise proposal. Although the administration would have found an ally for more far-reaching land reform in the Frente deputy, it was of course recognized that the whole legislature would have to approve before the reform could be enacted.

The resulting legislative proposal was much narrower in scope and more vulnerable to further legislative undermining. And where the initial proposal had been administratively cumbersome, the compromise proposal was far worse; each transfer of property from landowner to peasant required *fifty-one* procedures (Werlich 1978, p. 285). Where the administration proposal included the large commercial estates, the APRA-UNO amendments excluded them. Cash compensation was increased. Even without the elaborate procedures necessary to effect a land transfer, the compromise measure would at best benefit only about a tenth of the peasants qualifying for land.

The potential for legislative undermining came from two aspects of the compromise proposal. First, although the constitution was to be amended to permit the government to compensate landowners with bonds rather than cash, the Congress as well as the executive was involved in establishing each year's quota of bonds, their interest, and their duration. Second, the law specified that the land reform institute ONRA was to receive at least 3 percent of the national budget for each year of its operation, yet the legislature could deny ONRA these funds in subsequent years. In fact, because of the pressure of budget deficits, along with the reduced threat of land takeovers and violence, the legislature kept ONRA's appropriations at only 0.6 percent of the budget for 1964–1967 (Carroll 1970, p. 23).

Belaúnde was thus faced with the dilemma of deciding whether to accept the watered-down version or to hold out for a stronger reform measure. Deciding that it was the best he could expect, Belaúnde urged his Acción Popular and Christian Democratic legislators to accept the compromise bill, and it was enacted. The results were disappointing. Land transfers bogged down in the bureaucratic morass; the underfunded and understaffed ONRA could not keep up with the paperwork; the 11,000 families receiving land transfers—fewer than expected—got worse land than expected, at higher cost and with less financial support from the government for fertilizer, machinery, and the other requisites for small-farmer prosperity.[5]

TAX REFORM

As the military looked on with growing disquiet at the fiscal deficit, the Belaúnde administration made several futile efforts to overcome APRA opposition to tax increases. Haya de la Torre, the APRA chief, stood fast in his position of "No more taxes!", while APRA and UNO gained a short-term political advantage over Acción Popular in that the government appeared inept in its handling of fiscal affairs.

Initially the Belaúnde administration's tax policy was not directed toward progressive redistribution, nor did it enhance the government's capacity to extract resources from the domestic private sector. The government relied on increased import tariffs and the sales tax, which by mid-1964 had been raised 50 percent and 100 percent respectively (Webb 1977, p. 51). Other forms of taxation were changed in only minor ways. Once the industrial promotion effort was launched, tax changes to encourage investment, rather than to increase revenues, became the focus of new fiscal legislation. Tax policy was virtually an adjunct to the Industrial Promotion Law, with generous tax exemptions provided to encourage investment. The major increases in import tariffs of December 1963 and August 1964, balanced by exemptions for imported industrial inputs, were happily cast as both revenue producing and as stimulating to local industry; tax rate reductions for preferred industries, such as automobile assembly, were introduced to stimulate private investment in industries sheltered by the higher tariffs. The government, without definitive economic criteria for deciding which industries really should have been considered "preferred," and lacking any desire to antagonize business groups, granted exemptions on a more or less ad hoc basis (Kuczynski 1977, pp. 80–85).

In relinquishing its control over the specification of tariff exemptions (one of the few instruments it could manipulate without legislative approval), the administration contributed to the undermining of the progressivity and revenue capacity of the tax structure; more and more firms qualified for the exemptions, leading to greater profits for their owners and lower government revenues from import duties. The basic goal of channeling investment into the most useful sectors was blunted by the breadth of the exemptions permitted. Amplifying the decline in the revenue base was Belaúnde's attempt to contribute to development in the interior through tax exemptions for investments outside the Lima area. As investment in the Sierra and the jungle was not forthcoming to the degree the regime had hoped, revenue capacity was further weakened. In 1964 a 5 percent payroll tax was eliminated, to be replaced by a stamp tax which (though it had a lower exemption level) was only 1 percent of wages or salaries (Hunt 1971, p. 405). Finally, the pay-as-you-go provision of the personal income tax, an important aid to tax administration, was abolished by the Congress— without vehement administration protest (Kuczynski 1977, pp. 141–142).

These changes, particularly the tariff increases (which seemed to benefit modern-sector businesses and labor directly)[6] and the investment incentives, encountered little opposition, although the sales tax caused some grumbling. But by 1967 net tariff revenues were a smaller proportion of the total value of imports than in the two previous years, direct tax revenues were a significantly smaller share of total revenues than in 1963 (26 percent vs 32 percent), and the budget deficit was over 4 percent of the gross national product, compared to balanced budgets in the three years prior to the Belaúnde administration (Kuczynski 1977, pp. 80–87). Belaúnde's planners seem to have underestimated both the revenue requirements of their spending program (which itself was greater than anticipated) and the difficulty of increasing revenues once the spending programs—without their own sources of funding—were in place.

When the administration realized that taxing capacity had to be strengthened to keep up with expanding government spending, it turned to the all-too-obvious approach of increasing direct taxation, particularly via the income tax. This was a major error. Inasmuch as the tax reforms were designed to be progressive, the Belaúnde administration may have been mistaken in its belief that direct taxation was more progressive than the existing forms of indirect taxation. Webb (1977, p. 46) points out that the Peruvian tax system is "strong evidence against the usual supposition that a reliance on indirect taxes implies regressivity."

A more definitive error was the administration's failure to leave itself room for maneuvering with forms of taxation other than direct taxes when tax levels had to be raised to sustain the spending program. If the government had kept taxes higher in its early years, the deficit could have been made up through smaller, less politically vulnerable rate increases. Webb (1977, p. 52) notes, with considerable insight, that import duties were

> the most politically acceptable of the government proposals ... This measure not only offered the path of least political resistance (there is something unpatriotic about attacking a law that "protects national industry" and "defends the balance of payments"), it also promised more immediate and larger revenue yield than the income and property tax proposals. Also, changes in import duties are less visible to the general public, and can be disguised, as they were in 1964, as an "administrative updating" of import categories.

The administration tried to increase direct taxes in 1966, when finance minister Sandro Mariátegui submitted the 1967 budget with provisions for a new real estate tax, a new tax on enterprise-capital shares, and higher income taxes. The Congress refused to pass the tax measures but approved most of the proposed budget expenditures, thereby guaranteeing a high deficit. It should be noted, in terms of the importance of a legislative majority, that even some of Belaúnde's Acción Popular legislators came out against the increased taxes, as did some of the Christian Democrats. The finance minister accepted the budget without adequate revenue provisions and requested still higher import duties in a mildly successful attempt to offset the unexpectedly large spending increases (Kuczynski 1977, pp. 141–143).

By mid-1967 the revenue increases that could have been gained through indirect taxes were slim and obviously inadequate, forcing the government to propose again an undisguisable major increase in income taxation. There was no room for Belaúnde to nibble away at the deficit by introducing obscure taxes that would make a significant difference in the aggregate, or to earmark special tax sources for agencies beyond the reach of the APRA-dominated legislature. The opposition saw to it that the tax proposal for higher income and property taxes would create a political uproar.

The 1967 tax proposal was progressive, inasmuch as income and property taxes were paid by the well-to-do, but the basic motive was revenue generation. Earlier, the same motive had been responsible for the imposition of higher indirect taxes of a regressive nature. The description of the policy at any point in time as progressive or regressive depended on nondistributional considerations and on the exigencies of the moment.

APRA's opposition to further tax increases was both ironic and puzzling, inasmuch as the major thrust of the tax reform, namely significant increases in income and profits taxes, applied to fewer than 40,000 individuals and firms. Because of the very high exemption level, the personal income tax was applicable to only the top 1 percent of income earners (Kuczynski 1977, p. 87; Webb 1977, p. 190)— hardly the masses from which APRA intended to win support. The opposition to higher taxes was generated in part by the public's identification of further tax increases with the highly visible increases it had already felt (the doubling of the sales tax, for instance); there was little recognition that further changes would be of a different nature and that the burden would fall on different groups. The antitax sentiment also demonstrated the success of the Beltranistas in conveying the impression that the burden of higher taxes of any sort would be borne by all.

It is tempting to conclude that Belaúnde simply faced an impossible task in trying to get the Congress to accept tax increases in the only mode—direct taxes—that still had the potential for adequately increasing revenues. However, it is useful to ask what Belaúnde failed to do. There was no "grand gesture," no threat to bring the government to a halt or to penalize APRA constituencies. Although finance ministers and even prime ministers resigned over the issue in the short period of 1967–1968, they were expendable. At no point, until the military coup became an obvious possibility, was the legislative opposition confronted with any risk in pursuing its obstructive tactics.

Along with the 1967 devaluation the administration, while Congress was without a quorum, decreed a windfall export tax. Since the devaluation (in making Peruvian soles less expensive) was a distinct benefit to the export sector, the executive imposed a "retention of proceeds"—a tax labeled as such because the executive did not have the authority to enact taxes without legislative approval. More important from the government's perspective, the export tax had the capacity to cover half of the government budget deficit (Kuczynski 1977, pp. 171–173). However, the president would not allow the tax to stand, perhaps because the military insisted that Belaúnde come to terms with APRA (Astiz 1969, p. 120), or because Belaúnde personally objected to the fact that the tax constituted an illegal infringement on the authority of the Congress (Kuczynski 1977, p. 161).

Finally, in mid-1968, with the fiscal crisis still acute despite the devaluation and with APRA seeing its electoral future cut off if the military intervened, legislative opposition to tax increases relented. But it did not do so in the open arena of the legislature, where responsibility for the sacrifices necessitated by the economic crisis might be attributed to APRA and UNO. Instead, in June 1968 the Congress granted authority to the executive to "take the emergency measures needed to solve the structural imbalance in public finances, to strengthen the balance of payments, and to encourage the integrated development of our economy ... The measures taken under the authority of this law will be in the form of Supreme Decrees approved by the Council of Ministers, with the obligation of advising the Congress of each measure so taken."

Within the two-month period for which these powers were authorized, the Ministry of Finance and Commerce under Manuel Ulloa enacted many important tax reforms. In the much more closed arena of the ministry, in an atmosphere of crisis, Ulloa decreed higher or altogether new taxes on profits, interest income, real estate, corporate net worth, gasoline (with much steeper taxes on the higher octanes used by private cars than on the octanes used by buses), and various other items; the net effect was strongly progressive (Kuczynski 1977, pp. 230–233; Webb 1977, p. 53).

Thus, by the time Belaúnde was overturned, his administration had the ironic record of eroding the progressivity of the tax system through the regime's first four and a half years, then departing with significant redistributive improvements. The only reasonable assessment of the tax reform effort as a whole is that it was largely unsuccessful in changing the structure of tax incidence and in achieving adequate revenues for an increased public expenditure program. Among those who were taxed the burden may have become slightly less progressive, because the exemptions for the investments of the very wealthy reduced their burden, whereas the bulk of the modern sector could not readily escape the increased indirect taxes. However, since taxes of whatever form were extracted largely from the modern sector, while expenditures benefited both the modern and traditional sectors, the mere fact of higher tax rates was a progressive accomplishment.[7]

REACTIONS AND OPPOSITION TACTICS

Besides the legislative obstruction employed by the APRA-UNO opposition, the tactics used by Belaúnde's opponents were unconventional and in some instances notably subtle. Even the obstructionism in the legislature was unusual; unlike the typical strategy of opposing administration initiatives across the board, APRA exacerbated the fiscal crisis by taking the administration spending programs to their extreme, at the same time killing the revenue proposals.

Even more striking is the fact that Belaúnde was rarely accused of dishonest, selfish, or inappropriate goals, although his community-action program, Cooperación Popular, was criticized as being politically motivated and riddled with graft. Belaúnde was too popular, and his goals (abstractly defined) too representative of the country's reformist sentiment, for the opposition to attack directly. Instead, it based much of its attack on technique, where Belaúnde was weak and basically disinterested.

WINNING THE POLICY DEBATE

Insofar as Belaúnde was regarded as given to the grand gesture rather than to careful planning, his opponents were able to insinuate their influence in reformulating administration proposals in what they called sounder terms, which (as in the case of the land reform) often meant a substantive change in the objectives pursued by the policy. Belaúnde's critics kept the fiscal issue constantly in the public eye, through media efforts directed at civilians and the military alike. The administration was pinned between the high-spending, low-tax position of the legislative opposition, and the withering, logical, "rational" criticism of the orthodox establishment of Pedro Beltrán.

AVOIDING IMPACTS

Some of the reactions that had the greatest effect in blunting the effectiveness of Belaúnde's programs were simple accommodations to the government's rather clumsy economic regulations. For example, the financiers who were hemmed in by the administration's tight credit policies imposed in mid-1965—requiring 100 percent of new deposits to be placed in official reserves (to take them out of circulation)— merely shifted their deposits to the state development banks, which counted them as legal reserves but permitted financiers to continue lending the funds. Contrary to the administration's wishes and expectations, commercial bank credit increased by 29 percent during 1965 (Kuczynski 1977, p. 101).

Another tactic, employed in 1967, was to stockpile imports prior to the enactment of higher import duties. Because of the legislature's delays in considering the tax increase, importers had ample opportunity to prepare for it. It is also important to note that the importers and those who were stockpiling imports as intermediate products had the resources to purchase additional goods far in advance of their sale or use.

The stagnation of private investment has to be classified as yet another reaction to the government's policies and to the general political and economic climate. Agricultural disinvestment increased Peru's food import needs, contributing to the balance-of-payments problem. But the overall investment rate declined as well, in response to political tensions (such as those triggered by the 1967 devaluation), fears of inflation, and the maturation of previously expanding export industries such as fish meal. The administration's willingness to tolerate the deficit budgets formulated by Congress was in large part due to its awareness that the only way to fill the private investment gap was through expansion of the state's activities, even if this meant growing budget deficits. By 1967 capital flight accelerated greatly, contributing to the fiscal crisis of that year. Finally, the combination of lower private investment and the austerity measures the government was ultimately forced to impose created the recession of 1968 and contributed to the military's decision to intervene.

PRECIPITATING A DEVALUATION

The overvaluation of the Peruvian sol, originating prior to the Belaúnde administration but growing more exteme with the acceleration of domestic inflation, prompted the most direct economic undermining of the administration program. In 1967 the Central Bank was vulnerable to a foreign exchange shortage, yet the overall economic and trade situation of the country, according to many observers, was by no means desperate.[8] The government was negotiating with the International Monetary Fund, the U.S. government, and private foreign banks for loans to bolster the Central Bank's dollar reserves.

At that point, however, fish-meal exporters began to delay their export shipments. Other exporters retained their dollars rather than exchanging them for soles through the Central Bank. The fish-meal exporters demanded either devaluation or elimination of export taxes, but cutting export taxes would have worsened the already critical budget deficit. The fact that exporters articulated their demands in an overt attempt to influence policy suggests that their economic actions may have stemmed from the same motive, rather than from straightforward maximization of income security or profit in response to *prevailing* economic policies. While the withholding of export earnings may have been consistent with the strictly accommodationist rationale of deferring the redemption of export earnings until more soles could be obtained for dollars, the delay of fish-meal shipments cannot be explained as profit-maximizing within the context of existing policy.

These manipulations by the export sector, the general preference for imports, the foreign debt burden, the sluggish investment in domestic industry, and the flight of capital abroad all contributed to the rapid drain on Central Bank foreign reserves. By August 1967 the Central Bank had only U.S. $56 million in exchange reserves, having lost U.S. $39 million in that month alone (Dragisic 1971, p. 202). The administration had little choice but to order the Central Bank to desist from maintaining the sol at the long-standing rate of 26.82 to the dollar; the rate quickly readjusted to around 40 soles per dollar.

The devaluation triggered intense criticism of the government (but not, this time, from the Beltranistas). High inflation was feared. Yet another cabinet was compelled to resign, adding to the image of chaos and executive ineptitude. As the purchasing power of wage earners and salary earners declined, there were riots and serious strikes, even though APRA finally joined the administration in urging its union affiliates to restrain their wage demands.

This newfound cooperation from APRA enabled the Belaúnde administration to enact a stabilization program that eventually raised taxes, lowered expenditures, and perhaps improved the administration's image with the military. But the apparent abandonment of progressive objectives became a motive for military intervention. The stabilization program can be interpreted either as an APRA change of heart because of the increasing probability of military takeover, or as the government's acquiescence to APRA's less reformist economic preferences. In either case, the administration and APRA reached this rapprochement only through a program that obliterated the overt signs that Acción Popular was pursuing a strongly redistributive or even mildly progressive economic policy.

These external challenges were accompanied by internal disputes within Acción Popular that strongly paralleled the difficulties encountered by Frei in Chile at roughly the same time (Chapter 7). As the Belaúnde reforms stalled and the frustrations grew, the division between the "moderates" and the "hotheads" (*termocéfalos*) within Acción Popular became more acute. Belaúnde, whatever his disagreements with the succession of prime ministers and finance ministers serving under him, was held responsible for the government's economic performance. He was thus forced into the position of ultimately leading the moderate wing against the more radical members of his own party, including First Vice-President Edgardo Seoane. In early 1968 the delegates nominated Seoane as their 1969 presidential candidate, an act regarded as a rebuke to Belaúnde. This reaction was similar to the temporary wresting of control of the Chilean Christian Democratic party from Frei by more radical factions dissatisfied with the pace of reform. And, as in Chile, the net effect was to divide the party and push the president more firmly into the role of defending and representing the less ambitious positions that circumstances had forced him to take. Belaúnde's rapprochement with APRA, and the turnabout from progressive policy, was thus also prompted by his struggle to maintain his political base vis-à-vis this challenge from his own party's Left. To the degree that Belaúnde lost support within the party, he was motivated to cultivate the support of other, less progressive groups.

The factors enumerated above enable us to understand the economic aspects of the military takeover of October 1968. There were of course several noneconomic motives behind the decision of the armed forces to oust Belaúnde and institute the Revolution of 1968, but economic factors are undeniable: Belaúnde's promised reforms were not carried out, economic growth was a shadow of what it had been in the decade before, and the confrontation between the export orientation of the Beltranistas and the nationalist-developmentalism of the Left remained unresolved. When Belaúnde was seemingly committed to redistribution, the opposition managed to depict him as inept; when the understanding with APRA finally permitted Belaúnde to carry out his policies, these policies appeared far from progressive.

CONCLUSIONS

The mysterious turnabout of Belaúnde's fortunes in the last years of his term now makes sense. Belaúnde's assets were his popularity, the general sentiment for reform, the split between the coastal and the Sierra elite, and the extractable surplus provided by the prosperity prior to and during the first part of the Belaúnde era. His vulnerabilities too were highly visible: the expansion of his spending program was predicated on increasing the most blatant forms of taxation, facilitating an alliance of the very wealthy and the middle-income groups in the most visible arena, where opposition to further tax increases was most easily mobilized. His lack of interest in the details of economics left him vulnerable to the long-standing tactic of the conservative opposition—that of posing its positions as technically superior. Ultimately, the cumulative effects of private disinvestment, legislative obstruction, and inefficient social service spending cracked Belaúnde's rigid program of overvaluation and the pursuit of higher direct taxes. In spite of subsequent alterations in the program, the damage to Belaúnde's image of competence had been done.

Webb (1977, p. 50) referred to tax reform efforts under Belaúnde as "a case of a willing spirit but weak flesh." This metaphor has much validity for the Belaúnde reforms in general. Certainly the Peruvian executive did not have the degree of control over the economy and over economic decision making that was evident in Chile or even in Argentina. The formal institutions of economic policymaking—the Congress and the Central Bank—were not controlled, and many of the parameters of the economy were not under technical supervision, nor were they well monitored or intensively analyzed. Part of this lack of control was unavoidable, given Peru's constitutional structure and the lack of skilled economists, but part was by default.

Some of the constraints limiting the scope and success of Belaúnde's reforms were self-imposed, either by his unwillingness to circumvent the legislature through innovative—but not necessarily illegal—policy manipulations, or by simple lack of imagination. A democratically elected president is not betraying democratic mores by manipulating the executive-controlled levers of economic policy to achieve redistributive ends. To the degree that the opposition's capacity to mobilize against redisributive efforts is aided by the obviousness of the effort, Belaúnde's directness and lack of Machiavellian maneuvering, refreshing as they may have been, aided the representatives of economic privilege, to the detriment of the poor.

The other mystery—how at least mildly progressive measures could result in a worsening of the overall distribution of income—can be explained by examining the meaning and complexity of "income distribution," and the disregard by Belaúnde of certain aspects of economic policy. Redistribution within the modern sector does not offset a gap between the modern and traditional sectors; a measure that changes the relative shares within part of the overall distribution may not affect the relative shares of this part and others, or may, through its other effects, have an opposite impact on the overall distribution of income. There is no logical inconsistency in the possibility that a set of measures which is progressive in terms of its effects on the upper half of the income distribution may be regressive with respect to the overall distribution of income.

This possibility was actualized in the Belaúnde years. The remarkable pattern of tremendous attention to certain physical aspects of distribution while macroeconomic conditions pushed Peru farther along the path of duality between the modern and traditional sectors demonstrates how important the macrostrategic level of policy direction can be, and how easily the prevailing macrostrategy of development can be taken for granted. Industrial promotion can still dominate as the development strategy, without adequate provision for steering either its benefits or its productivity gains to the very poor.

CHAPTER 9
Argentina's Beleaguered Center

THE PERFORMANCE OF THE Frondizi and Illia administrations in Argentina graphically illustrates the tensions between the image and the reality of redistribution and effectiveness. After the military interregnum of 1955–1958 Argentina experienced bizarre fluctuations in income distribution under Arturo Frondizi, an ostensible populist who nonetheless imposed stabilization measures in December 1958 that resulted in the most severe drop of worker income of Argentina's postwar period. Because Frondizi seemed eager to cultivate working-class support in order to win the populist vote away from the Peronists, the income loss of the working class was both striking and puzzling. Whether it qualifies as an example of how redistributive intentions can be blocked by economic and political realities, or whether it simply reflects Frondizi's perfidy, is likely to remain a matter of controversy. What is clear is that Frondizi first raised labor's hopes, then crushed them dramatically, and—despite more promises—still could not make up for the initial decline in real wages by the time of his overthrow in 1962. Frondizi's tax reform, his only sustained progressive effort, made little difference in the equity of the tax system.

The 1963 election victory went to the Popular Radical party's Arturo Illia, much less of a populist and much less crafty than his predecessor Frondizi. Although Illia, by the almost universal consensus of the time, lacked any semblance of effectiveness, in retrospect the 1963–1966 period turned out to be moderately progressive and prosperous. Real wages crept up steadily, while the share of national income going to wage and salary earners also increased, but more erratically. The regime's economic management, labeled "do-nothing" and incompetent at the time, appears actually to have been relatively innovative and competent. Moreover, Illia's political rigidity—even his refusal to maneuver his Popular Radical party into coalition—did not stifle one of Argentina's most creative and open political periods, even though it was brief and uncertain.

In fact, it may be argued that the Illia regime's accomplishments were at least initially facilitated by the prevailing atmosphere of uncertainty and tentativeness. Modest but significant progress in income redistribution and administrative reform encountered little opposition, largely because it was not at all clear—even to many members of the Illia government—that such changes were actually going on. Later, the administration antagonized major economic groups by departing from the low-key gradualist approach of its first two years, but without losing its image of ineffectiveness. Finally, the Illia administration was subjected to the ultimate reaction of groups dissatisfied with economic policy, a concerted effort to remove the government through military intervention.

Frondizi inherited an economy undergoing a modest boom in terms of the most visible signs of prosperity, although Argentina's international financial situation was deteriorating. The interregnum government of Gen. Pedro Aramburu had unwillingly fueled an expansion of production through deficit spending and higher wages, ironically the same formula adopted by many populists. The strategy was hardly deliberate on the part of the military government. Wage increases were tolerated rather than promoted, and the administration attempted (unsuccessfully) to increase taxes to match higher government expenditures (Eshag and Thorp 1965, p. 18). Workers enjoyed their share of this prosperity by winning wage increases through a rash of strikes of relatively short duration,[1] for government and employers alike were not anxious for a showdown on the wage issue. Partly as a result of increased disposable income, the demand for imports rose and Argentina's supply of gold and foreign reserves declined.

The political climate bore little resemblance to the moderately positive economic picture. Although in economic terms organized labor scored modest gains during the Aramburu years, the labor movement was severely threatened by Aramburu's anti-Peronist decrees. Frondizi's promise of Integrationism—an alliance between the government and the unions ensuring labor movement autonomy and peaceful bargaining in wage negotiations—was perceived by union leaders as a notable improvement over the situation under Aramburu.

Moreover, Frondizi picked up Perón's often-flourished theme of nationalism. Striving to win the votes of the "partyless Peronists" through both secret negotiations and open politicking, Frondizi attacked the proposal that international oil corporations be invited into Argentina to revive the moribund petroleum industry. This was more a signal to Peronists that Frondizi was molding himself after their leader than it was a real commitment on Frondizi's part, for once he was elected, his turnabout was almost immediate.

In capturing the bulk of the Peronist votes, Frondizi found himself in the paradoxical position of holding almost complete control over the formal apparatus of governmental policymaking, but lacking effective autonomy because the military was poised to intervene in economic matters as well as in political affairs. Frondizi's party, the Unión Cívica Radical Intransigente (UCRI), held both houses of Congress, enabling him to secure passage of virtually all legislation he proposed. Yet the military, fearful of Peronism in a new guise, forced Frondizi to jettison his closest economic adviser, Rogelio Frigerio, the intellectual force behind Frondizi's brand of populism. He was replaced in June 1959 with Alvaro Alsogaray, brother of a prominent general and an ardent spokesman for laissez-faire economics. The stabilization program had been launched prior to this date; even so, throughout the Frondizi period the possibility of a return to the earlier progressive approach was made far less likely by the presence of Alsogaray and other neoliberal policymakers imposed upon the Frondizi administration.

In terms of political context, Frondizi conducted economic policy in Argentina in patently unfavorable circumstances. Until the military ousted him in 1962, Frondizi faced thirty-four uprisings, attempted coups d'etat, and other serious crises. Not only was his personal choice for economic czar overturned by the military, his astounding about-face in economic policy—from huge wage increases to the most drastic, antilabor stabilization program in recent Argentine history—created tremendous antagonism and suspicion.

FRONDIZI'S INITIATIVES

An important caveat must be stated at the outset with respect to Frondizi's early strategy of economic development and distribution.[2] If one accepts the cynical view of Frondizi's motivations—interpreting his prestabilization-program measures as maneuvers to create a climate of receptivity for his later policies—then these early measures cannot be regarded as a separate "strategy," but rather as a promotional tactic of the stabilization program. Richard Mallon and Juan Sourrouille (1975, p. 19) note:

> It is difficult to resist the impression that Frondizi's extravagant initial policies were motivated not only by a desire to fulfill campaign promises but also by the need to produce an economic crisis of sufficient proportions to justify a clean break with past policies so that he could introduce his own "developmentalist" strategy.

Nevertheless, the initial policies can be evaluated on their own terms, irrespective of the possibility that Frondizi had very different ulterior motives. Perhaps a sincere redistributionist could have introduced the wage increase package of May 1958. Whether or not Frondizi was sincere need not concern us at this point.

Frondizi's initial wage adjustment was consistent with the common populist rationale of providing greater disposable income for the urban worker, who would then stimulate production through his demand for consumer goods. The process of industrialization launched by Perón would be reinvigorated, but without the distortions, heavy-handed intervention, and corruption that marked the earlier process. The fact that the economy was already operating at nearly full capacity was a recognized problem, to be resolved through additional investment. According to Frondizi's campaign speeches, this investment was to come from domestic rather than foreign sources. However, even before his inauguration, Frondizi tried to disassociate himself from his campaign attacks on foreign capital (*Hispanic American Report* 1958, pp. 106–107, 220–221). To avoid squeezing the profit incentive for businesses and investors in general, the government did not impose price controls. Moreover, the tax reforms of the Aramburu government were left intact, at least initially, because of their hoped-for stimulation of domestic investment. They entailed lower taxes on reinvested profits, tax credits for investments in mining and for interest on foreign credits obtained to finance industrial imports, and exemptions on the inheritance tax for investment/savings instruments such as stocks and bonds. (*Hispanic American Report* 1958, pp. 278–279).

Frondizi also proposed to allow wage levels to be determined through collective bargaining between unions and employers, unencumbered by state interference. This was a politically motivated concession to the Peronists and also conformed to the Integralist principle of balancing the treatment of workers and entrepreneurs, who were to be equal partners in the "developmentalist" coalition.

Before any of these plans for matching higher spending by higher investment made headway, the May 1958 wage increase produced dramatic increases in inflation and balance-of-payments deficits. Was this simply by virtue of raising workers' wages roughly 10 percent higher than what they had been in 1956?

A 10 percent increase over the February 1956 level would not in itself have been excessive. That level (as opposed to the average for the rest of the year 1956) was rather modest, as indicated by the fact that it "was far below the expectations of labor . . . , but was termed 'provisional,' implying that new labor contracts would involve further increases" (*Hispanic American Report* 1958, p. 86). Considering that the 1958 adjustment entailed a moderate increase over a modest 1956 wage level, and that there was every expectation that inflation would eat away at the May 1958 wage gains,[3] the magnitude of the May adjustment would not seem excessive.

Nevertheless, it was a disaster of timing. The wage adjustment came precisely when the momentum of inflation was building—nearly 25 percent in 1957 compared to 13 percent in 1956. The ability of the economy to meet increased demand was severely hampered by a deteriorating industrial structure in desperate need of more investment. Imports had outvalued exports for the previous four years, and foreign exchange reserves had declined for the past five years (Díaz Alejandro 1970, pp. 353, 528). To increase wages at such a time, considering that higher disposable income of workers would increase aggregate demand that could not be met without increased imports, does bring into question the competence and intentions of the Frondizi government.

Two further considerations show how ill advised the wage adjustment was. First, if the wage increase through the general adjustment alone was moderate, this was not true of the combination of the general adjustment and the myriad negotiated wage increases that unions won through strikes and threats of strikes after the general adjustment had been decreed. The discontent of the unions with the general wage adjustment was not surprising; they immediately complained that it was not enough to cover anticipated future increases in the cost of living, and the Peronist unions had to make a show of strength in order to pursue their jurisdictional battles with the anti-Peronist, so-called democratic unions promoted by the government (*Hispanic American Report* 1958, p. 338). Any reasonable assessment of the overall impact of the wage policy, taking into account that the adjustment was only a starting point, would have had to anticipate much greater increases in labor costs.

Second, the lack of any provision for holding down prices not only allowed for the immediate translation of wage increases into price increases, but also provoked the unions into redoubling their efforts to secure yet higher wage increases. The Peronists saw the lack of price controls as Frondizi's cynical way of discharging his campaign commitment to raise wages, without ensuring that the wage adjustment would result in real income gains.

The ensuing free-for-all of strikes, nominal wage increases, and price rises culminated in some overall real wage gains for 1958 over the very low 1957 levels. According to the most reliable of several contradictory sets of official statistics, both skilled and unskilled workers gained 10 to 11 percent in 1958 after the 18 percent loss from 1956 to

1957 (Villanueva 1966, p. 76; Zuvekas 1966, pp. 28–30). Thus, real wage levels for 1958 were actually lower than in 1956 for both unskilled and skilled urban workers. More disappointing still was the overall economic picture as seen by the economist: foreign reserves declined, while the trade imbalance, fiscal deficits, and inflation all increased, even though real GDP increased impressively by 5 to 7 percent.[4] It must have been far more difficult for the general public to appreciate the severity of the economic crisis, given such esoteric indications as foreign reserve balances, than it was for government officials. As for inflation, which the public *could* appreciate, the solution of restraining prices must have seemed far more obvious than what actually followed with Frondizi's stabilization program announced in December of 1958.

One aspect of Frondizi's "progressive period" from inauguration to December 1958 that bears emphasis was its brevity. While short-lived progressive policies are not uncommon, these quickly terminated redistributive efforts, frequently launched at the very beginning of a regime, are often overlooked; economic historians seem to prefer to label the regime according to the policy it adopts after reversing its initial progressive path. This was the circumstance of Ibáñez in Chile and, to a certain degree, of Odría in Peru.

The rapidity of these reversals is usually viewed as evidence of the insincerity or superficiality of the leaders' redistributive commitment. It is presumed that they merely use progressive rhetoric to attain office, and, after a halfhearted attempt at implementing progressive policies, gladly revert to their true colors. However, this interpretation fails to take note of the fact that the redistribution-minded leader, even if utterly sincere, faces several problems that arise almost immediately after he embarks on a strongly redistributive program.

Often a leader and his advisers have no precise economic program when they first assume control. Once a program is formulated, it is rarely calibrated appropriately, in part because of lack of experience in estimating the relationship between the magnitude of change dictated by the program and the actual magnitude of change that will ensue. In part it occurs because the economy is particularly volatile when demand is elevated by higher incomes in the hands of the masses, and investors become skittish. Extreme economic and political reactions are provoked where none were anticipated. The new regime is often totally unprepared to accept these costs with equanimity and a long-range outlook. Nothing in populist rhetoric prepares the initially buoyant proredistributionist for the humiliation of increased inflation, a seemingly uncontrollable budget, and the apparent ingratitude of workers who undermine the economic balance by demanding even higher wages than the populist leader had intended. Moreover, once these problems begin to mount, the solutions seem to be found in a policy reversal rather than a recalibration of the existing program. The political pressures to make a bold new start in the opposite direction, to erase the initial humiliation, may be irresistible. The precipitous rise and fall of redistributive attempts within the span of a year or less can be likened to a game of chess in which, after a few moves, the progressive persona of the leader concedes the game to the conservative persona. This does not mean that the progressive has thrown the game, but rather that he has blundered early on and recongizes the impossibility of recovery.

FRONDIZI'S STABILIZATION POLICY

With increasing inflation and dangerously low foreign reserves, Frondizi accepted a very stringent IMF stabilization program. The program, examined in great detail in the economic literature on Argentina (Díaz Alejandro 1965; Eshag and Thorp 1965; García Martínez 1965; Zuvekas 1966), included the elimination of controls on prices, trade, and payments; the consolidation of exchange rates into a single, freely fluctuating rate; highly restrictive credit policy; removal of consumer and producer subsidies; tax increases; and severe wage restrictions. Since the stabilization program has been thoroughly analyzed elsewhere (and was certainly no instrument of progressive redistribution), it need not be reviewed in depth here. However, the program and its consequences warrant further examination because of the failure of the Frondizi government to induce or permit a more significant recovery of worker incomes after the initial impact of stabilization. Why did real wage levels recover so little in the four years that Frondizi remained in power? Why, after the stabilization program also failed to produce a sustained economic recovery, was it not then followed by a return to progressive policy?

The pronouncements made in launching the stabilization program, and the surprise expressed when the program plunged Argentina into a severe recession, reveal that stabilization may have been intended to be only a short-lived shock treatment, from which wages would recover in a healthier economic climate. After the "corrective inflation" resulting from the removal of price controls and other market distortions, the momentum of inflation would be blocked. With inflation checked and investment encouraged, higher production would soon boost employment and wage increases based on productivity gains.

Although there were short periods of improvement during Frondizi's remaining years, there was no sustained recovery. The year 1959 saw deep recession; there was modest growth in 1960–1961 (though much of the growth in industry was within the narrow confines of those sectors—like petroleum and the durable manufactures—that enjoyed tax subsidies from the government), and another recession in 1962–1963 (Eshag and Thorp 1965, pp. 24–31).

Since stabilization was not an immediate success, the unions soon discovered that they had to live indefinitely with the "new" Frondizi, now a convert to the free-market philosophy. This meant—it seemed—that the unions could negotiate their own wage increases. Although initially Frondizi strengthened the bargaining position of private employers by threatening to impose heavy fines on private firms acceding to unauthorized wage increases, after 1959 the government permitted private firms to negotiate wage increases with the unions, although the use of bank credit to finance wage increases was prohibited (Eshag and Thorp 1965, p. 24).

The question, then, is why the wage negotiations taking place in nearly all industries did not restore the real-wage levels of 1958. The workers did not simply accept the damage of a fixed price increase without attempting to regain their real-wage level. In fact, a frantic wage-price spiral was unleashed, with widespread strikes, but wage levels could not catch up with the cost-of-living increases that began with the enormous surge of 114 percent in 1959.

For 1959 alone, with the surprisingly accelerated rate of inflation, it is understandable that wage increases could not keep pace. Wage demands customarily take the existing inflation rate as a baseline, then add demands for real-income increases to the extent that workers and union leaders believe they can successfully push for real-wage improvements. Therefore, if the inflation rate increases after the agreements are reached, it can easily outstrip the nominal wage increases set by the agreements. Although this rule of lagging wages in the face of accelerated inflation can explain the situation in 1959, it cannot account for the remaining years. In 1960 and 1961 inflation decelerated, to 27 percent and 14 percent respectively, and the overall economy was recovering (Eshag and Thorp 1965, p. 23). It would seem that this period could have been the opportunity for a complete recovery of real wages, rather than the meager recovery indicated by the figures in Table 9. The trend in real wages from 1960 through 1962, for both skilled and unskilled workers, demonstrates the inability of the unions to recuperate after the 1959 decline.

One answer to the paradox is macroeconomic. In devaluing the peso and unifying the exchange-rate structure, Frondizi improved the

TABLE 9. INDEX OF REAL HOURLY WAGE IN ARGENTINA (1956 = 100).

Year	Unskilled	Skilled
1956	100	100
1957	82 (− 18%)	82 (− 18%)
1958	90 (+ 10%)	91 (+ 11%)
1959	74 (− 18%)	71 (− 21%)
1960	75 (+ 1%)	71 (0%)
1961	82 (+ 8%)	77 (+ 8%)
1962	79 (− 3%)	75 (− 3%)

SOURCE: Zuvekas 1966, p. 28.

relative position of the agricultural producers. Agroexporters were able to get more pesos for each dollar's worth of exported goods, while industrial producers and consumers had to pay more for imported machinery, intermediate inputs in the production chain, and consumer imports. For the consumer, imports and other goods depending on imported inputs became more expensive—as did food, because of the increased attractiveness of food export. The real value of wages was eroded in the most blatant way imaginable. Carlos Díaz Alejandro (1965, p. 113) notes that during this period "real wages appear to have borne most of the burden of transferring real income to rural producers." Still, this does not explain why the industrial wage earners were unable to pass their burden on to the industrial producers.[5] If forced to grant higher wages, nonagricultural employers were able to afford them because their own income shares did not decline at all.

A second economic explanation for the wage earners' failure to recapture former real-wage levels is that there was little incentive for employers to grant substantial wage increases or to avoid strikes by giving in to wage demands. In 1959 and early 1960 the contraction of demand (except in consumer durables), and the consequent overstock of inventory, discouraged many producers from settling wage disputes. The conservative *Review of the River Plate* noted in January 1960: "There are many sectors of industry and trade today where, because of declining sales and large inventories, the employers' interests are probably better served than their workers' by the implementation of a threatened strike."[6] In the partial economic recovery that ran from early 1960 to the end of 1961, the expansions came in capital-intensive areas of mining and foreign-owned mechanized manufacturing, keeping industrial employment low even though production overall went up (Eshag and Thorp 1965, p. 26). In normally labor-scarce Argentina the existence of significant levels of unemployment, and the continued sluggishness of demand for many labor-intensive goods, further undermined union bargaining positions. Finally, at the end of 1961 and all during 1962 a general recession kept employers unenthusiastic about acceding to real-wage increases in order to avoid losing production.

In addition, several government policies contributed, deliberately or not, to strengthening the bargaining position of the employers. The policy of attracting foreign investment favored capital-intensive manufacturing. In a situation of very scarce credit the government prohibited the use of credit to finance wage increases. Moreover, the government's massive reductions in public works also contributed to unemployment and thereby neutralized the unions' usual bargaining advantage of labor scarcity.

Perhaps the broadest generalization that can be drawn from these impediments to labor's capacity to regain its real-income levels is that measures seemingly far removed from wage policy had a major impact on wages. This point should be obvious enough, since any measure having an impact on the demand for labor, the overall level of production, or the rate of inflation will naturally affect nominal wage gains and the real value of these wages as the cost of living changes. The implication is that the usually overwhelming focus on "wage policy," narrowly defined, is woefully inadequate and may leave the other levers of economic policy to antiredistributionists.

The third answer is more political than economic. The drastic stabilization measures provoked drastic reactions from the unions, whose leaders feared both political and economic calamity. Their reaction to the imposition of apparently grossly uneven sacrifice was to escalate their wage demands into industry-wide and even general strikes that constituted political challenges to the regime (Bailey 1967). At the same time Frondizi's near-monopolization of economic policymaking made it clear that the economic program was his. Instead of relying on a pliable Congress to formulate the unpalatable measures of austerity, Frondizi acquired the executive power to impose or lift taxes, exchange controls, and manipulate other policy levers formerly held by the legislature (Randall 1978, p. 161; Wynia 1978, pp. 97–98). The decision to bypass Congress may have been designed to avoid the recriminations of the Popular Radical party minority in Congress, who were vociferous in attacking Frondizi for "selling out the country" through his proforeign-investment stabilization plan (Wynia 1978, p. 98). Even so, the cost to Frondizi of forgoing the opportunity to dilute some of the blame for unpopular measures may have been extreme.

First an abortive general strike in January 1959 was launched, partially to embarrass Frondizi by forcing him to cancel his upcoming visit to the United States. This would have denied him the opportunity to become the first Argentine president to make a state visit to his northern neighbor. The failure of the general strike, and Frondizi's highly publicized meeting with President Dwight Eisenhower, were hailed by Frondicistas as important political victories.

In March 1959 the Peronists urged the public to refuse to pay higher electricity rates; in 1961 the railroad workers' strike was accompanied by sabotage of rolling stock. These acts and dozens of similar confrontations blurred the line between politics and economics, a line that has never been clear in Argentina, even in the least combative of times. The result was that beyond any economic rationale Frondizi may have had for repressing wage levels, he had a compelling political reason to ensure that strikes failed to achieve their dual objective of improving wages and embarrassing the government. An unsuccessful strike came to be seen as a victory for the government. This was in sharp contrast to the early days of Perón, when the labor secretariat intervened repeatedly in labor-management negotiations to tilt the outcome in favor of the unions. When the dock strike disrupted port operations in early 1959, forcing him to authorize a 50 percent wage increase, Frondizi became more adamant about the wage demands of the striking bank employees (*Hispanic American Report* 1959, p. 227). Frondizi was equally adamant in facing down the railroad workers' strike of October 1961, after calls for a general strike went unheeded by much of the labor movement (in part because the railroad union was not Peronist); the government settled with the railroad unions only after the disintegration of the transportation system turned public opinion against the government in December of 1961, leaving over a hundred thousand railroad workers without one and a half months' pay.

The government's reluctance to permit union success even in the private sector was also revealed by an odd meeting in October 1961 between the General Confederation of Labor (CGT) and the Unión Industrial, the association of large-scale industrial firms. Many of these companies manufactured heavy machinery or consumer durables, for which demand was increasing, in contrast to other consumer goods. Breaking precedent, the two groups did not invite the government to their meeting, at which the Unión Industrial expressed its eagerness to accede to union wage demands. The CGT was equally amicable in its desire to deal with the employers without government involvement (*Hispanic American Report* 1961, p. 829). It seems reasonable to infer that both labor and managment saw the government as opposing quick wage settlements, and for that reason they were trying to reduce government involvement in labor-management negotiations.

Another plausible assessment of Frondizi's turnabout underscores the ability of economic reactions to change the course of economic policy. Kalman Silvert has argued that Frondizi put so much faith in the positive effects of a rapid economic recovery to smooth over confrontations about sharing the economic pie, that considerations of distribution—whether the rapid-recovery program would be progressive or regressive in the short run—were subordinated to finding a means to get the economy growing rapidly.[7] Thus, when the initial populist program ran into trouble, the stabilization program was adopted for one overarching reason: to stimulate the economy at almost any cost. That the recovery did not come until 1961, and then sputtered, is another issue.

If the shift in policy was basically a search for the formula to rapid recovery, it is also true that those with the potential to contribute to recovery had the power to reinforce or to undermine the initial policy. David Rock (1975, p. 205) notes that "Frondizi's initial attempt at conciliation with the unions was predicated on his confidence in the dynamic, politically integrative potential of a boom in foreign investment." It also required cooperation from the Argentine export sector to redress the balance-of-trade problem, and from the domestic manufacturing sector to expand the suply of consumer goods rather than simply raising their prices. But with the future clouded by the possibility of escalating inflation, investment to expand production did not materialize. The expectation of rapid growth through an ostensibly progressive policy (that is, the May wage increase) made little sense in light of the obvious dependence of the policy on the enthusiasm of those not benefiting from the redistribution. Similarly, the hope behind the stabilization program, that workers would accept economic deprivations without engaging in srikes, was also illusory.

Even so, after a year, another IMF mission came to Argentina and rated the stabilization program a success, urging its continuation and expansion. Missions came in each year and consistently urged more of the same, despite the fact that the economy did not respond as had been hoped. This is not the place to criticize the IMF and its approach to stabilization.[8] The point to be made is that there is an asymmetry between redistributive and regressive policy attempts, in that the redistributive efforts, if they go astray, are quickly abandoned; regressive attempts, if they do not produce more rapid growth, often result in conviction on the part of the leaders that the same measures have to be enforced with even greater vigor.

TAX REFORM

Aside from his soon-abandoned initial wage policy, the only aspect of Frondizi's economic approach that could qualify as a redistributive impulse was his attempt at tax reform. As usual, the motives were mixed. Frondizi hoped to reduce the chronic budget deficit by raising taxes while reducing expenditures, and the tax increases were to come from the higher-income brackets.

It was widely recognized that the tax system had two severe problems. First, the overall tax effort was inadequate, given the government's level of expenditure. The excessive spending of the government was a problem at least as serious as locating funding sources, and politically risky efforts were undertaken to reduce spending (Eshag and Thorp 1965, p. 21). However, the political reality was that the Frondizi government could not dismiss enough state employees or raise the rates for state-provided services enough to eliminate the gap between revenues and expenditures. Tightly related to this persistent gap was the problem of tax evasion. Severe underreporting of income was widespread because of the laxity in tax administration.

The difficulty of raising revenues was compounded by the fact that the stabilization program itself called for elimination of protectionist import duties. The IMF insisted on elimination of import duties on trucks, farm equipment, and other major items The emphasis on industrial promotion led to tax exemptions for earnings from "enterprises basic to national development" and for imports for the steel and aluminum industries (*Hispanic American Report* 1959, p. 626; 1960, p. 918; 1961, pp. 736, 1033). The objective of attracting foreign investment called for tax exemptions for industry as well. If total revenues were to incease, the remaining sectors necessarily had to shoulder higher tax burdens.

Another peculiar problem was that the social security tax, introduced by Perón as a means of increasing employer contributions to employee incomes, was subverted for use of the general treasury. Federico Herschel and Samuel Itzcovich (1957) point out that because social security contributions exceeded outlays, two-thirds of the contributions were lent to the government to finance general expenditures. This seemingly arcane problem had two implications. First, the social security tax, initially meant to be progressive, became a vehicle for taxing employees to support the general treasury. Thus, depending on the context, the social security tax could be progressive or regressive; the same instrument could be used for completely different purposes. Second, the practice of raiding the social security fund indicated how desperate the government was for revenues. This desperation, despite continual attempts to restrain expenditures, persisted throughout the Frondizi period, contributing to the pressure to impose regressive taxes.

Frondizi's tax reform measures included the following ostensibly redistributive provisions:

1. The basic rate of income tax was raised from 7 percent to 9 percent in January 1959, while the sliding rates were set to range from 2 percent to 45 percent.
2. At the same time, the income tax on businesses incorporated outside Argentina was raised from 35 percent to 38 percent, while the rate for Argentine businesses was maintained at 30 percent.
3. A 2 percent "patrimonial property tax" on holdings of more than 3 million pesos was introduced in 1961.
4. An emergency 20 percent increase on tax liabilities over 50,000 pesos annually was also initiated in 1961.

To reduce tax evasion the Frondizi administration in January 1959 raised the fines from 100 percent to 250 percent; strengthened the apparatus for tax administration; and concentrated on collecting taxes when they were due, to minimize the impact of inflation on their real value (*Hispanic American Report* 1959, p. 112; Pan American Union 1963, p. 105; Eshag and Thorp 1965, p. 22).

On the other hand, the Frondizi government needed revenues and investment even if the sources were not progressive. While income tax rates were increased, so too were sales tax rates. Excise taxes on automobiles—a progressive measure—were enacted, but so too were excise taxes on alcoholic beverages. Because the austerity program required tight credit, tax exemptions replaced credit as the most important instrument for stimulating local and foreign investment.

The results of these efforts are paradoxical. The administration was lauded for having improved the collection of taxes (Pan American Union 1963, pp. 43–44), an image it was trying to cultivate. Soon after Roberto Alemann replaced Alsogaray as minister of economics in 1961, he reported that tax revenues and the promptness of tax payment had increased dramatically (*Hispanic American Report* 1961, p. 735).

Nonetheless, there is stronger evidence that the higher tax rates merely provoked evasion and that many corporations retained taxes and employee social security contributions in order to finance their operations despite the shortage of credit. On the first point, the UN

Economic Commission for Latin America reported that whereas "declared income of enterpreneurs and rentiers in 1953 represented only about 30 percent of their taxable income, . . . in the late fifties and early sixties the proportion had dropped to below 20 percent" (UN 1969, p. 260). Thus while the administration was congratulating itself for collecting reported taxes on time, unreported taxable income was increasing. On the second point, Mallon and Sourrouille (1975, p. 145) argue that for capital-short firms during this period, "delayed payments (or nonpayment) of taxes and social security contributions to the public sector [were] the most important new source of financing."

The net result of Frondizi's ambivalent approach to taxation was that the scramble for higher revenues and investment completely offset the potentially progressive contribution of changing the rates of income tax. Although available studies of tax incidence do not permit a precise estimate of the changes in the progressivity of Argentine taxation specifically for the 1959–1962 years, the existing data indicate that the tax system may well have become more regressive. The UN Economic Commission for Latin America indicated that although the tax system was progressive overall, it became less so between 1953 and 1961. Analysis of the tax burdens in 1959 and 1965 showed that the tax system, slightly regressive to begin with, became a bit more so during the 1959–1965 period.[9]

Why did the redistributive impulse sputter when it came to Frondizi's tax reform? It was not (as one might infer from the harshness of his general economic program) that the tax changes were meant to be or perceived to be superficial. There were enough nongovernmental sources extolling the tax reforms to dismiss this possibility (Pan American Union 1963; *Hispanic American Report* 1959, pp. 52, 112). Assuming that the tax changes were serious efforts, there are two explanations for their failure. The first is the basic ineffectiveness of taxation when the government cannot eliminate tax evasion. Tax reform under Frondizi is a clear example of the illusory nature of redistributive instruments that are used because they *appear* straightforward in their effects. According to a naive model of policy impact—namely, that the changes legally decreed will have their "face value" effect—changes in taxes look as directly redistributive as changes in wages. But like wage policy, tax policy cannot close off all the avenues of escape for the prospective victims of redistribution. They may either avoid increased taxation by shifting away from more highly taxed economic activities, or they may just evade the taxes they cannot legally avoid.

The second explanation is the multiplicity of objectives motivating tax policy. To increase revenues, Frondizi resorted to regressive as well as progressive taxes, neutralizing the impact of the latter. To promote investment, Frondizi decreed exemptions on income derived from economic activities that the poor could not pursue.

ILLIA'S TURN

By 1962 Frondizi had not only antagonized labor, he had proved himself incapable of staving off the Peronists' resurgence. After Peronist victories in the gubernatorial and congressional elections of March 1962, the military intervened with a caretaker government that oversaw new general elections in July 1963.

The candidate of the Unión Cívica Radical del Pueblo (UCRP), Arturo Illia, was elected with only 25 percent of the popular vote, after machinations by the Peronists and the other principal parties failed. Unlike the 1958 election, in which Peronist support gave Frondizi a majoritarian mandate, Illia's victory brought the Popular Radicals into power practically alone, with neither the support nor the inconvenience of coalition partners.

The government's lack of popular support was an obvious fact of life throughout the Illia years. Also important was the uncertainty and confusion of the period. It began with the election campaign and continued throughout the years of speculation on whether the military would intervene, whether the Peronists would be allowed to run in particular elections, whether the government was overly ambitious or immobile, and so on. In 1962 the military factions of interventionists and legalists reached a point of divisiveness resulting in actual bloodshed. Throughout the Illia years the military seemed poised to intervene—yet was indecisive about its appropriate role. Many Peronists in the union movement called for open struggle, yet some of the most prominent contenders for leadership (such as Augusto Vandor) cooperated with the government.

The only economic interest group firmly supporting the administration was the small industrial entrepreneurs. They naturally were pleased that the big foreign firms and the larger Argentine companies enjoying close contacts with multinationals were not favored by the Illia administration as they had been by Frondizi. They were also gratified that the initial expansionary policies of the Illia administration provided them ample credit (Wynia 1978, p. 125).

The political weakness of the administration was partially offset by the initial economic conditions and the combination of good harvests and fairly high export-crop prices throughout the period. When Illia took office in October 1963, Argentina had suffered through nearly two years of recession. The provisional government that followed Frondizi exacerbated the recession through extremely tight credit policies, and foreign investment was wary of the uncertain Argentine environment. Consequently, industrial capacity was markedly under-utilized. Mallon and Sourrouille (1975, p. 26) estimate idle manufacturing capacity at more than 45 percent. As a result, unemployment rose to 9 percent, quite high by Argentine standards. It was an economic situation ripe for expansion stimulated by moderate increases in disposable income. Furthermore, the favorable export situation gave the administration room to maneuver in redistributing income. Even economic sectors squeezed by government policy found enough gain to continue their investments. During this period of confusion the Illia government managed to maintain a rather high level of economic expansion, with modest improvements in the distribution of income (Table 10).

From the standpoint of poverty alleviation, Illia's accomplishments were enhanced by the fact that wage policy focused heavily on minimum wages in a context where they actually had positive significance for the poor. Decent minimum wages, protected from inflation by cost-

TABLE 10. ARGENTINE INCOME DISTRIBUTION INDICATORS UNDER THE ILLIA ADMINISTRATION.

Year	Real hourly wage rates[a]	Wage and salary share of GDP[b]
Pre-Illia years:		
1959	146	37.7%
1960	151	38.0
1961	166	40.8
1962	163	39.8
Illia administration:		
1963	164	39.0
1964	175	38.9
1965	184	40.7
1966 (6 mo)	191	43.7

a. The base date was 1939 = 100. From Merkx 1968, p. 234, with data for 1966 from Epstein 1975, p. 625, adjusted to the 1939 base used by Merkx. Figures are based on collective bargaining agreements (*convenios*).
b. From de Pablo 1976, p. 46, based on Central Bank calculations of 1971.

of-living adjustments, were extended to rural workers. Economic expansion, combined with Argentina's labor scarcity, prevented the minimum wage from leading to employment reductions. In fact, unemployment decreased somewhat throughout the period (de Pablo 1976, p. 50).

This mild but nonetheless significant redistribution was accomplished along with moderate prosperity which cannot be fully explained by fortuitous harvests and high export prices (UCRP 1966, p. 18). The gross domestic product grew by nearly 4.5 percent per annum during 1963–1966, despite the recession of 1963 (the new administration was in control during only the last quarter) and the drop-off during 1966 when Illia was deposed in midyear (Banco Central de la República Argentina 1971). In the two full calendar years of the administration, 1964 and 1965, the gross domestic product grew at 10 percent and 9 percent respectively, with declining inflation, despite the increase in overall economic activity and real-wage levels. The figures in Table 11, calculated after the Illia government had been toppled, show that both wholesale and retail price levels dropped steadily from 1962 through 1966, with strikingly low inflation during the last six months of Illia's rule.[10]

The sharp drop in the first half of 1966 would seem to fly in the face of prevalent charges that the economy was on the verge of calamity. The decline in inflation came about because the Illia policymakers refused to allow the money supply to expand at the rate of increased prices resulting from the wage-price spiral that threatened to take off during 1965. The workers kept their wage increases, but their employers discovered that, with the reduced money supply, demand for their products could not be sustained if they raised their prices (Mallon and Sourrouille 1975, p. 29). This reflected the government's forcefulness, hardly the policy drift expected of the Illia regime.

What of arguments that the redistribution of the Illia years was the

TABLE 11. INFLATION DURING THE ILLIA PERIOD IN ARGENTINA.

Year	Wholesale price increase (percent)	Cost-of-living increase (percent)
1962	30.4	28.5
1963	28.7	24.0
1964	26.2	22.1
1965	23.9	28.6
1966 (6 mo)	9.7	6.2

SOURCE: República Argentina, Dirección Nacional de Estadisticas y Censos, 1966.

happenstance result of economic trends and political events beyond
the control of the government? Was Illia too weak to withstand wage
pressures that Frondizi could fend off? Edward C. Epstein (1975, pp.
625–626) argues:

> Although workers did better economically under Illia than under his
> predecessors, this was due more to the effects of the CGT than to any
> sympathy by Illia for the Peronist workers. Put another way, Illia was less
> able to resist workers' demands than Frondizi, owing to the former's
> political weakness.

This view is based on the premise that Illia's administration did not
favor higher real wages, but could not prevent them from rising. Yet
the relatively conciliatory relationship between Illia and the Peronist
unions under the leadership of Augusto Vandor, as contrasted with
the extreme confrontation during the Frondizi era, indicates that the
issue was not whether the Illia government could withstand the pressures of the unions, but rather whether the government and organized
labor could collaborate in the pursuit of partially shared goals.

   If a government's policies can be judged by the enemies it makes, the
Illia administration has an even stronger claim to progressivism. The
Rural Society, bastion of the conservative cattle and grain producers,
indeed saw a redistributive threat from the Illia policies:

> The Government will have to pay heed to the general demand for a
> change of policy, its fiscal and trade policies are destructive of the
> initiative and activities of private producers and traders, whom it further
> discourages with new and increased taxation, the suppression of former
> tax abatement benefits, and the restoration with retroactive effect of
> pernicious imposts and restrictions affecting both the export and import
> trades.[11]

Without evaluating the correctness of the Rural Society's conclusion
that these policies were counterproductive, one can see that the economic policies were a sharp enough challenge to the economic elite to
provoke a forceful response.

   Yet the Illia administration suffered from a fatal image of immobil-
ity. This image was developed by the press, then enjoying one of its few
periods of freedom from censorship. Jacobo Timmerman, publisher
of the influential magazine *Primera Plana,* created a devastating image
of Illia as a tortoise, moving with agonizing slowness in a country in
need of rapid solutions. Many elements of the union movement saw the
economy and their own economic standing as deteriorating—with
higher wages gained in spite of the government rather than because of
it, and likely to be lost at any time. Epstein (1975, pp. 626–627) notes:

The pessimistic evaluation of the economy by Peronists, probably conditioned by their union membership and by the Illia government's
general suspicion of the workers, actually was refuted by the economic
statistics of 1964 and 1965. In that interval, real wages for industrial
workers actually rose 8-½ percent. Nevertheless, many workers thought
otherwise.

At the same time, although inflation never accelerated, the business
sector's fear that it would do so was constant.

This was the blurred and ambiguous image of the government as
both active and paralyzed, as intent upon reinserting the state into
economic affairs (an approach seriously discredited by the Peronist
experience of 1945–1955) and yet incapable of action. Explaining how
this image came about goes a long way toward explaining the failure of
the Illia administration. It is not only a fascinating paradox, it also
accounts for the nearly unanimous acquiescence to the military coup of
1966. The groups fearing a repeat of Peronist-style state interventionism welcomed the coup with relief, while the groups demanding more
state activism were already frustrated with the administration's failure
to fulfill their expectations. The following account of the administration's initiatives and policymaking tactics demonstrates how this image
arose through the neglect of basic tactical considerations in the conduct
of policymaking.

ILLIA'S INITIATIVES

The broadest objectives of the Illia policymakers were to promote
rapid economic expansion along nationalistic lines, redistribute income moderately, and rectify serious imbalances in the economic
structure. This structure was deemed responsible for the chronic
budget deficits, vulnerability to world price fluctuations, and lack of
sustained growth.

Gary Wynia points out that the professional team chosen to run the
key economic ministries had been trained at the UN Economic Commission for Latin America (ECLA) and were imbued with the "structuralist" perspective then prevailing at ECLA under the leadership of
Raúl Prebisch (Wynia 1978, p. 115). This perspective rejected the free-
market approach because the prevailing structure of the economy was
viewed as profoundly distorted, not by the interventionist policies of
previous governments, but by the international economic system that
relegated developing countries to a position of dependence, deteriorating terms of trade, and built-in tendencies toward indebtedness,
unemployment, and inefficiency.

This outlook led the Illia economic policymakers to endorse an active role for the state. Because of the team's technical proficiency and training, state activism was to be coordinated through "central planning." The recently formed planning agency, CONADE, was directed to develop a five-year national economic plan and to provide technical coordination for all economic entities of the state. Because the Argentine economy was still very much under private-sector control, planning was limited to the public sector (it was to be "indicative"—that is, suggestive—for the private sector), a far cry from the Eastern European "centrally planned economies." The state would be called upon to fill the gap left by the departure of foreign enterprises no longer given a chance to exploit Argentina, but the state would not usurp the role of domestic private enterprise. The interventionism of the Illia administration consisted in price controls, not very stringent exchange controls introduced in 1965, and moderate expansions of existing state enterprises, including a free hand in oil exploration for the state oil company (YPF) without foreign competition. Even so, public endorsement of planning and state activism was quite risky in the Argentine context, because the association among state intervention, planning, and the Peronist economic debacle was still strong in the minds of the business community and the military.

The administration's wage policy reflected its limited willingness to have the state intervene in the private sector. Wages were to be determined through collective bargaining between employers and unions, with very little government involvement. The administration's influence on wages was to come via three means, none as direct as Frondizi's heavy-handed attempts to dictate wage levels. The first was a minimum wage adjustable at the rate of cost-of-living increases, justified by the rationale that a floor on wages would benefit the lower-income worker more than would intervention in the wage negotiations of the relatively well-to-do organized workers. Because of legislation still in effect from the Perón era (the Estatuto del Peón), the minimum wage extended to many low-income workers, including farm laborers. As usual, it was a benchmark for almost all wage negotiations. The second means was more subtle: credit policy was geared to the credit demand that would be generated by the private sector's granting of wage increases within the administration guidelines. Finally, price controls were implemented to ensure that wage increases were not simply eroded by inflation. These were probably regarded as the most interventionist aspect of the economic program, since after 1959 Frondizi had condemned price controls as the antithesis of his free-market approach.

An important qualifier must be added in assessing Illia's wage policy (or any wage policy in a country with a large state-enterprise sector). As even-handed as Illia was toward labor-management negotiations in the private sector, he could not avoid the wage issue with respect to state employees. Their demands came directly to the central economic team; how they were settled determined not only the magnitude of budget deficits but also the baseline for private-sector wage increases. The Illia administration resolved to keep public-sector wage increases just ahead of cost-of-living increases and not to tolerate greater increases. When public-sector unions rejected government wage offers, the resulting strikes (legal or not) naturally embarrassed the government considerably more than private strikes. The government ended up in a situation similar to that of Frondizi and other progressive reformists such as Frei and Belaúnde.

Despite the ambitiousness of this transformation and some of the UCRP rhetoric that accompaneid it, Illia's minister of economics, Eugenio Blanco, had had sufficient experience with Argentine economic cycles (he had been economics minister briefly during the provisional government of 1955–1958) to know that restimulation of the economy had to be balanced with some constraints on expansion of imports and foreign debt. Otherwise, the familiar balance-of-payments crisis and inflationary spiral would necessitate yet another stabilization program, with a fall in disposable income, real wages, and economic dynamism. Although the economic situation at the beginning of the Illia period clearly called for expansionist policies, it also required brakes on the "normal" dynamic of expansion experienced previously by the Argentine economy.

The strategy of the Illia government, then, was to expand the money supply and governmental expenditure initially, while encouraging moderate wage increases. In May 1965, after production had been restimulated, exchange controls were instituted to keep down imports. Wage increases were limited to increases in the cost of living, productivity, and increments that employers were willing to divert from profits (Mallon and Sourrouille 1975, pp. 28–29; UCRP 1966, p. 15). The exchange rate was kept mildly overvalued (that is, the value of the official-rate peso was kept slightly above the free-market value). The government thus was able to absorb some of the currency that would have been at the disposal of exporters to spend within Argentina (with some inflationary effect), but not enough to discourage exporters from offering their beef and grain to foreign markets.[12]

Finally, the omnipresent problem of the budget deficit brought up, once again, the issue of tax reform. Increased taxation of higher-bracket taxpayers of course was high on the agenda. But tax reform had an additional, nationalist meaning for the Popular Radicals, because many of Frondizi's tax exemptions were designed to encourage foreign investment and lending. The Popular Radicals saw the tax exemptions on interest on foreign credits—and on investments in the industrial subsectors most attractive to foreign investment—as not only regressive but as a sell-out of the nation's interests.

The tax reform policy had four major components. The most controversial was elimination of broad tax exemptions in both agriculture and industry, to be replaced by more restricted, limited-period exemptions carefully targeted to the subsectors and geographic regions where the government wished to promote greater investment. The second component, enacted all over Latin America during the 1960s, was reduction of the effective time lag between incurring the tax liability and paying the tax—a reform designed to neutralize inflationary erosion on tax revenues and to reduce the chances that the administration might simply lose track of tax obligations. The third component was devotion of greater resources to tax administration, and the fourth was avoidance of moratoria, pardons, and other "measures that enervate the morality of taxpaying" (UCRP 1966, p. 18). No longer would there be an incentive for the taxpayer to hold back his payment until the government, desperate for revenues, offered him immunity from prosecution in exchange for a given fraction of his liability.

One of the most striking features of the Illia approach is that, unlike most of Argentina's previous policies, it was calibrated. From the beginning it was recognized that the opportunity for immediate economic expansion was as much a danger as a boon. The initial approach did not overburden the adaptive capacity of the economy. There were no huge, abrupt changes in economic parameters. Exchange controls were reintroduced, but did not confiscate all the earnings of the agroexport sector, which was allowed to remain moderately profitable (Mallon and Sourrouille 1975, p. 28). As for inflation, Thomas Skidmore (1977, p. 172) has noted: "During [Illia's] four-year term, inflation averaged 25.7 percent, never dropping below 22 percent. This record is understandable, since the economic policy makers of the Illia government, realistically enough, expected only to stabilize the rate of inflation, not reduce it to zero."

How can this rare moderation be explained? Illia's distaste for the game of partisan politics kept him from promising very much, and therefore from having to launch heroic programs to maintain his credibility; but well-calibrated economic policies also reflected advances in economic planning that informed policymakers of the impact of their choices. For the first time budgetary requests were classified according to both economic category (important for anticipating the macroeconomic consequences of government expenditure) and program (UCRP 1966, p. 16). Also for the first time, the budgetary process for the entire federal government, including the state enterprises, was standardized and coordinated by the Ministry of Finance, the Central Bank, and the planning agency CONADE. These and several other improvements in the government's technical capacity to anticipate the magnitude of effects of economic policies led Mallon and Sourrouille (1975, p. 28) to conclude: "The increasing influence of competent technical staffs on the design of macroeconomic policies was also notable, particularly in the National Development Council (CONADE) and in the preparation of annual financial programs under the supervision of the Central Bank." This coordination made it possible to establish guidelines for fiscal policy that kept it compatible with the government's monetary policy (UCRP 1966, p. 19).

These newly acquired capacities permitted the Illia administration, once it recognized that the simple expansionary measures initially introduced could not work indefinitely, to cool off the economy without triggering the recessions that plagued both Perón and Frondizi. Furthermore, the increased competence in economic policymaking generated a strong predilection to disregard political considerations in favor of "technical" criteria.[13] This reflected UCRP's programmatic commitment to "strict constitutionality," which was interpreted as implying that the elected president need not pay attention to extralegal factors such as military pressures, the influence of major political forces that had lost the election, or other political facts of life. The government was to exercise full authority whether it had received a rousing majority mandate or a tenuous plurality, observing democratic procedures but not realpolitik. It was also the expectable desire of a party, out of power for more than thirty years, to take full advantage of its opportunities. Yet a basic source of the administration's aloofness was the outlook of its economic policymakers: their task was to find appropriate technical solutions, not to facilitate accommodation. Like the Frondizi administrators, the Illia policymakers ignored the participatory facet of planning; they too believed that they had the right answers for the economy, and that it was only a matter of exerting enough strength to implement them. Even the CGE, Illia's most committed support (and the same association of small industrialists that had been so successfully cultivated by Perón) was excluded from any significant role in economic policymaking.[14] By 1966, when things fell apart, the CGE and its members did not exert themselves to save the government.

The lack of legislative majority should have been a significant impediment to Illia's programs, especialy in light of his assiduous observance of democratic procedure. Illia, who would not rule by decree, had to operate through a legislature in which his party held less than a third of the seats. In fact, Illia's success in enacting his legislative programs from the beginning of his term until mid-1965 defied the logic that posits the legislative majority as a sine qua non of effectiveness in the legislative arena. Without granting governmental positions or any other major concessions, Illia was able to count on several legislative splinters to support the reforms proposed by his economic team, apparently because these small parties concurred with UCRP's policies. But the logic did apply after mid-1965, with fatal effects for the administration.

Before reviewing the sequence of events that ultimately brought down the Illia administration, let us examine the levels of investment and disinvestment, inasmuch as depletion of investment often constitutes a fatal weakness of redistributive attempts. Although overall investment did not decline—which explains why economic growth was sustained—some of the most visible components of investment dropped, with adverse political impact for the government.

Central Bank statistics show that after the 1962–1963 recession the levels of both private and public investment in Argentina improved substantially (Table 12). The investment of the public sector was aided by reductions in the deficits and personnel expenditures (in real terms) of the state enterprises, contrary to the popular perception that these

TABLE 12. INVESTMENT IN ARGENTINA, 1960–1966
(MILLIONS OF 1960 PESOS).

Year	Public investment	Private investment	Total investment
1960	918	1,258	2,176
1961	964	1,422	2,386
1962	810	1,385	2,194
1963	907	892	1,799
1964	904	1,362	2,267
1965	917	1,515	2,431
1966	747	1,510	2,257

SOURCE: Banco Central de la República Argentina 1976, pp. 192–193; CONADE 1971, p. 32.

entities were becoming more of a burden. According to official data, expenditures on state-sector personnel dropped from 3.08 billion constant (1970) pesos in 1962 and 3.02 billion in 1963, to 2.85 billion in 1964 and 2.73 billion in 1965. The deficit of state enterprises dropped from 2.85 and 2.61 billion pesos in 1962 and 1963 respectively, to 2.09 and 1.85 billion pesos for 1964 and 1965 (República Argentina 1970, p. 96).

The public sector's investment level was also aided by vastly increased tax revenues, which permitted the government to maintain a substantial capital budget level without creating an intolerable deficit. Illia's tax reforms were temporarily effective in raising revenues, but did not solve the underlying problem. The combination of strong economic recovery in 1964 and the elimination of numerous exemptions effective for that year led to an 80 percent increase in 1965 tax revenues over 1964 levels (which, to be sure, were quite low because the 1963 recession depressed that year's earnings and therefore the tax collected on it in 1964). With the elimination of even more exemptions for 1965, the central government's revenues for the first half of 1966 (that is, to the time of Illia's ouster) increased by 32 percent over the level of the same period for 1965 (UCRP 1966, p. 18). Nevertheless, the basic problem of tax avoidance and evasion remained. The swiftness of the tax changes in 1964 and 1965 may have caught high-income recipients off guard, but thereafter the old pattern was reasserted. Carlos Quinterno (1970, p. 263) reflects the standard view:

> The tax system, despite the always announced and always postponed basic reforms, continued as anarchic, confused and unjust as always . . . Fiscal evasion continued to proliferate, stimulated by the impossibility to control it, by the discouragement of the contributor confronted with such anarchy, and by the possibility of pardoning tax evasion [*blanquear las evasiones*], which occurred at the beginning of 1970.

Thus the resolve of the Illia administration to resist the short-term expedient of offering tax pardons in exchange for partial payments was ineffective; potential taxpayers still expected that the opportunity for absolution would arise sooner or later. They were correct inasmuch as the next government did resort to the *blanqueo* in order to raise revenues.

The immediate increases in tax revenues permitted Illia to increase fiscal expenditures, both in capital and current accounts, while simultaneously reducing the deficit. The administration was able to expand spending in all sectors, although there was no particular emphasis on spending in social sectors that would favor the poor. The government's concern for the poor was manifested, instead, in its minimum wage policy.

Private investment seemed to respond more to the actual growth opportunities available because of the expansion than to the image of ineffectiveness and stagnation. The greater difficulties encountered by multinational firms provided an opening for domestic Argentine entrepreneurs, and the investment opportunities appearing in specific sectors were attractive regardless of the overarching perceptions of malaise. As long as there was no concerted campaign to scare away investment, investors behaved as economic rather than political actors. In agriculture the good weather and favorable export prices kept cultivation levels high, despite the government's policies of higher taxes, higher rural wages, and exchange controls. In industry there was a burst of investment in machinery and equipment, but not in imported capital goods, because so much had been imported during the Frondizi years and underutilized owing to the recession of 1962–1963 (UCRP 1966, p. 18).

The "investment" shortage that did emerge was confined to liquid capital available to firms for day-to-day operations. The stock market was in a depressed state almost continuously through 1965 and 1966, kept near a state of panic by articles in the financial press such as "Investors Beware!" (*Review of the River Plate*, June 11, 1966, p. 383). The budget impasse held down the funds available to the government, and tight credit designed to check inflation added to the business sector's liquidity problems. This visible shortage of capital had more political impact than the fact that overall capitalization, despite the complaints from conservative quarters that the country was being decapitalized, was in fact gradually increasing.

THE OPPOSITION TO ILLIA

Illia was very much the man in the middle, attacked by both the labor-union Left and the business-sector Right. One of the most important questions in assessing the Illia experience is whether his political isolation, which by 1966 was almost complete, was an unavoidable cost of having steered a moderate and fair economic course in a country as polarized as Argentina. If so, one can only conclude that the price of achieving the government's policy objectives was its own demise. Alternatively, it is conceivable that the policy objectives could have been pursued through different tactics that might have avoided or mitigated the opposition of so many groups.

The government's policy of mild overvaluation of the peso, though

not enough to discourage agricultural investment, was resented sufficiently by the rural producers to earn their opposition. The rural
agroexport sector, stung by higher taxes as well, lost no opportunity to
convey the impression that the economy as a whole was in dire straits.
Perhaps no better example can be offered than the Rural Society's
"petition" of January 1965 to President Illia, a widely published appeal
for the government to discard its "wrong and dangerously harmful"
economic policies. It is noteworthy that the Rural Society could not
point to economic statistics to make its point, but instead employed the
negatively connoted terminology of economic disaster:

> It is indispensably and urgently necessary to combat and eradicate the
> ... present complete recession of confidence ... As Argentines, we
> have the right to demand this of Your Excellency; we cannot remain
> passive in the face of the imminent collapse of the Republic. We are
> complying with our duty in offering our co-operation in any positive
> action to be taken to achieve the goal of national recovery.[15]

The use of the terms "recession," "imminent collapse," and need for
"national recovery" would seem to imply tht the economy was in
disastrous shape. Yet in March of the same year the well-known
economist Carlos Moyano Llerena, a much-respected figure in business circles, had to concede that the economy was indeed going through
a rather protracted period of expansion—but that the signs of imminent recession would soon be appearing (*Review of the River Plate*,
March 19, 1965, p. 391).

The large-scale domestic-market producers turned against the Illia
government in 1965 after the administration refused to expand the
money supply in line with the wage increases that private producers,
disregarding government guidelines, granted their employees. The
Illia administration, we have seen, did not reward the early support of
the small entrepreneurial sector by granting it significant access to
policymaking deliberations. While there is no evidence that this sector
was actively cultivating military intervention, there is also no evidence
of its enthusiasm for protecting the regime.

A major segment of the Peronist unions opposed Illia because they
presumed that non-Peronists were antiworker; the Peronist CGT had
for years developed the image of Peronism as synonymous with
unionism (Epstein 1975, pp. 615–616). Moreover, Illia was perceived
to be the leader of the conservative wing of the Radical party, and
presumably even less disposed than other Radicals to espouse populist
policies.

The first phase of union opposition to the Illia government was
outlined in the *Plan de Lucha* (battle plan) of 1964. There are two more

or less complementary interpretations of the motivations of the Plan de Lucha. One is that the Peronist union leaders were protesting Illia's economic policies, presumably to force a policy change (Alexander 1979, p. 118). The other is that for the militants of the Peronist movement, this was to be the precursor of Perón's return. The economy's paralysis, through general and partial strikes and the occupation of factories (Hodges 1976, p. xv), would first trigger the military's ouster of Illia and then, with disruption continuing even under military rule, force the military to allow Perón to return.

After the Plan de Lucha crumbled in the face of Illia's refusal to react confrontationally as had Frondizi, a large portion of the Peronist labor movement shifted to a conciliatory position. Within Peronism a split had developed between the "right wing," oriented toward bargaining with government and management over bread-and-butter economic issues, and the "left wing," committed to using economic conflict to restore Perón as president. Led by the head of the Metallurgical Workers Union, Augusto Vandor, who presided over the "Group of 62" unions, the "collaborationist wing" was disposed to cooperate with Illia, to keep labor peace, and to define wage policy as an economic rather than a political issue. This uneasy détente held until late 1965, when Vandor's power within the labor movement was challenged by more combative leaders, with the tacit but always somewhat ambiguous support of Juan Perón himself. In the ensuing competition to show who was truly more militant, both Vandorist and anti-Vandorist unions became more combative. The administration, in turn, tried to undermine the Peronist unions by banning union political activity and changing the labor-law provisions that had facilitated single-union dominance over entire industries (Wynia 1978, p. 128).

The contentiousness of the unions was exacerbated by the government's insistence that nominal wage increases would be limited to 15 percent for 1966, in the hope that inflation would consequently be held to 12 percent for the year (*Review of the River Plate,* January 31, 1966, p. 127). Considering that the actual cost-of-living increase in 1965 had exceeded 28 percent, and that the monthly increases toward the end of 1965 were running on an annual basis at nearly 40 percent, the 15 percent wage guidelines had no credibility whatsoever. A clear departure from the gradualism and moderation that earlier marked the government's economic policies, they perhaps reflected the administration's desperation in the face of its image of paralysis and declining political support.

Prior to mid-1965 Illia enjoyed fortuitous legislative support from minor parties sympathetic to his economic program. The tax reforms for 1964 and 1965, the minimum wage legislation, and the price-control regulations were passed without major confrontations, elevating the Illia team's confidence that policy formulated in the economic ministries could be enacted more or less pro forma. Yet after the congressional elections of early 1965 the legislature became an ineffective arena, even for policy endorsement. With the election of more Peronist legislators and the defeat of a few UCRP candidates and allies, the administration's capacity to pass legislation formulated by its economic team declined drastically. The Peronist legislators, much like the APRA legislators encountered by Belaúnde in Peru, opposed even the progressive policies of the Illia administration, despite their own progressive commitment. From one perspective this may seem a selfish act of narrow partisanship; from another it may appear an unfortunate cost in the longer-term struggle for control and the opportunity to implement the full complement of Peronist policies. And, of course, Illia's own partisanship discouraged legislative cooperation from the Peronists. There is no indication that the government took account of this change by shifting policy or the mode of policy formulation either to circumvent the legislature or to accommodate to it.

By late 1965 the inflationary pressures became considerably more acute. Price controls gradually lost their effectiveness, and the wage-increase ceilings formulated by the government in line with its macroeconomic calculation of price rises of 20 percent and wage increases of 22 percent for 1965 were roundly rejected by the unions, which anticipated far higher cost-of-living increases. So confident were employers that they could pass on higher labor costs by increasing prices that many of them hastily granted high wage increases (*Review of the River Plate,* July 21, 1965, pp. 92–93).

The government faced a dilemma: intervene more directly to force down wage demands, or cap the inflationary pressures by using additional means to prevent price increases. It was at this point—with even conciliatory labor unions threatening that wage restrictions could be imposed only through violence—that the Illia administration came up with the idea of refusing government credit to finance labor costs in excess of the government guidelines. Since a good part of Argentine industry was dependent on government credit, the threat had a significant effect in keeping down the wage increases that employers felt they could afford to grant, and the inflationary spiral was avoided. However, this ingenious policy had its political cost: businesses felt that they were carrying the sacrifice in the fight against inflation, while unions regarded wage guidelines as not only contrary to their interests, but as proof that Illia really was antilabor in orientation.

ILLIA'S FALL

It was at this point that the Illia administration began to fit the preconceptions of its inefficacy. First, the legislature obstructed the budget package for 1966. Peronist legislators announced that they would tie up the budget and tax deliberations in order to protest the government's changes in the labor law (*Review of the River Plate*, March 22, 1966, p. 377); conservative legislators delayed in order to force greater reductions in the deficit. This was not the kind of acute confrontation that quickly signals a government that crisis prevails. Rather, the parrying and delays beginning with submission of the budget proposal in October 1965 dragged on into 1966. Finally, in May 1966, the government's budget package, and the tax reforms on the revenue side of the fiscal program, were voted down by a slim majority. The government faced the prospect of operating with considerably less revenue under the provisions of the 1965 fiscal program until a new budget could be passed. Moreover, the government could not pursue renegotiation of foreign debt until its budget requirements and revenues were established. The opposition formulated its own budget proposal that would have eliminated certain favored government programs. The administration still could have won, by arranging for the defeat of the Chamber of Deputies' budget proposal by two-thirds of the Senate, and Senate passage of the administration's budget proposal (which could be rejected in the chamber only by an unlikely two-thirds majority). But the most serious damage was the delay itself; as the budget tangle dragged into June 1966, the military saw it as confirming the ineffectiveness of the Illia government.

By early 1966 the military's worries about economic policy paralysis had already surfaced. The military was encouraged by the conservative, the Peronist, and the financial press to view the situation as urgently requiring changes of policy and personnel. For example, the *Review of the River Plate* (June 11, 1966, p. 370) told the public—and the military—that "responsible feeling in the Armed Forces is that a change of policies and of men in the higher levels of authority may be necessary to ensure that the problems with which the country is faced may be the more effectively and expeditiously solved." Such statements did not, of course, openly demand military intervention, but in the context of Illia's known commitment to maintain his economic team, they came as close as was necessary to making the point that a military coup would be welcomed. The military was apparently swayed by the opposition. The image of the government as being both dangerously interventionist and ineffective could hardly inspire any military faction to come to its defense. The electoral victories of Peronist candidates in the 1965 congressional elections, and the likelihood of further victories in 1966, also convinced the military that Illia's courting of the labor movement had failed to stop the resurgence of Peronism. The military finally took over on June 28, 1966, led by Carlos Onganía, the same general who had opposed the army's "interventionist" faction in the past.

The ultimate reaction against an economic policy is to force the policymaker out of office. Illia and his economic team had proved remarkably resistant to bargains, complaints, and threats. But they were terribly vulnerable in terms of image, and this permitted the opposition to attack the regime without sabotaging the economy (except for the disinvestment in capital markets, which had other justifications).

This economic policy motive is not the only explanation for the moves against the Illia administration: the president had antagonized virtually every political group through his narrow partisanship; he had antagonized the Peronist labor unions over the issue of power more than economics. Moreover, Illia had antagonized the military by trying to divide them through the elevation of General Onganía's subordinate as minister of defense; and the Peronists loomed as a major electoral force in the eyes of the still adamantly anti-Peronist military establishment. Nevertheless, it would be hard to argue that the economic motives for the coup were only secondary.

Several key individuals and groups supported the military coup d'etat for explicitly economic reasons. Frondizi himself, who of course defended presidential authority when he was in office, was not only still a bitter rival of the UCRP government, but had come to accuse Illia of squandering Argentina's development opportunities through what Frondizi saw as short-sighted parochialism. He issued a statement just before the coup, arguing that "when an antinational policy is being pursued, the armed forces cannot remain limited to their specific function."[16] By "antinational" Frondizi surely did not mean "antinationalist," since Illia's policies of canceling exploration contracts with foreign oil firms and instituting tougher foreign investment terms were far more nationalistic in the standard sense of the term than Frondizi's opposite position had been. Frondizi meant that the Illia economic strategy was not fulfilling Argentina's economic potential, which Frondizi viewed as achievable only through massive foreign investment. The military was called upon to carry out a "national revolution" expressly in order to avoid economic stagnation (Barrera 1973, p. 25).

CONCLUSIONS

The Illia experiment in "partisan populism" by a minority party ended in a political failure that surprised few observers of Argentine politics. Our analysis indicates, however, that the outcome was less cut-and-dried than one might imagine. The departure from gradual and often obscure redistributive policy to more blatant forms, the utter disregard for image making and policy presentation, the failure to accommodate to the new legislative reality after mid-1965, and other tactical short-comings have to be weighed with Illia's political precariousness as explanations of his demise. Moreover, Illia did nothing to block an opposition coalition, not only of the wealthy groups naturally fearful of redistribution, but also of the very economic sector benefiting, albeit modestly, from his policies.

One thing is quite clear: it does not take an economic reaction ending in overall economic catastrophe to bring down a redistribution-minded government. As in the case of Belaúnde in Peru, relatively superficial but acute crises, interpreted by the military (with the guidance of regime opponents) as signs of economic policy incompetence, can bring down a regime as surely as can economic collapse.

There are two important lessons in the contrast between Illia's politically fatal image and his actual record. The more obvious—and depressing—message is that doing good works does not translate into political credit. The other lesson is that a certain degree of confusion, and the image of "policy drift," can inhibit reactions against redistributive policies. This makes sense when seen within the theoretical framework that emphasizes the antiredistributive reaction sequence that is triggered by awareness that redistributive efforts are under way. Only in mid-1965 did the business community fully realize how far the Illia administration was willing to go to protect the real income gains of wage earners.

This is not to say that the confusion and vagueness of the government's image were deliberate or altogether advantageous. In retro-spect, UCRP officials readily admit that their administration was a public-relations disaster, with no sustained concern for the government's image. This was, to be sure, partially a principled rejection on Illia's part, in keeping with his position that the constitution established his right to rule irrespective of how the government was regarded. This vacuum left the government wide open to the propaganda of the opposition, even when the actual economic record was considerably better than the image being conveyed.

It is striking that the attacks on the administration's supposedly dangerous state-interventionist tendencies rarely focused on any concrete examples. It seems likely that the fears aroused by the regime's declared intention to play a more active economic role (by which the government apparently meant "rational planning" rather than significantly deeper penetration into the private sector) were triggering the reaction in lieu of actual, significant instances of state intervention. The five-year plan, which did not even come into effect until 1965, in actuality had very little in the way of state encroachment into the private domestic sector (CONADE 1965). The regime seems to have made enemies in an extremely inefficient way: not because of the policies it adopted, but because of the image it conveyed—an image that was not sustained by concrete policies that could have cultivated some countervailing support from their beneficiaries.

The Illia experience also confirms that the beneficiaries of redistribution are seldom satisfied with what they get and often end up exacerbating the political problems of the redistributive regime. This is not to say that demanding more is a form of ingratitude. The regime that can mobilize the capacity of the poor to demand more, and can establish their claim to greater benefits, is providing a more lasting contribution to economic equality than almost any short-lived economic policy. The unwillingness of beneficiaries to accept what governments offer them adds yet another reason for redistributionists to opt for quiet rather than strident redistributive policy. In the trade-off between mobilizing support and provoking opposition, the assumption that policy beneficiaries can be counted on as allies proves to be simplistic.

CHAPTER 10
The Logic and Tactics of Reformism

THE DEMOCRATICALLY elected, redistribution-minded reformist accepts certain political and economic constraints on the
scope of his or her actions. The economy's structure—its patterns of
ownership, the huge discrepancies between modern-sector and traditional-sector productivity, and so on—are typically changed only gradually, and sometimes only marginally, by the reformist. Moreover,
these changes must be cleared through the normal channels of government policymaking. Hence the reformist is subject to the obstructions
afforded by the existing institutional structure, which itself can be
changed only slowly, if at all. The opposition can maneuver over
familiar ground, where the wealthy have retained many of their levers
of political and economic influence. The reformist is always vulnerable
to the accusation that "more could be done," without the opportunity
of demonstrating that doing more could result in disaster.

In exchange for these constraints, the reformist has several advantages that provide openings for the "art of reform." He can benefit
from the sometimes considerable legitimacy of the democratically
elected leader who remains within the constitutional framework. Because reformism is not as necessarily antagonistic to middle-sector
interests as radicalism, the redistribution-minded reformist also has a
greater potential for forming politically powerful coalitions with these
interests. He may be able to avoid the unrestricted retaliation of the
opposition, and at the same time be able to win the support of
organized labor. The reformist also has the opportunity to operate an
economy which, because it has not been altered radically, is likely to
behave in more predictable ways than an economy undergoing radical
change.

This chapter focuses on the factors that explain why the reformists
encountered in this study failed in many respects, and succeeded in a
few, to take advantage of their opportunities. The difficulty of making
fruitful comparisons among the reformist regimes of Frei, Belaúnde,
Frondizi, and Illia is the general failure they all experienced, at least in

political terms. Only Frei served out his full term—and his party lost the crucial next election. In economic terms also there are only partial successes: the redistributive progress of Frei's first three years (although one cannot separate the later failures from the early initiatives); the economic and redistributive progress under Illia despite the political weakness of his administration; Belaúnde's partial victories in particular redistributive programs, despite the overall trend of income concentration. Nevertheless, differing degrees of success in specific programs do permit some useful comparisons, just as the general problems faced by all of the reformists provide insights into the dynamics of attempting redistribution in the liberal democratic framework.

COALITIONS AND "GRATITUDE"

What does it take to pursue the middle road of reformism successfully? The logic of the reformist's position argues for broad coalition building—and the subtlety, balance, and calibration necessary to cultivate such coalitions. The fact that the reformist does not necessarily frighten off politically important economic sectors ought to mean that the progressive reformist can form potent alliances. Yet the reformists examined in this study had only mixed success in aligning themselves with the two economic sectors theoretically most likely to be sympathetic with reformist aims: organized labor and the middle-income sector composed of white-collar workers, professionals, bureaucrats, and small-scale or medium-scale business interests.

Organized Labor

One striking puzzle concerning these progressive reformists is their notable lack of success in cultivating the support of organized labor. It is unexpected because the reformist's political strategy has typically emphasized organized labor as the beneficiary of progressive reform. The moderate redistributive changes envisioned by reformists usually entailed advantages for the lower-income segment of the modern, regulated enterprises. Within an existing economic structure this is the sector for which regulation is easiest and most direct, whereas reaching the remote farmer or the self-employed worker who plies the streets of the cities is far more difficult and is perceived as being far less controllable. Because the administrative capacity of the typical Latin

American nation permits the regulation only of firms of at least moderate size, there is a strong correlation between those who would benefit from progressive regulation of this sector and the membership of organized labor.

It is not surprising, therefore, that the predominant focus of reformist theory and rhetoric has been on labor-management relations: wage adjustments, minimum wages, the expansion of social benefits paid for principally by employers, working condition imrovements, and so on. Such programs do not entail the fundamental socioeconomic transformations that would threaten the organized labor movement from the Left; that is, a perception that their gains would be seriously undermined by income losses to even poorer population segments lacking modern-sector employment and organization. The "danger" that the benefits could bypass organized labor via massive transfers to the rural poor was precluded by the reformists' enthusiasm for industrialization. The benefits for marginal populations, whether urban or rural, were modest and typically were channeled through social service expenditures financed through greater taxation of high-income groups. There was no hint of major structural change to alter the dominance of the modern urban sector.

Yet the reaction of much of organized labor to the reformists' initiatives was antagonistic, as indicated by the high number of politically motivated strikes, criticisms of government policy, and support of opposition political groups. Despite the potential for alliance, organized labor behaved as if the reformist presidents were their natural enemies.

Why was collaboration with labor so elusive? Part of the answer lies in the choice of policy instruments. A more directly political explanation is that three of the four reformists attempted to gain control of the labor movement from the other political movements, which were nominally more radical in ideology. With the exception of Arturo Illia, the reformist presidents seriously aspired to create labor movements affiliated with their own parties. This naturally gave additional incentive for the Peronists in Argentina, the Socialists and Communists in Chile, and the Communists and Apristas in Peru to confront the governments on prominent economic issues such as the general wage adjustment.

By way of contrast, we have seen that Illia, until 1965, enjoyed rather congenial relations with that major part of the Argentine labor movement controlled by Augusto Vandor, despite the continual undercurrent of political competition with the Peronist movement. When the unions became more combative against the government (for reasons related much more to the internal dynamics of the Peronist movement than to Illia's actions), Illia's desperate efforts to limit union political activity and to impose wage constraints failed to reduce union opposition, and in fact hastened the Peronists' participation in calls for a military coup.

In retrospect, it seems clear that the 1960s reformist who embarked on both redistribution and takeover of the labor movement, even if done with perfect legality, had an excessively heavy agenda. In becoming a political competitor of the labor leadership, the reformist threatened a potential ally of considerable importance. Nothing detracted more from the reformists' perceived performance than their inability to avert the public displays of labor defiance which, more than the events in the countryside, were apparent to the urban representatives of other political and economic sectors.

REFORM-MINDED MIDDLE SECTORS

Perhaps an alliance with organized labor would have been less important if other alliance possibilities had materialized, particularly with the middle-sector groups who might be expected to benefit from a decline in the power of the economic elite, or simply be able to take advantage of the leakages of benefits directed principally to the poor. Indeed, the successes of the reformists in specific redistributive initiatives coincided with their temporary, issue-by-issue accords with such groups. Belaúnde's momentary unity with APRA legislators on the educational expansion program and Frei's legislative coalitions on specific tax and spending bills represented such alliances, whereas Frondizi moved so quickly from championing the workers to his probusiness stabilization program that a progressive redistributive alliance with middle-sector groups could not take shape. Illia's predicament was that no one seemed to realize that his economic policies would help anyone, despite the fact that both labor and certain business groups ultimately benefited.

All in all, the reformist's potential ability to form lasting coalitions with middle-sector groups that would oppose more radical approaches resulted in surprisingly little advantage to the leaders examined in this study. The reasons for this disappointing level of support can be understood by assessing what the reformists promised these groups and what was ultimately delivered. First, the reformist leaders promised economic growth, through an economic restructuring that would free the economy from the stranglehold of either foreign domination or the domestic oligarchy, or both, within a democratic political structure and an economy in which the state had a more active role than before, but not to the exclusion of the small-scale and medium-scale entrepreneur. Second, they promised enough reform to defuse the dissatisfaction of lower-income groups so as to avert class revolution or the rise of populist dictators. Third, the reformist leaders promised that particular segments of the middle sectors could share in the transfers directed primarily to the poor. Teachers, construction contractors, bureaucrats, and others astride the flow of benefits could themselves benefit.

The reformists were not perceived as having fulfilled the first two promises. Economic growth was weak, as in Belaúnde and Frondizi's cases; erratic, as in Frei's case; or overshadowed by the confusion of other events, as in Illia's case. The importance of growth in satisfying middle-sector backing is reflected in the fact that the strange reversal from populist to conservative policies that we witnessed among the populist authoritarians such as Ibáñez and Odría could be seen among the reformists as well. Even Belaúnde (in some of the stabilization measures adopted once the alliance with APRA was struck) and Illia (in his reversal on negotiating with the international banks) showed this tendency, but Frei and particularly Frondizi were remarkable in their turnabouts.

This can only be explained by noting that the progrowth reformist policymaker of the Frei or Frondizi mold was torn between two development strategies. The first was the populist gamble of relying on higher consumer demand to stimulate greater production, which in turn would increase employment and provide the incentives for capital expansion that would improve productivity rather than provoke inflation. This strategy could work only if sources of investment capital could clearly see that the initial redistribution of income in favor of the consumers—basically, the poorer segments of the populace—provided more of an opportunity than a threat to their existing and future investments.

The second strategy was to stimulate a business boom through policies directly providing higher profits to private-sector producers, even if the distribution of income tilted further in their favor. Such a strategy usually included easy credit, tax incentives, and even the easing of labor legislation, in order to boost investment. The erstwhile reformists, then, typically responded to the decline of private investment by shifting to this second strategy. It was, of course, not lost upon investors that a populist strategy could be undermined by their investment behavior.

Perhaps more important in the failure of the reformists to maintain support from middle-income groups was their inability to stem the polarization of politics and economic competition. The very rhetoric chosen by the reformists, and the prominently class-based economic instruments they chose to emphasize (wage policy and land reform, for instance) exacerbated the polarization. Naturally, the corporatist streaks revealed in attempts to dominate the labor organizations added to this polarization, insofar as reformism could be construed as an attempt to capture and emasculate the workers' movement.

The cynicism provoked by the reformists' adjustments following poorly calibrated, overly optimistic promises can be seen most graphically in the responses of their own political movements. Except for Illia, the reformist leaders were unable even to hold on to the political movements that brought them to power. The revolt within the Acción Popular of Belaúnde led to the party's takeover by the *termocéfalos* ("hotheads") and their nomination of Seoane as their next presidential candidate. Frei expended much of his energy and political capital in putting down the revolt of the left wing of the Christian Democratic party, and the leftist Unidad Popular coalition that defeated the Christian Democratic candidate Radomiro Tomic in the 1970 election incorporated a considerable contingent of Christian Democratic defectors. Even Frondizi ultimately lost much of his Radical Intransigente party, when in 1963 the pro-Frondizi wing had to separate from the party to form the MID (Movimiento de Integración y Desarrollo), both becoming minor parties in terms of electortal strength. Only Illia, who openly swore off extraparty alliances in order to enhance the policy-making importance and patronage of Popular Radical party loyalists, was able to emerge with his party intact.

What soured the relationships between the reformist presidents and their own party bases was the inability of the top officials to pursue as progressive a policy as the party activists favored. Except for Illia, who stubbornly pursued nationalistic policies despite the damage to the balance of payments that the reduction in oil production caused, the reformists were seen as betrayers of progressive party principles. Starting out as strongly populist in tone, the reformists attracted reform-minded elements of the middle sectors, while antagonizing more conservative elements. The leaders' subsequent inability to match performance to stated or implied objectives antagonized their original suporters, without attracting the conservatives, because no progress was made in halting the advance of political forces to which the conservatives objected even more. Thus Frondizi was not successful in gaining the support of Argentina's conservatives when he shifted abruptly from progressive to regressive economic policies; when the Peronists threatened to win the next election, Frondizi stood practically alone. The obvious implication is that if a populist image is cultivated at the outset, a policy reversal cannot offset the loss of original support. The reformist is better off maintaining his original policy direction, or starting out with a less blatant populist image.

THE PATTERN OF REACTION

Three types of reactions to redistributive efforts are worthy of note: legislative obstruction, disinvestment, and appeals for military intervention. The first is predictable, given the particular situation of the democratic reformist; the second straightforwardly reflects the apparent failure of growth and the inability of reformists to threaten punishments for disinvestment. By contrast, the appeal to military intervention is at first glance surprising, in light of the reformists' self-imposed restraint.

Legislative opposition and obstruction were employed against every reformist regime. Yet, contrary to the widely accepted view that a legislative majority as a sine qua non for successful reform, Illia and Belaúnde launched progressive initiatives without being in command of the legislature. Moreover, as Belaúnde demonstrated in his eleventh-hour coalition with APRA, a legislative majority or minority need not be a fixed entity, but may be a creature of constantly changing composition.

Reformist experiences also reveal much about the legislature as a policymaking arena. In theory the legislative arena would be expected to be "open" in the dual sense of being responsive to attempts at influence by a broad spectrum of political and economic interest groups, and of being accessible to monitoring by such groups. In practice, effective access is not that open, since it depends on having a fairly large contingent of sympathetic legislators. Moreover, much of the bargaining over legislation goes on in back rooms rather than in open session. In terms of the accessibility of understanding, legislated policies tend to be more widely publicized than policies formulated in other arenas, but they are not necessarily more easily understood or monitored. The legislation on education expenditure in Peru is a good case in point; it is not certain that the legislators clearly understood the implications of their own legislation.

The pattern of disinvestment in response to reformist initiatives was the most straightforward economic reaction. The only unresolved issue is whether, short of promising and providing a more positive investment climate, the reformists could have prevented disinvestment without abandoning their basic programs. Although it is not difficult to imagine sanctions for disinvestment—taxes based on potential rather than actual performance (which have been applied to land), threats of greater state intervention in sectors where private investors are not contributing as much as the government insists—the reformists were basically passive. This can be explained by their method of operating through rewards rather than threats, also by the fact that the reformists simply did not anticipate the investment problems they would encounter.

The most distressing feature of their experience was that despite the relative mildness of their challenges to the established economic order, the political response to three of the four reformist governments was to call for military overthrow of the regime. Since Argentina, Chile, and Peru are being examined here for reasons quite removed from the political failures of their reformist leaders, the difficulties experienced by the reformists must be regarded as more than an artifact. Even if military intervention is not inevitable, it is striking that the opposition to Frondizi, Illia, and Belaúnde chose to call for their overthrow, and succeeded. Analyzing why this was so will help us to understand the reformist's vulnerabilities, although it is well beyond the scope of this study to account for the failure of Latin American democracy, given that this has been the *problematique* of Latin America for at least the past two decades.[1]

There are two interrelated questions. Why was the military predisposed to appeals from opposition groups? Why did these groups pressure the military to intervene?

In all three instances of coups against the centrist leaders, the military acted at least in part to prevent governmental power from being transferred to a nominally "populist" movement that the military had long considered unacceptable—and that the military had previously deposed. The coup that overthrew Belaúnde was motivated by animosity toward APRA, which appeared likely to win the next presidential election, as well as by the belief that necessary reforms were not being carried out and that the economy was collapsing through the ineptness of the government. In Argentina both Frondizi and Illia were deposed in large part because of the resurgence of Peronist strength.

It was not particularly relevant that these "unacceptable" parties were by this time no longer radical and in fact hardly progressive; military disapproval endured, perhaps because of the parties' presumed irresponsibility and corruption. In Peru many of the military officers had moved so far to the left that an APRA electoral victory was opposed on the grounds that the party was both too corrupt and too conservative to solve Peru's socioeconomic problems.

When these governments did not win enough support from organized labor to change the military's expectations of a Peronist or an APRA comeback, the governments were seen as having failed according to the standards they had set for themselves. The image of ineptness was reinforced by the regime's political failure to wean labor away from antagonistic labor movements. It could be argued that the military's expectation that deep-rooted political movements such as Peronism and APRA could be so quickly destroyed was unreasonable. Yet, as we have seen, the expectation was not strictly of the military's own making.

There are three essential conclusions. First, the military did not intervene because of fears that competing political movements represented greater progressivity. Chile is the only case where this threat was real. Second, it was the ineffectiveness—of the incumbent regime and what was feared from the allegedly irresponsible populist rival—that accounted for much of the military's decision to intercede. Third, and most important for the strategies of reform, it has been convincingly demonstrated that intervention is likely only after the military is convinced that there is enough unity within its own ranks and among "acceptable" civilian groups with respect to the necessity and advisability of such action. Meticulous case studies of the coup d'etat process, most particularly the work of Guillermo O'Donnell (1973, 1978) for Argentina, John S. Fitch (1977) for Ecuador, Arturo Valenzuela (1978) for Chile, an Alfred Stepan (1971) for Brazil, reveal that the military goes through an elaborate behind-the-scenes consultation and soul-searching routine to ensure that a consensus exists. The obvious implication is that support for the regime by a major political-economic group (other than the party or parties in power, of course) can be a major deterrent, if not an automatic veto, on the decision to go ahead with military intervention.

Concerning why certain opposition groups resorted to the appeal for military intervention as their form of political retaliation against reformist or centrist governments, it is of course necessary to specify which groups were so disposed. In Peru, APRA, although it had provided the major legislative obstruction to Belaúnde prior to the economic crisis of 1967–1968, had the most to lose from military intervention; it therefore collaborated with the government in its last-ditch effort to resolve the economic crisis that ultimately brought on the military coup. The appeals for military intervention came instead from industrialists, from the commercial and banking sectors, and from the conservative UNO political group that had been left isolated when APRA allied itself with Belaúnde.

In Argentina the appeal to the barracks during Frondizi's regime came tacitly from opposition political parties (who demanded his resignation as a condition for supporting the government after Frondizi's party lost the 1962 by-elections to the Peronists), as well as from the major business organizations. When Illia was president, political groupings (including Frondizi's) isolated from Illia's minority government called for a preemptive strike against the Peronists. As O'Donnell (1978, p. 163) notes, the same "major business organizations" that urged Frondizi's overthrow called for Illia's removal as well.

In each of these cases the economic and political fortunes of the wealthy segments of the population were jeopardized more by the political movement threatening to win than by the incumbent regime. First, with the looming threat of government takeover by a civilian group widely seen as disdainful of democratic practice, the adherence to constitutionality by the reformer was far less a positive consideration to the groups opposing the rise of Peronists in Argentina or Apristas in Peru. This accounts for the fact that Illia and Belaúnde, the two leaders most intent upon following constitutional procedure to the letter,[2] were vulnerable to the opposition's charge that they were paving the way for the destruction of the very democracy they claimed to represent. Since no long tradition of unbroken democratic rule was at stake, advocating yet another overthrow of an ineffective civilian government was not as momentous as it would have been, for instance, in Chile. In the Argentine and Peruvian cases legitimacy was more strongly linked to perceived effectiveness than to democratic practice.

Second, since they could not predict the future radicalism of the Peruvian military and the chaos of the Argentina in the decade of the 1970s, these groups probably believed that they had little to lose from the overthrow of governments that had not offered them opportunities for meaningful influnce.[3] The only way these groups representing higher-income segments could have shared political power was to unite with an elected or militarily imposed regime, because they could not marshal electoral support for their own candidates. Yet Belaúnde, Frondizi, and particularly Illia all adhered to a notion of narrow party partisanship, according to which the president had no obligation to seek political or economic counsel from other political groups or lobbies. This disdain for alliance left the opposition with few qualms about calling for the ouster of an aloof government.

One common element of the opposition's strategy against all of the reformist regimes pursuing redistribution for any length of time was the effort to create an image of ineffective government. Rather than emphasize the danger of the regime's excesses (which was the opposition's primary promotional tactic against the populists), the opponents of reformist redistribution tried to depict the government as confused, indecisive, and incapable of maintaining the overall health of the economy. Of course, the relative temperance of the reformist's program is less amenable to criticisms of excess than other programs, but it is also difficult to detect the progress actually made by the reformist. This was most notably the case for Illia and Belaúnde, who were ousted by military officers who believed themselves to be more reformist than the regime they deposed.

What lessons are to be drawn from the fact that the appeal to the coup was so common in spite of the relative mildness of the reformist's program? First, the theoretical or "logical" advantage the reformists derived from operating within constitutionality was very weak in the era when more ominous movements appeared to be on the verge of success. Mildness of government action is no guarantee of mildness of opposition reaction. Being democratic and even-handed is not enough. In particular, the reformist needs allies from among the groups to whom the military looks for signals of the advisability of intervention. Because this may well mean cultivating the support of higher-income groups, the reformist must balance his noble desire to equalize the burden of redistribution with the infeasibility of attempting redistribution without powerful allies. It is not necessary to have the support of *all* higher-income groups to forestall military intervention and to undertake reforms, and this is an important source of strength for reformist attempts at redistribution.

Our cases also establish the central importance of the image of effectiveness. Undoubtedly the inept appearance of the reformists was partially determined by factors outside their control. The era of the 1960s was a poor one for pursuing less than radical strategies. It is a commonplace that the Alliance for Progress decade was marked by rapidly rising aspirations throughout Latin America, in terms of both growth and redistribution. The possibilites that the demands of lower-income groups would exceed the capacities of reformist strategies, and that business-sector expectations of rapid growth would be similarly disappointed, were very much a part of the Latin American climate of the time.

Nevertheless, the reformist has some control over perceptions of ineffectiveness. Less exaggerated promises would have had some impact on rising expectations, and would certainly have made modest progress less embarrassing. For example, it was not politically essential for Belaúnde to say in 1966 that a devaluation was not only unneces-sary, it would also be treasonous. Frei did not have to promise—and loudly publicize—land and housing reforms of such magnitude that their fulfillment was beyond financial feasibility even under the most optimistic scenarios. More devotion to the details of policymaking undoubtedly would have improved Belaúnde's image of not really caring about economic constraints.

It seems almost obvious that effectiveness, in the reformist's delicate position between promoting change and conserving the basic institu-tional framework, requires careful calibration—perhaps more so than for the authoritarian populists or radicals. However, the reformists' potential advantage of operating an understandable or predictable economy was enjoyed only by Illia and Frei. The widespread percep-tion during the Illia years that nothing was being done came about because nothing wrenching was done. Illia came off as a "do-nothing," but he avoided the acute disequilibrium that forced his predecessor Frondizi to abandon his progressive program altogether. Frondizi's massive early wage increases, whether cynically designed to be infla-tionary or not, certainly had this effect. Frei, despite his grand rhetoric, was the master of piecemeal change. His progress in social service spending, formulated and financed in bits and pieces, was certainly disappointing to those whose aspirations had been roused. It was also what kept the Chilean economy from veering into hyperinflation, depression, or agricultural collapse. Without the rhetoric, the progress made certainly would have been more appreciated and perhaps more politically potent.

It is important to keep in mind, then, that the image of decisiveness and effectiveness is not equivalent to the image of boldness and commitment to ambitious change. Highly publicized, sweeping steps not only forewarn and mobilize opposition, they also make it difficult for the policymaker to achieve his proclaimed goals. Belaúnde, Frei, and Frondizi showed no lack of wide-ranging objectives; nonetheless their effectiveness was widely questioned. When their ambitious plans could no longer be followed and a reversal in direction was necessary, they appeared to be vacillating rather than pursuing a decisive and well-calibrated strategy.

We can elaborate these general points by reviewing how the reform-ists wielded the primary policy instruments of their redistributive efforts. Their most common vehicles of redistribution were wage policy, social service spending, and tax reform. These measures were applied quite differently from one regime to another, permitting us to isolate some successful strategies and tactics.

WAGES AND CONFRONTATION

Frei and Frondizi used the general wage adjustment as the major pillar of redistribution. In contrast to Perón's subtler policy of support for or against union positions in hundreds of labor-management negotiations, the emphasis on general wage adjustments was the most open, ambitious, and direct appeal for working-class support; the most direct exposure of how far the government thought it could go; and the most blatant statement of distribution, whether progressive or not. Illia and Belaúnde did not use the general wage adjustment as a redistributive instrument, preferring instead to allow unions and management to set private-sector wage levels, though within parameters set more or less indirectly by government credit policy. These variations highlight the flexibility of choice of redistributive vehicle, and specifically that an "obvious" instrument like general wage adjustment is in fact optional. Even within the same country—Argentina—one reformist chose to emphasize general wage adjustments and the other did not.

The use of general wage adjustments to improve workers' real wages had four effects, none of them fortuitous for the government. The pattern occurred not only under Frei and Frondizi with respect to both public-sector and private-sector workers, but under Illia and Belaúnde with respect to public-sector workers whose wages had to be set through government policy. First, with no viable price-control policy, inflation ate away at initial wage gains. Second, no matter how well calibrated the general wage adjustment itself may have been, wage increases above this guideline undermined the planned balance of labor costs, consumer demand, and prices. Third, the real-income gains granted to workers covered by general wage adjustment regulations were not credited to the generosity of the government, but were perceived as labor's victory over government opposition. Finally, the government did not satisfy labor. The level of confrontation of unions and government was steadily high, regardless of the real-income gains, and the struggle for the control of labor complicated the calibration of wage-increase demands that could produce real-wage gains.

What is the political dynamic underlying this pattern? When wage-level determination comes to be controlled, partially or wholly, by the government, the demands of labor leaders become confrontational. The involvement of the government makes wage issues more political. When a labor leader heads an organization competitive with the government party's own organization, it becomes politically costly for the labor leader to accept the government's wage adjustment, no matter how fair it may be. The government gets the credit if a wage adjustment is perceived as generous; the reactions to wage adjustments deemed inadequate—often general strikes—can easily mar the "performance" of the government in operating the economy.

This test of strength is even more pronounced because the impact of wage-policy decisions, if general wage adjustments are involved, is so broad and so public that the leadership of organized labor cannot afford to sit by without reacting. Wage adjustments are not sufficiently segmented, and are certainly not sufficiently esoteric, to escape the glare of public awareness.

It could be argued, of course, that public awareness is precisely what the redistributive-minded reformist requires to cultivate support; surely this has been a prime motivation behind general wage adjustments. Yet the limited gratitude of organized labor brings into question whether rallying support is worth the costs of raising aspirations and triggering opposition. This crucial issue is treated in some detail in my concluding chapter.

If wage increases were an indispensable element of successful redistribution, the above conclusions would be distressing indeed. However, the very status of wage policy as a redistributive instrument, even aside from the technical and political obstacles, is highly problematic for devloping countries.

The primary limitation lies in the fact that it is not only extremely difficult to effect real-income changes by raising wages, it is also unlikely that real-wage increases will have a positive impact on the incomes of the poor in a developing country like Chile or Peru. Argentina—which is unusual by virtue of its labor scarcity, relatively small rural population, and more predominant modern sector—is in a different situation.

As long as the distinction between "income from labor" and "income from capital" is presumed to reflect the income differential between workers and owners, relative wage levels seem to represent the balance between the rich and the poor. This differentiation is at least somewhat misleading, even in countries at Argentina's level of development and beyond, where highly paid corporate executives and employed professionals receive the bulk of their earnings in the form of wages.[4] It is more fundamentally misleading for developing countries, in which the poorest segments of the population—the landowning peasantry and the urban unemployed—do not derive their incomes from wages. The majority of wages go to organized white-collar and blue-collar workers in the modern (high-technology, high-productivity) sectors and in government, and they are usually in the top half of the income pyramid.

Because of the dual-sector nature of most Latin American economies, incomes of the largely urban, modern sector are far higher than incomes of the largely rural, traditional sector. Transfers of income within the modern sector due to higher real wages of the workers covered by minimum wage regulations and wage covenants end up having little impact on redistributing income to the very poor. Workers in industry, mining, transport, government, communications, and other largely "modern" activities may be poorer than their employers, but they are usually far better off than the self-employed who till tiny farm plots, push carts through the city streets, shine shoes, or sell jars of herbs. In Chile in 1968, for example, of the fifth of the total work force designated as self-employed (*trabajadores por cuenta propia*), less than half earned more than the *sueldo vital* (the benchmark salary for white-collar workers) (ODEPLAN 1971, pp. 45–46).

To be sure, the wages of the landless peasantry, and of small farmers who work for others as well because their own land is too small to sustain full-time work, are a valid reflection of the incomes of at least one segment of the very poor. Yet quite often, particularly prior to the mid-1960s, agricultural wages were explicitly excluded from wage-setting legislation. Even in the 1970s, as Richard Webb (1974, p. 4) points out with reference to developing countries in general, "most wage policy, in practice, applies to urban and modern sector workers only. A discussion of rural wage policy is therefore more an examination of what ought to be than of what exists." Likewise, the wages of workers employed in tiny operations of the informal sector are often either excluded from wage legislation or present insurmountable obstacles of enforcement. Consequently, the issue of wages has generally been the question of how to divide resources within the modern urban sector. This is certainly a matter of redistribution, but where there is a large impoverished traditional sector, it has only indirect consequences for the very poor.

Even these indirect consequences of modern-sector wage increases tend to harm rather than help the very poor. Higher wages for middle-income workers raise the prices of some of the goods that the poor have to purchase, and lower the willingness of employers to hire more workers. Politically, wage increases may "use up" the redistributive capacity of a regime predisposed to accomplishing some income redistribution.

It is worth recalling that even under Juan Perón, the redistribution-ist most closely associated with industrial workers, the major redistribu-tive effects benefiting the poor were not those that provided higher wages to the already privileged industrial working class. Rather, they were the elevation of previously unorganized and low-paid industrial workers to a newly privileged status (in postwar Chile and Peru the industrial workers were already privileged in contrast to agricultural workers and small-plot farmers), the expansion of this industrial-worker sector at the expense of the grain and beef producers, and, finally, the provision of full employment. If a large pool of unemployed had remained, or if masses of peasants had remained in the countryside, the maintenance of high wages for organized workers would have had regressive rather than progressive impacts.

This disconcerting assessment of the redistributive potential of wage policy is, fortunately, not the whole story. If wage policy focuses on raising the nominal wages of workers currently covered by governmental wage regulation (for example, via the typical general wage adjustment), it is unlikely to be either effective or beneficial to progressive redistribution. But if wage policy focuses on expanding the coverage of wage regulations, the dynamic is profoundly changed.

Although at any point in time there is a rather clear distinction between wage earners covered by governmental wage regulations and everyone else,[5] over time the coverage can be extended. Granting inclusion to formerly excluded segments of the work force is a bona fide way of elevating poorly paid workers to a substantially higher income level. Expansion of the coverage of the minimum wage is progressive, although raising the real level of the minimum is likely to be regressive insofar as it provokes the substitution of capital for labor by employers faced with higher labor costs. Reducing the minimum number of employees a firm must have to be obligated by official wage guidelines, as long as such actions do not stimulate layoffs to avoid coming under the regulations, would have the same progressive effects.

SPENDING AND TAXING

If even the adept reformist was not notably successful in cultivating the support of organized labor, he was able to gain the cooperation of crucial parts of the middle sectors in the progressive expansion of social service spending. In particular, he allied himself with those middle-sector service providers who stood to benefit from increased spending in the areas of housing, health, and particularly education. Obviously, such alliances lead to outcomes that do not meet the standards of thorough equity: there is no basis in equity for one middle-income group to benefit from governmental policy over another. Moreover, there is the danger of increasingly greater leakage to middle-income groups of benefits originally targeted for the poor, as Frei's experience with public housing amply demonstrated. As a matter of fact, our cases provide no examples of social service expansion without benefits to at least one higher-income group.

Measurement of the success of directing benefits to the poor through the budget must be tempered by considerations of the deficit. A significant increase in social service spending by itself is a hazardous and inadequate way of redistributing income, for the simple reason that the lack of corresponding increase in revenues can ultimately force the imposition of stabilization programs or even the overturn of the government, as occurred most graphically in Peru when Belaúnde was ousted. Coupled with the fact that there is no better way of undermining the government's image of effectiveness than to leave it without sufficient funds for its own programs, the natural antagonism toward increased taxation expressed by representatives of middle-income groups has often led to the denial of revenue sources for new expenditures, even if such expenditures were supported by large legislative margins. Revenue generation is part of the problem of social service spending expansion, not a separate issue.

The prospect for raising taxes proved to be better than one might expect considering the extractive nature of taxation and the fact that tax legislation had to go through the public display of legislative consideration. However, improvements in taxing capacity did not emerge along the commonly accepted lines of stronger emphasis on coherence and substitution of direct for indirect taxation. The need to form legislative coalitions dictated more tentative progress. A union of tax-system rationalizers and redistributionists is possible for forcing consideration of tax reform, but it is unlikely that the two sides will agree on the nature of the changes. The most successful tax changes, in terms of their contribution to redistribution, have been the piecemeal additions, earmarked for social service expenditures, that passed through the legislature with the support of social service providers. Indirect taxes, long maligned by the purists as necessarily less progressive than direct taxes,[6] are often more equitable in practice, because many direct taxes such as those on income and property, can be evaded. "Tax reform" initially may be put on the agenda through the coalition of redistributionists seeking higher taxes and tax-system rationalizers seeking greater coherence. But if the rationalizers continue to view progress as the development of an elegantly simple fiscal system based on direct taxes, they will be disappointed when the coalition-seeking reformist has to turn to earmarked taxes to develop enough support.

The more successful ploys by clever reformists like Frei imply that just because a reformist operates in a liberal democratic framework does not mean that each of his policy measures is or ought to be subjected to public scrutiny tantamount to a plebiscite. Clarity, when it mobilizes a powerful opposition, is counterproductive. Frei, particularly in the first half of his tenure, kept the opposition constantly off guard; yet when he was unambiguous in his intentions, his policies drew more opposition than support. Where Frei seemed to be groping, as in the progression of half-defeated tax measures, he succeeded. Illia, by circumstance rather than design, took the image of fumbling to such lengths that the economic opposition was hardly mobilized, although the political opposition capitalized on this representation by convincing the military that intervention was necessary. Certainly it is not the ineptness that is essential for success, but rather the lack of clarity which fails to signal the potential opposition what redistributive policies might accomplish.

This raises a philosophical question. Are elections per se, and adherence to legal procedures, sufficient to discharge the responsibility of an elected official to openness and responsiveness to the popular will, on the grounds that following constitutional rules fulfills all obligations that the constitution's authors deemed necessary?

According to all Latin American constitutions, certain policies must be formulated openly, inasmuch as the Congress controls specified parts of the policymaking process such as the formulation of tax and budgetary instruments. This may be construed as an institutional commitment to a certain degree of policy-formulation openness, but it is a self-discharging commitment. The same constitutional specifications contribute to meeting this responsibility to openness, since they ensure that some policy formulation will take place in such open forums as the legislature.

There would seem to be no valid basis for protesting redistributive effort through instruments of less open formulation if the officials involved do not violate constitutional rules. Objections would have to be based on an abstract argument that openness, beyond that which is mandated by the constitution, is desirable. Given the evidence gathered in this study to the effect that openness of formulation may be seriously detrimental to the success of redistribution, openness can hardly be justified as a tactic. If the economic well-being of the poor is a fundamental concern, it is difficult to argue that openness beyond what is constitutionally required ought to be regarded as a principle of higher moral order than progressive redistribution.

THE IMPORTANCE OF CONTEXT

The success of the reformist, because he works within the boundaries of established institutions, is particularly sensitive to the limitations and opportunities of the institutional structure. For this reason the redistribution-minded reformist has to be more aware of the terrain of the policymaking process than the radicals or authoritarians who strive to change this structure. It is tempting to underrate the importance of institutional arrangements, on the grounds that they reflect basic power relationships, which are therefore the more appropriate focus of explanation. Since the powerful can alter institutions as well as policies, it may be argued, why not concentrate exclusively on "who has power and why" instead of on the more tedious questions of "what are the mechanisms through which their attempts must be channeled?"

Yet for the reformist—and even for leaders with less commitment to existing institutional arrangements—these institutions have a persistence that obviates continual adjustment of intrainstitutional power balances in response to changes in the overall power balance. Rules and habits take time to change. This is also an important shortcoming of the assumption that political power, defined as a broad measure of capability, predetermines the success of redistributive attempts. Political power outside the specific policymaking process—in the abstract, as it were—does not translate straightforwardly to power within that process. Institutional advantages for one group or another may be present within the arrangements in ways that are not congruent with the existing distribution of power.

The institutional arrangements in Chile and Peru, particularly the balance of power between the executive and Congress, were very important in setting the bounds of redistribution under Frei and Belaúnde. Frei inherited an executive-legislative structure in which the executive was dominant. This was not because of Frei's popularity or the political strength of the centrists at the moment, nor even because of the power of the "interclass alliance" supporting him, but rather because the Ibáñez dictatorship of 1927–1931 put an end to the Parliamentary Era by strengthening presidential power enormously. Belaúnde, in contrast, faced a far more powerful legislature, not because his support was weak, but because of powers vested in the Peruvian Congress by the 1933 constitution and the success of the 1945 Congress in reversing the 1939 plebiscite outcome that gave the president veto power. Through the same constitutional occurrences decades before his administration, Belaúnde was saddled with a legislature safe from electoral pressures for the same term as his.

Of course, even a reformist can try to change the institutional structure; and all did try in either major or minor ways. Both Frei and Belaúnde attempted to alter congressional-executive relations as well as the basic power of the state to control the economy (as in the case of the constitutional amendments concerning expropriation of property without immediate cash compensation). However, efforts to change institutions tend to be more provocative than efforts to change policies because future outcomes on other, as yet unspecified issues are involved. The fundamental challenge for the reformist is to steer through the existing institutional framework with enough understanding and guile to achieve progressive ends without destroying the system. During the 1960s this was a difficult task indeed, but it may be easier in the current era of lower expectations and at least partial discrediting of the more radical approaches.

IV

THE RADICALS

THE EMERGENCE OF RADICAL regimes in a number of Latin American nations in the late 1960s and early 1970s can be linked to their prior experiences with reformism. However, it would be misleading to conclude that the shift to an approach rejected by the reformists themselves signified the failure of reformism. While the appearance of radical regimes in countries like Peru and Chile certainly reflected a measure of frustration with the less radical efforts preceding them, the reformist record has to be assessed in light of two additional considerations.

First, reformism did not give way to radicalism in all cases; reformists in Venezuela and Colombia continued to contend with less reform-minded centrists rather than yielding power to radicals. The inevitability of the demise of reformist efforts is by no means established.

Second, even where radical regimes followed reform regimes, the reformists' successes, as much as their failures, contributed to the rise of radicalism. Where progressive reforms simply failed to make good on the promises of the reformists, leading to greater impatience and support for extreme solutions, it is of course justifiable to speak of the failure of reform. But the creation of higher aspirations must also be taken into account: reformist efforts that produced their intended changes could and often did create demands and expectations of further change. The success of reformist efforts in producing concrete results can make fundamental change seem more feasible; radical change can be seen as an extension or escalation of prior reforms rather than a repudiation of the reformist experience. This does not mean, of course, that reformist attempts which trigger the victories of more radical regimes constitute political success for the unseated reformist; he will get little consolation from progressive achievements that contribute to his own demise. Nevertheless, the failure of a regime to stay in power, even if it is overturned through coup d'etat or revolution, does not necessarily signify the failure of the regime's efforts in the realm of economics or social justice.

In short, the rise of radical regimes in Latin America stemmed from a mixture of rising expectations spurred by some reformist success and frustration because of the limits to that success.

Although the radical impulse was very strong in all three countries examined in this study, it was expressed in very different ways. In Chile the Marxists had long been a well-established political force in electoral politics, accepted as a legitimate contender in partisan politics, although their acceptability as a winner was the key untested issue. In Peru, where well-articulated ideological leftism had never been very strong, it was the military under General Velasco that formulated its own version of radical transformation of the country, with all the expected ambivalences related to mobilizing a rather passive population while still maintaining discipline. Argentina's radical impulse, like everything else in that country, was cast in the shadow of Perón; the radical program articulated by stand-in president Hector Cámpora reflected the views of part of the Peronist Left, while the critique of Peronist policy reflected the views of those who rejected Peronism's perceived betrayal of leftist principles. Because the radicals within the Peronist movement soon lost out in the competition to define the economic approach of the government, there was no significant period of radical economic policy in Argentina.

CHAPTER 11
Collapse in Chile

B ETWEEN 1970 AND 1973 Salvador Allende in Chile undertook the most extreme redistributive effort of the three countries we are examining. It was a brave, and in many ways an exhilarating, period. It was also an economic and political catastrophe, resulting in an extremely bloody military takeover, political repression, and regresive economic policies that are still in force today. Allende's three years have been meticulously analyzed and documented, and yet a bitter controversy persists over the lessons of his rule. Interpretations of the Allende period fall into two rough categories: those which maintain the inevitability of Allende's downfall, and those which claim that particular decisions taken along the way explain why the experiment turned into disaster. Theorists committed to the idea that rapid and profound economic transformation cannot be carried out within the established political framework argue that the Chilean case only confirms that economic revolution requires political revolution, particularly when the existing structure is backed by the United States. Other theorists maintain that a democratic transformation to socialism can succeed if it is not carried out with excessive rapidity, or carried to excess. These analysts assert that the Allende objectives were feasible, the tactics in error.[1]

The perspective adopted here is that Allende's conduct of economic policy prevented a fair test of his positions. Whether the vested interests of the status quo ante system would have been willing and able to topple the constitutional regime if the government had adopted a more carefully planned economic strategy, and had avoided some of its obvious political mistakes, remains essentially unanswered. An analysis of how the Allende program unraveled is nonetheless critical for understanding the concrete mechanisms—the proximate causes—of the failure.

Nothing in this analysis is meant to imply that economic issues were more important than political issues, or that Chile did not experience a clash between radically different ideologies. The confrontation was

indeed of high importance; many of the "economic" actions taken by
the various actors were politically motivated, and many of the reactions
to economic policy were triggered not just by the content of the policy
but also by the fact that it was the Allende regime enacting them. The
emphasis of this chapter on the economic side of the Allende experience is meant to highlight how the formulation of economic policy
exacerbated the political conflict and undermined the coalition that
Allende hoped to forge with a broad enough alliance of economic
sectors to stave off the political opposition.

   Two questions concerning Allende's conduct of economic policy are
vital to an understanding of the economic and political collapse. The
first is why the administration lost the support of domestic industrialists and the "petit bourgeoisie," who had been courted and favored
in Allende's electoral campaign and early policies. Perhaps the most
important feature of the Allende experience that made it conceivable
that his objectives could have been achieved was the initial support,
albeit tentative, that Allende was offered by middle-class sectors.
Retrospective analyses, focusing on the ultimate class polarization that
was so evident by 1973, tend to ignore the strength of Allende's initial
position. Yet the vehement opposition of this sector during Allende's
last year shattered any remaining chance that the government could
reverse either the economic decline or the extreme political polarization.

   The economic decline of the middle sectors is easy to document. It is
harder to explain why the government allowed the decline to go so far.
If the income redistribution under Allende is judged in terms of the
targets set by his own economic team, it becomes painfully clear that too
much was accomplished in too short a period. The Allende planners
intended to increase the share of national income going to wage and
salary earners from 51 percent to 60.7 percent, or 9.7 percent more of
the total GDP. In fact, their share of domestic income went up 11
percent in 1971 alone! In light of this extremely abrupt change, it is not
surprising that the income shift was "accompanied by sizable disequilibria in the balance of payments, and increases in the fiscal deficit
and the deficits of the enterprises in the area of social ownership of the
economy. At the same time there [was] a downturn in investment"
(Foxley and Muñoz 1976, p. 144). To these already awesome problems
one must add the inflation rate, which rose from 20 percent in 1971 to
78 percent in 1972 and 235 percent in January–August 1973, before
the military coup (Stallings 1978, p. 247).

   Table 13 summarizes the distributional impacts of the Allende
program. Even with the increase in industrial production[2]—a
straightforward result of higher demand generated by much higher

TABLE 13. MACROECONOMIC TRENDS IN CHILE UNDER
SALVADOR ALLENDE, 1970–1973.

Year	Index of minimum agricultural wage (1968 = 100)	Index of industrial remuneration (1968 = 100)	Index of industrial production (1968 = 100)	Inflation (annual consumer price increases) (percent)
1969	97.9	104.6	104.2	30.7
1970	118.5	113.4	104.0	32.5
1971	164.3	144.0	119.3	20.1
1972	177.4	149.6	122.6	77.8
1973 (8 mo)	120.5	117.4	115.2	235.2

SOURCE: Stallings 1978; pp. 247, 250, 253.

wage levels—the effective scarcities of goods for the middle sectors grew dramatically in 1972 and exploded in 1973. Many lower-income individuals who previously had been out of the market for beef, consumer durables, and other products were in a position to purchase these items by 1971. Long lines and emptied shops were a reality, with a profound impact on those who previously had counted on the availability of these goods. The fact that there was no "shortage" compared to the previous supply was hardly a solace to the middle sectors. Whether or not total production was higher, the sacrifices that Allende had promised would be reserved for the big monopolists were experienced also by middle-income families in their inability to buy in 1972 what they had been able to buy previously.

These economic consequences of the unplanned abruptness of the redistribution had a shattering effect upon the shopkeepers, truckers, and other self-employed, small-scale operators whose support was essential for keeping the right-wing opposition at bay. It was not the degree of redistribution per se that could be faulted, but rather the disintegration of the economy, and of the relations among political groups, resulting in part from the rapidity of the redistribution.

The second question concerning Allende's economic policy is why the administration's investment strategy, designed to avoid the usual syndrome of disinvestment and inflation generated by rapid state-sector expansion and progressive redistribution, failed so miserably. The reactivation of the economy in 1971 provided what seemed to be the opportunity for an economic expansion that could have combined higher consumption with higher investment and productivity—ideal circumstances for reducing, or even eliminating, the pain and political strain of redistribution. Of course, the disaffection of the middle sectors is one answer. However, the investment response of the state sector (Table 14) was even more disappointing than the expected decline of private investment.

The reasons lie primarily in Allende's lack of control over the political groups that favored redistribution, and in the absence of technical competence of the economic policymakers. To be sure, the political opposition and the threatened economic elite spared no opportunity to undermine Allende's policies. Yet this was fully anticipated by the government, which had designed its investment model to overcome the disinvestment of the "economic oligarchy." The crushing blow came with the loss of middle-sector support, which accompanied the sharp economic deprivation of this segment beginning in late 1971. The economic decline, in turn, was an unintended consequence of poor calibration, the failure of the state sector to maintain savings and investment, and the attack on the rectitude of the bourgeoisie by the more radical elements of the Unidad Popular coalition.

Although the state sector was supposed to offset the disinvestment of the private entrepreneur, without control state investment declined in the face of large wage increases given to state employees. And the pace of economic change was far more rapid than the government had anticipated, leading to a rapid deterioration of the middle sector's income shares in the face of unexpectedly high inflation. While this was partly a result of poor planning and of the Right's actions to cut off moderate options, it was exacerbated by the pressure by the left wing of the Unidad Popular to transform the economic system as rapidly as possible. Leftist forces, as much as the opposition, goaded Allende into accelerating the pace of economic change beyond the tolerance of the economy.

TABLE 14. FIXED INVESTMENT IN CHILEAN INDUSTRY
(MILLIONS OF 1965 ESCUDOS).

Year	State	Private
1969	315	262
1970	350	260
1971	373	93
1972	219	39
1973 (8 mo)	192	21

SOURCE: Stallings 1978, p. 248.

THE BACKGROUND

Although previous chapters detail much of the background pertinent to Allende's administration, the election of 1970 and the nature of the Unidad Popular coalition are also important. These factors left the administration poorly prepared to handle the technical aspects of economic policymaking and the political aspects of coalition bargaining.

POLITICAL ASPECTS

The 1970 election was a three-candidate contest in which the right-wing contender, former president Jorge Alessandri, was thought to be the strongest. The Christian Democratic candidate, Radomiro Tomic, was a champion of the left wing of his party, reflecting the party's disillusionment with Frei's Revolution in Liberty; his positions were so close to those of the Unidad Popular that the Christian Democrats and the UP were widely expected to split the support from the electoral Left, leaving Alessandri with the Center and the Right.

The fact that these election predictions were wrong—Allende gained a plurality of 36.6 percent, compared to 28.1 percent for Tomic and 35.3 percent for Alessandri—explains in part why the Unidad Popular team (that is, those advising Allende and those likely to be given high-level governmental positions in the event of his election) failed to develop economic plans prior to its victory. It was certainly not for lack of capability, since the "economic cabinet" of the Allende administration comprised respected university economists engaged in teaching, research, and writing at Chile's prestigious national university and at several of the economic research institutes of international reputation.

The Unidad Popular coalition consisted of the large Communist and Socialist parties, the modest Radical party, and various smaller groups. Although the first two parties had long histories as separate entities, the alliances within the Unidad Popular coalition were far more complicated than the competition between these two dominant members; cross-party alliances were in fact more important. The Communist party, more cautious and even more conservative ideologically than the Socialists, lined up with the moderate wing of the Socialist party, including Allende himself. The rest of the Socialist party, led by Senator Carlos Altamirano, did not formally include the far-left MIR (Leftist Revolutionary Movement), but the MIR usually backed the radical faction of the Socialist party in its confrontations with the government. The MIR's tolerance of the Allende government was shaky at best, despite the fact that the regime was further to the Left than any of its predecessors. Many MIR activists were prepared to defy any government operating within the liberal-democratic framework.

Allende's narrow plurality in the election was matched by the Unidad Popular's position in Congress. The 1969 congressional elections had left the Unidad Popular with 61 of 150 deputies and 19 of 50 senators;[3] after the 1971 congressional elections the Unidad Popular accounted for 57 of the deputies and 17 of the senators. The Unidad Popular thus faced a majority opposition (since the Christian Democrats generally sided with the right-wing National party legislators); but the opposition lacked the two-thirds majority in the Chamber of Deputies to override presidential vetoes.

ECONOMIC ASPECTS

President Eduardo Frei had left the Chilean economy in a mixed state. The government's foreign reserves were very high, at U.S. $343 million, because of high world copper prices and high production levels. Moreover, two additional huge copper mines (Andina and Exótica) began production just in time for the Allende regime, more than making up for the declining production of the three old major deposits and largely offsetting the decline in world copper prices after Allende took office.

On the other hand, the domestic economy itself was in recession, due to the stabilization program that Frei had implemented and the business sector's reaction to Allende's election. Therefore an immediate problem of the Allende government was to reactivate the economy. In the short run, this was a great advantage, because it provided the administration the opportunity to apply "Keynesian" rationales and policies of higher government spending, credit expansion, and wage increases that were also politically popular. In the long run, however, the opportunity proved to be fatal. The administration found it impossible to restrain expansionary measures once they were launched.

ALLENDE'S INITIATIVES

Although the drama of the Allende years was dominated by the issue of nationalization[4]—the conversion of privately owned firms to state ownership—other aspects of economic policy were equally important (in highly interrelated ways) in determining distributional changes and political reactions.

WAGE POLICY

The approach to reactivation adopted by the Allende planners was, essentially, to increase the incomes of wage and salary earners. The formulation of wage policy, however, involved three levels. First, the government had to decide on the role of its representatives on the tripartite arbitration boards responsible for resolving collective bargaining wage disputes. The decisions of these boards were important in establishing the parameters of wage negotiations even if the unions had the option of rejecting them. If a strike was declared illegal because the union refused to accept the board's decision, the union's leadership and members faced the possibility of legal reprisals that significantly worsened the union's bargaining position (Angell 1972, pp. 75–76). Under Frei, governmental representatives on the boards typically pressured for wage restraint, particularly during the three years preceding Allende. Under Allende, however, the government representatives on the arbitration boards backed the workers' demands.

Second, the calculation of official wage adjustments was to be made through a formula that would increase workers' real wages.[5] The administration granted cost-of-living adjustments equal to the previous year's inflation rate. Since the inflation rate in 1970 had been higher than the rate for 1971 (35 percent vs 22 percent), this meant a very substantial increase in real wages, with even higher adjustments for workers earning less than twice the minimum salary.[6] Frei, we remember, had also decreed cost-of-living adjustments pegged to the previous year's inflation rate, where this rate was higher than that of the effective year. An important difference, however, is that the Frei planners relied almost exclusively on this differential in inflation to provide real-income increases for wage earners, whereas under Allende this adjustment was in addition to other increases (such as the adjustment for the low-income groups, the even larger minimum-wage increase, and government support for the unions in collective bargaining), without any evidence of attempts at careful calibration.

Third, the administration had to formulate a wage-policy position for the growing state sector. When Allende took office the public sector already accounted for over 13 percent of the country's total employment (ODEPLAN 1971, p. 69), and nationalization promised to increase this proportion dramatically. Therefore the trends in public-sector wages had not only their obvious implications for the budget, but also a very strong effect on overall wage rates. Moreover, the state sector under the Allende administration was supposed to provide the investment increases that the private sector could not be expected to provide; wage levels within the state enterprises were thus important in determining how much reinvestable profit would be left over after the state employees had been paid.

Despite the danger of higher wages eating into the investable capital of state enterprises, the Allende administration did not intend to restrain public-sector wages as Frei had attempted to do. This was a pivotal decision. The administration decided to forego the opportunity to control state-sector wages to offset the negative effects of other aspects of governmental economic policy, in order to extend to state employees the same income increases going to private-sector workers. This decision reflected the Unidad Popular's alliance strategy—to maintain the loyalty of bureaucrats and skilled state workers—rather than its commitment to progresive redistribution, for the state-sector workers were better off than many private-sector employees or self-employed workers.

These wage policies did not discriminate to any significant degree against higher-income employees. Allende was very explicit that the wage policy was designed to cement the alliance among wage and salary earners (including professionals and bureaucrats) of all income levels. Minister of Finance Orlando Millas argued that "everything that the People's Government has done has resulted in higher living standards and better possibilities for the . . . middle sectors. And we will continue with these policies since all revolutionary processes get strengthened precisely through the alliance between the working class and the middle strata."[7] Thus it was not an attempt to redistribute income from white-collar to blue-collar workers (*empleados* to *obreros*), but rather an attempt to benefit the whole wage-earning and salary-earning sector at the expense of employers.

It is important to note that although Allende and his closest associates intended to maintain the loyalty of the middle sectors, their efforts to enact redistribution without blatant rhetoric were continually undermined by the rhetoric of the far Left, including the main wing of the Socialist party within the Unidad Popular coalition.

PRICE CONTROLS

An important adjunct to wage policy was the regime's commitment to keeping down the prices of basic commodities so that inflation would not reduce the purchasing power of nominal wage gains. Of course, price controls were not new to Chile, but the expansion of the state sector reduced the possibility that the private sector could disregard them. The administration set up state distribution centers, predominantly in working-class areas, to prevent black markets from forming to allocate scarce commodities at higher prices. Finally, violation of price controls was risky for any business that was vulnerable to accusations or even takeovers by its workers. Many factories had worker vigilante committees that watched for any hint of illegality.

PUBLIC SPENDING

Reactivation was the initial rationale for significant increases in government spending. But more fundamentally, the Allende administration was committed to expanding social service programs in order to help economically marginal populations. The specific programs selected were those that could provide jobs, since the open unemployment rate in Santiago prevailing when Allende took office exceeded 8 percent. Major programs in housing, urban sanitation, and irrigation were undertaken. Housing starts for 1971 by the public sector alone were more than triple the total starts in the previous year. Fiscal spending (that is, the national government's spending excluding state enterprises) increased from 19 billion escudos in 1970 to 33 billion in 1971, an increase of more than 70 percent (de Vylder 1976, pp. 55, 61). Moreover, the emphasis on construction, as opposed to other sorts of social service projects, resulted in greater demands for materials, like concrete and wood, which were in relatively short supply.

EXPANDING THE SOCIAL AREA

The government's commitment to socialism was expressed most straightforwardly in its initiatives to extend state ownership to the principal means of production, euphemistically labeled the "Social Area" (Martner 1971, p. 32). When Allende first came to office, the top-priority targets for state takeover were obvious: foreign-owned firms, the largest industrial enterprises, and the banks. To maintain the cooperation of the domestic industrialists, merchants, and small-scale businessmen, Allende proposed to limit the nationalization to firms at the "commanding heights" of the Chilean economy. At the Talca International Fair in March 1971, Allende (1973, pp. 109–110) made it clear that his strategy was to maintain a sharp distinction between big

businesses, multinational corporations, and "monopolists" on the one
hand, and the small to medium businesses on the other:

> When we speak of structural changes and social transformations we are
> planning, we are expressing ideas which are already in the minds of the
> majority of the people of Chile. We know that the programme we have
> initiated damages both national and international interests, both where
> monopolies are concerned and in the field of import and export. At the
> same time we must realize that the programme of Unidad Popular offers
> the soundest and broadest guarantees of security for small- and medium-
> scale industries ... These firms will receive the thoroughgoing and
> powerful support of the Unidad Popular government.

The first initiative was a legislative proposal for the nationalization
of the 253 largest firms, accompanied by guarantees that smaller firms
would not be expropriated. The government's bill did not fare well in
the legislature, because the Christian Democrats introduced their own
legislation, a constitutional amendment calling for congressional approval of each expropriation. The Christian Democratic bill passed,
Allende vetoed it, and the ensuing controversy over whether the
Congress did or did not override this veto effectively blocked the
passage of any substantive new legislation on nationalization.[8] As so
often happens when the legislative avenue is blocked, the administration relied on existing legislation. In this instance it was a 1932 law,
Decreto Ley 520, that permitted the government to requisition or
intervene in companies experiencing difficulties in producing essential
goods. In the politically chaotic Great Depression years a Socialist
republic had reigned for twelve days; Decreto Ley 520 was one of its
creations that was never rescinded.

However, Decreto Ley 520, even if applied sparingly by the Allende
administration, did not specify which firms were subject to nationalization. The administration still could state explicitly which firms or
categories of firms would be subject to expropriation (even without
new legislation such a list was finally announced in 1972), or could
undertake a plebiscite on the issue—but instead it relied on its verbal
references to the "commanding heights of the economy" to reassure
the owners of lesser enterprises. This left the administration with more
flexibility than would be afforded by a list or formula dictating the
firms to be nationalized, and such vagueness may have been politically
convenient for relations within the Unidad Popular (because of differences between the moderate and radical factions over the pace of
transformation). Yet Decreto Ley 520, inasmuch as it was designed as a
means of preventing shortages rather than as a vehicle for permanent

nationalization, exacerbated fears that the administration would undermine the legal basis of the Chilean system. It also left many producers, even those of small or medium scale, fearful of expropriation.

By early 1972 the economic problems brought into question, even inside the government, whether state takeovers should be carried further, and at what speed. Within the ruling coalition the debate over nationalization revolved around the pace of the process. The Communists, the Radicals, and the moderate (Allende) wing of the Socialists argued for gradual nationalization. This was known as the policy of consolidation, for which it was argued that the transformation of the private industrial sector into the "social area" (the state sector) should proceed only as rapidly as was consistent with the simultaneous requirement to consolidate the soundess of already-nationalized firms, in terms of productivity and the adequacy of available investment. Given the finite supply of state-controlled resources at any point in time, these would not be adequate to maintain the investment levels of state industries if the state sector were expanded without first ensuring that previously nationalized industries were contributing to rather than draining away the state's overall resources. Since the changeover from private to state ownership was expected to cause temporary declines in production, in spite of the general policy of retaining the existing management wherever possible, the overall levels of production would suffer if new administrative problems were encountered before the old ones could be resolved. Existing state enterprises were to add to the viability of future state enterprises, not compete with them. The other rationale for the consolidation strategy was encouragement of the rest of the private sector through assurances that nationalization would not extend beyond the "monopolists." The moderates argued that unless nationalization proceeded slowly, and with guarantees to certain sectors that they would not be included, disastrous disinvestment would result.

Not surprisingly, this position was challenged by more radical elements within the Unidad Popular coalition. The radicals argued that the problems facing the country were caused by the coexistence of private and state ownership, rather than by the intrinsic weakness, temporary or otherwise, of state ownership per se. As long as major portions of the means of production remained beyond the direct control of the state, haste was essential for ensuring that the transformation would indeed go through. This was a delicate argument to make publicly; it implied that one could not count on the Left's remaining in power indefinitely, or that Allende and his moderate faction could not be trusted to pursue the total transformation to socialism even under auspicious economic conditions. In private, the Altamirano Socialists mocked the Communists, accusing them of being "bourgeois" at heart.[9]

STATE ENTERPRISE MANAGEMENT

Within the Unidad Popular there were two philosophies, of untested compatibility, concerning the management of the state sector. The centralized planning of the Soviet Union and Eastern Europe was attractive to some, yet the ideas of worker participation and "popular planning" were also in vogue—among Christian Democrats no less than among Unidad Popular supporters.[10] Although there was much talk of the value of coherent planning, the initiatives of the Unidad Popular government were in the direction of worker participation in policymaking. Within state enterprises worker representatives joined "management," ostensibly representing the interests of the state, in decision making at all levels, including the setting of wage levels. Worker representatives, not surprisingly, urged higher wages; management, as we have seen, was under little pressure from the administration to restrain state-sector wage levels more than private-sector increases.

The state sector was given one special policy-implementing role: to restrain inflation by holding down the price levels of state-produced items. This was a clear expression of the tendency to entrust policy objectives to the instruments over which the government presumably had the greatest control.

TAX REFORM

Although the new state enterprises were presumed by many Unidad Popular activists to be immediately self-financing, more sober assessments recognized that expansion of the state sector combined with increased social service spending again required tax increases. Extracting resources from private hands remained an issue even for the socialist economy of Allende, but of course it was a "mixed" rather than a fully socialist economy.

The tax reforms proposed by the Allende government involved simplifying the tax structure—which was expected to eliminate many of the loopholes through which the wealthy avoided taxes—and increasing the progressivity of the tax rates. Because the reforms involved the total tax structure, they were presented as an entity, rather than through piecemeal accompaniments of particular spending programs. The budget and the tax package were submitted together in an effort to force the legislature to meet the financing needs of the government. If the legislature balked, the onus for inadequate taxes would (it was presumed) be laid to the Congress, thus strengthening Allende's position should he call for a plebiscite.

LAND REFORM

The leaders of the Unidad Popular considered their commitment to the peasant to be deeper and more thoroughgoing than Frei's. According to Unidad Popular agricultural authorities (Jacques Chonchol and Rolando Calderón, for instance), the Christian Democrats had left the rural capitalist structure intact, neglected to provide adequate support for even the limited number of land recipients, and created a new agricultural elite through the *asentamiento* (the collective form that gave control and profits to each expropriated estate's former permanent employees) which still excluded the rural landless and minifundistas.

The Unidad Popular program therefore not only concentrated on expropriation (through the use of existing legislation, it turned out), but also on organizing new structures of cooperatives and collectivization, and an enormous flow of government financial support to the agricultural sector. Stefan de Vylder (1976, p. 192) points out that Allende's goal of increasing the number of tractors in the "reformed sector" by 50,000 over five years would have resulted in nearly one tractor for each family in that sector. In emphasizing agriculture's need for investment rather than neglect or outright resource extraction (as had often been the case in the past), the Allende government may have overcompensated, in that heavy resource flows into agriculture meant mechanization and hence lower labor absorption in a sector with a serious problem of underemployment. Whether, and to what extent, this problem may have emerged is not known, because of the shortness of the Allende experiment. It is obvious, however, that the resources poured into agriculture were yet another drain on the resources of the government.

THE INVESTMENT MODEL

The objective of transferring property to the social area was not merely an end in itself (though it was, of course, an important end). A further rationale for nationalization was that the surplus generated by formerly private enterprises could be devoted to the economic development of the country, rather than being diverted to foreign owners or to the foreign bank accounts of the Chilean economic elite. According to this reasoning, the private investment decline triggered by the state's encroachment on the foreign and domestic monopolists would be more than offset by the investments made by the enlarged state sector. Sergio Bitar (1979, p. 106) notes that "the model assumed that profits from the Social Property Sector would compensate for the increase in public spending, thus reducing the inflationary impact of the deficit caused by reactivation and salary increases."

A second source of investment expected to offset the decline of funds from large-scale private enterprise was the small-scale and medium-scale entrepreneur, who was to be reassured by precise definition of the limits of nationalization and wooed by the expanded demand created by the reactivation program.

Finally, the investment program of the Unidad Popular was firmly focused on long-term productivity increases. Aside from the stimulus of the reactivation program, there was no provision for improving productivity in the next one to four years. This was consistent with the "structuralist" view of development, which emphasized the need for infrastructure (from irrigation to housing) and an adequately capitalized agricultural sector. The Unidad Popular leaders could argue that their programs were not shortsighted, as previous investment programs had been. The trouble was that the Allende program could not survive the short term.

ALLENDE'S BOLD START

The economic downturn which confronted the Allende government by the time it took office in November 1970 provided the government with an opening for reactivation of the economy. It was hoped that this economic surge could provide higher revenues to pay for expanded social services, political credit for the administration (especially welcome after the opposition's predictions of imminent disaster), and an advantage in the 1971 congressional elections, which would improve the Unidad Popular's legislative strength (as Frei's Christian Democrats had gained in the 1965 elections shortly after he had assumed office). Moreover, the Allende planners believed that the reactivation could be accomplished without appreciable inflation, because of high levels of idle productive capacity and unemployment, and ample international reserves and government revenues due to strong copper sales and prices abroad (Bitar 1979, p. 106).

The reactivation policy was a success. Gross national product increased by just over 9.5 percent, based on the redistributive success of increasing workers' disposable income through wage increases. Indeed, there was an exaggeration of intended policy effects in the wage trends. The general wage adjustment for 1971 was set at 35 percent, since that had been the cost-of-living increase for 1970. Yet the unions, knowing that the government would not resort to the traditional strike-breaking actions of previous administrations, used their vastly improved bargaining position to gain much higher wage concessions. The state enterprises, naturally loath to take what would appear to be a regressive stand, increased wages beyond the 35 percent guideline. The workers' bargaining position was strengthened because the arbitration boards were now stacked in favor of the workers' wage demands, and because private employers recognized their vulnerability to worker takeovers. The average nominal wage increase turned out to be 50 percent for 1971, equivalent to an astounding 34 percent real-wage increase (Stallings 1978, p. 200).

The nominal wage increases resulted in higher real incomes because price controls were extremely effective, even though higher wages were pushing production costs dramatically upward. From July 1970 to July 1971 the average increase in blue-collar wages was 2.8 times the increase in the cost of living for the same period. Significantly, the increase in white-collar salaries was 2.9 times this cost of living increase. From October 1970 to October 1971 the wage increase was 2.9 times the cost-of-living increase, while the salary increase was 3.35 times the cost-of-living increase, indicating that the advance of real incomes was actually accelerating (Instituto de Economía 1972, pp. 38–39).

The increased demand sparked increased production, which grew by 14 percent in 1971. Some observers have interpreted this development as indicating that the small-scale and medium-scale producers were happy with the course of economic policy (de Vylder 1976, p. 62). However, in many instances the production increases may have been desperate efforts to cover rising costs by greater unit sales, because price increases could not cover growing labor costs. Even during the boom year of 1971 many major and smaller-scale firms earned lower profits than in 1970, and many lost money in 1971 (Instituto de Economía 1972, p. 31).

Although the advance in real worker incomes resulted from stringent price control implementation, by the beginning of 1971 it became evident that the controls could not be sustained. The problem was not so much the black market or the flaunting of price-control regulations, as had been the case with previous efforts. Rather, the limits on the effectiveness of price controls were on the supply side, and were indeed the consequences of the previous year's success in wage increases and price freezes. Where prices could no longer cover the producer's costs, scarcity occurred. Furthermore, the state enterprises were running deficits because of their commitment to sell at controlled prices. And price controls on domestic goods stimulated importation because of the reduction of domestic production, thus contributing to the serious foreign reserve drain. Gradually, and reluctantly, the government permitted price increases. Often these were still below the inflation rate and were granted only when the situation with respect to a given commodity had become desperate; frequently they came too late to induce the manufacturers to continue unprofitable production.

In April 1971 the workers of the enormous Yarur textile factory seized the installation and requested that the government take it over under the provisions of the Decreto Ley 520. The Yarur requisition request was supported by the radical faction of the Unidad Popular, including Economics Minister Pedro Vuscovic, but was opposed by the moderates of the Unidad Popular and by Allende himself (Stallings 1978, p. 136). The radicals prevailed, and within three days of the occupation the factory was requisitioned. Because of the swiftness of the government's response and the prominence of the Yarur case (it was one of the nation's largest private firms, owned by a very powerful industrial family), the Yarur takeover encouraged a spate of further occupations in factories large and small. Many of these occupations also led to government takeovers, so that the tenuous confidence of domestic industrialists that they would be spared from nationalization quickly evaporated.

The rapidly growing state sector was not, as had been hoped, a counterweight to the disinvestment of the private sector. De Vylder's (1976, pp. 130–163) assessment of the Allende regime's performance reveals that the government was no more successful in controlling the state than in regulating the private sector. In the mining of copper, Chile's most important export, the relatively well-paid workers resorted to costly strikes to press for wage increases beyond the government's guidelines, with sixty-seven work stoppages at the troubled Chuquicamata mine in 1972 and a two-month strike at the El Teniente mine in 1973. Copper production stagnated in 1972 and dropped by 2 to 5 percent in 1973. Even greater declines were registered in iron and coal production (de Vylder 1976, p. 132).

In industry the problem was different but more devastating. The levels of production did not decline, but state workers received wage increases at the same rates as private-sector workers, and even more lucrative improvements in fringe benefits. Combined with managerial inefficiency, bloated employment rolls, lower per-worker productivity,

and price controls on most state-produced products, the state enterprises lost enormous amounts of money in 1972 and 1973. It is
estimated that seven of the ten industrial sectors controlled by the state
ran deficits in 1972, mounting a total deficit of 20 billion escudos (de
Vylder 1976, p. 154), equivalent to nearly a third of the central
government's fiscal expenditures. To cover these losses, the government increased the money supply drastically, leaving no possible way
of avoiding galloping inflation. This answers part of the riddle of why
high production and disaster went hand in hand. State enterprises kept
producing at nearly full capacity, but had no resources to expand. The
year 1973 saw a decline from 1972 levels as blockages and disruptions
mushroomed, but total production still easily exceeded the 1970 level.
The most telling costs, then, were not production declines but the
liabilities of keeping up that production: inflation, the fiscal crisis, and
political polarization.

The overestimate of potential production was based on the mistaken
assumption that because a high degree of excess capacity had been
identified, the opportunities for industrial expansion triggered by a
massive increase in demand were correspondingly high. When idle
capacity was calculated at approximately 25 percent to 32 percent as of
1970 (Instituto de Economía 1972, p. 77; Sigmund 1977, p. 137), it was
assumed that the 14 percent increase in manufacturing production in
1971 far from exhausted the potential for further expansion, even
with little increase in new-capacity investment. It turned out, however,
that the growth in production for 1972 was only 2.8 percent, whereas
the money supply more than doubled (de Vylder 1976, pp. 90, 95).

It is a well-known fact of economic life that average idle-capacity
figures disguise the bottlenecks in particular industries and phases of
production that severely limit the utilization of part of that idle
capacity. If the Allende planners had simply been wrong in their
calculations of how much of this idle capacity indeed could have been
utilized, their failure might be explained as an isolated error. However,
the problem was more profound; apparently they chose to ignore
technical issues.

Similarly, the Allende administration seemed to overlook the realities of monetary effects. De Vylder (1976, p. 56) points out that the
Allende government restricted the scope of monetary policy even
more than previous administrations, which traditionally ignored the
opportunities to channel credit systematically into priority areas, or to
use discount rates to regulate the demand for credit.

This pattern was general. Throughout the first two years of the
Allende administration there was an unmistakable air of neglect toward conventional balancing of macroeconomic parameters. There is

strong evidence that the Allende economic team was well aware of the destabilizing effects of its initial program. Gonzalo Martner, head of the planning agency ODEPLAN, made the following observations at a round-table discussion in May 1971:

> Achieving an *ex ante* harmonization of the various agents and variables intervening in the economic process is not a basic requirement for us. The compatibilization of the economy is our goal, not our point of departure ... I see in all of this discussion a conflict of mentality. For some of the participants in this forum it appears that what interests them the most—and in this they may be influenced by all of their academic training—is to maintain the harmony of the various economic variables; every dissonance, every imperfection, alarms them. We do not think in terms of this traditional rationality. On the contrary, we know that certain incompatibilities will be produced, and we are wiling to confront them. Because our interest, I repeat, is to construct a new economy. And we cannot accomplish that unless certain dislocations [*desajustes*] are produced along the way.[12]

There are two plausible explanations for this attitude. One is that the economic team had to justify a program dictated by political considerations (principally the internal politics of the Unidad Popular), and Martner was putting the best face on a difficult situation. The second explanation is that the Allende planners were smitten with the anti-technical romanticism that we have seen in other redistributionists, such as Belaúnde. Alec Nove (1976, p. 75) has described this attitude succinctly, if bluntly:

> Among the errors that can be diagnosed was one that could be called economic naivete ... There is little realization that real incomes depend decisively on productivity. Wage constraint is equated with impermissible "reformism" or with betraying the working class. By some UP leaders inflation was blamed on capitalism and curable by altering *las estructuras* [the structures], enlarging the Social Property Area, freeing Chile from subordination to foreign capital, and carrying out land reform ... The fact that a large expansion of the money supply would stimulate a speed-up in inflation was either forgotten or regarded as unimportant. So was the pressure of rising wages upon costs. By contrast, there was a gross overestimation of the antiinflationary effects of price control, and an underestimation of the effect of such control in stimulating imports.

LAND REFORM

The course of land reform followed a pattern similar to that of wage increases, in that the Allende administration found it less difficult than had been expected to implement radical changes, but far more difficult to control the pace and consequences of those changes. Illegal land takeovers (*tomas*) were, if anything, encouraged by the existence of a regime sympathetic to dramatic land reform. Rather than waiting for the government programs to allocate land to them, more peasants than under the Frei administration merely took over land. Official figures indicate 1,278 illegal occupations in 1971 alone, compared to 320 for the entire period of 1960–1969.[13]

The increase in takeovers, which contrasts sharply with Belaúnde's experience in Peru, where the much less ambitious land reform program quelled unrest and illegal activities, has been explained by Kyle Steenland (1977, p. 10) as the result of the government's explicit policy of refusing to use the police to intervene in rural or urban takeovers. This certainly accounts for the peasant's belief that participating in tomas did not expose them to prohibitive risks, but it does not explain their motives for participating in the first place, if their acquisition of land was assured for the very near future without such takeovers. Perhaps the reason is that the occupations were known to bolster the government's position in expropriating land without protracted appeals by the landowners. Steenland (1977, p. 10) argues that "the illegal occupations were of great benefit to the Popular Unity since they cut off the farm owner's profits immediately and made him more willing to sell out to CORA rather than follow a two- or three-year bureaucratic appeal process in the Agrarian Tribunals." In at least some instances, MIR peasant organizers argued that the takeovers would aid the government (Steenland 1977, p. 76).

Despite success in eliminating the large landholdings, the land reform did not resolve the problems of inefficient production. After good harvests in 1970–1971 and 1971–1972, the harvest of 1972–1973 was a disaster, entailing a 22 percent decline in major crops and requiring the government to import far more food than before (Instituto de Economía 1973, p. 138). The failure could be traced to three factors. One was the bad weather; but Chile had suffered through bad weather before without an agricultural catastrophe. Second, some land was left uncultivated. Another factor was the CIA-supported truckers' strike beginning in October 1972, just at the time when transport of seed and fertilizer was critical for planting. The agricultural failure was even more catastrophic than simply the need to import more foodstuffs. Because the Allende government had poured resources into the provision of credit and mechanized equipment for agriculture, the lack of productivity increases meant that yet another flow of governmental expenditure was not offset by productivity gains and paybacks. Many government loans to cooperatives were never repaid (de Vylder 1976, p. 190). Supplying imported food thus involved a double drain on the government's resources

These flaws did not signify, of course, that modifications over time could not have been made. But the agricultural production declines that occurred in 1972–1973 came when the Chilean economy had no capacity to accommodate another failure. The drop in agricultural production meant that the scarcity caused by increased demand had become in addition a real scarcity of diminished supply; the balance-of-payments situation was rendered nearly hopeless by the need to import food. The Right's claim that the economy was literally falling apart had its most graphic demonstration.

REACTIONS AND OPPOSITION

The initial responses of the wealthy after the Allende election were predictably reactive. There was a run on the banks, but the government extended them more credit—effectively increasing the money supply—in order to avert a banking collapse. There was also a sharp drop in private investment, construction, and consumption of consumer durables (Bitar 1979, p. 105). It is clear that the wealthy were rushing to convert to liquid assets in order to minimize their vulnerability to future attacks, but their actions were defensive rather than subversive. Many of the wealthier families opted for extended stays in Argentina, the United States, or other havens, leading to the common perception of the wealthy as bewildered and nearly paralyzed—for the time being.

From the start, the large-scale business sector tried to convey the dismal prospects for private investment and production. An "investment strike" was expected to materialize and deepen. Through 1971 the private-sector entrepreneurs did in fact respond to the incentive of increased demand by expanding their own production. But private investment declined in every year of the Allende administration. In both 1971 and 1972 even total investment declined absolutely (Instituto de Economía 1973, p. 138).

The reactions of landowners threatened with expropriation were keyed to the specifics of the 1967 Agrarian Reform Law that the Allende administration was forced to use after failing to pass its own land reform legislation. Because the 1967 law exempted landholdings of under 80 basic irrigated hectares, some 1,500 farms were divided into smaller units. The resulting 4,500 farms were retained by their original owners, who were reluctant to cultivate—if only because of the uncertainty of the land's ultimate fate. By 1972–1973, the total area under cultivation declined to 80 percent of its 1969–1970 level (de Vylder 1976, p. 199).

The economic sectors initially threatened by the Allende program recognized that to change policy, either directly or by precipitating a change in the government itself, required organizational action as well as economic action. Their disinvestment was both anticipated and planned. If government plans proceeded, simple disinvestment would merely rescue part of the industrialists' resources as their firms were taken over; it would not protect their ownership. Moreover, as long as the "monopolists" were distinguished from other producers, the chances were small that anyone would come to their defense, at the risk of antagonizing the government. The large-scale producers therefore decided to include the associations of the small-scale manufacturing, service, and commercial concerns in a broad organization led by SOFOFA. In late 1971 the Frente Nacional del Area Privada (National Private Sector Front) was formed as the coordinating organization for all *gremios* (employers' associations or guilds) (Stallings 1975, p. 348). Apparently the opportunity to associate with the powerful SOFOFA industrial elite was sufficiently attractive to the gremios of truck drivers, grocers, and the like to offset any fears of retaliation from the government, or perhaps the economic losses of the small-scale operators had already convinced them that a confrontation with the government was inevitable.

By uniting with the lower-middle-class organizations, the industrialists widened the social and political gap between this crucial economic segment and the government. While Allende promised that the socialist attack on private capital extended only to large enterprises, the decision of the gremio leaders to join with the industrialists signified that they did not find Allende's promises credible. Over the years 1972 and 1973 the gremio members and their families moved steadily toward allegiance with the beleaguered large-scale and medium-scale industrial and commercial sectors.

This identification was manifested most clearly in the October 1972 truckers' strike, perhaps the most decisive signal to the military that the Allende regime had to be overturned.[14] This strike was not the first mass demonstration of dissatisfaction with Allende policies. In December 1971 there was a massive and well-publicized March of the Empty Pots, a generally peaceful rally in which housewives manifested their displeasure with the shortages of food and other basic items. The demonstration was obviously not spontaneous, and the Unidad Popular could claim that the housewives were the relatively well-to-do, spoiled bourgeoisie unwilling to accept the implications of equity. The march was interpreted as a symbolic act, although it did contribute to the political polarization when Allende, instead of trying to reassure the middle sectors that their problems were taken seriously by the government, responded sarcastically that the shortages resulted from food hoarding by residents of the wealthy neighborhoods.

The truckers' strike, in contrast, was a serious threat to Chile's economy, because of the country's dependence on road transport. The fact that it was well organized increased its importance; the military could see both the alliance of the middle-sector oposition and the truckers—certainly one of the most modest income-earning segments of the "middle"—and the capacity of this segment to disrupt the economy at will.

Tax reform initiatives were blunted by the Chilean congressional opposition in almost precisely the same manner as congressional opposition in Peru had undermined Belaúnde's fiscal policies. The opposition could have refused higher taxes and cut government spending accordingly. Instead, the tactic was to further exaggerate the spending burden and hence the discrepancy between revenues and spending. In early 1973, in the face of already uncontrolled inflation, the opposition passed legislation calling for even higher wage levels than the massive increases the executive had requested. When Allende vetoed that bill, Congress rejected the executive's tax increase proposals. The congressional opposition flaunted its control over taxation by passing a simplified tax structure, as Allende had proposed, but one that actually reduced the burden of high-income taxpayers. Less than half of the increased spending was covered by revenues (de Vylder 1976, pp. 92–93, 223).

Part of the strategy of challenging the legislature to respond to the executive's demand for a higher overall tax package was to threaten the Congress with a plebiscite if it failed to grant the increase. However, by late 1972 and early 1973 the Allende administration had already lost the support of the middle-sector voters whose backing would have been necessary for a decisive Allende victory. With its control over tax policy thus guaranteed, the congressional opposition used the revenue deficit to humiliate the administration and undermine the fiscal viability of its spending program.

The decision to moderate the pace of nationalization, and to be explicit about which firms were subject to state intervention, was accompanied by a change in the top economic team. Pedro Vuscovic,

the minister of economics who had spearheaded the strategy of accelerated state takeovers, was replaced by Carlos Matus, an economist
of the moderate Allende wing of the Socialist party. Orlando Millas, a
leading proponent of the consolidation argument, became minister of
finance. This new team tried to check the momentum of economic
disintegration. The state sector was finally directed to bring its prices in
line with costs; the exchange rate was made more realistic; Allende
broached the possibility of returning some of the intervened firms—
technically only temporarily controlled by the state. But by the end of
1972 it was too late, both in terms of the state of the economy and in
terms of the level of opposition to any government policy. Massive
strikes, growing shortages, pitched battles in the streets between right-
wing and left-wing groups, and acute dissatisfaction within the military
despite an eleventh-hour inclusion in the cabinet of top-ranking military officers, brought on the military takeover of September 1973.

These reactions of Allende's opponents are noteworthy. For one
thing, by 1972 the opposition showed practically no restraint whatever—a very rare situation in light of the fact that economic actors
usually find it prudent to hedge, even under governments they detest.
In Chile under Allende the situation was literally one of economic war.
The decisions to leave land uncultivated, close down factories, and
otherwise undermine the economy constitute the most clear-cut instance of economic action designed literally to force replacement of the
regime, with complete disregard for short-term economic rationality.

Except for the alienation of the lower middle sectors and *their* reactions, the responses of the owners of land and factories did not in themselves doom the Allende economic strategy; rather, they left the
government to its own devices—macroeconomic policy and state enterprises—which led to a spectacular undoing. The strength of the
reactions left the Allende government with no room for error in its
conduct, a fact completely overlooked by the blasé policymakers and
the Unidad Popular's Left.

CONCLUSIONS

Allende and his fellow moderates of the Unidad Popular failed in their
political-economic alliance strategy with the middle-income population for three broad reasons. First, they could not, or would not,
calibrate the pace of transformation from a technical point of view.
This accounts for the almost hopeless disequilibrium stemming from

the supposed success of the initial reactivation program. The poorly-thought-out economic program that overestimated the capacity for industrial expansion and the ability of the state to increase investment can account for the massive inflationary pressures and scarcities for the politically pivotal middle sectors.

What accounts for this failure of the economic program, other than almost self-imposed naiveté? Of the many assumptions underlying the Allende program, one of the most critical was that the state sector would control the economy's parameters. This accounted for much of the optimism of the early phase of Allende's administration: the state would invest to keep up productivity, despite the expected withdrawal of private capital; the state would keep prices in line; and the state would reward its own workers—to a reasonable degree. A constant feature of the internal debate within the Unidad Popular was the disagreement on whether greater state control over economic parameters was worth alienation of the middle-sector groups that feared expansion of the social area. We have seen that the premise underlying this debate, namely that formal state control would increase the government's effective control, was faulty.

Finally, the breakdown of the proposed alliance with the middle sectors was exacerbated by the blatant image of class struggle projected by the Unidad Popular, despite Allende's own inconsistent attempts to reassure small-scale and medium-scale entrepreneurs that the government would safeguard their interests. Not only did the actual economic trends belie these assurances, but the pronouncements of Altamirano and others, addressed more to internal debate within the Unidad Popular than to optimal presentation to the public at large, undermined whatever hope remained for the beleaguered government.

CHAPTER 12
The Peruvian Military

THE MILITARY GOVERNMENT of Gen. Juan Velasco Alvarado (1968–1975), in carrying on the progressive reforms in Peru that Belaúnde failed to achieve, provides a striking exception to the common pattern of military regimes dedicated to preserving the status quo. In their commitment to wrest economic control from the domestic elite and foreign corporations, the military radicals did indeed transform the economy. If radicalism is taken to mean expansion of the state, the Peruvian military was radical. What remains to be explained, however, is why their redistribution per se did not go much further than Belaúnde's.

Unlike Allende, who imposed a full-blown redistributive program at the start, Velasco's efforts emerged gradually. Despite some radical rhetoric and the uncompensated expropriation of the U.S.-owned International Petroleum Corporation (IPC) oil properties, the Velasco government took little action in the domestic economy that could distinguish it from other military governments—until land reform was extended to the coastal plantations in mid-1969. In 1970 the General Industrial Law greatly expanded the role of the state in basic industries and established worker participation in private-sector corporate management. In 1971 a broad-gauged governmental agency, SINAMOS (Sistema Nacional de Apoyo a la Movilización Social, or National System to Support Social Mobilization), was established to mobilize workers and peasants in a host of "popular" (but government-channeled) movements. In 1973, however, after riots and other expressions of popular opposition, SINAMOS was downgraded. In 1974, with inflation and balance-of-payments problems rising as a result of the lack of domestic private investment to augment existing capacity, the government continued its expansion and at the same time undertook massive borrowing from abroad rather than increasing taxes. It was successful in securing short-term foreign loans, despite the many expropriations of foreign property, but fiscal problems, inflation, and strikes mounted. These problems, in addition to political confrontation and Velasco's declining health, led to his replacement in 1975 by Gen. Francisco Morales Bermúdez. Morales Bermúdez instituted a wage-freeze stabilization program that cut sharply into the wages of industrial workers. The economy remained depressed.

Of all the cases examined in this study, Velasco's regime is the only true military government committed for any length of time to redistribution. Military men like Juan Perón attempted redistribution, but not as leaders of military governments. The redistributive potential of the military can therefore be glimpsed in the Velasco case, with the obvious caveat that it is only one regime at one point in time. The fact that Velasco's was an institutionalized military government—acting formally on behalf of the armed forces—is of some relevance to the level of coercion at the government's disposal, and obviously to how far the government could go without provoking military intervention. The often-cited proposition that coercion by the military is necessary to achieve significant redistribution can be explored through the Peruvian case. The striking result is how tenuous the control of the Velasco government was, despite being a military regime.

Other aspects of the military nature of the regime are important. The increase in military expendures was a direct result and placed a heavier burden on public finances already severely strained by the redistributive initiatives. In addition, the military's conception of national strength, equating industrialization with military potential, helps to explain the regime's promotion of the modern sector.

Although these characteristics differentiate the Velasco regime from civilian regimes, many of the same dilemmas emerge. The problems of disinvestment, of beneficiaries' expectations outstripping the regime's capacity to satisfy their demands, and of calibrating the transformation are the same. The factors that account for the success of Velasco's efforts in changing the economy's structure, to the extent that he did succeed, are also largely the factors that explain the success of nonmilitary governments: pragmatic improvisation, ambiguity, the calculated use of threats, rewards, and alliances without undue concern for microequity. The factors accounting for the Velasco government's failures to redistribute as much income as had been intended, and to maintain the pace of economic growth in the process, also were the same as those hindering other governments.

Another broad issue illuminated by the Velasco experience is the importance of initial redistributive commitment. In Velasco's case the mixed collection of military officers and their civilian associates did not at first evidence a strong or unified commitment to radical transformation and redistribution (Cotler 1970). The chronology reveals that the deepening of the revolution grew out of short-term political considerations rather than a fixed initial commitment.

VELASCO'S RECORD

In retrospect it is easy to get the impression that the Peruvian military helped the poor through strongly nationalistic measures, and in so doing wrecked the economy. In 1968 Peru apparently sacrificed its international economic connections by expropriating U.S. property without compensation. Shortly thereafter it instituted worker participation and profit sharing in the private sector over the strong objections of the business community and enacted a land reform extending even to the efficient coastal plantations. Nonetheless, it ended up in the humiliating position of negotiating with the International Monetary Fund for a bailout.

This image is deceptive. For the entire 1968–1975 period, the growth in gross national product averaged a rather steady 6 percent. However, subsequent stabilization programs, necessitated by economic disequilibria clearly attributable to Velasco's policies, resulted in a decline in per capita GNP of roughly 2.5 percent annually for the next three years and very high inflation (by Peruvian standards), reaching more than 55 percent by 1978 (FitzGerald 1976, p. 63; 1979, p. 112; Thorp 1979, p. 112).

The impact on the the country's productive capacity was also mixed. As Table 15 indicates, gross capital formation was maintained at just under 16 percent of gross domestic product. This rate was somewhat lower than in previous years (21 percent for 1960–1964 and 18 percent for 1965–1968). The decline was thus part of a long-term secular trend; how much of it was due to government policy is debatable. Although the rate of capital accumulation was lower, there was no decapitalization of the Peruvian economy despite profound changes in the economy's ownership structure; capital investment was roughly double the level of depreciation (FitzGerald 1976, p. 22).

This investment came at a high cost. Table 15 shows that gross investment was low during the first five years of the Velasco period, not because private domestic investment declined (after the uncertain year of 1969 it was not much below the 1965–1968 rate), but because of the net outflow of foreign capital. By 1974, however, there was a reversal: private domestic savings declined in the face of inflation, while foreign borrowing took up the slack. Yet the terms of the loans were so short that the debt burden, exacerbated by the need to repay Belaúnde-era

TABLE 15. INVESTMENT AND SAVINGS IN PERU UNDER JUAN VELASCO.

Year	Gross investment (% of GDP)	Private domestic savings (% of GDP)	Public domestic savings (% of GDP)	Foreign savings (% of GDP)	Debt service (% of exports)	Inflation (%)
1960–1964	21.1	19.0	1.6	0.6	—	—
1965–1968	18.1	15.6	−0.6	3.0	—	—
1969	13.3	11.9	2.0	−0.6	15	7.8
1970	12.9	15.1	1.9	−4.1	16	6.6
1971	15.0	15.3	0.5	−0.8	24	3.8
1972	14.2	14.4	0.5	−0.8	23	4.9
1973	15.7	15.5	−0.3	0.5	33	14.7
1974	18.9	12.9	0.6	5.4	—	16.6
1975	19.7	8.7	1.2	9.8	—	20.0
1976	17.8	12.0	−0.3	6.1	39	34.5
1977	15.1	13.2	−2.5	4.4	—	38.0

SOURCES: Fitzgerald 1976, p. 71; 1979, pp. 243, 304, 310.

262

loans coming due at that time, increased the debt service ratio dramatically. Moreover, the state was unable to generate savings from its own enterprises and instead served as a channel for short-term foreign loans through its deficit spending on capital improvements.

The severe downturn following 1975 must be laid to Velasco. The depression occurred because the atmosphere engendered by Velasco led to a drop in domestic saving and foreign investment finance. Even though state action prevented a major decline in overall investment, the vast sums of money borrowed abroad had to be repaid; the cost was in the austerity measures required by foreign lenders through their insistence on IMF terms. Rosemary Thorp (1979, p. 110), certainly no advocate of orthodox economic measures, concludes "that such policies . . . appear in the circumstances to be the only option, given the structure of the international system, the effect of the international recession on base metal prices, and the country's internal situation." As a model of long-term economic growth, the Peruvian experiment of state-led development was not successful. Thorp, despite her sympathy with Velasco's attempts to change the elite-dominated export-led economic model, maintains "that in forty years Peru has not faced a problem of such severity."

This does not, however, speak to whether the experiment was a success in terms of the struggles for economic control and redistribution. Nor does it speak to the issue of whether the Velasco regime was able to impose its preferred policies and implement its economic model, regardless of whether the economic model accomplished its objectives.

In terms of the Velasco government's political objective of sharply curtailing the economic power of the multinational corporations and the coastal elite (who dominated both the agroexport sector and large industry), and of increasing the state's power in setting the economy's parameters, the accomplishments are impressive, even discounting the retrenchment under Morales Bermúdez, who "reprivatized" some of the industry taken over by the state under Velasco. E. V. K. FitzGerald (1976, p. 28) concludes:

> The main result of these reforms [of the 1969–1973 period] has been to break much of the economic power of the domestic elite, to reduce substantially the foothold of foreign enterprise in the economy, and to introduce a certain degree of worker participation. This, in turn, combined with the expansion of public enterprise, has led to the emergence of the state as the dominant force in the economy. The process of surplus mobilization has been fundamentally altered, but not so as to bestow total control to the state—as final domestic output remains in the non-state sector.

Yet if the regime was successful in gaining far more control over the economy, it did not reverse the trend toward greater income concentration. The modern industrial sector continued to grow more rapidly than the traditional sectors found both in the countryside and in the metropolis of Lima. The official real-wage level for 1968–1972 rose 5.5 percent annually (Webb 1977, p. 247) but "wage-earners" in Peru, especially those whose compensation shows up in official statistics, are decidedly not among the poor. Under Belaúnde, official real wages had declined modestly; under Velasco, the "labor elite" was a primary beneficiary of economic growth, while the poorer sectors benefited far less (if at all) because the bulk of redistribution remained within the modern industrial sector. The lack of intersectoral redistribution meant that the income transfers by and large remained within the richest quarter of the population. Since practically the only source of higher income for the peasantry was redistributed land, and arable land in Peru (3 percent of the total) is pitifully scarce to begin with, the improvements for the bottom half of the population were bound to be extremely modest by the very nature of the redistributive strategy employed (see Table 16).[1] The plantations were to be run as cooperatives, but with strong central planning from Lima (Harding 1975, p. 251). Compensation was to be in the form of long-term bonds, some cash, and an option to convert the bonds to cash committed to industrial investment.

Even with respect to the intrasectoral redistribution within the industrial sector, the Velasco government's achievements in transfer-

TABLE 16. DISTRIBUTIONAL EFFECTS AND CONSEQUENCES IN PERU
UNDER JUAN VELASCO.

	Earnings (thousands of 1963 soles)			Share of national income[a] (percent)			
Year	Blue collar	White collar	Peasants	Profits	Blue collar	White collar	Peasants
1960	10.9	30.9	6.6	26.5	22.7	22.2	13.4
1965	13.0	38.9	7.2	25.5	23.4	23.8	11.5
1970	13.2	39.9	9.3	27.2	21.6	24.4	11.8
1973	16.1	43.0	7.4	28.0	23.9	24.4	7.9
1976	15.2	42.1	8.9	29.8	22.1	23.9	8.9
1978	10.5	—	8.8	—	—	—	—

SOURCE: Fitzgerald 1979, pp. 129, 172.
a. Excludes the share of "nonagricultural independents"—the self-employed, ranging from professionals to own-account peddlers.

ring company ownership shares to employees fell far short of the estimates. The fact that only 17 percent of ownership shares had been transferred by the end of 1975 was a source of disappointment and frustration for the military (FitzGerald 1979, p. 125).

Land reform in general was successful within the constraint of overall scarcity. FitzGerald (1979, p. 109) estimates that roughly a quarter of the peasant families received substantial benefits. In the beginning the administration tolerated landowners' efforts to sub-divide their own land and thereby avoid expropriation, but then the government made a sharp reversal which ultimately achieved its target of transferring 7.3 million hectares from all Sierra farms of over 30 hectares and all coastal farms of over 50 hectares (Caballero 1977). Because this land went mostly to the permanent workers and tenant farmers of the former estates, it left almost nothing for the landless peasant. Although an outside assessment may regard the land reform as successful within the range of the feasible, the disappointment of those who were still landless was a crucial political factor.

Of course, these statistics reflect the condition of wage earners during the Velasco period only. They do not reveal the potential for future redistributive gains or losses that the political changes wrought under Velasco may yet bring. The long-term redistributive implications of liquidation of the coastal elite's economic control (resulting from takeover of the major industries and the coastal plantations) should not be underestimated, despite the retrenchment after Velasco was replaced in 1975.[2] Workers and peasants today remain mobilized to a greater extent than they were prior to the Velasco era. These transformations make the Velasco experience more akin to the Perón experience than to the redistributive attempts of many others (including Allende) whose changes have vanished in the reactions following their defeats. On the other hand, the economic sacrifices endured under Velasco's successors are also relevant to the assessment.

BACKGROUND TO THE MILITARY RADICALS

The most important fact about the Velasco administration, other than the background of the Belaúnde period, was the lack of a definite, unified, and fixed ideological stand among the top-level military officers controlling the government. Undoubtedly, one important source of inspiration was the Center for Higher Military Studies (CAEM), the army's premier training organ and think tank for advanced officers.

CAEM's very subject matter, including public administration and political analysis, encouraged military activism in national affairs and belief in the military's competence to oversee Peru's development.

However, "the" ideology espoused by or developed at CAEM encompassed at least two very different strains. Developmentalists (or conservatives) emphasized productivity as the primary goal, to which redistribution was a means. Radicals urged redistribution for the sake of equity. The developmentalists' advocacy of wresting economic control from the oligarchy was based on their perception of the oligarchy's lack of economic dynamism, not the fact that its members were too wealthy. The developmentalists did not oppose foreign investment per se, whereas the radicals opposed all foreign investment, regardless of how it was applied, on the grounds that it entailed the loss of national autonomy. The developmentalists were not enthused about worker participation because it increased the risks of inefficiency and hence of slowed growth, whereas the radicals favored worker mobilization because it would increase the workers' power and their share of the rewards (Philip 1978, pp. 82, 114). In sum, the differences between the two groups were fundamental and quite significant in terms of policy choices, not just as abstract theoretical disputes.

The way the Peruvian military came to a radical position is an example of the limited degree to which initial redistributive commitment determines the course of redistributive efforts. Attempts to delineate the CAEM ideology seem to imply that the military's political and economic approach was determined in the classrooms of the center, with the Velasco era simply playing out this approach. However, many of the leading military figures of the Velasco administration were former Belaúnde supporters who had become disillusioned either with Belaúnde himself or with prospects of fundamental reform within a liberal democratic setting. Moreover, military officers representing both variants of the CAEM philosophy were in evidence within the Velasco regime at the outset; only gradually did the radicals win out (Philip 1978, pp. 82–92).

The adoption of a radical position can be explained in terms of the other issues that arose in the early days of the Velasco regime and the political challenges that Velasco had to face. In seeking popular support and backing from the military nationalists to be able to remain in office past the mandatory retirement age, Velasco found it convenient (and not inconsistent with his own ideological predispositions) to bring up the International Petroleum Corporation question as the first major issue addressed by the new government (this was long before any clearcut victory of the radicals over the developmentalists). The IPC was the primary nationalist issue of the day; inept handling of the negotiations and contract by the Belaúnde administration was one of the major irritants that had precipitated the 1968 revolution. In raising this matter—which resulted in expropriation of the IPC holdings and a protracted conflict with the U.S. government over compensation—the Velasco regime found itself in opposition to those groups and individuals who defended the IPC. These included the coastal economic elite, still represented by Beltrán's *La Prensa,* which attempted to discredit the military government's handling of the IPC case. The military's confrontation with the oligarchy, which was seen in any event as the ally of the United States, increased the antagonism between the military and the coastal elite and thereby strengthened the hand of those members of the government who favored more radical attacks on the wealth and power of the elite. Nationalism, in the Peruvian context, was easily converted into antioligarchical sentiment. This was a significant if not dominant element in the radicalism of the Velasco regime.

Interestingly, the rejection of the economic role of the elite did not concomitantly entail a rejection of the elite's favorite growth strategy, export-led industrialization. One plausible interpretation of Peru's historical pattern is that the export boom had run its course, thereby eliminating the justification for export-led industrialization (Thorp and Bertram 1978, chap. 14). Yet there was no reevaluation of the basic economic strategy of industrialization financed by expansion of the export sector.

The absence of any clear definition of the military's ideology was important in establishing the initial reception of military rule. The government was not universally seen as radical; in the minds of many Peruvians and outside observers it was equally plausible that the new rulers were nationalists of a conservative bent (Werlich 1978, p. 297). Vehement opposition and active efforts by conservative political forces to undermine the government, which in retrospect might be expected, simply did not materialize.[3] Several leading elite families, including the Prados, at first supported Velasco because they expected that the military leaders would prove to be moderate, or even conservative (Philip 1978, p. 86). In the first few months of the government Velasco attempted to broaden military support for the regime by bringing in senior officers in addition to those who had participated directly in the coup. One of these was Gen. José Benavides, wealthy in his own right and with close ties to the Peruvian elite and foreign firms such as the Cerro de Pasco conglomerate, was selected as minister of agriculture. Landowners took this as a signal that Velasco's land reform proposals

were so much rhetoric (Philip 1978, p. 82). The elite's initial perception, as well as their lack of opposition to the new government, were
strikingly similar to the reception of the 1943 military takeover in
Argentina by the Grupo de Oficiales Unidos, from which Juan Perón
emerged. The inability of the Argentine elite to anticipate the radical
turn that the regime would take under Perón was a major factor in
explaining the weakness of opposition in the early stages, when that
government was in its most vulnerable state (see Chapter 3).

VELASCO'S INITIATIVES

The initiatives of the Velasco administration provide further evidence
that the magnitude of state expansion was dictated by the developmentalist impulse and the lack of private-sector response more than by
any set plan for full state domination. The government's actions in
1969 gave little indication of radicalism with respect to the domestic
economy. Even though the Belaúnde economy, restrained by defla-
tionary policies provoked by the fiscal crisis, declined in terms of per
capita GNP by 1.4 percent and 2.4 percent for 1967 and 1968, the
Velasco administration resisted the opening for a strong reactivation of
the sort that Allende launched in Chile in 1971. Instead, Velasco
continued the Belaúnde policies of reduced public expenditures and
tighter restrictions on credit and imports (FitzGerald 1976, pp. 18, 62).

When reactivation became feasible, the Velasco government, in line
with its diagnosis of Peru's economic stagnation as caused by suppression of the potentially dynamic domestic entrepreneur, kept manufacturing profitable through easy credit, protectionism, and tax
incentives.

ALLIANCE STRATEGY

This courting of entrepreneurs can be explained by noting the
attempt to forge an interclass alliance. Velasco's alliance strategy with
respect to the middle sectors was strikingly similar to Allende's, in that
the small-scale and medium-scale domestic entrepreneurs—as opposed to the foreign and domestic "monopolists"—were to be wooed in
order to avoid private disinvestment.[4] The workers were also to be part
of the alliance, but only through new institutions created by the
military. There were no provisions for civilian participation in governmental decision making, yet as pressures mounted from civilian sup-

porters of the revolution, the organization called SINAMOS was created in mid-1971 to coordinate and mobilize the participation of citizens through new and existing labor unions, peasant cooperatives, community development organizations, agrarian reform movements, and so on. Citizen representatives were elected to the councils of the various SINAMOS entities, whose heads were functionaries of the centralized SINAMOS bureaucracy. It was simultaneously a channel for participation, a reform designed to make the bureaucracy more responsive to the workers and the marginals, and a vehicle of corporatist penetration and control. Stepan (1978, chaps. 5, 6) points out that for the formerly unorganized or weakly organized, SINAMOS provided initial mobilization; but for the already-mobilized, SINAMOS was competitive with existing organizations such as peasant leagues and industrial unions. SINAMOS thus represented institutionalized governmental support for the pursuits of these organizations, but only as far as the government wished to go—and in the directions of its choice (Dietz 1977).

Although both the alliance strategy and the economic growth model included the domestic entrepreneur, plans evolved to mobilize peasants and industrial workers through land reform, tax reform, expansion of the state, and wage policy. Apparently the administration did not recognize that these measures would undermine the rationale for cooperation by the investing sectors, large or small, domestic or foreign.

LAND REFORM

The moderate progress in land reform under Belaúnde did not diminish either the broad consensus for agrarian reform or the pressure from peasants for their own land, although the violence in the countryside of the early 1960s had subsided. The land reform undertaken by Velasco was a combination of compensated expropriations in the Sierra, designed and administered much as Belaúnde's had been, plus expropriation of the large coastal plantations that Belaúnde had left intact on the grounds that their efficient operation could not tolerate tampering. This argument found little sympathy among the military radicals, who blamed the coastal elite for Peru's economic backwardness and had vast confidence in their own abilities to direct state enterprises. The plantations were to be run as cooperatives, but with strong central planning from Lima (Harding 1975, p. 251). Compensation was to be in the form of long-term bonds, some cash, and an option to convert the bonds to cash committed to industrial investment.

TAX REFORM

For the state to generate significantly greater savings for productive investment, the savings from the state itself (the surplus, if any, from state enterprises) would have to be augmented by further extraction from the private sector. The Velasco administration, like Belaúnde's, proposed to increase direct taxation through corporate profit and property taxes, and to increase the equity of indirect taxes by augmenting the burden on luxury goods. Because the Velasco administration did not have to reckon with legislative obstructionism, like the APRA-UNO opposition that had blocked Belaúnde's tax reform for so many years, it was hopeful of increasing the overall tax incidence from 15 percent as of 1970 to 18 percent by 1975 (FitzGerald 1979, pp. 201–203). At the outset, though, the Velasco administration implemented the tax reforms already legislated by Belaúnde and announced that additional changes would be forthcoming. Perhaps begun as a tactic to avoid antagonizing potential private investors, the delay turned out to be permanent.

WAGE POLICY

The Velasco administration's attitudes toward unions, labor, and wages reflected the same ambivalence we have seen in the populist authoritarians—Perón, Odría, and Ibáñez. The union movement was a threat to the military's control; the two major labor federations being the Communist-dominated CGTP (Confederación General de Trabajadores del Perú) and the APRA-dominated CTP (Confederación de Trabajadores Peruanos). Although the Communists supported the Velasco government in its early years, the regime nonetheless considered both of these confederations as obstacles to the government's own plans to mobilize workers for the revolution (Cotler 1975, p. 73; Philip 1978, pp. 128–130). The government therefore launched not only SINAMOS but also its own union confederation, CTRP (Confederación de Trabajadores de la Revolución Peruana).

On the issue of specific wage levels the Velasco administration did not have a clearly formulated position. The incomes of workers in industries covered by the General Industrial Law were to increase through profit sharing. Wages were to be negotiated in standard collective-bargaining fashion, except that worker representatives were to be involved in management decisions. It is difficult to determine what the government's preferred rate of real-wage increases might have been, if in fact it was even formulated as an explicit objective.

The fact that the Velasco government by and large tried to compete with, rather than suppress, the labor unions affiliated with the CGTP and CTP was important in maintaining union strength in bargaining with employers. In the private sector the government permitted strikes and walkouts which, along with the populist rhetoric of the government, strengthened the union bargaining position by signaling employers that they had little to gain by resisting wage demands. Ample credit and the absence of effective price controls on nonagricultural products reinforced this willingness to grant wage increases.

In the public sector, which expanded under Velasco's nationalizations, the government's relationship with labor was more confrontational, since the unions represented a more direct challenge to the military's authority in setting wages and keeping up productivity. Strikes in state enterprises (including the copper mines) and government services (such as education) were illegal, and the military was prepared to break them up and jail union leaders.

STATE EXPANSION

The rationale behind the expansion of the state sector was that the dominance of the economic elite and the multinational corporations had inhibited Peru's development. Because the domestic elite and the multinationals were neither highly entrepreneurial nor interested in increasing their investments, the development of the economy could be spurred, it was felt, by making room for small and medium-sized businesses, such as those that had ignited the fish-meal boom with their willingness to take risks. The state's intervention was intended to release the energies of the "marginalized" private entrepreneurs rather than to sweep aside private initiative (Thorp and Bertram 1978, p. 303).

Therefore the Velasco regime planned for state expansion in those areas where the largest firms had dominated—in basic industry and minerals—and in the industries where private finance was simply not forthcoming. So, for example, the state took over the fish-meal industry—but only after the industry had collapsed because of overfishing and ecological changes. The state was to avoid involvement in consumer-goods industries, retailing, and general commerce. The later (post-1973) encroachments into these private-sector areas were the result of the government's frustration at the lack of private investment response, not part of the original conception.

STYLE

Whether deliberately or not, the Velasco administration operated in an atmosphere of ambiguity and contradictory signals, starting with the original uncertainty regarding its revolutionary commitment and its fairly successful attempt to minimize the significance of the IPC takeover by claiming that it was a special case (Philip 1978, p. 3). This ambiguity was reinforced by the selection of apparently conservative men like José Benavides for key posts. Moreover, the General Industrial Law appeared both conservative and radical; the governmental agency SINAMOS seemed to be both an earnest effort to mobilize independent action on the part of urban and rural workers and a calculated means to control them; and the general treatment of foreign capital provided both lucrative opportunities and severe deprivations. The government's orientation was not necessarily inconsistent; it was simply pragmatic in its balancing of radical and nonradical components.

It is ironic that although the Velasco regime extemporized constantly and effectively, there was a strong official stigma attached to improvisation. From the Statute of the Revolutionary Government on the day of the coup, which criticized the Belaúnde government for improvisation (among other things), to the comprehensive Plan Inca unveiled by Velasco in 1974 with the improbable claim that he had prepared it before the coup, the military government strove to identify itself with premeditated grand schemes.

THE VELASCO PROGRAM IN ACTION

The way the Velasco regime moved toward firmer state intervention can be seen concretely in the development and consequences of the General Industrial Law decreed in September 1970. This law, formulated within the military government in considerable secrecy and without outside consultation, can be interpreted as either vague or flexible. But it was clearly a compromise between the radicals and developmentalists (Petras and LaPorte 1971). There was some emphasis on encouraging private investment through tax incentives, credit, and import protection for business activity in certain sectors, with additional incentives for investment outside the greater Lima area. The radicals' objectives were expressed in provisions that reserved "basic industry" to the state (existing private investment in these industries to be taken over gradually, with compensation); fade-out requirements for new foreign investment (also to revert gradually to the state); and worker participation (through "workers' communities") in the management and profits of private companies.

Although the General Industrial Law was not as radical as Velasco's rhetoric, the business community's reaction was extremely negative. Far more attention was paid to what seemed to be the opportunities for open-ended state incursions into the private sector than to the opportunities for private-sector expansion in sectors not part of basic industry. The worker-participation provision was singled out for the most criticism, but the ambiguity of the whole package provoked fear in all sectors of industry. Since the business community had not been consulted in the formulation of the law, it had no reason to attribute the imprecision to anything but the antibusiness sentiments so often expressed in the government's rhetoric.

Once the immediate economic crisis leading to Belaúnde's ouster had eased, the Velasco regime turned to reactivating the economy. This was to be done through the hoped-for alliance between the state and the domestic entrepreneur. In order to stimulate private investment, the government eased the credit restrictions in force in 1969 and boosted state investment. It also permitted wages to rise, utilizing the same argument voiced in Chile at almost the same time: existing idle capacity would enable the economy to grow rapidly when higher wages placed greater disposable income in the hands of the consumption-oriented masses. The main differences between Peru and Allende's Chile were that Velasco's policies were applied more gradually, and the Peruvian population affected by official wage regulation was far smaller because of Peru's relatively low proportion of workers in industrial establishments. Therefore the Velasco government could use wage policy to reactivate the economy, but the immediate redistributive benefits would accrue to the modern, urban industrial work force of the top quartile of overall income distribution. Consequently, the transfers under Velasco were smaller and less abrupt that those under the Allende reactivation policy.

The response of the manufacturing sector to the economic reactivation was similar too to the Chilean reaction in 1971–1972. Production indeed went up, but private investment was not forthcoming to increase capacity, even though manufacturing was highly profitable. By 1973 manufacturing capacity was fully utilized, but demand did not slacken; urban wages remained high through the pressures of strikes and the safety valve of the opportunity to pass additional costs on to the consumer through price increases. The result was inflation and increased imports (FitzGerald 1976, pp. 62–63).

The lack of private investment response, shown in Table 15, left the government a short-term option of increasing state investment, since state enterprises for the first time played a major role in the economy. The lack of investment response from the private sector, as well as the desire for more control, induced the government to shift more and more of the economy to state enterprises. The need for further investment in these sectors compelled the government to permit state enterprises to make fixed investments beyond their revenues (though still at a lower rate than the economic plans called for), thereby requiring transfers from the central budget. Although the situation was not as extreme as under Allende (when state enterprises were running large deficits in both current and capital outlays), the overall deficits of the Peruvian state enterprises created a serious central budget deficit. The investment crisis was transformed into a fiscal crisis. The government was left with two options: increase taxes or borrow abroad.

In choosing the option of borrowing, which converted the fiscal crisis into a crisis of foreign debt and balance of payments, the Velasco government made a pivotal decision that precluded significant redistribution and necessitated austerity measures to address the debt problem in 1975–1978. In fairness to the Velasco planners, it must be noted that the severity of the debt crisis was due to the failure of the oil companies to make their expected discoveries—and the consequences of undertaking a major tax reform were of course unknown.

LAND REFORM

In June 1969 agriculture minister Benavides resigned. Within a fortnight the Velasco government enacted the Agrarian Reform Law and occupied the coastal sugar plantations of the north. The sudden action gave the coastal elite no opportunity for countermeasures. With the coastal plantations taken over, the struggle for land redistribution concentrated on the more traditional haciendas, first on the coast and then in the Sierra. Unlike the lightning expropriation of the major plantations, the implementation of the rest of the land reform had to be gradual.

Active opposition to the Agrarian Reform Law was limited by two provisions. First, a property could be expropriated in toto if the owner violated the labor legislation. Many landowners were unwilling to undertake disruptive actions, such as dismissing workers, for fear of incurring expropriation through this provision. Second, the confidence of landowners that they would be able to ride out the land reform effort was encouraged by the same apparent loophole that existed in the land reform legislation in Chile under Frei and Allende. The landowner could divide his property among family members and associates, bringing each unit below or at least near the legal limit, which varied according to location and type of land. There were requirements that land be cultivated by the owners, but they did not deter many landowners from dividing their property under the assumption that this superficial change would exempt them from expropriation. The confidence of many landowners that they could circumvent the land reform law in all likelihood forestalled some of the disinvestment that one would have expected. Yet in 1970, largely in response to the unrest of peasants who were increasingly critical of the government's "empty rhetoric," the administration tightened the regulations on subdividing estates and abruptly expropriated some of the subdivided haciendas (Harding 1975, p. 240). Some of the parceling already accomplished still went unchallenged, but the combination of initial false confidence on the part of the landowners and subsequent reversal by the government facilitated significant reform.

The landowner reactions had the secondary consequence of forcing many marginal peasants off the land. Colin Harding (1975, p. 238) reports:

> In the scramble to parcel up estates which took place all along the coast in the months following the publication of the law, ... the permanent and temporary laborers came off very badly, despite the avowed intention of the ministry of agriculture that "permanent laborers should be furnished with land in zones not yet affected by the agrarian reform and in which parcellation by private initiative is carried out." One author estimates that in the Canete valley, south of Lima, two thousand permanent laborers (40 percent of the total labor force) were deprived of their jobs because of the smaller labor requirements of the new parcels of land.

Thus the efforts by landowners to minimize the impact of the land reform law deprived many of the very group the law was supposed to benefit. The blame was directed against the government, resulting ultimately in stronger pressures to deepen the land reform.

As in Chile, land reform in Peru could not be tightly controlled by the government, even though that government was a military regime. When, early on, the coastal areas were announced as the first targets (partly because the small number of coastal plantations offered an administratively easier task than the myriad landholdings of the Sierra), peasant leagues of the Sierra led land takeovers (as in Chile, called *tomas*). This had two consequences. First, the small-scale and medium-scale farmers whom Velasco had tried to reassure became fearful that land reform would be carried beyond their interests. Furthermore, the tomas gave the impression that the government's land reform was reactive—that the government was unwillingly giving in to pressure from the peasants. The corollary impression was that the government deserved no credit for the initial measure of success of land reform, and that in fact it was preventing additional land reform

measures. Landless and nearly landless peasants must have had difficulty appreciating the extent to which further land redistribution was
limited by the absolute scarcity of arable land.

REACTIONS AND OPPOSITION

A few generalizations can be made about the reactions of those
potentially deprived by Velasco's redistributive plans. The lack of
clarity of the new regime's economic objectives virtually precluded
immediate response. George Philip (1978, p. 96) notes that "many
civilians were taken by surprise, both by the coup itself and by the
growing radicalization at the beginning of 1969." Moreover, the strategies of threatened sectors in both agriculture and industry were similar
in that they focused on uniting small-scale, medium-scale, and large-
scale operators in their opposition to the policies.

However, it is useful to distinguish between the reactions of industrialists and large-scale landowners, because the former were significantly more successful in fending off Velasco's measures. Although by
1974 the remaining medium-scale landowners (including the former
owners of large haciendas) succeeded in joining with small farmers to
undermine the power of SINAMOS, by then the battle against the
original large-scale landholders had largely been won.

LANDOWNERS

The landowners' reactions, except for the abortive attempts to
subdivide their properties, were surprisingly rare and ineffective, even
taking into account the widespread recognition that the time for land
reform had come. Certainly their responses could have been more
aggressive: landowners could have disrupted agricultural production,
slaughtered their livestock, or mobilized their permanent hacienda
sharecroppers who might have feared that outside workers would
benefit at their expense. Yet, as in Peronist Argentina, the landowners'
complaints were heard in their journals; they were plaintive appeals
for a rational agrarian policy rather than calls for action. The explanation perhaps parallels the reasons why Argentine landowners did not
disrupt the agricultural economy when Perón began to expropriate
their profits. In Argentina, the landowners still had much to lose—
their property. In Peru, it appeared to many landowners that their
land too might be spared if they avoided antagonizing the unpredict-

able and apparently somewhat vindictive government. Because the scope of the land reform was left unspecified at the beginning, and only the largest properties were initially affected, these landowners were isolated from the potential support of smaller *hacendados*. When the land reform effort turned to the next level of landholdings, with hints (like the subdivision option, for example) that it would go no further, these targets were isolated in turn from the support of the smaller landholders, and so on.[5]

When in 1972 the National Agrarian Society (SNA) began to protest rather vehemently against land reform, the government simply abolished the association. In the place of SNA and all the peasant leagues, the administration established the National Agrarian Confederation (CNA) as the only legitimate organ for representing farmers' interests. The remaining landowners, who no longer controlled the production or transport of crucial commodities, had no recourse for opposing this action by disrupting the economy.

The legal monopoly of CNA, subordinate to SINAMOS and prohibited from acting as an interest group, finally united the remaining landowners, along with new land recipients and sharecroppers who aspired to own their plots, into local movements opposing the government's plans for further collectivization. Harding (1975, pp. 248–250) gives the example of the Frente de Defensa del Agro Arequipeño (Front for the Defense of Arequipan Agriculture), which supplanted the local agrarian league set up under the CNA and extracted promises of no further expropriations in that area. This sort of coalition was broad enough to dissuade the government from direct confrontation. Already facing opposition to further collectivization reforms from unionized plantation workers, the regime found it easier to deal with the "unrecognized" groups than to coerce them into compliance.

RURAL WORKERS

The major force that blocked further equalization of rural income, then, was not the landowning sector but the agricultural workers who were privileged by virtue of their employment in the relatively high-paying commercial subsectors of agriculture or their status as full members of newly established cooperatives. As in the industrial sector, alternative forms of cooperative or collective farms could have spread the benefits to the formerly transient workers, or even encompass *minifundistas* who had not been employed on the farm prior to land reform. To resist the government's efforts to make these changes, workers benefiting from the existing arrangements resorted to strikes, raids on SINAMOS offices, and straightforward uprisings. The government faced, often simultaneously, land takeovers where the land transfers were not yet completed and strikes where the first transfers had already occurred.

The coordinating focus of opposition to further land reform was APRA, which controlled the unions of the sugar plantations and had founded many of the peasant leagues. The confrontation thus took on partisan political significance, since APRA was fighting for the restoration of civilian rule. By 1973 large segments of the rural proletariat came to regard SINAMOS and the government's land reform in general as a fascist means of military control. The riots of November 1973 and the subsequent disruptions directed against SINAMOS can be interpreted as the conseqences of APRA's success in turning these segments against the military government despite its still-populist policies.

In essence, the government had not seen that the abstract distinction between landowners and the peasantry was in reality blurred. For small landholders and for those who received plots or became part of a profitable cooperative, there was no incentive to support further land reform, and much to fear from it. With insufficient land for everyone, some of the reform schemes and new organizational forms had the potential of reducing the resources available to those who had already benefited. The cost of making this error was not so much in the failure to redistribute land as in the overall weakening of the military's resolve to encourage participation and further reform throughout the economy.

THE INDUSTRIAL SECTOR

In assessing the industrialists' reactions, it should be kept in mind that the relationship between industrial and commercial sectors and the government was not one of out-and-out confrontation until 1974. The business sector and the Velasco planners discussed, bargained, and agreed to myriad special arrangements. The criticisms of the secretive formulation of the General Industrial Law apparently were heeded. Policy formulation became more open, particularly in matters that concerned the ministries (largely controlled by more moderate military officers) and the business sector. The formulation of the "industrial community" arrangements, for instance, went through several modifications on the basis of reactions by the business community.

To the degree that the industrial and commercial setors were dissatisfied with Velasco's policies, they tried to circumvent the impacts of the offending programs. For example, industrialists were able to blunt the impact of the Industrial Community Law provision that required the transfer to workers of new share issues at a rate of 15 percent of book profits. By various bookkeeping expedients such as increasing the salaries of owner-managers, many firms managed to reduce their net profits.

More important, they responded by withholding their own investment and by discouraging the investment of others. There was an investment strike similar to the one in Chile. FitzGerald (1979, p. 61) notes that "private capital reacted against the new regime as soon as it became clear that the promised reforms would actually be implemented. In particular, the rate of manufacturing investments fell sharply to a level little above that needed for replacement, even though profitability rose steadily." Big business discouraged investment by conveying a highly negative image of the economy and by drawing smaller entrepreneurs closer to the industrial and commercial elite.

Until the 1974 takeover of six major Lima dailies, the regime's industrial policies were criticized from the pages of *La Prensa* and other newspapers despite some government harrassment. These criticisms were accepted by domestic investors, large and small, and were fed to potential foreign investors via the international press.[6]

To overcome the attraction of profitability for the small-scale and medium-scale entrepreneurs legislated into manufacturing ventures, the National Society of Industries (Sociedad Nacional de Industrias, or SNI), like the Chilean SOFOFA during the Allende years, shifted its tactics to incorporate smaller-scale entrepreneurs and thereby broaden the opposition to government policy. Alberti (1977, p. 68) reports that owners of the smaller manufacturing firms were given an increasingly important role in SNI affairs. At the same time, these entrepreneurs came to identify themselves with the industrial elite. The government's divide-and-conquer tactics, which were successful in the agrarian sector, did not work in industry.

For nearly five years the Velasco government acceded to the obvious power of the private business sector by making ministerial-level accommodations. As the urgency of attracting capital mounted, the government put off a sweeping tax reform and was content to tighten the administration of Belaúnde's tax reforms. By the end of Velasco's term, even though the administration of taxation was superior, the tax burden on businesses was actually less than before, owing to the tax incentives of the General Industrial Law (FitzGerald 1979, p. 203).

Only in 1974, when the government became thoroughly disillusioned with the lack of investment response, was a more radical plan contemplated: a proposal—never implemented—to transform all firms affected by the General Industrial Law into cooperatives within ten years. As the regime cast about to find a viable investment vehicle, the further withdrawal of private investment increased the government's resolve to strengthen its capacity to capture private savings and convert them into productive investment. Yet the five years of governmental pragmatism in dealing with the business sector undoubtedly forestalled a drastic investment strike and production sabotage, which would have brought on an economic crisis much sooner. By the same token, the increasing regidity of the government exacerbated the economic crisis that emerged in 1974.

ORGANIZED LABOR

Strong opposition also came from organized workers of the modern industrial sector, although they benefited economically from the Velasco reforms. Their resistance derived as much from politics as from economics. By taking over industries, the state became more directly involved in the labor-management confrontation over wages. As in other instances of increased state involvement, (Perón, Frondizi, and Frei), the strike became a combined political and economic act. Moreover, the incursions of SINAMOS and the government-sponsored trade union confederation CTRP gave the Communist and APRA union leaders additional motivation to oppose the government. The issue of wages was obviously both an important and a convenient rallying point. FitzGerald (1979, p. 61) notes:

> After an initial period of consternation at the rapid succession of reforms and the disorientation resulting from the radical rhetoric of SINAMOS, the trade unions began to regroup, particularly under the influence of the communist CGTP. More importantly, the workers in nationalized industries came to realize that state management would be little different from private management—a specific manifestation of the internalization of the class conflict within the state itself: the annual average of days lost through strike action rose from about one million in 1969–73 to over three million in 1974 and 1975. General strikes followed in both 1976 and 1977.

The most serious challenge to the regime came with the November 1973 riots in the southern cities of Arequipa, Cuzco, Puno, and Ayacucho. The disruption was intitiated by a strike of the teachers' union SUTEP (Sindicato Unico de Trabajadores de la Educación Peruana, or United Peruvian Educational Workers Union), an Aprista union that had been challenged by the government-backed competitor. The strike spread to students opposing the regime's repression, small farmers opposed to SINAMOS efforts to control the peasant leagues, and various other supporters of APRA and Acción Popular. The riots paralyzed the South and provoked a state of siege, hundreds of arrests, and an unknown but probably large number of casualties.

The riots were damaging to the Velasco administration in two ways. First, they strengthened the more conservative military officers who feared the instability that could emerge from further mass mobilization. Second, because SINAMOS was widely held responsible for provoking the riots, it had to be severely weakened to allay the fears of the military. A conservative general was placed in charge of SINAMOS and its activities were sharply curtailed.

While these civilian reactions led to changes in government policies, they also led to a political repression that played into the hands of the military "moderates" who opposed both political confrontation and further economic radicalism. The takeover of the Lima newspapers in July 1974 provoked riots in the city's wealthier neighborhoods. When the government closed other publications for disclosing a military scandal, bombings of government offices ensued. Finally, in February 1975, major riots and looting broke out in Lima during a police strike. The government responded by suspending the constitution and attacking the rioters with regular army troops.

All of these disruptions were connected to the economic condition of the country and to the government's increasing defensiveness. Press coverage of the economy was negative, and the military felt that the investment climate could not tolerate such unpatriotic reporting. Increased tension was provoked by the strikes, the demands for relief from growing inflation, and the government's efforts to control the dissent.

One of the most significant economic policy reactions to the increasing disruption of the urban work force was the use of the state agricultural purchasing agency, EPSA, to subsidize urban food prices. This was done both by importing food and by keeping prices paid to local producers low. Both tactics discouraged domestic agricultural production, and the low prices also diminished the progressive impact of Velasco's policies, inasmuch as the small farmers who might have gained from higher food prices were of lower income levels than the urban groups benefiting from the subsidies.

OPPOSITION WITHIN THE MILITARY

Ultimately the military removed Velasco,[1] and his replacement by General Morales Bermúdez signaled an end to the efforts at progressive restructuring. Military "opposition" thus was crucial, even though the military's reactions reflected those of society as a whole. If there were significant divisions within the military over the preferred scope of reform, how did the radicals dominate initially and why did their dominance decline?

The policymaking structure instituted by Velasco helped to magnify the power of the younger radical officers by placing them in positions of authority exceeding that of the ministries, which were staffed by senior officers and tended to be more conservative. Velasco set up a presidential secretariat, the Comité de Asesores a la Presidencia (COAP), staffed by young colonels, to formulate broad policies and to coordinate the ministries. But the system created a discrepancy between the plans formulated and publicized by the government and the actual microdecisions made in the ministries. The decisions affecting specific firms were made rather pragmatically, while the pronouncements and image of the regime remained radical through the actions of COAP.

By 1973, in the wake of rioting and economic downturn, Velasco faced opposition within the military itself. Philip (1978, p. 144) points out that the military developmentalists and radicals at the outset had common purposes—to destroy the dominance of foreign and oligarchic capital—but by 1973 the developmentalists' goals were either accomplished (greater state control, land reform) or shown to be infeasible (complete independence of foreign capital). At the same time, the government's continued efforts to mobilize workers despite the failure of SINAMOS, and the declining levels of investment, raised fears among the developmentalists that Velasco was leading the country into chaos. The riots of November 1973 and the increasing level of strikes gave credence to these fears. Moreover, developmentalists concerned with the economic situation recognized that foreign finance was both essential and not to be taken for granted, especially since Velasco was apparently renewing the attack on the private sector through the social property enterprise scheme and other more desperate ideas formulated by COAP (such as turning all major firms into cooperatives). The moderates, on the other hand, attempted to maintain productive relations with business and labor leaders through the ministries; eventually, they began delicate attempts to remove Velasco who, as his health deteriorated, was perceived as increasingly erratic.

Additional opposition came from officers labeled hard-liners; they opposed political mobilization on the grounds that it was an opening for Communism and the destruction of law and order. These elements, ensconced in the military since the beginning of the Velasco regime, had been forced to bide their time until the radical tendencies could be attacked as undermining public order and generating the economic crisis. Given the dominance of radicals in COAP and of moderates in the ministries, the hard-liners had difficulty penetrating the process of economic policy formulation within the government and turned to actions outside the policymaking process.

Their initiatives were directed, with some support from APRA, against the Communist-affiliated segment of the labor movement. They were epitomized by the activities of the right-wing labor movement MLR, which was actually created by an active-duty military officer, Gen. Javier Tantalean, after the CGTP (also headed by Tantalean) had been dismantled following bloody confrontations with the Communist unions in 1972. The MLR was a strike-breaking operation, designed to increase the government's control, but it obviously sharpened the confrontation between "mobilized" civilians and the military government. Since the Communists basically supported the government during Velasco's tenure, the competing labor organization set up by military officers such as Tantalean obviously was not sympathetic to the program of the radical officers dominant in the government as of 1970. The radicals could block the MLR effort to maintain control, and to hamper Communism, only when the MLR itself threatened domestic stability, as it did in 1972. But when the situation in the cities and countryside became increasingly unstable for reasons other than Tantalean's ventures, support for his efforts grew within the military.

Politics and economics became increasingly intertwined. Opposition to the government's policies, including the radical economic measures (such as union strikes to forestall more equitable reforms in the sugar cooperatives, or newspaper articles criticizing government policies), provoked military efforts at repression. Yet advocacy of political repression was not consistent with the political mobilization that was unleashed (but not fully controllable) through the military's economic and social programs. Thus the radicals supported mobilization only if it was channeled in controlled directions, while the hard-liners also opposed mobilization—but not of their favored groups (such as, in Tantalean's case, APRA).

Within the military, then, it was not simply a confrontation between hard-liners of conservative economic persuasion versus economic radicals favoring political mobilization. Some of the radical officers, in fact, came to be regarded as hard-liners (Philip 1978, p. 152). Rather, it was a combination of economic radicals responding to the attacks on their programs by invoking political repression; of economic conservatives using the state of confrontation to attack both Communists and military radicals as the sources of intolerable disruption; and of developmentalists who opposed both the further radicalization of economic policy and the repression.

When General Morales Bermúdez finally put together the long-rumored coup in August 1975, the changeover was neither a clear-cut rejection of radical policies nor a victory for the hard-liners (many of whom were displaced from positions of importance following the coup). The new regime promised to further the revolution, though correcting for its "deviations," but the economic crisis required the abandonment of further radical reforms. The government argued that the implementation of austerity measures was unavoidable.

REACTIONS OF FOREIGN CAPITAL

The initial reaction of foreign capital to the IPC takeover and the other nationalistic acts of the Velasco government was the expectable withdrawal of investment shown in Table 15. Subsequently, however, foreign funds in the form of loans and selective investments in minerals became an exceedingly important element in Peru's overall financing. Maintaining the investment level was a real achievement, even if it did entail building up a huge foreign debt. It should not be taken for granted that a highly nationalistic government, which had antagonized the major power in the hemisphere and had enunciated a policy of reducing the control of foreign capitalists over its economic affairs, could still attract foreign loans and investment capital. Moreover, it should not be presumed that the Velasco administration simply undertook a suicidal strategy of incurring an unpayable debt rather than face the need to accommodate to reduced investment funds. The gamble taken by the Peruvian government might have paid off if the expected oil export boom had materialized. Instead, the oil finds were disappointing in relation to the amount invested; other mineral extraction efforts were of long gestation under even the best of circumstances; and the expansion of exports simply did not materialize to save Peru from its crushing burden of debt.

Attraction of foreign funds required the Peruvian government to demonstrate its creditworthiness and to provide secure opportunities for profitable investment. These two requirements were interrelated, in that Peru's creditworthiness hinged on maintaining high export earnings through mineral exports (particularly oil and copper), and this was the area in which foreign capital could be used to increase production rapidly. To avoid debt default, the foreign debt had to be renegotiated. This in turn required demonstrating the eonomy's capacity to pull in foreign reserves, to offset the U.S. government's pressure against Peru and the negative assessment of Peru's credit worthiness presented by the World Bank. Peruvian leaders faced two dilemmas. First, the possible inconsistency of the nationalist demand for control over Peru's natural resources (which the military government itself made into the symbol of national autonomy through the IPC expropriation) and the granting of foreign rights in this most sensitive sector could be a political liability. Second, the government had to reassure key sources of foreign funds, even while closing in on foreign-owned resources in other sectors. The climate for any cooperation from foreign funding sources seemed extremely negative. In 1969 the United States had reacted to the expropriation of the IPC by suspending the Peruvian sugar quota and had successfully applied pressure on the World Bank to freeze long-term credits for Peru. The World Bank decision influenced other long-term lenders to do the same. The Peruvian government went ahead with expropriations of the holdings of W. R. Grace and ITT; it began to enforce the 200-mile fishing limit; it reclaimed the mineral concessions that had not yet been exploited; and in 1970 it passed the Industrial Law, with its restrictions on foreign participation in basic industries.

Still, these events and the U.S. government's attitude did not deter the American-owned Southern Peru Copper Corporation from negotiating for the Cuajone copper field concession. Nor did they deter the major oil companies from signing service contracts with the state oil company PETROPERU, stipulating that the oil companies would retain roughly half of the oil found in exchange for bearing the full costs of exploration and development. The fact that these contracts were signed in 1971—well before the oil embargo and the oil price rise—dispels the possibility that the oil companies were desperate for new sources.

Moreover, the international banks were willing to lend billions of dollars to Peru despite the World Bank evaluation, despite the Velasco regime's moves to nationalize the banking sector, and despite growing recognition that the debt would have to be renegotiated. When the renegotiation was agreed to in 1972, the burden of debt payback was displaced to 1976. It was certainly true that lending by the commercial banks was of shorter duration (three to five years) and at higher interest rates than the World Bank or bilateral official lending would have been. Nonetheless, the volume of available funds was impressive. Foreign investors and lenders displayed a high level of responsiveness to selective incentives. While the Cerro de Pasco conglomerate was being nationalized, other mining companies were still interested in dealing with the Peruvian government. The lack of a concerted effort by "international capital" to punish the Velasco regime is an important lesson for other governments that may wish to undertake nationalist measures. The Peruvian case indicates that international capital does not enforce liberal principles for the benefit of international capital as a whole, but responds to particular investment opportunities as they arise.

CONCLUSIONS

Before drawing conclusions about why the Velasco administration succeeded in some of its efforts and failed in others, it is important to clarify why it did not undertake a fundamental redistribution despite all of its rhetoric and the price it paid for being "radical." Richard Webb (1977, p. 87) notes that the redistribution, being basically intrasectoral, could not redress the major income discrepancy, which was between the modern industrial sector and the rest of the economy. To determine why the Velasco regime did not make the income distribution more equitable overall, we need to analyze why intersectoral transfers were not undertaken.

These transfers could have had two forms: immediate transfers of wealth, income, or services to the lower-income sectors, particularly to the rural sector; or policies (for example, taxing or pricing) to encourage growth of the agricultural sector and urban employment to absorb the underemployed of the urban traditional sector. Yet the revolution seems to have been conceived almost totally in terms of ownership; its efforts were oriented to wresting ownership of the means of production within each broad sector away from the original owners and bestowing it on the workers previously associated with it. To judge by the Velasco administration's total lack of enthusiasm for Belaúnde's emphasis on expanding the social services that might aid the poor, the Velasco programs probably appeared to the radicals in the administration to be hopelessly slow and "reformist." Once the government had embarked on the transfer of ownership, maintaining the appropriate economic environment, even if it involved sacrificing opportunities for tax and pricing reforms, seemed imperative. The government—and for that matter all the other political actors—accepted the marxist presumption that the most fundamental issue was ownership.

Another explanation is that the regime made the initial decision to rely—in part—on private investment, and the consequent need to keep the investment climate positive required that the government forgo fundamental redistribution. There is certainly some truth to the proposition that the Velasco government held off its tax reform in order to maintain this investment climate, even if its efforts ultimately proved futile. As in Allende's Chile, the state-sector enterprises were not helpful in contributing to available investment capital. If the state had, by some maneuver acceptable to the rest of the military, overnight converted the entire corporate industrial sector to state enterprise, the capital still would not have been adequate.

The Velasco case is important in explaining the successes and failures of all efforts that were launched. Because the commitment to economic transformation deepened over time—in sharp contrast to the more common pattern of declining interest—the Velasco regime demonstrates the weakness of positing that the level of initial commitment determines the success of redistribution. Furthermore, the Velasco experience helps to explain why it is that so often the reaction of the opposition blunts the commitment to redistribution, even though in this case it seems to have accentuated the commitment. For the Velasco regime the actions of industrialists and landowners to circumvent the official decrees spurred further action by a government that could remain in office for a protracted period. The deepening of the revolution may have been motivated by the early frustrations, but a necessary condition was the economic success of the years prior to 1974. The government's ability to remain in power without sharply reversing its populist orientation lay in the economy's acceptable GNP growth until 1974. When the overall economic performance turned sour, the regime became as vulnerable to unrest and to military takeover as any civilian regime facing the same problems.

The Velasco regime also provides an excellent example of the advantages of segmenting the opposition. Cynthia McClintock (1983) points out that the landowners, against whom Velasco was quite successful, were "confronted sequentially and separately"; but "in the industrial sector 'large' and 'small' industrialists felt challenged simultaneously." The same dynamic held for the regime's initial success and later problems with organized workers. Initially, the takeover and structuring of cooperatives, both agricultural and industrial, gave the government the opportunity to work out arrangements without the concerted opposition of labor in general. By 1974 the sheer magnitude of strikes and other coordinated efforts by the labor movement (led by both Aprista and Communist confederations) prevented the government from either repressing them all or buying off the most dangerous of the groups.

A key tactic for segmenting the opposition was ambiguity. The Velasco regime was successful in disarming the opposition only when there was considerable doubt about what the regime intended to accomplish. Where the Velasco regime was clear in its intentions—as in the cases of SINAMOS and the worker participation scheme—it was far less successful.

Yet ambiguity has also been invoked as an explanation for Velasco's ultimate failure. McClintock (1983) in particular emphasizes the importance of the lack of support, which she attributes to the regime's "stealth"—the very factor that enabled Velasco to perpetrate the reforms despite potentially great opposition. McClintock's thesis is that if Velasco had been more straightforward in his actions, particularly in including beneficiary groups in the planning of the reforms, he could have counted on the support of the already benefited groups such as the newly landed peasantry, members of cooperatives, and so on.

What is unclear is whether those already benefited would have risked their own gains to further the revolution. We have noted the phenomenon of ungrateful beneficiaries of the Prado reforms. The actions of organized workers, both industrial and agricultural, suggest a completely "rational" defense of their positions in the face of the regime's more ambitious plans to extend benefits to poorer segments of the population. The reason why the overall income distribution did not improve was the combination of the government's stimulus of growth in industry rather than agriculture, and the success of the industrial workers and the ultimately landed peasantry in preventing further redistribution. There is no evidence that potential support was lost through ambiguous policies that were too subtle or circuitous for their beneficiaries to recognize.

It is also notable that the Velasco regime was effective in transforming the economy in precisely those areas where the groundwork had already been laid by the Belaúnde government. This was not simply because Belaúnde and Velasco had the same concerns. It was because the technical preparation of such plans is a lengthy and essential step, regardless of whether the government is a military one that can—in theory—impose policies by fiat. Although the Velasco regime was successfully improvisational in keeping the industrial and commercial sectors from open rebellion, its improvisations in developing new forms of cooeprative and state-sector enterprises were not successful. In other words, the regime's pragmatism mitigated the antagonism of the business sector but did not come up with new redistributive models.

CHAPTER 13
Common Predicaments

SALVADOR ALLENDE AND Juan Velasco, radical in such different ways, afford a fruitful opportunity for comparative analysis.
Their ideological stands were so different that comparisons on that
dimension reveal more than the fact—important in its own right—that
it does not take a fervent Marxist to create an enormous state sector in
an attempt to restructure economic privilege. The tactical-strategic
questions most usefully addressed concern the value of improvisation,
economic realism as opposed to romanticism, and the degree of control
that the central government can expect to exert over the state sector.
Also significant are the issues of whether Velasco's corporatist approach was a limiting factor in his program of economic change, and
how "radicalism" relates to income redistribution.

The common elements of the Allende and Velasco experiences
provide an illuminating profile of radical efforts at redistribution. In
terms of conceptions and broad strategies, there are four key
similarities.

First, the radicals of both countries expected their own crisp distinctions among classes and subclasses to be held by everyone else. Allende
assumed everyone would accept the distinction between "monopolists," who were the enemy, and the rest of the middle class, who were to
be spared from victimization and would participate enthusiastically in
the economic boom because they had nothing to fear. Velasco anticipated that the large industrialists and the latifundistas would be
similarly isolated in the minds of all other elements of their own
respective sectors. For both men the "workers," whether organized or
not, whether employed in the modern sector or not, were to be a
unified class willing to support measures benefiting any of their breth-
ren. This presumption led both leaders into excessive optimism concerning their capabilities of forging a delicate alliance among selected
segments of each broad class or sector. It also led the planners of both
regimes to assume that more private investment would be forthcoming
than actually materialized. This miscalculation set off the overblown
reactivation programs that culminated in economic disaster.

Second, both regimes employed a level of provocative rhetoric that antagonized some of the economic sectors that the regime intended to court as allies. The rhetoric may have been motivated by the desire to discredit those portions of the upper-income and middle-income sectors who were not to be included. Instead, it only served to frighten and mobilize all of these groups against the government. In an important sense the blatancy and hyperbole of both regimes were wasteful; proredistributive support was already strong and in no need of bolstering in the sectors where the governments intended to extend benefits, and both governments eventually suffered from the excess of demands that could not be met at the planned pace of transformation.

Third, both governments relied on the state sector to fill the investment gap and consequently were highly vulnerable when the state sector proved less adequate than previously believed to generate savings and investment. The presumption that Stefan de Vylder (1976, p. 115) attributes to Allende's planners applies equally well to Velasco's:

> Through the nationalization of monopolistic enterprises huge surpluses which had earlier "disappeared" in the form of capital flight, tax evasion, unproduction, speculative investment, etc. were to be recuperated for development needs ... In this "new economy" the state-owned sector was to become large and centralized enough to be "dominant" and permit firm public control of the economy.

Fourth, despite the theoretical importance given to state investment, both regimes showed an unwillingness, or inability, to force the state sector into cost savings that would have permitted them to contribute to overall investment levels. in both cases the expected "surplus" was drained by public-sector wage increases, and in Chile this was reinforced by placing much of the burden of holding down prices onto the state manufacturing firms.

REACTIONS

The reactions against these regimes also show some similarities which are noteworthy, either because they are characteristic of the dilemmas faced by radical redistributive efforts, or because they are surprising in light of the presumed radicalism of the regimes.

Despite the boldness of the governments' own programs, they were outstripped by independent and illegal actions by many low-income elements, who tried to force more rapid wage increases and property transfers. There were record numbers of land takeovers, factory takeovers, strikes, and other confrontations with the wealthy. These simultaneously pushed the government into more radical or faster-paced transformations than intended, and magnified tensions over the pace and scope of the transformation. These actions were accompanied by ample criticism, on the part of the more radically oriented political groups, of the regimes' inadequate commitment to rapid redistribution, despite the fact that the leaders regarded themselves as fully radical. We have seen that the progressive measures of the reformists, rather than winning the backing of beneficiaries, created greater demands and increasing dissatisfaction. It is far more striking that the same occurred for the radicals.

The organizational reactions against redistributive initiatives in both Chile and Peru included efforts by industrialists and landowners to expand the membership of their formal associations to include smaller-scale owners, in order to enlist their aid in opposing government policy. Partly as a result of these tactics by larger-scale operators, there was increasing polarization between the government and smaller-scale middle-sector groups, as more of these segments shifted to open opposition to the regime.

Furthermore, efforts by large-scale industrialists to organize "investment strikes" upset the government plans for economic expansion to accommodate greater disposable income in the hands of low-income individuals. These were successful to a large degree in Chile despite the reactivation policy, and to a moderate degree in Peru. The investment strikes had one very important implication. The withholding of investment, a manipulation of economic resources alone among the potential resources of power, had a sufficiently severe effect on these two economies to constitute a crisis. This is not to say, of course, that the other, more straightforwardly political actions of the opposition groups in Chile and Peru were unimportant. But unless a redistribution-minded government solves the problem of providing adequate investment, either through alliance with private-sector investors or through the state's resources, it cannot avoid a harrowing economic crisis. It is useful to explore further why these two regimes failed to provide for their nations' investment needs.

REALITY AND ECONOMIC ROMANTICISM

One of the issues facing all radical regimes is deliberate disregard of harsh economic realities and of the need for careful calibration, whether through advance planning or immediate response to unfolding events. Attention to detail, when the world seems to require radical transformation, is often regarded with disdain by radicals, giving rise to economic "romanticism" or "naiveté."

One aspect of this naiveté was the reliance on an investment model that overestimated the contribution of the private sector in an environment hostile to private enterprise. The reactivation plans that created inflation by pushing demand far beyond available capacity were remarkably similar in conception and performance. In both cases the ambitiousness of the reactivation could be justified only if an enthusiastic private sector response were forthcoming. In Allende's case the hostility was not all of his making, since the left wing of the Unidad Popular was clearly trying to prod the administration into even more radical policy positions. Yet both Allende and Velasco should have been able to anticipate that the rhetoric of officials and their associates precluded optimism. They should have either devised a viable strategy for doing without private investment—an option which I shall argue was infeasible—or scaled down the pace and magnitude of the reactivation and the redistributive goals tied to it.

Both regimes also were overly optimistic about the capacity of the state sector to provide a viable alternative to private investment. It is striking that in both Chile and Peru the growth of public-sector investment fell far shorter of expectations than did private-sector investment. To be sure, private investment expanded more slowly than did public investment in Peru (FitzGerald 1976, p. 84), and in Chile neither grew. But the essential point is that low or negative growth rates in private investment were anticipated, whereas both regimes pinned their hopes—and set other economic parameters—on the assumption that the state sector would invest at high and predictable levels.

Why this miscalculation? It seems that the state is often regarded as an instrument of policy; since it is "part" of the government, it is presumed to afford far more control than does regulation of the private sector, which is a more indirect and hence presumably more hazardous means of setting the economy's parameters. Neither Allende nor Velasco adequately appreciated the degree to which the state sector constituted an interest group that could pressure the central policymakers for higher wages, better fringe benefits, and (perhaps most important of all) decision-making autonomy that frustrated any hopes of coherent central control.

For all the concern over control and the use of direct interventionist policies, neither Velasco nor Allende took advantage of the government's increased control over the economy to rectify its imbalances. In addition to the failure to use state enterprises to increase savings, both governments effectively took over the banking system but did not employ monetary policy to avert the ill effects of other policy measures. Lessened effective control cannot be laid to a weakening of formal control, since the opposite occurred. Instead, as the quotations from Allende officials in Chapter 11 showed, there was an almost ideological condescension toward calibration, despite lip service to the importance of planning.

Even radicals, then, have to attend to detail if they are to survive. If calibration is indeed no less important for the success of a radical, a fusion between radical commitment and concern for detail must be found. Their theoretical compatibility has been maintained by many sources.[1] However, we have also seen that improvisation is a vital element in preempting opposition reactions and coping with the unexpected repercussions of redistributive initiatives. Hence it is not just a matter of fusing radicalism and planning, but the more complex combining of radicalism, planning, and improvisation. In untangling and addressing this issue, we rely on the superior tactical performance of Velasco—who remained in office for seven years and accomplished many of the objectives he set out to achieve—despite the concomitant economic crisis, whose magnitude should by no means be minimized. The opposition of the middle sectors forced the Velasco economy into stagnation, but not into collapse.

AMBIGUITY AND IMROVISATION

We have assessed Allende's lack of plans as a serious liability in his conduct of economic affairs, but Velasco's as an advantageous source of improvisation. Is this inconsistent, or are there different sorts of improvisation that can contribute to the design of the "right" kind of flexibility? There are indeed three dimensions by which Allende's and Velasco's improvisation can be distinguished.

Let us first clarify whether there is in fact a necessary trade-off between advance planning and improvisation. Our concern here is not with formal plans, but with technical preparation done in advance of applying policy. Why not formulate flexible plans designed to meet all plausible contingencies, "improvise" with these plans as the guide, and thereby have the best of both worlds? Because in practice it is never possible to plan for all contingencies; something—minor or major—is bound to go wrong. Then, the need to diverge from the recommendations expressed or implied in the advance studies may either generate resistance or, if accepted, incur political and psychological costs for the government.

Resistance, political or psychological, occurs when advance planning advocates positions with which specific individuals or groups come to identify. These policies have a certain claim upon those who commissioned their preparation. To ignore the advice of months or years of study, even when it no longer appears to be relevant, can be embarrassing, indicating either incompetence earlier or impetuosity now. The costs of changing may entail antagonizing certain individuals or groups. Thus, when the Allende government finally decided that "consolidation" rather than further expansion of the state sector was necessary, the left-wing Unidad Popular elements participating in the formulation of plans for the social area felt more betrayed than if the acquisition of state enterprises had been hit-or-miss.

Moreover, any plan signals the intentions of the government, whether correctly or not. Advance technical preparation can rarely be so hermetically conducted that expectations of government action based upon these preparations do not arise. Consequently, where advance planning is likely to guide future action, it reduces ambiguity; where it does not ultimately guide action, it may increase ambiguity and surprise. In neither case, though, is it neutral with respect to creating expectations.

In short, there are some trade-offs between advance planning and improvisation that in practice can be minimized but not altogether eliminated, and there are distinct mentalities of planning and improvisation that can rarely coexist. It is worthwhile to ask when one ought to be emphasized over the other. What was there about Allende's situation or approach that made improvisation so damaging?

First of all, Allende's measures for redistributing income operated at the most aggregate level of macroeconomic policy. General wage adjustments bolstered by across-the-board price controls, dramatic changes in the aggregate money supply, and so on, were nonsegmented, largely undifferentiated policy levers that were certainly powerful in their impact, but were also prone to catastrophe if badly calibrated. Velasco operated on a less aggregate level of policy—disallowing specific landholding parcellations designed to evade expropriation; implementing industrial-community profit-sharing plans that affected only large industrial establishments, and these only gradually; arranging better bargaining positions of workers, but without dictating general wage adjustments; limiting price controls to a few items such as food; and so on.

Second, the measures employed by the Allende planners had nearly instantaneous impact, as opposed to the gradual effects of the Velasco policies that permitted adjustment as economic trends were seen to be off the track. The initial errors of Velasco's policies resulting from ad hoc formulation were relatively more remedial through further improvisation, whereas in the Allende case enough damage was done by the catastrophic redistribution (a tenth of the national income) effected in 1971 alone to undermine the entire experiment.

Allende also found, primarily for political reasons,[2] that the direction and effects of his policies were irreversible as long as he stayed in power. Because of his start with such extreme measures, the technical weaknesses caused by the lack of careful planning could not be offset by improvisation. Velasco, starting out modestly and finding his revolution deepening, was able to improvise first in expanding the scope of the reforms (particularly land reform), then in restricting some of the more flamboyant initiatives in the industrial sector when the economy began to disintegrate. Velasco was saved from his own administration's misconceptions and incompetence by his willingness and capacity to abandon one scheme and pick up another—whether on his own or because he was prodded by the military establishment. His establishment was a closed institution in which changes of heart could be agreed to without embarrassing public confrontations. Allende, much more locked in by the deliberations and desires of the more open Unidad Popular, could not backtrack without engaging the more radical elements in a public confrontation that imposed political costs on Allende and led to even more polarized conditions because the radicals' demands were channeled so publicly.

Finally, in Allende's case, there was never any doubt of the regime's commitment to radical transformation; the question was whether any middle-sector group would be spared the deprivation of redistribution. In Velasco's case, the ambiguity concerned whether any basic transformation would be carried out. Consequently, Velasco could use improvisation and the absence of carefully formulated plans to maintain the uncertainty of whether even the ultimate victims of redistribution (for example, the landowners eventually forced to give up their land despite parcellation) should openly oppose the government. This ambiguity was damaging when it antagonized groups who were not targeted, but was the trade-off for keeping the actual victims off guard. In Allende's case the principal victims were all too clear from the beginning; whatever uncertainty was involved—specifically whether lower-middle-income segments would suffer economic deprivation— only raised the level of anxiety among hoped-for allies.

Many of these differences stem from the fact that the Allende program was simply more radical in its aims than anything that Velasco contemplated. This is not to criticize the ambitiousness of the Allende reforms, but simply to assert that an extremely radical program can less afford looseness in its conception. If a leader is intent on signaling his intention to make radical transformations and forgoes the advantages of ambiguity, he must be prepared with careful plans to calibrate policy in order to minimize the damage of expectable reactions.

CORPORATISM AND REDISTRIBUTION

The issue of whether the Velasco regime was "corporatist," and what implications this might have, is more fruitfully addressed in this comparative chapter than in the narrative review of Velaso's efforts because the contrast with Allende is helpful in understanding why Velasco turned to state control over interest group actions. If the Velasco regime could be characterized as "corporatist," does this account for the limited degree of redistribution carried out? Did his attempts to take over lower-income-group organizations represent an effort to dampen working-class demands as dictated by corporatist philosophy, or did they reflect the failure of redistributive efforts that had run their course, or the need for calibrating a redistribution that had gone as far as it could under prevailing economic conditions? Were the political goals of reworking societal structures inconsistent with further redistribution? Is the redistribution effected by corporatist-minded leaders a secondary tactic directed at the more fundamental goals of stability and control—a crumb thrown to the poor to entice their participation in government-sponsored arrangements—and hence inherently limited in scope?

Many aspects of Velasco's approach were more reminiscent of Perón than of the Marxist strategy in Allende's Chile. The rhetorical appeal to interclass cooperation, the preoccupation with controlling the participation mobilized by the government, the effort to create a system of representation in which state-sponsored organs held a monopoly of organization for important sectors—these were the common elements linking Velasco and Perón.[3] They are the hallmarks of the philosophy and strategy labeled organic statism and corporatism, respectively. Organic statism has been defined by Alfred Stepan (1978, pp. 26–27) as "a normative vision of the political community in which the component parts of society harmoniously combine to enable the full development of man's potential, [although] such harmony does not occur spontaneously in the process of historical evolution but rather requires power, rational choices, and decisions, and occasional restructuring of civil society by political elites."

This philosophy is typically a guide and a rationale for corporatist political arrangements, defined by Philippe Schmitter (1974, pp. 93–94) in terms of formal institutional characteristics as "a system of interest representation in which the constituent units are organized into a limited number of singular, compulsory, noncompetitive, hierarchically ordered and functionally differentiated categories, recognized or licensed (if not created) by the state and granted a deliberate representational monopoly within their respective categories in exchange for observing certain controls on their selection of leaders and articulation of demands and supports." According to this definition, by 1972 if not sooner the Velasco regime was highly corporatist in its intentions.[4] The Confederación Nacional Agraria was a classically corporatist initiative according to Schmitter's definition, inasmuch as it was intended to monopolize representation of the rural sector and was accompanied by the formal dissolution of competing agrarian representational institutions. While SINAMOS and the union movement CTRP were not given formal monopolies, they were clearly intended to supplant or absorb existing structures representing peasant, blue-collar, and low-income community groups.

One can argue that the Velasco administration was considerably more corporatist in orientation than the Perón administration, inasmuch as Velasco tried to impose formal monopolies of representation, whereas Perón actually required competing parties to remain active—the better to divide them in their frustration of having to participate in the effectively rigged electoral game. Moreover, although Perón had elaborated a philosophy of Justicialismo that was explicitly organic statist, he seemed to glory in competitive victories (even if the game was not fair) rather than being appalled with competition as is congruent with the organic view of social harmony.

If Velasco's regime was the clearest example of corporatism among the redistributive-minded governments we have examined, to what extent does this characterization explain the magnitude of redistribution undertaken by the government? With respect to the extent of redistribution consistent with a corporatist or organic statist viewpoint, Stepan (1978, p. 33) makes the crucial point that "a just and stable organic order is not necessarily to be equated with the established order. The concept of the common good, with the moral obligation it imposes on the state to achieve the general welfare, leaves open the possibility that the state can formulate and impose on its own initiative major changes in the established order so as to create a more just society." In other words, corporatism may call for fundamental change. Stepan goes on to demonstrate the co-occurrence of organic statist beliefs and advocacy of improved material conditions for the poor in the writings of the Catholic church.

Thus adherence to an organic statist philosophy does not preclude advocating a transformation of the socioeconomic order to a condition of greater economic justice. Nor, despite the fact that corporatist philosophy was most loudly proclaimed by Benito Mussolini (and therefore is often regarded as inherently regressive in income-distributional terms because of Mussolini's use of corporatist control to hamper the Italian labor movement), is there a priori presumption in the organic statist philosophy that the existing distribution of income ought to be made more regressive. In fact, Guillermo O'Donnell (1974, p. 67) asserts that there have bene strong links between corporatism and populism in Latin America. Corporatism is seen as an approach to the problem of "incorporating the popular sector economically and politically, using it to break the domination of the oligarchy, but also controlling it to prevent the emergence of autonomous organizational bases, leaders, and goals that might carry its political activation beyond the limits acceptable to the new bourgeois and state-based sectors." Thus a corporatist approach to arranging links between the government and interest groups has been, in at least some Latin American cases, a concomitant of improving the economic lot of lower-income populations. Perón's own approach certainly fits this model.

However, unlike the Marxist view that the ideal final distribution is equality of economic benefits, and the liberal view which does not take a position on a specific ideal distribution, the organic view may posit a distribution—reflecting some degree of income inequality—such that the economy functions harmoniously and economic actors are compensated according to the differentiated contributions they make. Justifications for rewarding some more than others may include the need to stimulate incentive; the pursuit of other goals of the society (such as a military buildup financed through reduced consumption by the masses); or the intrinsically greater value of work based on higher skill, intelligence, or willingness to take risks. The question, then, is whether the balance of rewards achieved in Peru at some point during the Velasco administration was regarded as adequate by leaders holding organic statist views and therefore obviated further efforts to achieve redistribution.

Two different arguments, one involving the economic vision of the corporatist and the other his political vision, could be made to link the

Peruvian military's corporatist or organic-statist views to the abandonment of redistributive efforts. First, the distribution of income, taking
into account its change through the reforms applied, might have been
regarded as already optimal. The changes achieved after the first few
years of the Velasco regime, for instance, could be interpreted as
having satiated the military's modest impulse to redistribution. Second,
if the increased social mobilization inaugurated in lower-income sectors through redistribution were seen as threatening the government's
control and the harmonious conduct of political, social, and economic
relations, then the political vision may have been perceived as jeopardized by further redistribution.

It is unlikely that the Peruvian military decided that redistribution
had gone far enough, or that income distribution in Peru had reached
the point at which the economic order was just and harmonious. Peru is
cursed with disparities of income that will put off for a very long time
the issue of whether the lower-income segment as a whole is overreach-
ing in its demands for a greater share of the nation's wealth—although
the demands of organized labor, to the extent that they can be met only
at the expense of the welfare of poorer individuals, is already an issue.

Once Velasco made the decision that redistribution in the agrarian
sector had gone as far as it could, he had two options for coping with
demands for further redistribution, on the one hand, and landowners'
demands for retrenchment on the other hand. He could simply turn
down the demands for and against further redistribution articulated
by autonomous organizations representing the various rural groups of
landowners, cooperative workers, landless peasants, and so on. Following the liberal pluralist model of keeping the state out of interest-group
affairs, the regime then would have faced the issue of how to suppress
the disruptions created by these groups when the government refused
to meet their demands. Alternatively, Velasco had the option of trying
to moderate the demands by asserting control over the channels
through which the demands were articulated. The activist stance of the
regime, and the early commitment to enhancing participation—in
evidence long before SINAMOS was initiated—led him to this second
option.

So Velasco chose the corporatist path of damping economic demands, but it does not appear to be consistent with Peru's situation to
say that the corporatist impulse required the damping of economic
demands. These attempts to control the land-hungry peasants, organized workers, and urban marginals are explicable in terms of the
restraint necessitated by immediate economic problems and political
pressures from groups other than the very poor—teachers, sugar
workers, and miners.

The contrast with Allende's experience provides some insight into why the Velasco regime ended up with elements of repressive corporatism as well as radicalism. Allende's failure was, in large part, the result of his inability to rein in the Unidad Popular. As provocative as Allende's personal program for redistribution was, his associates in the left wing of the UP movement threatened middle-sector economic actors far more and were bound to provoke complete polarization unless some control was applied by the president. Allende did not take advantage of presidential power, as Frei did, to discipline his own movement (though, to be fair, Frei did have an easier task, inasmuch as the Christian Democrats were a single party rather than a coalition of parties like the Unidad Popular). Velasco, partly because of his military background and partly because of the different power relations prevailing under a military dictatorship, was more preoccupied with, and more capable of, asserting limits on the expression of demands for more economic transformation than the regime was willing to undertake.

"RADICALISM" AND REDISTRIBUTION

The primary criterion by which the Unidad Popular government and the military radicals of Peru were definable as "radical" was their demonstrated willingness to expand state ownership of the economy. However, there was strikingly little relation between redistribution and the macrostructural characteristics normally associated with economic radicalism. The structural changes in ownership achieved by Velasco, though they were considerable, did not result in an overall improvement of the distribution of income. The bulk of the redistribution effected by Allende came from a combination of wage increases and price controls applied to private and state corporations. The proportion of private to state enterprises was largely irrelevant to the imposition of these policies.

Moreover, even the Chilean redistribution was largely limited to the relatively well-to-do workers in the industrial and agricultural sectors. Recall de Vylder's (1976, pp. 184–185) assessment of Allende's land reform:

> Little was thus achieved in terms of a modification of the very uneven distribution of labor in relation to available land ... The 100,000 smallest *minifundistas* ... continued to have at their disposal less than two physical hectares of land per family, and they continued to overex-

ploit their tiny holdings just as before, while vast amounts of land in other parts lay idle ... Only the full integration of small holders and unattached day laborers as beneficiaries would have made possible a radical improvement in the poor and irrational utilization of rural Chile's land and manpower. Such an integration would also have been required to relieve the misery of the hard core of rural poor, who benefited little or not at all from the Unidad Popular's land tenure reform.

In regard to the expansion of the social area in the Chilean industrial sector, de Vylder (1976, p. 155) noted in parallel fashion:

> The policy of "nationalizing" no more than some twenty per cent of the industrial labor force, giving these twenty per cent vast material and nontangible privileges (influence, prestige, etc.) while leaving the situation for the great majority—and, let me repeat, the poorest section—of the workers more or less unchanged was bound to give rise to new inequalities and to generate (or perhaps accentuate) splits within the working class.

The results are highly depedent on the fact that these economies were (and still are) characterized as dual economies, with huge discrepancies between modern-sector and traditional-sector incomes, largely but not completely overlapping the urban-rural separation. As Richard Webb (1977, p. 87) points out, changes in ownership structures within a given sector affect the distribution of income within that sector, but not the intersectoral distribution which is so fundamental to overall income distribution when there are immense intersectoral differences.

CHAPTER 14
Conclusions

THE MOST COMMON IMAGE of the struggle for redistribution has been one of open confrontation between the fully committed proredistributionist leader and the united, devious, unqualifiedly vindictive opposition. If valid, this image of the hero of the poor confronting the united front of the rich would be a gloomy one for the reformist, though perhaps a source of inspiration for the radical.

The image is at once pessimistic and cynical. It is rare enough to find a leader who is fully and irrevocably committed to redistribution when his own political survival is so often at stake. The prospects of redistribution are also limited if it is assumed that the die is cast in the initial commitment and heroism of the leader. More pessimistic still is the assumption that redistribution is of necessity highly confrontational. If indeed the redistribution-minded leader had to proceed against out-and-out opposition, particularly against a united enemy, the climate of investment would be so poisoned that decent aggregate economic performance, so important for the general welfare and the durability of the redistributive reforms, would be virtually precluded. The cynicism comes in the assessment of leaders who end up aiming for, or achieving, only modest degrees of improvement in economic justice. If the image of the redistributive struggle is that of an all-or-nothing confrontation between the rich and the poor, in which the poor either do or do not have enough power to triumph, moderation and caution come to be regarded as cowardice or lack of commitment to the cause.

The analysis strongly contradicts this image. Initial commitment is hardly a guarantee of success, nor is its absence a disqualification. There have been leaders who, like Allende, failed in their efforts to achieve lasting redistribution despite having been committed for decades to the redistributive cause; others, like Perón and Velasco, to a large extent adopted redistribution as a tactic, and it eventually became a central defining characteristic or principle of their regime.

The case studies also show that the image of the poor confronting the rich is profoundly misleading. On the one hand, the most effective strategy for securing the political viability of a redistributive policy often is to gain the backing of a selected part of the higher-income population. We have seen cases (Frei and Allende) in which errors in tactical choice can explain a failure that at first glance appears to have been a clear-cut case of the poor against the wealthy, whereas in fact the administration has antagonized previously noncombative elements of higher-income sectors. On the other hand, one of the most serious problems of carrying out redistributive programs is that the already-benefited poor often resist the spread of benefits to other segments of the needy.

Rejection of a deterministic view of the politics of redistribution naturally leads to the question of what can be done. Obviously, redistribution is not doomed to failure; there have been enough successes among the prominent debacles to dispel fatalism. But once an administration adopts its ideologically determined model of development and macrostructural form, can anything more be added, in terms of strategy and tactics, that will make a difference to the outcome?

Two arguments have been raised against the presumption that the choices subsidiary to the broadest issues of growth model and role of the state do make a difference. The first argument is that these broad choices—rapid industrialization as opposed to an agricultural emphasis, export-led growth versus import substitution, foreign against autonomous financing, socialism versus laissez-faire capitalism versus state capitalism, and so on—determine the bulk of the variation in distributive shares. There is no doubt that these choices, if implemented, are very important. We have seen that the metropolis-centered, proindustrial, export-led growth model chosen or taken for granted by a succession of Peruvian regimes resulted in continued income concentration despite the leaders' probably sincere belief in their own commitment to progressive redistribution. Yet this argument disregards the fact that the growth model and the broad institutional structure must be implemented in order that their effects, whatever they may be, be felt. If lower-level strategies and tactics must be carefully selected to guarantee the political survival of the redistributionist's program, then these "details" become crucial.

Furthermore, the commitment to a particular grand strategy of growth, or to a particular structure of state and economy, often emerges from the array of specific measures the government ends up applying, rather than being the fixed point of departure. It is highly unlikely that Perón, Frondizi, or Velasco chose a model at the outset and then proceeded unwaveringly to implement it.

The second argument maintains that the distributional choices emerge from tacit accords among economic policymakers, so that through a process of "mutual accommodation" the impact of any given policy instrument will be balanced by the implementation of other instruments that provide the "proper"—that is, tactily-agreed-upon—distributive result (Lindblom 1977). This argument may be used to posit that it is not worthwhile to focus on the tactics of choosing particular economic instruments to convey a redistributive effort, since the impact of any given instrument is bounded by the joint impact of the accords.

This argument of mutual accommodation probably has considerable merit in stable, developed countries characterized by good information and agreement (tacit or explicit) on distributive shares at least within a given government. But for most developing countries it is not plausible to expect smooth accommodation, not only because of the lack of consensus on distributive shares, but also because of poor communication among different governmental entities. It is in the disjunction of these entities on the issue of redistribution that some of the most important points of leverage have been found; for example, the military "radicals" of President Velasco's coordinating office COAP were able to push beyond the relative conservatism of the officers in the ministries to effect radical reforms in several areas, without the emergence of any consensus. Finally, there are marked fluctuations in income distribution over time in at least Argentina and Chile, which would deny the existence of a stable mutual accommodation over distribution. These fluctuations represent the effects of different economic instruments applied without the use of countervailing instruments by other economic policymaking entities. What made Frondizi's shift in the treatment of organized labor so abrupt was the fact that the initial wage increases were not accompanied by offsetting measures, and the subsequent stabilization program consisted entirely in instruments that cut into real-wage levels.

DIMENSIONS OF CHOICE

We are left with an inelegant reality: the choice of strategy and tactics makes a difference. But strategy and tactics of what sort? Insofar as contextual factors varying from one case to another will undoubtedly condition the success of any concrete choice, comparative examination can at best point to a design for analysis and choice, rather than dictating concrete actions. We can enumerate many aspects of choice, but surely not all conceivable dimensions are likely to be important. For instance, the choice among economic planning techniques is unlikely to make much difference; nor is the choice of foreign banks to be solicited for loans. The cases we have examined point to four relevant dimensions; specific instrument selection, repesentation, linkage, and timing. The rationales for focusing on thee aspects are given below.

INSTRUMENTS

Economic reactions very often arise in direct response to the concrete measures undertaken by the government. These measures or instruments themselves convey many of the concrete and symbolic elements of the struggle over income redistribution, ranging from the feasibility of implementation to the combativeness of the issue. Moreover, because different instruments are formulated in different arenas (for example, an open forum like the legislature or a relatively closed one like the Central Bank), the choice of instrument also determines the access of various pressure groups to the policy formulation process. Some instruments are highly visible, stimulating the mobilization of support and opposition, while others are intrinsically esoteric. Certain instruments, in affecting only a part of the population, are less likely to mobilize other actors, even if in the final analysis the interconnectedness of the economy guarantees that benefits going to one recipient influence how much will go to all others.

PRESENTATION

We must also conclude that the presentation and image of a redistributive effort are extremely important, no matter how superficial they may seem to the writer who chronicles the economic history of the era after the fact. This conclusion is unavoidable because of the astounding discrepancies between the perceived and actual trends in distribution and growth in most of the cases we have examined. In Argentina, the reputed agricultural disinvestment under Perón never occurred; the following period of La Revancha (the "revenge" against Peronist labor) actually saw real-income increases for organized labor; and Illia's supposedly inflationary "do-nothing" period in truth resulted in both growth and progressive redistribution with fairly low inflation. In Chile, Frei went from defeat to defeat in engineering one of the few effective tax changes in Latin America. In Peru, under virtually every "progressive" administration (including those of Belaúnde and Velasco), the overall distribution of income actually deteriorated. Treacherous as these discrepancies may be for the economic historian, they give the redistribution-minded leader much-needed room for maneuver. The fact that more often than not these discrepancies worked to the detriment of the proredistributive government reinforces our assessment that the manipulation of the symbols associated with redistribution is not only relevant, it also has been badly handled.

LINKAGE

Our case histories strongly indicate that the linkages of different instruments are important, not only because the economic impact of a one instrument is affected by the impacts of others, but also because the political feasibility of formulating and implementing an instrument is conditioned by other policies in force and by other issues in debate. The coalitions to be formed by the redistribution-minded leader depend on the economic policies directed toward the nonpoor coalition members as much as they do on the specifically redistributive instruments. Perón's credit subsidies to the emerging medium-scale entrepreneurs gained their support for his wage policies, just as Belaúnde's exchange-rate policy was probably quite important in ensuring the acquiescence of middle-income sectors to the government's spending programs for the poor. Similarly, the earmarking of tax sources to spending programs under Frei was an essential element in the political viability of these tax increases.

The tactics of linkage take on a dual importance in that they influence both the perception of redistributive policy and the Realpolitik of coalition building. The problems for the policymaker are, first, to decide which measures to initiate in combination (that is, more or less simultaneously), and second, to determine the extent to which they ought to be presented as a combination. Naturally, at any point in time there are innumerable measures that represent ongoing governmental activities and regulations, constituting a "combination" in a literal sense. I refer here to a "combination" in the narrower sense of a set of measures of recognized political or economic relevance to one another.

TIMING

There are three different but "obvious" tactics for timing the redistributive effort. Because each has been credited with high importance by one authority or another, they cannot be dismissed as trivial; yet obviously the disagreement on which is correct leaves undetermined the issue of which is the optimal approach.

If it is assumed that the government has its greatest power when it is first installed, and its capacity to gain compliance recedes as its mandate erodes, then the general advice will be to initiate as strong a redistributive effort as possible, as soon as possible. According to this argument, any attempt to moderate or delay a redistributive effort entails an irreversible loss of opportunity by the regime to effect its reforms. Peter Cleaves (1974, p. 321) argues for the Chilean case that "the most propitious period for a Chilean regime to implement the ideological aspects of its policy is during its first years of government. If the regime does not move swiftly in the initial months, the opposition usually sees to it that many of its programs never materialize."

Alternatively, if it is assumed that an economic system is more tolerant of redistribution at different points in time, depending on the overall level of prosperity—and hence the level of "surplus" that can be extracted from some economic actors for the benefit of others— it follows that redistributive efforts should not necessarily be launched when the new regime comes to power, but rather during the upswing of the business cycle. Insofar as disinvestment resulting from redistribution is seen as a threat to the continuity of the redistributive program, the initiation of such a program may be scheduled to occur when the investment climate is otherwise particularly propitious, either for local or foreign investors or both.

Finally, since each redistributive instrument faces a different process of formulation, application, and reaction, and because the rationale for each instrument in terms of additional objectives will also vary, it is plausible that the optimal timing for the introduction of redistributive efforts cannot be established generally with either of the preceding methods. Rather, each instrument's peculiarities will yield a different approach to timing. For example, progressive tax reform has its greatest appeal during fiscal crisis, when attention is focused on the need to balance the budget by increasing revenues. Obviously, fiscal crisis is not necessarily to be expected at the beginning of a new administration, or in times of economic upswing. Moreover, if one economic instrument is to be linked to another, its application must be timed specifically according to the opportunities to implement the other instrument.

STRATEGIC CONSIDERATIONS

The economic policymaker faces a crucial political choice in guiding his selection of economic measures and the tactics for presenting, timing, and linking them: whether to select measures and tactics that are likely to mobilize support, or to choose "quieter" approaches that eschew mobilization in order to keep potential opposition from arising as well. In theory, neutralizing opposition and mobilizing support can be consistent—when, for instance, so much support is mobilized that the opposition does not dare to oppose. Yet no case has emerged in which the size or intensity of support deterred the opposition, in part because the opposition can oppose in many ways that do not entail overt political confrontation.

For the redistributive-minded policymaker, the decision to be either strident or subtle must hinge on the relative strengths of support and opposition in influencing the fate of redistribution. My evidence strongly suggests that the traditional emphasis on cultivating support even if it tends to mobilize opposition is counterproductive. The emphasis of most redistribution-minded leaders has been on support mobilization, and these efforts often have run into catastrophic problems that can be traced to mobilization of opposition beyond what would have been necessary. Moreover, the mobilization of supposed support rarely pays off for the proredistributive regime, either because the already-benefited segments turn around to block redistribution to the remaining poor, or because their raised aspirations remain unsatisfied.

THE NATURE OF SUPPORT

Perhaps the most widespread presumption that political science offers to the analysis of policymaking is that one seeks support from the beneficiaries: those who have benefited from one's policies in the past or who stand to benefit in the future. The classic model of the relationship between government and populace has emphasized the exchange of support for satisfactions. The government satisfies the demands of some or all of its people, who in turn support the regime. When political competition is added to the model, the contest over the right to rule becomes one of matching up the strength of the current rulers and their beneficiaries against the strength of their various competitors. In this model, then, the competition in the political arena is won by the side that has satisfied, or is expected to satisfy, groups capable of providing the support of greatest magnitude, resources, and intensity.

Implicit in the model is the importance to the existing political leaders of ensuring that those who will receive benefits from the regime (that is, those whose demands are met) will appreciate their benefits and will translate that appreciation into support; they must be mobilized. Hence the value of identifying, organizing, and stimulating the participation of groups favored by policy is stressed in the bulk of the literature on political strategy.

The shortcomings of this model in explaining redistributive policy-making lie in the fact that the support of beneficiaries is of limited political value: those who have already benefited from redistribution are not likely to behave in grateful ways, and those who may benefit from contemplated redistributive policies are often incapable of being mobilized sufficiently to help the government vis-à-vis typical opposition tactics. This assessment contrasts with Albert Hirschman's (1963, p. 252) proposition that the reformer generally underestimates the support he can marshal, and overestimates the strength of the opposition. Our cases do not confirm this; on the contrary, both support and opposition can be treacherous.

The well-known phenomenon of rising expectations explains why beneficiaries of redistribution are not content with income transfers already effected through government policy. Once a regime has decided that a particular sector has improved its income share to the optimal level (in the eyes of the government policymakers), any visible measures to limit further improvements are likely to be resisted vigorously. Because wage increases have been such a prominent tool of redistribution, this phenomenon is most prominently seen in the apparent ungratefulness of the organized-labor sector. A outstanding example is the deteriorating government-labor relations in Chile under Frei, where the advances of blue-collar real income during the first three years had no restraining impact on subsequent wage demands. The same problem undermined the state-sector investment strategies of Allende and Velasco, as the unionized public employees in newly nationalized industries were able to secure wage increases that eliminated any possibility of significant state savings and investment. Even Juan Perón had to clamp down on the labor movement of his own creation in order to keep wages from disequilibrating the economy.

It can always be argued that the problem is not in the greed of those who have already benefited, but rather in the insufficient generosity of the leader. However, the leader must consider the macroeconomic consequences of his "generosity" to a given group, in terms of both the possibility of deterioration in overall growth and the denial of benefits to other, perhaps even poorer, low-income groups. There are many subsets of "the poor," often with opposing interests with respect to a given economic policy. Food subsidies for the urban poor, generally engineered to the detriment of the rural poor, is the classic example. The implication is that mobilizing "the poor," far from being a straightforward task, turns out to be a complicated and often unrewarding exercise insofar as the differences among lower-income seg-ments are likely to be substantial and politically divisive.

COALITIONS

Our examination of redistributive efforts results in several insights into the importance of coalitions.

First, allies from among the nonpoor have been essential to every redistributive success we have seen. Sometimes they have been crucial in promoting the formulation of a redistributive policy in a relatively open policymaking forum. This was true of educational reform in Peru under Belaúnde and social service expansion under Frei in Chile, both conducted in the legislature. In other cases their significance has been in responding to investment opportunities, keeping up the overall level of investment to avert the deleterious effects of production stagnation. Thus Perón had his allies among the small-scale to medium-scale business sector; and Velasco had some assistance in keeping up private investment from the businessmen dealing with (and profiting handsomely from) the expansion of the state sector. Moreover, if the redistributionist fails to hold onto part of the middle sectors and a coalition of the wealthy is allowed to form, the results are likely to be devastating. In Chile, Frei's power was reduced dramat-ically when the industrial entrepreneurs were pushed into the arms of the rural interests over the issue of the property amendment; while Allende's government was destroyed by the shift of lower-middle-income groups from neutrality to open opposition after 1971.

Second, the sectors that swung over in support of the victims of redistribution, and tipped the balance to crush the redistributive effort, often were not intended by the policymakers to suffer eco-nomically. They identified with the opposition either because of sym-bolic tactics adopted by the opposition, such as their inclusion in associations of the wealthy (such as the SOFOFA in Chile and the SNI in Peru); because sloppily formulated economic policy actually did result in their deprivation, as the case of Chile under Allende; or because the ambiguity of governmental intentions led them to regard the government and its policies as threatening.

Finally, we must recognize that coalition tactics involving the non-poor are usually at variance with the overall equity of the redistribu-tion. This does give the opposition of both the Right and the Left ammunition against the regime, in the form of the argument that the administration's policy in fact helps the rich, albeit only a portion of the rich. Yet, as we have argued, this cost must be balanced against the near

impossibility, in nonrevolutionary situations, of significant redistribution without the support of some nonpoor groups.

THE NATURE OF REACTIONS AND OPPOSITION

The traditional benefits-support exchange model is also inadequate
to account for the patterns of reaction seen in redistributive attempts.
The model presumes that reactions to policy are exclusively channeled
through expressions of political support or opposition, even though
governmental actions go through all channels. In other words, although the regime's actions impinge upon all arenas of social interac-
tion, reactions to these programs are presumed to be registered
directly and only through politics. If this were true, it would follow that
if the government had the strength to implement a given economic
policy, and if its "net" political support were enhanced by adopting
that policy, then the government would be well advised to move in that
direction. What this model does not take into account is the possibility
of responses outside the political arena, particularly economic reactions. The potential victims of redistribution, even where they do not
have the strength to prevent the implementation of redistributive
policies, nonetheless can undermine them through other means. This
oversight is no worse than the model adopted in many economic
analyses of redistribution, namely that the significant reactions are
exclusively economic, but in disregarding economic and political interactions it tends to underestimate the importance and versatility of
opposition reactions.

Our profiles of redistributive efforts and the reactions to them
reveal four broad modes of reaction by the threatened higher-income
groups.

1. Influence over Policy Formulation

Even when the most severe breaches between the policymaker and
the opposition exist (as during the Allende period), there will be
attempts on the part of those threatened by redistribution to affect the
formulation of policy. The opposition, acting through its representatives in the legislative process (when a legislature exists) or through
other official representatives, may try either to dilute the redistributive
impact of policy or, as we have seen most graphically in the case of
government social service spending under Belaúnde and Allende, to
exaggerate the policy sufficiently that it will fail because of the economic disequilibria produced. The opposition also attempts to influence policy formulation indirectly, by expressing, usually through

the print media, how disastrous the economic policies are for the country as a whole.

2. Economic Adjustment

Economic accommodation, defined as change in economic behavior designed to maximize profits or economic security under the prevailing economic policy regime, is the reaction that accounts for the weaknesses of some of the most prominent redistributive instruments, including wage increases and tax reforms. Economic accommodations may simply dilute the impact of redistributive policies, often resulting in disillusionment of the groups hoping to benefit, and the withdrawal or weakening of their support for the regime. We have seen how Frei and Velasco disappointed their hoped-for constituencies among urban workers and ended up struggling to check the economic demands of these groups, which threatened the viability of the overall economic strategy.

Alternatively, even if the accommodation is not motivated by the political intent to force replacement of the policy, the economic problems triggered by accommodation, such as inflation or disinvestment, can force policy changes or even the replacement of the regime if the policymakers have not adequately thought about the indirect consequences of their measures.

3. Economic Retaliation

We have also come across several examples of economic reactions entailing the immediate sacrifice of economic gain for the purpose of provoking policy change, either by forcing existing policymakers to change their measures in the face of disastrous economic consequences (such as production stoppages), or by forcing removal of the policy-makers themselves. Although in practice the same acts that further an actor's short-term economic interests may be chosen to embarrrass the administration and to undermine prevailing policies, this is not always the case. The factory owners' sabotage in Chile during the Allende regime is perhaps the most clear-cut example.

The distinction between economic accommodation and economic retaliation is important for two reasons. First, the analytic models necessary to anticipate the two responses are different; accommodation can be understood from a strictly economic perspective, whereas the likelihood and nature of retaliation can be understood only by taking the political context into account. Second, the tactics for avoiding retaliation are different from the tactics (if any) for minimizing accommodations that might undermine the redistributive effort. The tactics for blocking retaliation, as we have seen most clearly in the case of Perón and to some extent in that of Velasco, involve keeping the redistributive victim from losing all, but leaving the government the option of its own retaliation.

4. Political Retaliation

In addition to the customary jockeying for political power, we have seen numerous attempts to undermine the political position of policy-makers whose economic measures are threats to various economic sectors. Although dissatisfaction with economic affairs is rarely the only motive behind efforts to overthrow a government, it is equally rare that this motive is altogether absent. Frondizi's effort to secure the ouster of Illia because the latter was employing the "wrong" economic strategy provides the most obvious example, but the right wing's disruption leading to the overthrow of Allende, and the pressures on the Peruvian military to remove both Belaúnde and Velasco, are examples too of political retaliation based on at least in part on economic motives.

The existence and common use of all of these modes of reaction implies that the redistribution-minded policymaker cannot count on the reactions to his policies to remain strictly in the political arena—as the standard political models seem to presume. Nor can he depend on economic reactions remaining strictly economic. Thus, if the victim is more versatile than one imagines, even if the initial political balance seems to be strongly in support of the redistributive measures, avoiding the mobilization of the opposition is more important than in other policymaking spheres.

TACTICAL IMPLICATIONS

PRESENTATION

The general rule in presenting redistributive programs, on the basis of the experiences of the leaders examined here, seems to be "less is better." Blatant attempts seemed to gain little support, while provoking great antagonism. Of course, this finding must be balanced against the leader's need to be elected or otherwise placed in leadership in the first place; it is impossible to determine the extent to which bold promises were necessary for winning, even if sometimes the rhetorical flourishes were clearly nonessential self-indulgences. Even if the emergent leader has made blatant declarations in order to reach power, he still has some discretion over whether to proceed openly or obliquely. The rationale for the oblique approach is manifest throughout the case studies, in the successes of subtlety and the ease with which open attempts at redis-

tribution have been undermined. The "ethics of openness," as analyzed in Chapter 1, do not seem to be more compelling than the ethics
of distributive justice.

With respect to ambiguity we have seen, in examining Perón's tactics
and in comparing Allende and Velasco (see Chapter 12), that ambiguity which keeps intended victims from believing that they have
nothing left to lose is a great advantage, whereas ambiguity that
frightens unintended victims is an enormous disadvantage.

INSTRUMENTS

Once we recognize that "properties" of different policy instruments
influence the outcomes of redistributive attempts, two issues arise. The
analytic issue is how to characterize a given instrument in such a way
that its likely success as a vehicle of significant redistribution can be
assessed. How many properties or dimensions are involved; do they
constitute a manageable list; and what are these properties? The
second issue concerns the theory of redistributive strategy: what are
the broad guidelines for selecting the instruments, as well as the modes
of presentation and coalition tactics? Of course, a government must
have a "wage policy" and a "tax policy" and so on, if only in the sense
that the government has to decide whether to take any action at all in
each of these areas. The issue is where the government decides to
concentrate the redistributive effort.

The list of potentially important characteristics of the instruments of
economic policy is formidable. It includes dimensions of the nature of
the instrument per se: its scope of impact, degree of differentiation,
complexity, ease of calibration, directness of extraction from one
group to another, degree of institutional change for formulation or
implementation, degree of qualitative change in form or coverage, and
relevance to the achievement of objectives other than redistribution.
Theodore Lowi's (1964) distinctions among distributive, redistributive, and regulatory measures—all of which can influence the distribution of income—would also fall within this set of dimensions.

Another set of dimensions concerns how an instrument is viewed: its
provocativeness, perceived complexity, the apparent extent of departure from existing practice, and the degree to which it symbolizes
policy success or failure of (for instance, devaluation is often construed
as signifying the failure of preceding policies).

Still another set of dimensions pertains to the nature of the policymaking arena in which the instrument is formulated: whether that
arena is fragmented, conflict-prone, widely accessible to interest
groups, highly influenced by the participation of tecnicos, and subject
to public awareness. Since the policymaker rarely has the authority to

shift the arena in which a particular instrument must be formally authorized, the nature of the arena for each instrument is largely a given. For example, tax reform under normal liberal-democractic practice requires legislative approval; hence tax policy is an instrument characterized by the openness and public awareness inherent in the legislative arena.

The strategic importance of avoiding the mobilization of the victims of redistribution points to several of these dimensions of instruments as important in designing redistributive efforts. The logic of keeping the opposition off guard and divided calls for instruments that are formulated in rather closed arenas that are sufficiently differentiated (with different rules applying to different conditions and, in effect, to different cases) to keep the opposition from uniting. Moreover, since the formulation of more esoteric instruments is more likely to be reserved to policymakers operating in relatively closed policymaking arenas, the actual and apparent complexity of redistributive measures is an additional advantage, as long as proredistributionists can maintain the loyalty of individuals with sufficient expertise to operate these instruments. The economic romanticism of many progressive-minded individuals, including some (like Allende's planners) with adequate technical training, can of course undermine this advantage.

Since blatancy does not pay, the selection of instruments to carry the redistributive effort ought to avoid the combative arenas, the image of direct extraction, and the impression of entailing qualitative change in institutions and policy. Often the most effective redistributive measures have been the subtle changes in quantitative parameters (for example, the increase in hidden tax rates rather than the establishment of new forms of taxes) and in the coverage of existing programs (minimum wage and health-system coverage, for instance).

One more dimension of instruments is important, but with varying consequences. It is clear that the existence of multiple objectives complicates the politics over a given economic instrument, but no general conclusion is warranted as to whether this property improves or detracts from the success of redistribution carried out through that instrument. Often the alliances between proredistributionists and middle-income groups have been formed around a measure that serves middle-sector interests as well as redistribution. For example, land reform has motives of both redistribution and productivity. The widespread support for improved agricultural productivity has made it easier in both Chile and Peru to launch a redistributive land reform, but this motive also prevented the land reform from reaching some of the poorest potential land recipients. The momentum of tax reforms that ultimately resulted in higher taxation began with the additional objective of rationalizing the fiscal system, but it is not clear that the rationalizers aided in actually implementing new taxes, which were more often than not highly irregular from the perspective of a fiscal purist. Credit policies and regional development policies have been reconsidered regularly, because the same instruments could be redirected to emphasize aggregate economic growth. The only general lesson to be drawn from the recognition that many redistributive instruments will be called upon to serve other objectives is that the proredistributionist must be particularly sensitive to the danger that an articulate opposition can capture the instrument through persuading policymakers that these other objectives are more desirable than progressive redistribution.

LINKAGE

The most obvious linkage strategy proposed to achieve redistribution is the comprehensive application of all available redistributive instruments. This position has been espoused not only by the most ardent proredistributionists, on the grounds that more is better, but also economic theorists who argue that unless all available instruments are addressed to redistribution, the targeted victims of extraction will escape by shifting their economic activities to areas that are not subject to redistributive efforts, or that benefits will leak to the nonpoor, or both.[1] The importance of coalitions with the nonpoor and the might of a united opposition make it clear that the comprehensive approach is untenable. This is not to say that the approach is without short-term political advantages: the all-out redistributive program may commit the government to a redistributive course despite second thoughts by the proredistributionist's colleagues in government; it can also be rationalized as the surest way of accomplishing some redistribution while the proredistributive leader is still in charge.

However, we have seen that essential coalitions between the poor and key middle-income groups are far less likely to succeed if the policies of redistribution leave no opportunities for the middle-income groups, or even selected elements of the wealthy, to be lured into alliance. Moreover, the technical problems of calibrating an all-out program of redistribution are so awesome that the economic dislocations have been devastating, as the Allende debacle so clearly demonstrated.[2]

If the all-out approach of linking all possible instruments in the redistributive effort is rejected, there remain a host of linkage tactics to be selected according to the specifics of the situation. The guiding principles must be the cultivation of an adequate coalition through

Peru, with its smaller population of university graduates, the economics profession had been considered even more "backward" (Kuczynski 1977, p. 17). Yet now a new generation of highly trained Peruvian economists, generally with U.S. degrees, dominates the Belaúnde government, utilizing quite sophisticated planning methodologies; it may recalled that Belaúnde's "plans" were little more than lists of investment preferences, without reconciliation of revenue, expenditure, or monetary and investment objectives.

The key question, then, is whether the control and expertise generated by these developments can be harnessed by proredistributive leaders. If deliberate economic naiveté continues to be the style of the progressives, these changes are likely to remain the advantages of the wealthy.

Notes

1 INTRODUCTION

1. The most comprehensive compilation of data relative to distribution is in Jain 1975.
2. For literature on achieving redistribution see, for example, Myrdal 1957, 1968; Fuchs 1967; Cardoso and Faletto 1970; Adelman and Morris 1973; Foxley 1976; and Frank and Webb 1977. For "redistribution *and* growth" see Cline 1972 and Chenery 1974.
3. The seminal work was of course Rostow 1963.
4. They are weak because distributional data are often available only for special census years. They are unreliable because income is frequently misreported and because estimation methods often vary from one year's study to the next.
5. See, for example, Adelman and Morris 1973; Chenery and Syrquin 1975; Jackman 1975; Ward 1978; and Fields 1980.
6. See, for Argentina, Díaz Alejandro 1970; Mallon and Sourrouille 1975; de Pablo 1976; Randall 1978; Wynia 1978; and de Pablo 1980. See, for Chile, Molina 1972; Ffrench-Davis 1973; de Vylder 1977; Stallings 1978; and Foxley, Aninat, and Arellano 1979. See for Peru, FitzGerald 1976; Kuczynski 1977; Webb 1977; Thorp and Bertram 1978; and FitzGerald 1979.
7. For a discussion of the problems of assessing tax and expenditure incidence, and for a survey of incidence studies, see Tanzi 1974 and De Wulf 1975.

2 MATCHING TACTICS, CONTEXT, AND THEORY

1. "Urban" is defined as settlements of over two thousand.
2. The income share for wage and salary earners does not reflect how the Peruvian poor were faring, since even the poorest small farmer was classified in the statistics as an "owner."
3. See especially Freels 1968 on this division.
4. Calculated from Payne 1965, p. 130; and Astiz 1969, p. 214.
5. Most notably the railroad workers' union (La Fraternidad), which was dominated by Radical party loyalists.
6. There have been numerous attempts to assess whether production is increased more by concentrating income, because of the greater propen-

sity of the wealthy to save and invest, or by expanding the domestic market through more equitable distribution of income. These attempts take various allocations of income and wealth as already established through prior policy and then trace the impact on production and productive capacity of the variations in savings, investment, and consumption that each allocation implies. See Cline 1972.

7. Because its inclusion would make the connection between success and effectiveness tautological, it is convenient to exclude one aspect of governmental effectiveness from our definition, namely leadership's capacity to judge how far it ought to go.

3 ARGENTINA'S MACHIAVELLIAN MASTER

1. Because he was a rising member of the military junta that took over the Argentine government in 1943, the beginning of Peron's "rule" cannot be firmly dated. By 1946 he was formally in control as president, but even before that he had enacted several extremely important redistributive measures.

2. Depending on which definitions and which calculations of national income and its shares are used, the highest labor proportion of national income was achieved in either 1950 or 1952. See Silverman 1969, pp. 242–245.

3. See Whitaker 1964, pp. 123–127, 136–139; and Díaz Alejandro 1970, chap. 2 and pp. 260–269.

4. Díaz Alejandro (1970, chap. 1) traces these problems to the pre-Depression economic structure. The impact of structural weaknesses was delayed by the influx of foreign reserves during World War II.

5. From an economic point of view, the urban nature of Argentine poverty can be explained by the fact that Argentine beef and grain production required far less labor than the more intensive agriculture typical of the Latin American large estate (*hacienda*) and small plot (*minifundium*). In the early 1960s only a quarter of the net income of the Argentine agricultural sector went to labor (Ferrer 1964, p. 519). This was far less the result of low agricultural wages than of the small agricultural work force required to tend the herds and to cultivate the vast fields of wheat and corn of the Pampas. See also United Nations 1969, pp. 28–35.

6. According to UN 1969, pp. 58–59, less than 40 percent of the families in the bottom two deciles of income recipients were in agriculture as of 1961.

4 THE DEBACLE OF CHILE'S GENERAL OF HOPE

1. Angell (1972, p. 3) characterizes Ibáñez as "posing as a populist."

2. Cavarozzi 1975, pp. 162–163. Brian Loveman, however, maintains that blue-collar real wages increased from 1940–1944 to 1950–1954 (Loveman 1979, p. 262).

3. *El Mercurio,* March 5, 1947; cited in Cavarozzi 1975, p. 172.

4. Paul Drake's conclusion that the Communists "held most labor demands in check" during this period (Drake 1978, p. 287) may have been valid for the

1938–1943 period, but cannot account for the fact that strike activity—both legal and illegal—was very high from 1945 through 1947. See Loveman 1979, p. 266.

5. The following account is based on Bray 1961, pp. 49–50, and Cavarozzi 1975, pp. 216–241.

6. It was not much different, though, from the problems of interparty coalitions, such as those faced by Allende from 1970 to 1973.

5 THE FALTERING REDISTRIBUTIONIST IMPULSE IN PERU

1. Cited in Thorp and Bertram 1978, pp. 188–189.

2. This account is based on Dragisic 1971, pp. 57–58.

3. Ibid., pp. 117, 130–136.

7 GRADUALISM IN CHILE

1. Thomas Edwards (1972, pp. 25–26) points out that "the settlement of 100,000 families would require expropriation of nearly 60 per cent of Chile's irrigated land, somewhat higher than CORA's [the Agrarian Reform Corporation] earlier estimate of 40–50 per cent. Either level was clearly beyond the grasp of the Chilean government between 1964 and 1970, however, when settlement costs are considered. Based on its experience to 1967, CORA estimated the cost to the government of settling 60,000 families by 1970 would amount to $370 million in 1968–1970. Reduction of this cost could come only through reducing investment in housing, rural road building, machinery, and working capital to support the new settlers; this was unacceptable because of the debilitating effect it would have on productivity in the agricultural sector."

2. Other "international" economic issues, such as nationalizing the copper mines (which were largely U.S. owned) and renegotiating the foreign debt, also preoccupied government policymakers.

3. That is, housing undertaken largely by private contractors operating under contracts and specifications from CORVI.

4. Merrill (1968, p. 156) notes: "Educated in the traditional manner to value great green areas, wide avenues, and a low building area–lot size ratio, many administrators adhere to standards and codes contained in outdated municipal regulations."

5. The rise in the rates of sales taxes had uncertain distributive implications, since the progressivity of the complex set of sales taxes is the subject of debate. See Ffrench-Davis 1973, pp. 153–186; Stallings 1975, pp. 521–522. In any event, the increase obviously gave the government far more revenue to spend. The increase in both the rate and efficiency of the income tax was, in the Chilean context, clearly progressive.

6. This account of Frei's tax initiatives is based largely on Ffrench-Davis 1973, pp. 169–180.

7. Frei's agrarian reform efforts are reviewed extensively in Kaufman 1972; Molina 1972, pp. 89–84; and Loveman 1976.

8. Cited in Edwards 1972, pp. 29–30.

9. That is, earning more than the lowest white-collar salary (*sueldo vital*) as distinct from the lowest blue-collar wage, which was considerably less.

10. Sáez called for compensation in bonds for any wage increase above the cost-of-living increase; Frei compromised with the Communists by deleting the clause. See Sigmund 1977, p. 67.

11. Cited in Stallings 1975, p. 291.

8 REFORM IN PERU

1. The Acción Popular–Christian Democratic coalition won 44 percent of the seats in the Senate and 36 percent in the House; UNO won 16 percent and 19 percent respectively.

2. Bourricaud (1970, p. 231) notes that "Belaúnde ... achieved Presidential power after a campaign of only six or seven years ... This in fact was from the outset his main, even his all-sufficient, answer to the question 'What is to be done?'" With reference to the 1962 election campaign, Bourricaud (p. 304) adds, "Belaúnde's dominating principle appears to have been his claim to legitimacy and his refusal to regard the Presidency as negotiable."

3. Some of the northern sugar-plantation owners were associated with APRA and therefore excluded from APRA's expropriation plans.

4. Horton (1974, p. 44) offers the following quote from a Cajamarca landowner: "The Agrarian Reform Law will soon be approved, and will certainly affect [the hacienda] Udima. Therefore we should plan to dedicate all our attention in the years in which the firm can still do so, to extract the maximum possible surplus from the *colonaje* and from the *haciendas* cattle ... We should eliminate the stables and the cheese factory, the alfalfa fields, land reclamation projects, etc., the purchase of feed concentrates and all the other activities which force the *hacienda* to spend money which is never transformed into profits." The capital removed from agriculture was largely turned to urban-oriented activities of construction, manufacturing, and finance. See Thorp and Bertram 1978, p. 283.

5. Roughly 14,000 families received land from 1964 through 1969, with increased application of the land reform act by the military when it took over in late 1968 (see Carroll 1970, p. 25; Harding 1975, p. 234; Kuczynski 1977, p. 69). Of these, many received land already expropriated under previous administrations or were simply given title to the land they already occupied.

6. The second-order effects, such as the higher cost of living, were more problematical.

7. This point is made most cogently by FitzGerald 1976, p. 43.

8. The argument and citations on this point are provided in Astiz 1969, pp. 119–131.

9 ARGENTINA'S BELEAGUERED CENTER

1. Gary Wynia (1978, pp. 72, 102, 156) shows that the average strike duration for 1956–1957 was 8.60 days, compared to an average of 11.75 for the period 1947–1949, 14.48 for 1950–1954, and 9.10 for 1959–1961.

2. The logic of the program is expounded in Frigerio 1962 and Frondizi 1963.

3. The *Hispanic American Report*, May 1958, p. 278, notes, "The cost of living was expected to soar even higher—it increased 30 percent in 1957—since no price control measures were contemplated. It was assumed that producers would pass along the higher wage costs in higher prices."

4. Zuvekas 1966, p. 23. Zuvekas also notes that the contemporaneous official figures reported a GDP growth rate of only 2 percent.

5. Díaz Alejandro (1965, pp. 112–114) notes that urban nonwage income recovered after 1955, rather than declining as did urban wage income. Nonagricultural private business did not lose any ground in its national income share from 1956–1958 to 1959–1961, and in fact producers in mining and manufacturing gained substantially in income shares, from 14.8 percent in 1956–1958 to 17.4 percent in 1959–1961. The gain from 14.5 percent to 15.1 percent for agriculture was offset by the drop in governmental wage income from 7.1 percent to 6.3 percent.

6. Cited in Díaz Alejandro 1965, p. 171.

7. Cited in Goldwert 1972, p. 172.

8. Many critiques on this subject can be found in Thorp and Whitehead 1980.

9. Whereas in 1953 direct taxes reduced the richest decile's share of total income from 37.0 percent to 35.1 percent, by 1959 the reduction was from 42.3 percent to 41.3 percent (UN 1969, p. 260). In other words, the share of total income redistributed through taxation declined from 1.9 percent to 1.0 percent. For 1961, when the richest decile's share was 39.1 percent before taxes, it was reduced by 1.5 percent to 37.6 percent after taxes. This would seem to be a slight recovery. Later studies (CONADE 1967; Bobrowski and Goldberg 1970) examined the overall progressivity of tax incidence, rather than only the effects on the top decile, and covered the period experiencing the full effect of the Frondizi changes. It is reasonable to conclude that they are sounder evaluations of the trends in the equity of taxation than the UN study, and that their findings of a deterioration in the equity of the tax burden are more compelling.

10. It must be kept in mind that the operative effect of inflation has as much to do with the expectation of higher inflation rates as with actual increases. Throughout the Illia period the prevailing view of almost all sectors was that price levels were about to take off at any moment. This perception was fueled by periodic large monthly increases which, when calculated on an annual basis, were indeed high. It was always with a degree of perplexity that Illia's critics, such as the *Review of the River Plate*, reported that the inflation rate never became as disastrous over a prolonged period as they had predicted.

11. Cited in the *Review of the River Plate*, January 30, 1965, p. 137.

12. The *Review of the River Plate*, April 20, 1965, p. 73, representing the viewpoint of the export-import sector, admitted that "in the case of the meat export trade, overseas beef prices are probably sufficiently high to obviate the need for exchange devaluation to stimulate increased exports."

13. This point is elaborated by Quintero 1970, pp. 209–214, 259–264; Mallon and Sourrouille 1975, p. 28; and Wynia 1978, pp. 118–120.

14. Wynia (1978, p. 125) points out that the CGE pressed for establishment of a Socioeconomic Council that would guarantee them an input in economic policymaking that they could not command by virtue of their economic strength alone.
15. Published in the *Review of the River Plate,* January 30, 1965, p. 137.
16. Cited in Barrera 1973, p. 25.

10 THE LOGIC AND TACTICS OF REFORMISM

1. Among the many works on the general question of the "breakdown" of democracy in Latin America, see O'Donnell 1973; Linz and Stepan 1978.
2. For Illia, practically every source evaluating his administration makes this point; for Belaúnde, Kuczynski (1977, p. 282) notes that Belaúnde "was unwilling to short-cut constitutional procedure even in times of great crisis."
3. Wynia (1978, esp. chap. 9) makes this point convincingly for Argentina.
4. The distinction between "salaries" and "wages" is not maintained in most national accounting schemes, largely because of the ambiguity of the terms.
5. The only complication comes in treating part-time wage earners.
6. For example, Tanzi (1974, p. 73) asserts that "the predominance of indirect taxes and the limited use of capital and income taxes as well as the evasion or erosion of the latter, has almost inevitably made difficult the achievement of any redistributive power."

11 COLLAPSE IN CHILE

1. See, for example, the viewpoints expressed in O'Brien 1976; Gil, Lagos, and Landsberger 1979; and Sideri 1979.
2. The production increase is confirmed by figures of the Industrial Promotion Society (SOFOFA), which calculated an index of physical production in order to avoid any distortions that inflation might impart to the valuation of production. The SOFOFA figures (which, if biased, would be antigovernment) also show higher production throughout the Allende years. With 1969 industrial production as a baseline of 100 (a higher level than in any previous year), the SOFOFA figures for the next four years were 103.5, 114.7, 117.6, and 106.7 (Stallings 1978, p. 253).
3. This includes Socialists, Communists, and Radicals, who joined together in the 1970 presidential election and agreed to form a legislative bloc.
4. I use the term "nationalization" here instead of the more precise term "statization" because of the latter's awkwardness and state of disuse. Nationalization as employed here does not imply the conversion from foreign to national ownership, although in practice *some* of the nationalized firms were indeed foreign owned before they were taken over by the state.
5. Note that unionized workers covered by collective bargaining agreements were not formally affected by the official wage adjustments, which pertained to public-sector wages and minimum wages, but were formally only

"recommendations" for private-sector workers earning above the minimum wage. However, the general wage adjustment did have very important indirect effects on the range of the plausible outcomes of collective bargaining agreements. See Stallings 1978, pp. 168–169.

6. Stallings 1978, p. 128. The minimum salary, or *sueldo vital*, was the minimum for white-collar workers and should not be confused with the minimum wage, or *salario minimo*, which was generally only half the minimum salary.

7. Cited in de Vylder 1976, p. 91.

8. The controversy concerned whether a two-thirds majority was necessary to override the presidential veto—or only a majority, since the bill was in fact a constitutional amendment.

9. Alex Nove (1976, pp. 54–55) noted: "It was, above all, the Communists who sought to reassure the middle classes ... They were outflanked from the left not only by the Miristas, who were urging seizures of property and challenging the very concept of legality, but by the other members of the coalition (I recall the mocking tones of Chilean postgraduates whom I met at an international seminar in the summer of 1971: the Communists were a bourgeois party, they insisted)."

10. See Foxley 1971 for an anthology of essays by Chilean economists and politicians on the subject of worker particiation.

11. The bases for believing that the actual money (or nominal) wage increases were greater than the Allende planners had intended include the fact that price controls were probably designed to encourage workers to moderate their nominal wage demands (Nove 1976, p. 59), and the later efforts on the administration's part to reduce real wages.

12. In *Panorama económico*, no. 261 (May 1971) pp. 17, 21.

13. Steenland 1976, p. 10. Loveman 1979, p. 322, offers the even lower figure of 220 tomas for 1960–1969.

14. According to a *New York Times* interview with Chilean military officers after the coup, their decision to intervene came in October 1972. See Sigmund 1977, p. 226, for a review of when the Right, Left, and military turned to strategies of armed action. The timing, however, remains controversial.

12 THE PERUVIAN MILITARY

1. This point is made not only by FitzGerald and Webb, but also by Figueroa (1976, pp. 168–169). However, Figueroa's estimates of the maximum redistribution that could be yielded by the Velasco reforms are in some instances flawed. For example, he begins with H. Van de Wetering's estimates of 7,859 million soles of value added in agriculture potentially affected by land reform, and then takes 14 percent of this figure (Van de Wetering's estimate of the proportion of *total* value added subject to land reform redistribution), to arrive at the potential value of redistribution. This double counting of the 14 percent leaves Figueroa with a figure of potential redistributive impact that is less than one-seventh of Van de Wetering's estimate.

2. The sugar plantations have subsequently been reprivatized, and the expansion of the social property sector canceled.

3. Only later, in 1974–1975, did the Peruvian revolution deepen to such an extent that the upper-income groups came to regard Velasco as evil incarnate.

4. Speculation on whether the Velasco administration was genuinely interested in protecting domestic entrepreneurs is not terribly enlightening, since the government was constituted of individuals with unquestionably different ideological outlooks and sympathies.

5. This pattern is noted in McClintock 1983.

6. For example, the consulting firm Business International (cited in Philip 1978, p. 125) reported back to U.S. and European investors on the dissatisfaction of foreign and domestic firms after the General Industrial Law was decreed in 1970.

7. The intramilitary confrontations are recounted in detail in Philip 1978, pp. 136–153.

13 COMMON PREDICAMENTS

1. The Marxist planning literature, typified by the works of Oscar Lange (Lange and Taylor 1938), is one source; the Alliance for Progress is another.

2. Allende, for example, lacked control over the left wing of the Unidad Popular, and over the peasants and workers involved in land and factory takeovers.

3. In Velasco's case, the vehicles were SINAMOS and the Confederación Nacional Agraria; in Perón's case, it was the CGT, CGE, and Congress combined.

4. The corporatist features of the Velasco regime are reviewed at length in Stepan 1978, and in Cotler 1972, Malloy 1974, and Collier and Collier 1977.

14 CONCLUSIONS

1. See Chenery et al. 1974, especially chap. 6.

2. Frondizi's economic crisis of 1958–1959 may also be regarded as an example of an "all-out" redistributive program resulting in intolerable economic problems that necessitated a drastic change. However, the question of whether this was due to technical miscalibration or deliberate manipulation remains unresolved.

3. See Chapter 13. This is most typically the case for radicals of the Allende and Velasco mold, who, for example, boldly expanded the state sectors without much concern over existing managerial capacities, financial viability, or contribution to needed investment. However, economic romanticism or naiveté is not the exclusive property of radicals—Belaúnde demonstrated that it can also afflict reformists.

References

Adelman, Irma, and Cynthia T. Morris. 1975. *Economic Growth and Social Equity in Developing Countries*. Stanford: Stanford University Press.

Alberti, Giorgio, Gorge Santisteven, and Luís Pasara. 1977. *Estado y clase: la comunidad industrial en el Perú*. Lima: Instituto de Estudios Peruanos.

Alexander, Robert J. 1951. *The Perón Era*. New York: Columbia University Press.

───── 1962. *Labor Relations in Argentina, Brazil, and Chile*. New York: McGraw-Hill.

───── 1979. *Juan Domingo Perón: A History*. Boulder, Colorado: Westview Press.

Allende, Salvador. 1973. *Chile's Road to Socalism*. Harmondsworth, England: Penguin.

Angell, Alan. 1972. *Politics and the Labour Movement in Chile*. New York: Oxford University Press.

Arbildua, Beatriz, and Rolf Lüders. 1968. Una evaluación comparada de tres programas anti-inflacionarias en Chile: una década de historia monetaria, 1956–1966. *Cuadernos de Economía* 5(14):25–105.

Astiz, Carlos. 1969. *Pressure Groups and Power Elites in Peruvian Politics*. Ithaca, New York: Cornell University Press.

Bailey, Samuel L. 1967. *Labor and Nationalism in Argentina*. New Brunswick, New Jersey: Rutgers University Press.

Banco Central de la República Argentina. 1971. Origen del producto y distribución del ingreso, anos 1950–1969. *Boletin Estadístico* Suplemento - Enero. Buenos Aires.

───── 1976. *Cuentas nacionales de la República Argentina: Series históricas*. Buenos Aires.

Banco Central del Perú. 1966. *Cuentas nacionales del Perú 1950–1965*. Lima.

Barrera, Mario. 1973. Information and Ideology: A Case Study of Arturo Frondizi. *Sage Professional Papers in Comparative Politics*, Series 1, No. 44.

Bhagwati, Jagdish. 1978. *Anatomy and Consequences of Exchange Regimes*. Cambridge, Massachusetts: Ballinger.

Bitar, Sergio. 1979. The Interrelationship between Economics and Politics. In *Chile at the Turning Point: Lessons of the Socialist Years*, ed. Federico Gil. Philadelphia; Institute for the Study of Human Issues.

Blanksten, George. 1953. *Perón's Argentina*. Chicago: University of Chicago Press.

Bobrowski, Luís, and Samuel Goldberg. 1970. Presión tributaria por niveles de ingreso: un análisis comparativo. *Finanzas Públicas: Segundas Jornadas* (Cordoba, Argentina):391–445.

Bourricaud, François. 1969. Notas sobre la oligarchía. In *La oligarchía en el Perú*, ed. Instituto de Estudios Peruanos. Lima: Instituto de Estudio Peruanos.

———— 1970. *Power and Society in Contemporary Peru*. New York: Praeger.

Bray, Donald. 1961. Chilean Politics during the Second Ibañez Government. 1952–58. Doctoral dissertation, Stanford University.

Bustamante y Rivero, José. 1949. *Trés años de la lucha por la democracia en el Perú*. Buenos Aires: Artes Gráficas.

Caballero, José M. 1977. *Agrarian Reform and the Transformation of the Peruvian Countryside*. Cambridge University Centre of Latin American Studies Working Papers Series, No. 29.

Cardoso, Fernando, and Enzo Faletto. 1970. *Dependencia y desarrollo en América Latina*. Mexico City: Siglo XXI.

Carri, Roberto. 1967. *Sindicatos y poder en la Argentina*. Buenos Aires: Editorial Sudestaba.

Carroll, Thomas F. 1970. *Land Reform in Peru*. Washington, D.C.: U.S. Agency for International Development.

Cavarozzi, Marcelo. 1976. The Government and the Industrial Bourgeoisie in Chile. 1938–64. Doctoral dissertation, University of California, Berkeley.

Chenery, Hollis, and Moises Syrquin. 1975. *Patterns of Development. 1950–70*. New York: Oxford University Press.

Chenery, Hollis, Montek S. Ahluwalia, C. L. G. Bell, John H. Duloy, and Richard Jolly. 1974. *Redistribution with Growth*. London: Oxford University Press.

Cleaves, Peter. 1974. *Bureaucratic Politics and Administration in Chile*. Berkeley: University of California Press.

Cline, William R. 1972. *Potential Effects of Income Distribution on Economic Growth: Latin American Cases*. New York: Praeger.

Collier, David. 1975. Squatter Settlements and Policy Innovation in Peru. In *The Peruvian Experiment: Continuity and Change under Military Rule*, ed. Abraham F. Lowenthal. Princeton, New Jersey: Princeton University Press.

Collier, David, and Ruth Collier. 1977. Who Does What, to Whom, and How; Toward a Comparative Analysis of Latin American Corporatism. In *Authoritarianism and Corporatism in Latin America*, ed. James M. Malloy. Pittsburgh: University of Pittsburgh Press.

CONADE (Consejo Nacional de Desarrollo), República Argentina. 1965. *Plan Nacional de Desarollo 1965–69*. Buenos Aires.

———— 1967. *Estudio sobre política fiscal en Argentina*. Buenos Aires.

———— 1971. *Plan Nacional de Desarrollo y Seguridad*. Buenos Aires.

Cook, Cheryl A. 1976. Macroeconomic Development and Public Policy in Argentina. 1930–1965. Doctoral dissertation, Yale University.

Cooper, Richard N. 1971. Currency Devaluation in Developing Countries. In *Government and Economic Development*, ed. Gustav Ranis. New Haven, Connecticut: Yale University Press.

Cotler, Julio. 1970. Political Crisis and Military Populism in Peru. *Studies in Comparative International Development* 6:95–113.

—— 1975. The New Mode of Political Domination in Peru. In *The Peruvian Experiment: Continuity and Change under Military Rule*, ed. Abraham F. Lowenthal. Princeton, New Jersey: Princeton University Press.

de Pablo, Juan Carlos. 1976. *Un esquema de política económica para la Argentina.* Buenos Aires: Ediciones Macchi.

—— 1980. *Economía política del Peronismo.* Buenos Aires: El Cid.

de Vylder, Stefan. 1976. *Allende's Chile: The Political Economy of the Rise and Fall of the Unidad Popular.* London: Cambridge University Press.

De Wulf, Luc. 1975. Fiscal Incidence Studies in Developing Countries: Survey and Critique. *IMF Staff Papers* 12:61–129.

Díaz Alejandro, Carlos. 1965. *Exchange Rate Devaluation in a Semi-Industrial Country.* Cambridge, Massachusetts: MIT Press.

—— 1970. *Essays on the Economic History of the Argentine Republic* New Haven, Connecticut: Yale University Press.

—— 1971. The Argentine State and Economic Growth: A Historical Review. In *Government and Economic Development,* ed. Gustav Ranis. New Haven, Connecticut; Yale University Press.

Dietz, Henry A. 1977. Bureaucratic Demand-Making and Clientelistic Participation in Peru. In *Authoritarianism and Corporatism in Latin America,* ed. James M. Malloy. Pittsburgh: University of Pittsburgh Press.

Dragisic, John. 1971. Peruvian Stabilization Policies. 1939–1968. Doctoral dissertation, University of Wisconsin.

Drake, Paul. 1978. *Socialism and Populism in Chile. 1932–52.* Urbana: University of Illinois Press.

Eckstein, Shlomo, Gordon Donald, Douglas Horton, and Thomas Carroll. 1978. *Land Reform in Latin America: Bolivia, Chile, Mexico, Peru and Venezuela.* World Bank Staff Working Paper No. 275. Washington, D.C.

Edwards, Thomas L. 1972. *Economic Development and Reform in Chile: Progress under Frei. 1964–1970.* Latin American Studies Center Monograph Series, no. 8, Michigan State University, East Lansing.

Elliot, Charles. 1975. *Patterns of Poverty in the Third World.* New York: Praeger.

Epstein, Edward C. 1975. Politicization and Income Redistribution in Argentina; The Case of the Argentine Worker. *Economic Development and Cultural Change* 23:615–632.

Eshag, Eprime, and Rosemary Thorp. 1965. Economic and Social Consequences of Orthodox Economic Policies in Argentina in the Post-War Years. *Bulletin of the Oxford University Institute of Economics and Statistics* 27:1–44.

Ferns, H. S. 1973. *The Argentine Republic.* London: David & Charles.

Ferrer, Aldo. 1964. Commentary. *In Inflation and Growth in Latin America,* ed. Werner Baer and Isaac Kerstenetsky. New Haven, Connecticut: Yale University Press.

—— 1967. *The Argentine Economy.* Berkeley: University of California Press.

Ffrench-Davis, Ricardo. 1973. *Políticas económicas de Chile 1951–1970.* Santiago: Ediciones Nueva Universidad.

——. 1976. Policy Tools and Objectives of Redistribution. In *Income Distribu-*

tion in Latin America, ed. Alejandro Foxley. Cambridge: Cambridge University Press.

Fields, Gary. 1980. *Poverty, Inequality, and Development.* Cambridge: Cambridge University Press.

Figueroa, Adolfo. 1976. The Impact of Current Reforms on Income Distribution in Peru. In *Income Distribution in Latin America,* ed. Alejandro Foxley. Cambridge: Cambridge University Press.

Fitch, John S. 1977. *The Military Coup d'Etat as a Political Process: Ecuador, 1948–1966.* Baltimore, Maryland: Johns Hopkins University Press.

FitzGerald, E. V. K. 1976. *The State and Economic Development: Peru since 1968.* Cambridge: Cambridge University Press.

―――― 1979. *The Political Economy of Peru 1956–78.* Cambridge: Cambridge University Press.

Fodor, Jorge. 1975. Perón's Policies for Agricultural Exports 1946–48: Dogmatism or Commonsense? In *Argentina in the Twentieth Century,* ed. David Rock. Pittsburgh: University of Pittsburgh Press.

Foxley, Alejandro, and Oscar Muñoz. 1976. Redistribution, Growth and Social Structure. In *Income Distribution in Latin America,* ed. Alejandro Foxley. Cambridge: Cambridge University Press.

Foxley, Alejandro, Eduardo Aninat, and J. P. Arellano. 1979. *Redistributive Effects of Government Programmes: The Chilean Case.* Oxford: Pergamon Press.

Frank, Andre Gunder. 1967. *Capitalism and Underdevelopment in Latin America: Historical Studies of Chile and Brazil.* New York: Monthly Review Press.

Frank, Charles, and Richard C. Webb, eds. 1977. *Income Distribution and Growth in the Less-Developed Countries.* Washington, D.C.: Brookings Institution.

Frankman, Myron J. 1974. Sectoral Policy Preferences of the Peruvian Government 1946–68. *Journal of Latin American Studies* 6:289–300.

Freels, John W. 1970. *El sector industrial en la política nacional.* Buenos Aires: Eudeba.

Frigerio, Rogelio. 1962. *Los cuatro años (1958–62): política económica para argentinos.* Buenos Aires: Ediciones Concordia.

Frondizi, Arturo. 1963. *Política económica nacional.* Buenos Aires: Ediciones Arayu.

Fuchs, Victor. 1967. Redefining Poverty and Redistributing Income. *Public Interest,* Summer:88–95.

Garcia Martinez, Carlos. 1965. *La inflación argentina.* Buenos Aires: Guillermo Kraft.

Gil, Federico. 1965 *The Political System of Chile.* Boston: Houghton Mifflin.

Gil, Federico, Ricardo Lagos E., and Henry A. Lansberger, eds. 1979. *Chile at the Turning Point: Lessons of the Socialist Years. 1970–1973.* Philadelphia: Institute for the Study of Human Issues.

Goldwert, Marvin. 1972. *Democracy, Militarism and Nationalism in Argentina: An Interpretation.* Austin: University of Texas Press.

Harberger, Arnold. 1977. Fiscal Policy and Income Distribution. In *Income Distribution and Growth in the Less-Developed Countries,* ed. Charles R. Frank and Richard C. Webb. Washington, D.C.: Brookings Institution.

Harding, Colin. 1975. Land Reform and Social Conflict in Peru. In *The Peruvian Experiment: Continuity and Change under Military Rule*, ed. Abraham F. Lowenthal. Princeton, New Jersey: Princeton University Press.

Herschel, Federico, and Samuel Itzcovich. 1957. Fiscal Policy in Argentina. *Public Finance* 12:97–115, 208–228.

Hillaker, Grant. 1971. *The Politics of Reform in Peru*. Baltimore, Maryland: Johns Hopkins University Press.

Hirschman, Albert O. 1963. *Journeys toward Progress*. New york: Anchor.

Hodges, Donald C. 1976. *Argentina 1943–1976: The National Revolution and Resistance*. Albuquerque: University of New Mexico Press.

Horton, Douglas E. 1974. *Haciendas and Cooperatives: A Study of Land Reform and New Enterprises in Peru*. Cornell University Latin American dissertation Series No. 67. Ithaca, New York.

Hunt, Shane. 1971. Distribution, Growth and Government Economic Behavior in Peru. In *Government and Economic Development*, ed. Gustav Ranis. New Haven, Connecticut: Yale University Press.

Instituto de Economía, Universidad de Chile. 1956. *Desarrollo económico de Chile 1940–1956*. Santiago: University of Chile.

———— 1963. *La economía de Chile en el periodo 1950–1963*. Santiago: University of Chile.

———— 1972. *La economía chilena en 1971*. Santiago: University of Chile.

———— 1973. *La economía chilena en 1972*. Santiago: University of Chile.

Jackman, Robert W. 1975. *Politics and Social Equity*. New York: Wiley.

Jain, Shail. 1975. *Size Distribution of Income: A Compilation of Data*. Washington, D.C.: World Bank.

Jaquette, Jane S. 1971. The Politics of Development in Peru. Doctoral dissertation, Cornell University.

———— 1972. Revolution by Fiat: The Context of Policy-Making in Peru. *Western Political Quarterly* 25:648–666.

Kaldor, Nicholas. 1964. Economic Problems of Chile. In *Essays on Economic Policy*, vol. 2. London: Duckworth.

Kaufman, Robert R. 1972. *The Politics of Land Reform in Chile. 1950–1970*. Cambridge, Massachusetts: Harvard University Press.

Kenworthy, Eldon. 1973. The Function of the Little-Known Case in Theory Formation, or What Peronism Wasn't. *Comparative Politics* 6:17–46.

Kinsbruner, Jay. 1973. *Chile: A Historical Interpretation*. New York: Harper.

Klaren, Peter. 1973. *Modernization, Dislocation, and Aprismo*. Austin: University of Texas Press.

Knight, Peter T. 1975. New Forms of Economic Organization in Peru: Toward Workers' Self-Management. In *The Peruvian Experiment: Continuity and Change under Military Rule*, ed. Abraham F. Lowenthal. Princeton, New Jersey: Princeton University Press.

Krueger, Anne O. 1978. *Foreign Trade Regimes and Economic Development: Liberalization Attempts and Consequences*. Cambridge, Massachusetts: Ballinger.

Kuczynski, Pedro-Pablo. 1977. *Peruvian Democracy under Economic Stress: An*

Account of the Belaunde Administration, 1963–1968. Princeton, New Jersey: Princeton University Press.

Kuznets, Simon. 1969. *Modern Economic Growth.* New Haven, Connecticut: Yale University Press.

Lange, Oscar, and Fred M. Taylor. 1938. *On the Economic Theory of Socialism.* Minneapolis: University of Minnesota Press.

Levinson, Jerome, and Juan de Onis. 1970. *The Alliance that Lost its Way.* Chicago: Twentieth Century Fund.

Lindblom, Charles E. 1977. *Politics and Markets.* New York: Basic Books.

Linz, Juan, and Alfred Stepan, eds. 1978. *The Breakdown of Democratic Regimes.* Baltimore, Maryland: Johns Hopkins University Press.

Loveman, Brian. 1976. *Struggle in the Countryside: Politics and Rural Labor in Chile 1919–1973.* Bloomington: University of Indiana Press.

——— 1979. *Chile: The Legacy of Hispanic Capitalism.* New York: Oxford University Press.

Lowenthal, Abraham F., ed. 1975. *The Peruvian Experiment: Continuity and Change under Military Rule.* Princeton, New Jersey: Princeton University Press.

Lowi, Theodore. 1964. American Business, Public Policy, Case Studies, and Political Theory. *World Politics* 16:677–715.

Mallon, Richard, and Juan Sourrouille. 1975. *Economic Policymaking in a Conflict Society.* Cambridge, Massachusetts: Harvard University Press.

Malloy, James M. 1974. Authoritarianism, Corporatism, and Mobilization in Peru. *Review of Politics* 36:52–84.

———, ed. 1977. *Authoritarianism and Corporatism in Latin America.* Pittsburgh: University of Pittsburgh Press.

Mamalakis, Markos. 1976. *The Growth and Structure of the Chilean Economy.* New Haven, Connecticut: Yale University Press.

Mamalakis, Markos, and Clark W. Reynolds. 1965. *Essays on the Chilean Economy.* Homewood, Illinois: Irwin.

Martner, Gonzalo, ed. 1971. *El pensamiento económico del gobierno de Allende.* Santiago, Chile: Editorial Universitaria.

McClintock, Cynthia. 1983. Velasco, Officers, and Citizens: The Politics of Stealth. In *The Peruvian Experiment Reconsidered,* ed. Abraham Lowenthal and Cynthia McClintock. Princeton, New Jersey: Princeton University Press.

McCoy, Terry. 1969. *The Politics of Structural Change in Latin America.* University of Wisconsin Land Tenure Center Research Paper No. 37.

Merkx, Gilbert W. 1968. Political and Economic Change in Argentina from 1870 to 1966. Doctoral dissertation, Yale University.

——— 1969. Sectoral Clashes and Political Change: the Argentine Experience. *Latin American Research Review* 4:89–114.

Merrill, Robert N. 1968. *Towards a Structural Housing Policy: An Analysis of Chile's Low-Income Housing Program.* Cornell University Latin American Studies Dissertation Series.

Molina, Sergio. 1972. *El proceso de cambio en Chile: la experiencia 1965–1970.* Santiago, Chile: Editorial Universitaria.

Myrdal, Gunnar. 1957. *Rich Lands and Poor.* New York: Harper.

―――― 1968. *Asian Drama.* London: Allen Lane.

Nove, Alec. 1976. The Political Economy of the Allende Regime. In *Allende's Chile,* ed. Philip O'Brien. New York: Praeger.

ODEPLAN (Oficina de Planificación), República de Chile. 1971. *Antecedentes sobre el desarrollo chileno - 1960–70.* Santiago.

―――― 1975. *Geografía de la pobreza en Chile.* Santiago.

O'Donnell, Guillermo A. 1973. *Modernization and Bureaucratic Authoritarianism: Studies in South American Politics.* University of California Institute of International Studies, Politics of Modernization Series.

―――― 1976. *Estado y alianzas en Argentina, 1956–76.* Buenos Aires: Centro del Estudio del Estado y Sociedad.

―――― 1977. Corporatism and the Question of the State. In *Authoritarianism and Corporatism in Latin America,* ed. James M. Malloy. Pittsburgh: University of Pittsburgh Press.

―――― 1978. Permanent Crisis and the Failure to Create a Democratic Regime: Argentina, 1955–66. In *The Breakdown of Democratic Regimes: Latin America,* ed. Juan J. Linz and Alfred Stepan. Baltimore, Maryland: Johns Hopkins University Press.

Pan American Union. 1963. *The Alliance for Progress: Its First Year: 1961–62.* Washington, D.C.: Organization of American States.

Payne, James L. 1965. *Labor and Politics in Peru.* New haven, Connecticut: Yale University Press.

Peralta Ramos, Monica. 1978. *Acumulación de capital y crisis política en Argentina (1930–1974).* Buenos Aires: Siglo XXI.

Petras, James. 1969. *Politics and Social Forces in Chilean Development.* Berkeley: University of California Press.

Petras, James, and Laporte, R. 1971. *Perú: ¿transformación revolucionaria o modernización?* Buenos Aires: Amorrortu Editores.

Philip, George. 1978. *The Rise and Fall of the Peruvian Military Radicals, 1968–1976.* London: Athlone Press.

Pike, Frederick B. 1967. *The Modern History of Peru.* Lodon: Weidenfeld & Nicolson.

Quijano Obregón, Anibal. 1971. *Nacionalismo, neoimperialismo, y militarismo en el Perú.* Buenos Aires: Ediciones Periferia.

Quinterno, Carlos A. 1970. *Historia reciente: la crisis política argentina entre 1955 y 1966.* Buenos Aires: Libreria Huemul.

Quiros Varela, Luis. 1972. Chile: Agrarian Reform and Political Processes. In *Allende's Chile,* ed. Kenneth Medhurst. London: Hart-Davis-MacGibbon.

Ramos, Joseph R. 1970. *Labor and Development in Latin America.* New York: Columbia University Press.

Randall, Laura. 1977. Lies, Damn Lies, and the Argentine Gross Domestic Product. *Latin American Research Review* 12:137–158.

―――― 1978. *An Economic History of Argentina in the Twentieth Century.* New York: Columbia University Press.

Ranis, Peter. 1966. Peronismo without Perón Ten Years after the Fall (1955–1965). *Journal of Inter-American Studies* 6:112–128.

Reed, Irving B., Jaime Suchlicki, and Harvey Dodd. 1972. *The Latin American Scene of the Seventies: a Basic Fact Book.* University of Miami (Florida) Center for Advanced International Studies Monographs on International Affairs.

República Argentina, Dirección Nacional de Estadísticas y Censos. *Boletín de Estadística.* Various issues. Buenos Aires.

República Argentina, Secretaria de Estado de Hacienda. 1970. *Sector público argentino, esquema de ahorro-inversión y financiamiento.* Buenos Aires.

República Peruana, Instituto Nacional de Planificación. 1966. *La evolución de la economía en el periodo 1950–64.* Lima.

República Peruana, Oficina Nacional de Estadística y Censos. 1971. *Anuario estadístico del Perú 1971,* vol. 29. Lima.

Rock, David. 1975. The Survival of Peronism. In *Argentina in the Twentieth Century,* ed. David Rock. Pittsburgh: University of Pittsburgh Press.

Schmitter, Philipe. 1974. Still the Century of Corporatism? *Review of Politics* 36:85–131.

Sideri, Sandro. 1979. *Chile 1970–73: Economic Development and its International Setting.* The Hague: Martinus Nijhoff.

Sigaut, Lorenzo. 1972. *Acerca de la distribución y niveles de ingreso en la Argentina 1950–1972.* Buenos Aires: Ediciones Macchi.

Sigmund, Paul E. 1977. *The Overthrow of Allende and the Politics of Chile, 1964–1976.* Pittsburgh: University of Pittsburgh Press.

Silverman, Bertram. 1969. Labor Ideology and Economic Development in the Peronist Epoch. *Studies in Comparative International Development* 4:243–258.

Silvert, Kalman H. 1966. *The Conflict Society.* New York: American Universities Field Staff.

Skidmore, Thomas E. 1977. The Politics of Economic Stabilization in Postwar Latin America. In *Authoritarianism and Corporatism in Latin America,* ed. James M. Malloy. Pittsburgh: University of Pittsburgh Press.

Sommerfeld, Raynard M. 1966. *Tax Reform and the Alliance for Progress.* Austin: University of Texas Press.

Stallings, Barbara. 1975. Economic Development and Class Conflict in Chile. Doctoral dissertation, Stanford University.

———— 1978. *Class Conflict and Economic Development in Chile.* Berkeley: University of California Press.

Steenland, Kyle. 1977. *Agrarian Reform under Allende: Peasant Revolt in the South.* Albuquerque: University of New Mexico Press.

Stepan, Alfred. 1971. *The Military in Politics: Changing Patterns in Brazil.* Princeton, New Jersey: Princeton University Press.

———— 1978. *The State and Society: Peru in Comparative Perspective.* Princeton, New Jersey: Princeton University Press.

Sunkel, Osvaldo. 1970. Cambios estructurales, estrategias de desarrollo y planificación en Chile 1938–1969. *Cuadernos de la realidad nacional* (Chile) 4(3):31–49.

Tanzi, Vito. 1974. Redistributing Income Through the Budget in Latin America. *Banca Nazionale del Lavoro Quarterly Review* (Rome) 27(108):65–87.

Thorp, Rosemary. 1967. Inflation and Orthodox Economic Policy in Peru. *Bulletin of the Oxford University Institute of Economics and Statistics* 29:185–210.

Thorp, Rosemary, and Geoffrey Bertram. 1978. *Peru 1890–1977: Growth and Policy in an Open Economy.* New York: Columbia University Press.

Thorp, Rosemary, and Lawrence Whitehead, eds. 1979. *Inflation and Stabilization in Latin America.* London: MacMillan.

UCRP (Unión Cívica Radical del Pueblo). 1966. *La política económico del Gobierno Constitucional.* Buenos Aires: UCRP.

United Nations. 1949. *Economic Survey of Latin America.* New York: UN Economic Commission for Latin America.

——— 1955. *Foreign Capital in Latin America.* New York: UN Department of Economic and Social Affairs.

——— 1959. *The Industrial Development of Peru.* Mexico City: UN Department of Economic and Social Affairs.

——— 1964. *The Economic Development of Latin America in the Post-War Era.* New York: UN Economic Commission for Latin America.

——— 1965. *External Financing in Latin America.* New York: UN Economic Commission for Latin America.

——— 1966. *The Process of Industrial Development in Latin America.* New York: UN Economic Commission for Latin America.

——— 1968. *El desarrollo económico y la distribución del ingreso en la Argentina.* New York: UN Economic Commission for Latin America.

——— 1969. *Economic Development and Income Distribution in Argentina.* New York: UN Economic Commission for Latin America.

——— 1971. *Income Distribution in Latin America.* New York: UN Economic Commission for Latin America.

U.S. Treasury Department. 1947. *Census of American-Owned Assets in Foreign Countries.* Washington, D.C.: Government Printing Office.

——— 1960. *U.S. Business Investments in Foreign Countries.* Washington, D.C.: Government Printing Office.

——— 1974. *U.S. Investments Abroad, 1966. Final Data.* Washington, D.C.: Government Printing Office.

Valderrama, Mariano. 1976. *Siete años de reforma agraria peruana.* Lima: Universidad Catolica.

Valenzuela, Arturo, 1978. *The Breakdown of Democratic Regimes: Chile.* Baltimore, Maryland: Johns Hopkins University Press.

Villanueva, Javier. 1966. *The Inflationary Process in Argentina,* 2nd ed. Buenos Aires: Instituto Torcuato di Tella.

Ward, Michael D. 1978. *The Political Economy of Distribution.* New York: Elsevier.

Webb, Richard C. 1975. Government Policy and the Distribution of Income in Peru, 1963–1973. In *The Peruvian Experiment: Continuity and Change under Military Rule,* ed. Abraham F. Lowenthal. Princeton, New Jersey: Princeton University Press.

——— 1977. *Government Policy and the Distribution of Income in Peru.* Cambridge, Massachusetts: Harvard University Press.

Weil, Felix. 1944. *Argentine Riddle.* New York: John Day.

Werlich, David P. 1978. *Peru: A Short History.* Carbondale; Southern Illinois University Press.

Whitaker, Arthur P. 1964. *Argentina.* Englewood Cliffs, New Jersey: Prentice-Hall.

Wynia, Gary. 1978. *Argentina in the Postwar Era: Politics and Economic Policy Making in a Divided Society.* Albuquerque: University of New Mexico Press.

Zimmerman Zavala, Augusto. 1974. *El Plan Inca, objectivo: revolución peruana.* Lima: Empresa Editora del Diario Oficial "El peruano."

Zuvekas, Clarence, Jr. 1966. Economic Growth and Income Distribution in Postwar Argentina. *Inter-American Economic Affairs* 20(3):19–38.

PERIODICALS

Hispanic American Report, Stanford University, Stanford, California.

Panorama económico, Santiago, Chile.

Review of the River Plate, Buenos Aires, Argentina.

Index

DATE DUE

DEC - 2 2004			

GAYLORD   PRINTED IN U.S.A.